MOTORCYCLE TUNE-UP
AF566606

Introduction

Spurred on by rising fuel prices and a troubled economy, more people are buying and riding motorcycles than ever before. Also, cycle riders are doing their own tune-up and repair work to save themselves bucks. That's what this Petersen book is all about. By keeping your motorcycle in a good state of tune, you not only save money, you gain in knowledge by doing the work yourself. Increased fuel economy, improved performance and a better appreciation of your own abilities are all dividends of doing your own maintenance.

Owning and riding your motorcycle is really only half the fun. The real satisfaction comes from being able to understand the way it works and fixing things that go wrong yourself. This book tells it all: How to troubleshoot problems, how to tune your engine, and what types of tools you'll need to do the job. Information contained in this book applies to *all* motorcycles, with several chapters devoted to *specific* tune-up information for the most popular bikes. There are plenty of pictures to make step-by-step tuning easy, and our artist has detailed the workings of all parts of the motorcycle with explicit artwork to make your job even easier.

While much of this book is aimed at the new motorcycle owner, there is plenty of valuable information to refresh the mind of the more experienced rider/tuner. After you've used this book, you'll want to keep it in your toolbox for future reference, along with a shop manual and the owner's manual for your motorcycle. Armed with all this information, you should have the safest, sweetest-running bike in town . . . and you'll have done it yourself!

—Don Whitt

ACKNOWLEDGMENTS

We would like to thank the following people and companies for their cooperation in providing material and technical assistance for this book: Ron Lovil of Suzuki, Jenine Black and Tom Berkley of Yamaha, Doug Freeman of Kawasaki, Ken Luehmann of Honda and Brian Slark of Norton/Triumph. Thanks also to the following for their help in the actual preparation of this book: Dain Gingerelli, photographer; Eric Bean and John Collins, photographic assistants.

ISBN 0-8227-0110-3

BASIC MOTORCYCLE TUNE-UP

Written by Richard Bean. Edited by Don Whitt.

COVER

Keep in tune with the times. We'll show you how to save money and gasoline by doing your own tune-ups. To set an example, Motorcyclist Magazine's associate editor, Rich Cox, gaps a plug on a Honda 750 Four while Larry Griffin of PPC Photographic records the scene. Detail photos of tune-up procedures provide a sneak preview of the material inside. Photos were shot by Eric Rickman with setups courtesy of Fred Vanacore of Racecrafters. Cover design by Dick Fischer.

**Library of Congress
Catalog Card No. 75-45500**

Table of Contents

I. Tools & Techniques

What's a Tune-up?

Those few hours spent tuning your motorcycle in the driveway will pay off in money saved, both in labor costs and improved mileage.

Most new motorcycle owners will tell you that a tune-up is what the mechanic at the dealership does to your new motorcycle when you take it in for servicing. They don't really understand the principles of preventive maintenance or know what tools are required. Let's define a tune-up by first looking at what happens to the engine in your motorcycle while you are riding it.

When you first pick up your bike at the dealership, it has been examined by a mechanic, and all of the necessary adjustments to make it run according to factory specifications have been done. You don't have to put the motorcycle together yourself or make any adjustments; you just ride it. At that time it is in a state of tune prescribed by a book for mechanics called the "shop manual."

As you ride your motorcycle, however, a certain amount of "aging" creeps in. Moving parts wear slightly, air and oil filters begin to fill up with unwanted contaminants and parts such as spark plugs, wiring, cables and soft materials begin to wear out. As this aging process continues, the motorcycle's performance begins to drop, ever so slightly at first, then noticeably. At some point, engine performance will become so poor that certain adjustment or replacement of parts is necessary to restore the engine to normal working order. Adjustment or replacement of parts is a tune-up. It's as simple as that.

A more complete definition of a tune-up is: performing the work necessary to restore the motorcycle to the condition it was in when you bought it. The bible for this process is the factory shop manual for the particular bike you are working on. There are a lot of books on the market which lump together all the tune-up specifications (specs) and procedures for motorcycles of all kinds, but the factory book is the best and most detailed.

One thing to remember about a shop manual, though, is that it was designed and written for professional mechanics, so unless you are better than just average about mechanical things, it's best to stick to a more basic kind of motorcycle book as your guide.

Along with the shop manual, you might also include the owner's manual that came with your bike. It contains the basic information necessary for minor tune-up and servicing. Furthermore, if you wish, it is sometimes possible to get the parts book for your bike to help identify and obtain replacement parts. These parts books (available from the dealer) may cost you a few dollars, but compared to the cost of your motorcycle and the money you can save by doing your own work, they are a cheap and worthwhile investment.

Riders of any age can learn the tune-up business. All it takes is the ability to read simple instructions and follow through. A tune-up book like this one and the shop manual for your bike are all you need.

I/Minor Tune-up

Minor tune-up is considered work in which no major components (like the head, piston, rings or valves) are removed from the bike. A good general reference for this kind of tune-up is the owner's manual that came with your bike when you bought it.

The parts for a tune-up (in this case for a Honda 350) consist of plugs, ignition points, carburetor rebuilding kits and condenser. The whole package is available at your dealer for about $20.

Parts used in a minor tune-up are:

AIR and OIL FILTERS (most bikes don't have an oil filter, but some large street bikes do),
SPARK PLUGS,
IGNITION POINTS and other related IGNITION COMPONENTS.

Adjustments common to a minor tune-up are:

SPARK PLUG GAP,
IGNITION POINTS SETTING,
IGNITION TIMING and adjustment of the
CARBURETOR and
VALVES (on four-stroke models; two-stroke engines don't have valves).

Correct spark plug gap is important for good performance. Gapping tool should be of the round wire gauge type for best results. A flat feeler gauge will not measure the gap properly if the underside of the ground electrode is pitted.

Other items covered in a thorough tune-up should be:

CHAIN and
CLUTCH ADJUSTMENT,
BATTERY INSPECTION,
WHEEL SPOKE and
TIRE INSPECTION,

plus others which are covered in greater detail in the chapters "Your First Four-stroke Tune-up" and "Your First Two-stroke Tune-up." Additional information can be found in the chapter on "Preventive Maintenance."

I/Major Tune-up

Major tune-up involves partial disassembly of the engine to inspect the condition of the cylinder head, cylinder, piston and rings. Repair work more extensive than this is generally considered an overhaul.

A major tune-up includes everything covered in a minor tune-up and may go much farther, even to removal of the cylinder head and the cylinder (sometimes called the "barrel") from the engine so that work may be done on the piston and rings. This includes, in a four-stroke engine, the valves and other parts of the valve-actuating mechanism which are carried in the head.

If, in the course of a major tune-up, you discover engine problems that mean disassembling the lower case halves, you are past the major tune-up stage and into what mechanics call an "overhaul." At this point it might be wise to consult an experienced mechanic for help, as getting into the lower end of a motorcycle engine requires special tools and information beyond the scope of this tune-up book.

To perform a minor or major tune-up at home

When performing a major tune-up on your engine, carefully check the pistons and rings for signs of wear that could allow oil particles and vapor from the crankcase to enter the combustion chamber.

The lower half of the engine is highly complicated and requires special tools and knowledge to work on. If you suspect problems in this area, better leave it to a mechanic.

isn't hard if you follow certain rules. You will need a place to work that is well lighted and well ventilated, a minimum number of tools (see the chapter "Tools for Tuners") of the correct sizes and types and, last but certainly not least, this book and/or your owner's manual or the shop manual for your bike.

After you have decided on a place to work, a garage or driveway being the most obvious choices, the first step is a good cleaning of your bike. Nothing is more difficult than trying to do careful work on a bike that is dirty or greasy. This is especially true for bikes ridden off-road. A good place to clean your bike is at the local carwash. Be careful not to spray water directly on a hot engine. Let it cool for several minutes before washing it, but it will clean up better if the engine is still warm. Riding it home will generally dry it enough to work on.

If you don't have a carwash nearby, the same job can be done on a driveway or lawn. A pan of warm water mixed with detergent soap or one of the liquid cleaners should do the trick.

WARNING: NEVER CLEAN YOUR BIKE WITH GASOLINE OR OTHER INFLAMMABLE SOLVENTS. HOT ENGINE PARTS OR THE IGNITION CAN SET THESE LIQUIDS ON FIRE, RESULTING IN SERIOUS DAMAGE AND INJURY. ALWAYS CLEAN A COOL ENGINE, USING ONLY AN APPROVED CLEANING SOLVENT SUCH AS GUNK, STODDARD CLEANING SOLVENT OR, FOR CARBURETORS, GUMOUT OR PARTS DIP.

The local pay carwash is an ideal place to get the grit and grease off your bike. Not only does it make the work easier, but a layer of dirt can hide broken parts or other troubles. Parking the bike on the front lawn for washing is also good.

Pick a good spot to work on your motorcycle. The driveway will do in fair weather, but any location chosen should be well lighted and ventilated.

Stoddard Solvent is a kerosene-like material used by the military and service stations for cleaning vehicles because it is *fairly* safe. Under no circumstances should you use gasoline or other highly inflammable liquids. The danger of fire is too great. Also, always work in a well-ventilated space when using *any* solvent or other chemical to clean parts. Liquids such as carburetor cleaner are very toxic (poisonous), and inhaling vapors can make you ill. Keep the garage door open if you're working inside.

WARNING: WHEN TUNING OR CLEANING YOUR MOTORCYCLE, BE CAREFUL NOT TO TOUCH THE EXHAUST PIPE OR OTHER METAL PARTS THAT MIGHT BE HOT ENOUGH TO BURN YOU. HOT ENGINE PARTS CAN CAUSE SEVERE BURNS.

CAUTION: IF YOU PARK YOUR BIKE ON AN UNPAVED SURFACE, PUT A BOARD OR OTHER FLAT, HARD OBJECT UNDER THE TIP OF THE KICKSTAND. IF YOU DON'T, THE WEIGHT OF THE BIKE MAY MAKE THE KICKSTAND DIG IN AND THE BIKE WILL FALL OVER. THIS IS ESPECIALLY LIKELY WHERE WATER USED FOR WASHING HAS SOFTENED THE GROUND.

Really stubborn grease and dirt can easily be removed with an approved cleaning agent, such as Stoddard Solvent. For best results, the engine should still be slightly warm, but be careful never to use solvents on a hot engine. They might catch fire.

This can happen to you if the ground soaks up too much water. The kickstand can sink in and the bike will topple over. Placing a board under the kickstand solves the problem.

Once you have cleaned your bike and moved it to a good place to work on it, the next step is to gather up your tools, books and a quantity of clean rags. Get all the materials you will need together *before* you start your tune-up. Having to get up and search for tools or parts in the middle of a job can make you lose track of what step in the tune-up you were doing, and a mistake can be costly.

Take a few minutes to read through the portions of whatever book you are using that concern your bike and get a good idea of the exact sequence of steps you will be performing. If you are new to tuning or working on your motorcycle, going quickly through the steps without actually doing any adjustments will familiarize you with the locations of the various parts and help keep you from overlooking anything or misreading a step.

One important point to remember: When removing parts from your bike, take care to do the job in such a manner that you remember how things came apart. With small parts it is often necessary to lay them out on a clean cloth or newspaper so that they won't get lost or dirty. Work carefully and follow the step-by-step instructions in the book. If you experience any difficulty, don't hesitate to ask someone more knowledgeable for help. Often you will learn more if you do your first tune-up with a friend who is a good mechanic looking over your shoulder.

Normal tune-up means following directions developed at the factory. Highly qualified engineers and mechanics have spent considerable time working on your motorcycle, and the tune-up specifications given in the shop manual or this book are the recommended settings for normal operation. Do not change any of these settings or adjustments without consulting a mechanic. Remember, a tune-up is designed to restore the engine in your motorcycle to the state of tune it had when it left the dealer's showroom. If you desire to tune your bike to obtain some different level of performance, such as increased economy, consult that chapter in this book.

Once you have read this chapter, you can go on to the more specific tune-up information contained in this book. For four-stroke engines, start with "Your First Four-stroke Tune-up." For two-stroke engines, see "Your First Two-stroke Tune-up." Don't forget to read the next chapter, "Tools for Tuners," *before* starting to work on your motorcycle.

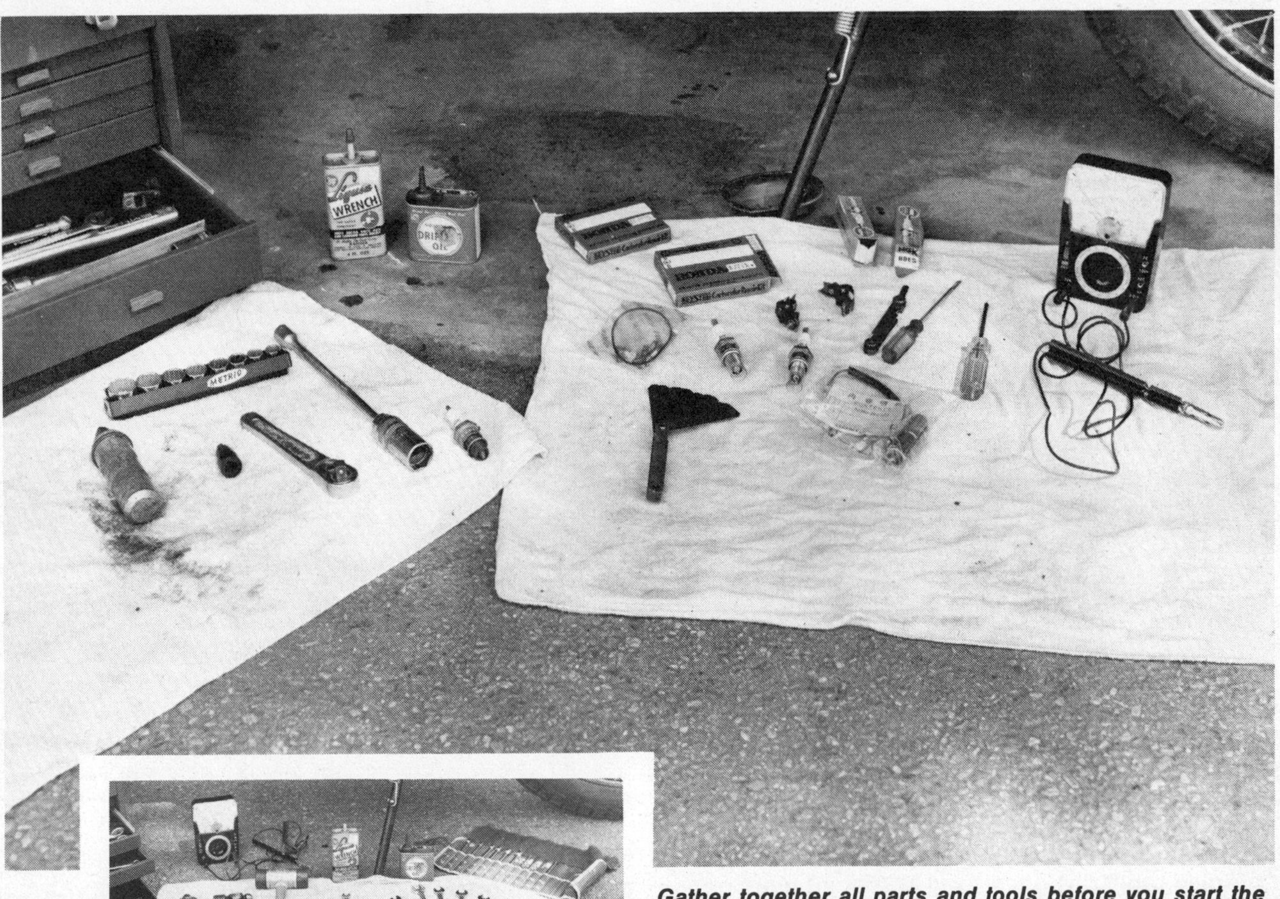

Gather together all parts and tools before you start the job. If you have to stop halfway through to get a tool, you might forget where you are and overlook something important.

Laying out all parts and tools on a clean cloth is helpful too. It makes things easier to keep track of and keeps tools and parts cleaner.

1/ Tools for Tuners

A good set of tools is a must for tune-up work. You needn't spend a fortune, but buy the best you can afford. Good tools will make the work easier.

The majority of all motorcycle tune-up work and preventive maintenance is done with simple hand tools of the type you are probably already familiar with. Only a few special tools are needed in even the most extensive tune-up work, and these are generally tools designed to fit a specific part of *your* motorcycle rather than all motorcycles. These tools are usually available at your dealer.

When purchasing hand tools for your motorcycle, there is only one rule to remember: Buy the best tools you can afford! That doesn't mean you need to spend a fortune buying all sorts of exotic tools; just try to get the best tools for the job. Cheap tools are generally found in discount stores or on sale in parts stores. If you are uncertain about a tool, compare it with its counterpart from Sears, Proto or Snap-On. If the tool doesn't have the same clean finish and good fit of tools like the ones mentioned above, stay away from it. High-quality tools may cost a little more, but they will always save you money in the long run.

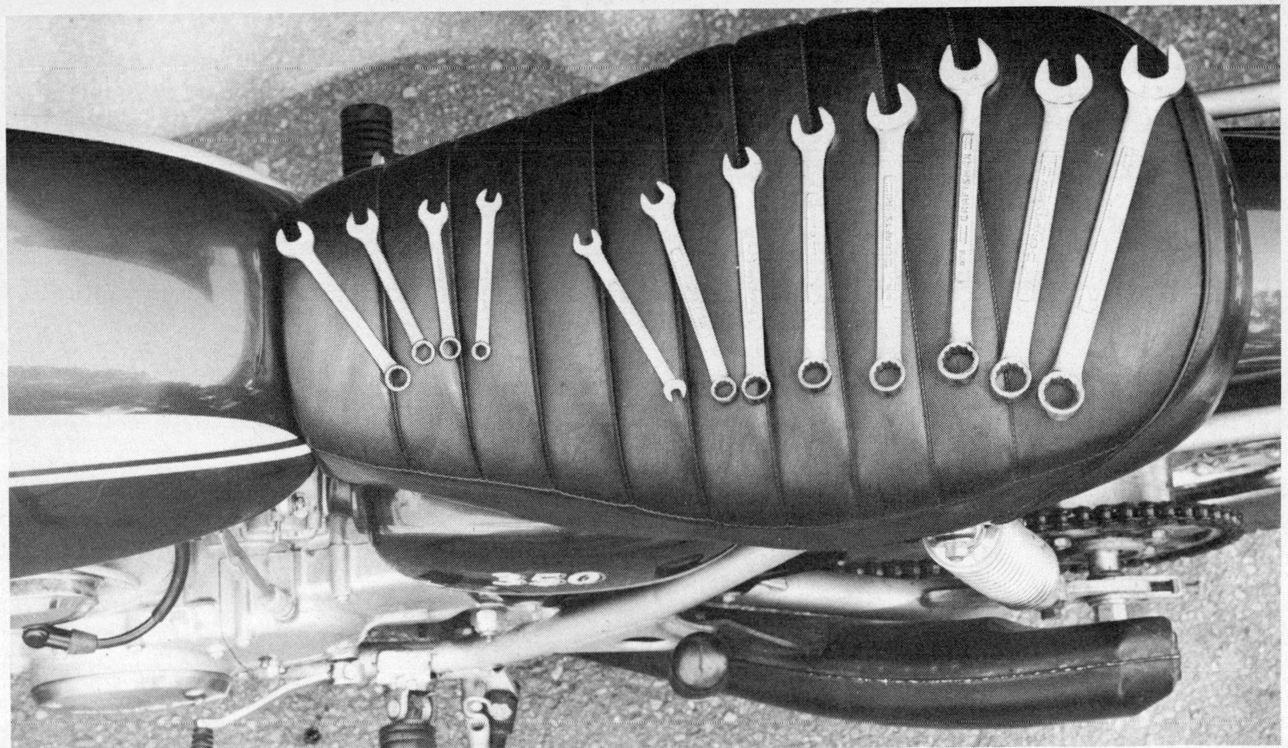

A full set of combination wrenches is a must when working on a motorcycle. Most motorcycles require metric sizes in tools.

The logical starting place in hand tools is with a set of wrenches. The vast majority of all motorcycles are fitted with parts in metric sizes, which are different from American part sizes. Some American wrenches will fit your motorcycle, but a complete wrench set in metric sizes will give you the ability to perform a lot more maintenance. (NOTE: Some older English motorcycles were built with a size system of parts and fittings called "Whitworth." If you own one of these bikes, you may have to purchase all your tools from your dealer.)

Next you'll want to add pliers. Regular pliers in one or two sizes are a good idea, and a pair of needle-nosed pliers can be very helpful in getting into tight places. Another adjustable tool is the crescent wrench, which operates like an open-end wrench but is adjustable for size.

Pliers of the Channellock type open up wide to handle big nuts and bolts, such as those found on wheels and forks, while vise-grip pliers are useful on hard jobs and often make a good temporary substitute for a small vise. One each of these hand tools will make a lot of jobs easier.

CAUTION: DO NOT USE PLIERS OR ADJUSTABLE WRENCHES IF YOU HAVE THE PROPER SIZED BOX-END OR OPEN-END WRENCH. ADJUSTABLE WRENCHES AND PLIERS MAY SLIP AND HURT YOU OR DAMAGE THE SURFACE OF NUTS AND BOLTS.

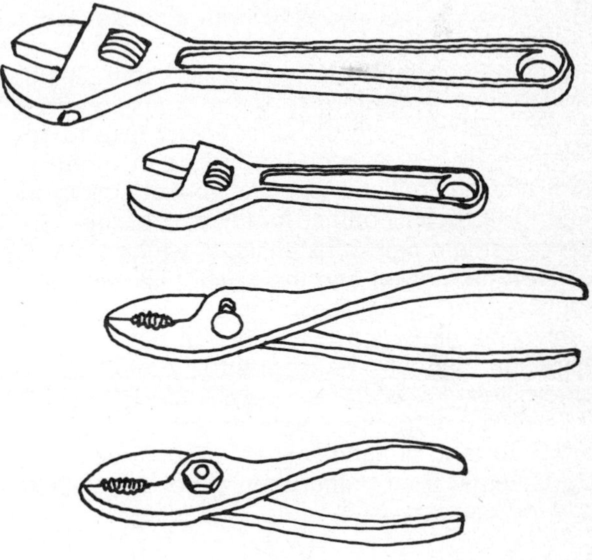

Standard pliers and crescent wrenches in one or more sizes will make the work easier at times. Don't use pliers or adjustable wrenches when you have the right size box- or open-end wrench. You can damage boltheads with the former tools if you are not careful.

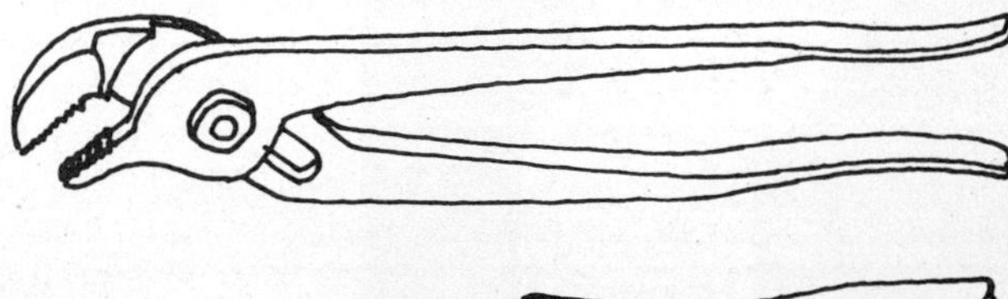

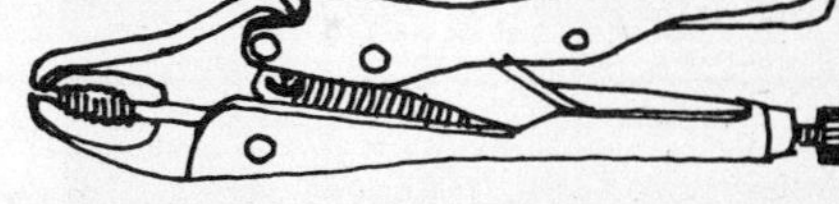

A pair of vise-grips and some large Channellock pliers should be in the tool kit on your bike if you ride off-road at all.

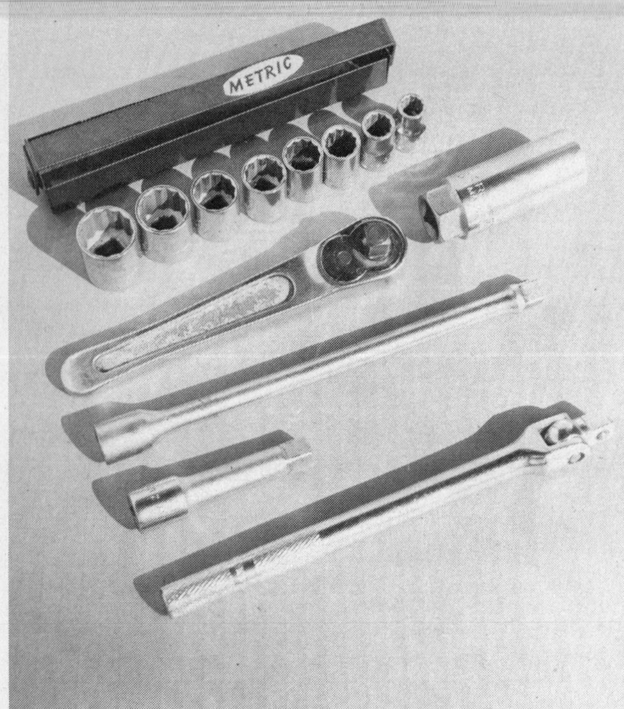

A metric socket set (shown at left) with extensions in 4- and 6-inch sizes is a good bet. Include a small breaker bar and a spark plug socket to break loose those stubborn plugs from the head.

A socket set, consisting of a ratchet handle and a set of sockets in metric sizes, will speed up work. There are many places on any motorcycle where it is far easier to work with a socket and extension than a hand wrench.

Additions to the basic socket set should include regular blade and Phillips screwdriver tips and a set of Allen-head drivers. Check your bike to see if it uses Allen screws on the engine or other parts and buy only the specific socket sizes you need to fit them. Another handy part of the socket set is a pair of extensions, which fit between the socket and the ratchet handle for reaching into tight places. If you have the money, a universal joint adapter will let you get at boltheads that can't be reached any other way on some bikes.

We recommend the ⅜-inch drive for your socket set and attachments as the best all-around size for most uses, rather than either the ¼-inch or ½-inch sizes.

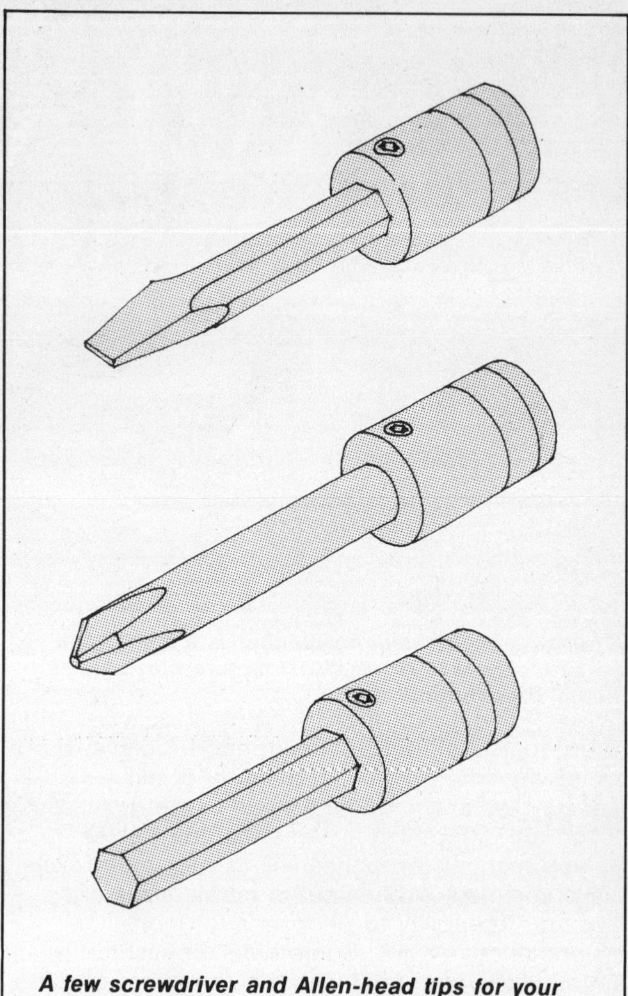

A few screwdriver and Allen-head tips for your socket set will come in handy. They really speed up removal of engine side covers and the clutch cover.

Sometimes the only way to get at a troublesome bolt is with a long extension and a universal joint adapter (as shown below).

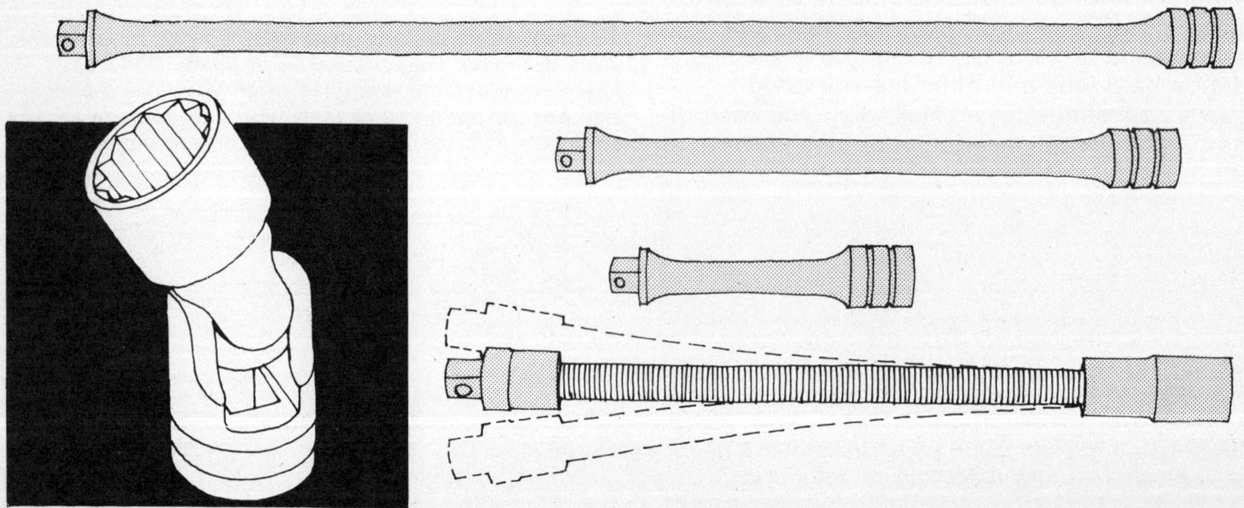

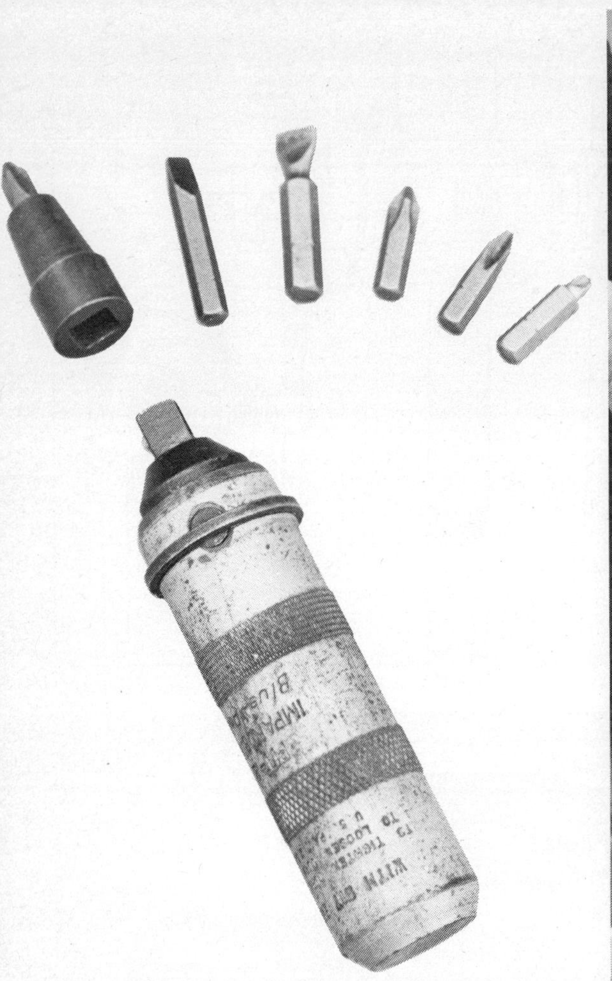

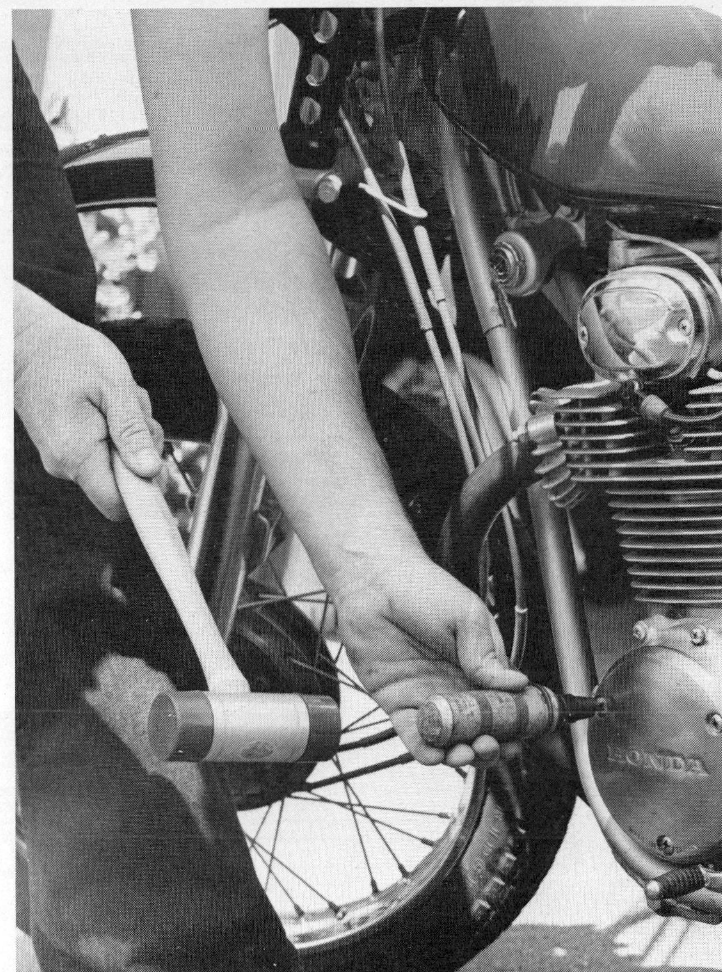

A hand-held impact tool and a good collection of bits are a standard motorcycle tool good for breaking loose case and cover screws. The tool provides a twisting force when struck with a soft-faced hammer.

One of the handiest items ever developed for mechanical use is the impact driver, with an assortment of Phillips and slotted screwdriver bits. This tool is primarily used on the side covers of motorcycles. The screws holding these covers tend to become very hard to remove, and they strip their threads easily if you try to remove them with an ordinary screwdriver. Using the impact tool, which is put into place on the screw and then struck with a soft-faced hammer, you can break loose the most stubborn screw without damage to it or to the case.

Speaking of hammers, there are two types that most motorcycle mechanics have in their toolboxes. One is the standard ball-peen hammer. The other is a soft-faced hammer, which usually has one face of medium-hard rubber and the other of hard plastic. This soft-faced hammer will probably be a favorite, as it can be used in a variety of ways on your motorcycle without leaving marks or breaking any of the cast metal covers or other parts.

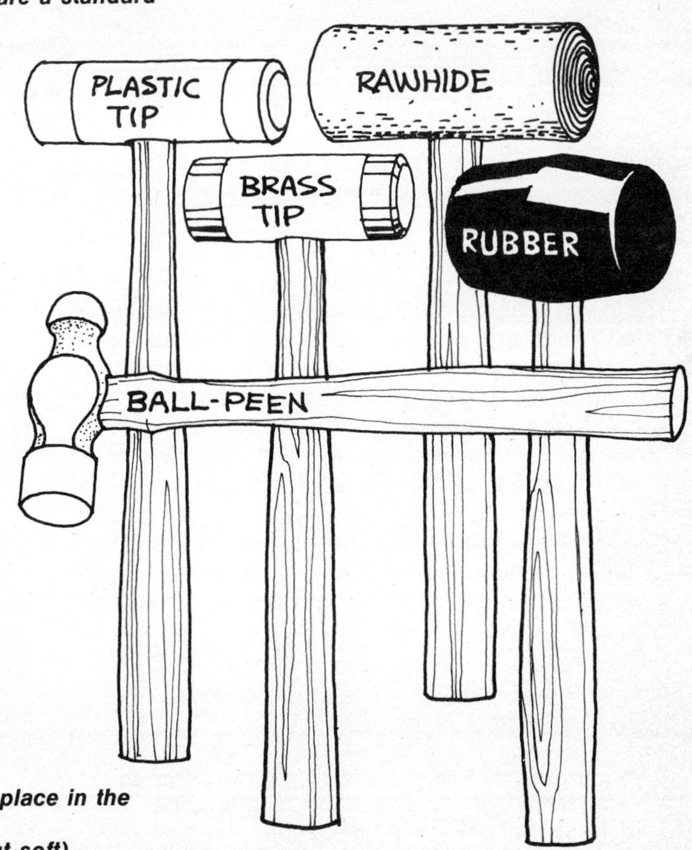

Both the ball-peen and soft-faced hammers have their place in the motorcycle tuner's toolbox. You'll find that the soft-faced hammer gets a lot of use on alloy (strong but soft) engine parts.

A chain-breaking tool is a good item to have for preventive maintenance and repair of your chain. This tool can remove individual links in your chain when necessary. As a matter of fact, this is one item that should be carried in the tool kit on your bike, along with a couple of spare links. Chains do break, and it usually happens when you are riding far from home or a garage.

If you haven't already done so, we recommend that you discard the cheap, stamped tools that come in the tool kit of most motorcycles and replace them with a selection of quality tools from your toolbox. If you are ever stuck with a sick bike while out riding and don't have good tools, it can be a long walk back to town.

A chain-breaking tool (right) is necessary to remove and install links in the chain.

A full set of screwdrivers, both slot and Phillips head, should be one of your first tool purchases. Buy as many sizes and lengths as you can afford; you'll need all of them sooner or later.

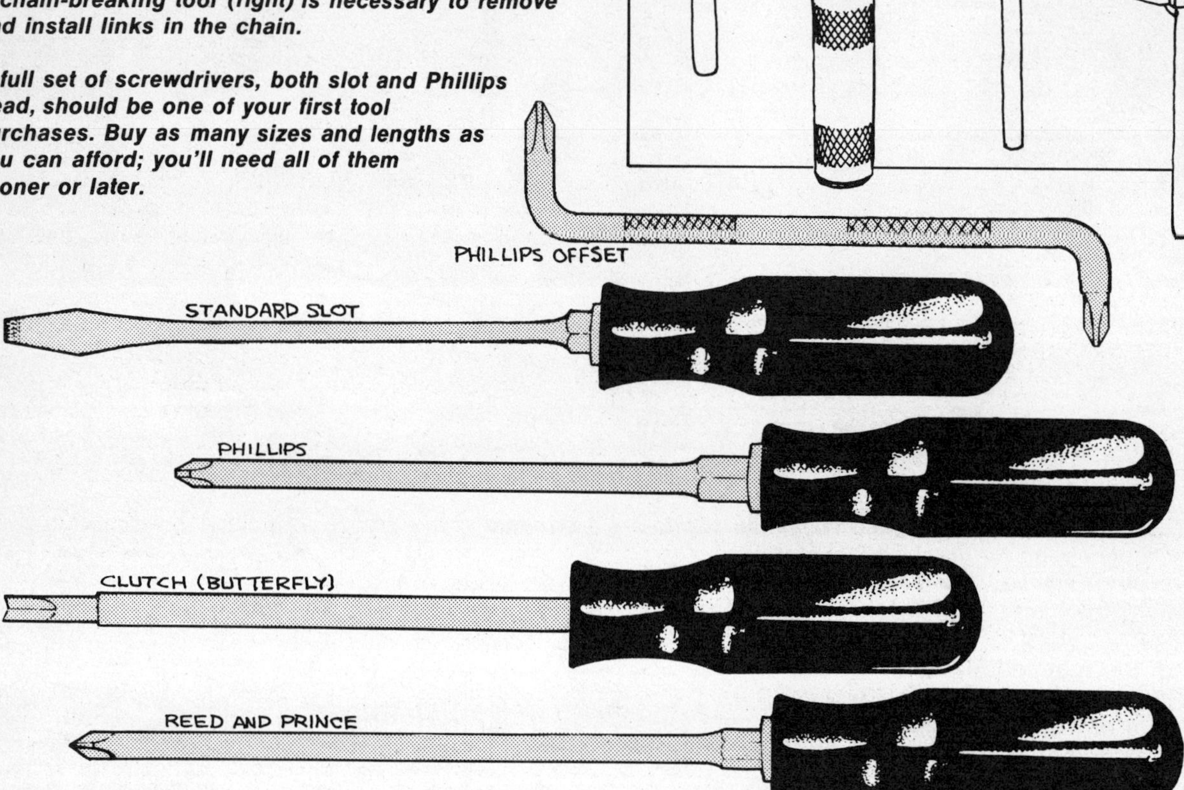

A good selection of screwdrivers with both slot and Phillips tips and in a variety of sizes is a must for any motorcycle work. Here, as with sockets or any other tools, buy good quality. A bad screwdriver will cause more grief than almost any other tool in your toolbox. A good selection of shaft lengths is important also. It's suprising just how often you wind up with a screwdriver of the right tip size, but in a length that won't allow you to get at the very screw you need to work on. It's advantageous to have the right tools on hand at the time you need them. Chasing tools in the middle of a job is time-consuming, and there is always the possibility of making a mistake or forgetting a step in the job.

Here's a good example: If the only screwdriver you have with the right tip size is too long to get a straight shot at the screw head you're trying to work on, it's worse than no screwdriver at all. A stubby model would be just the ticket here.

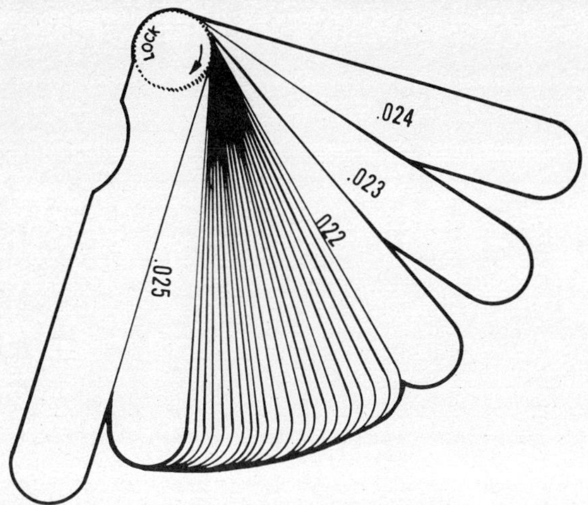

Feeler gauges and spark plug gapping gauges are precision tools. Buy good ones and take care of them. They are easily damaged, so put them away in the toolbox drawer when not in use.

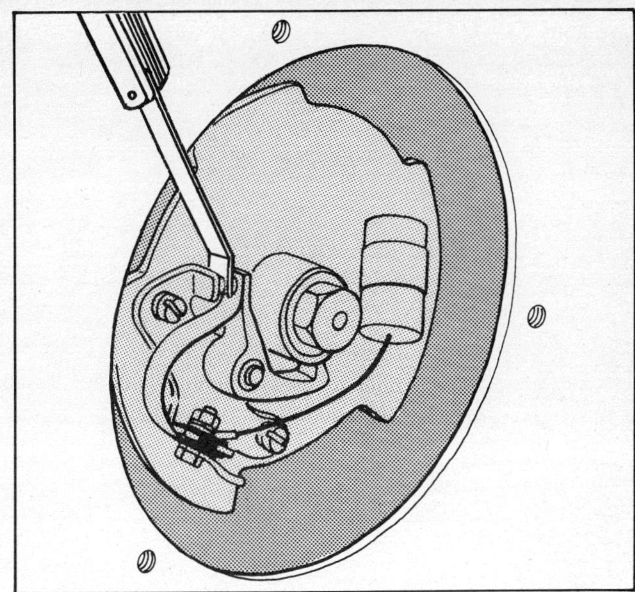

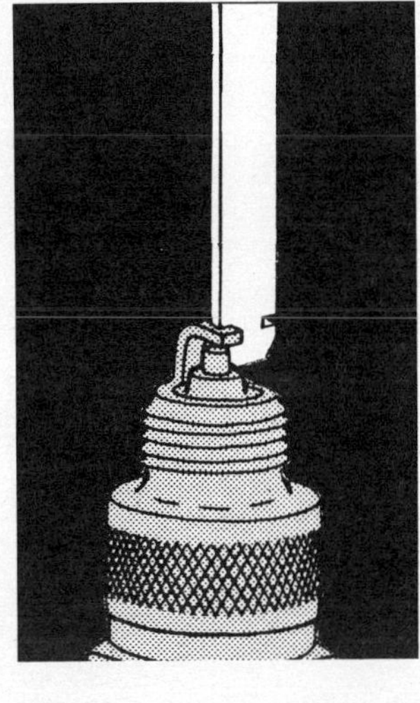

There are two measuring tools which fall in the special hand tool category. Both are needed for tune-up work. The first is a set of feeler gauges. They are used for a number of chores, from setting valve clearances on four-stroke engines to checking the ignition point gap.

The other necessary tool is a spark plug gapping tool. It may look as if a feeler gauge of the correct thickness would do the gapping job, but the underside of the ground electrode can become so badly pitted that the only correct way to measure the gap between it and the center electrode is with a gauge made of round wire.

The primary use of the feeler gauge is setting the opening on the ignition points (below). It is important that the gauge be kept clean, free of oil or grease which can change the reading and cause problems with the operation of the ignition system.

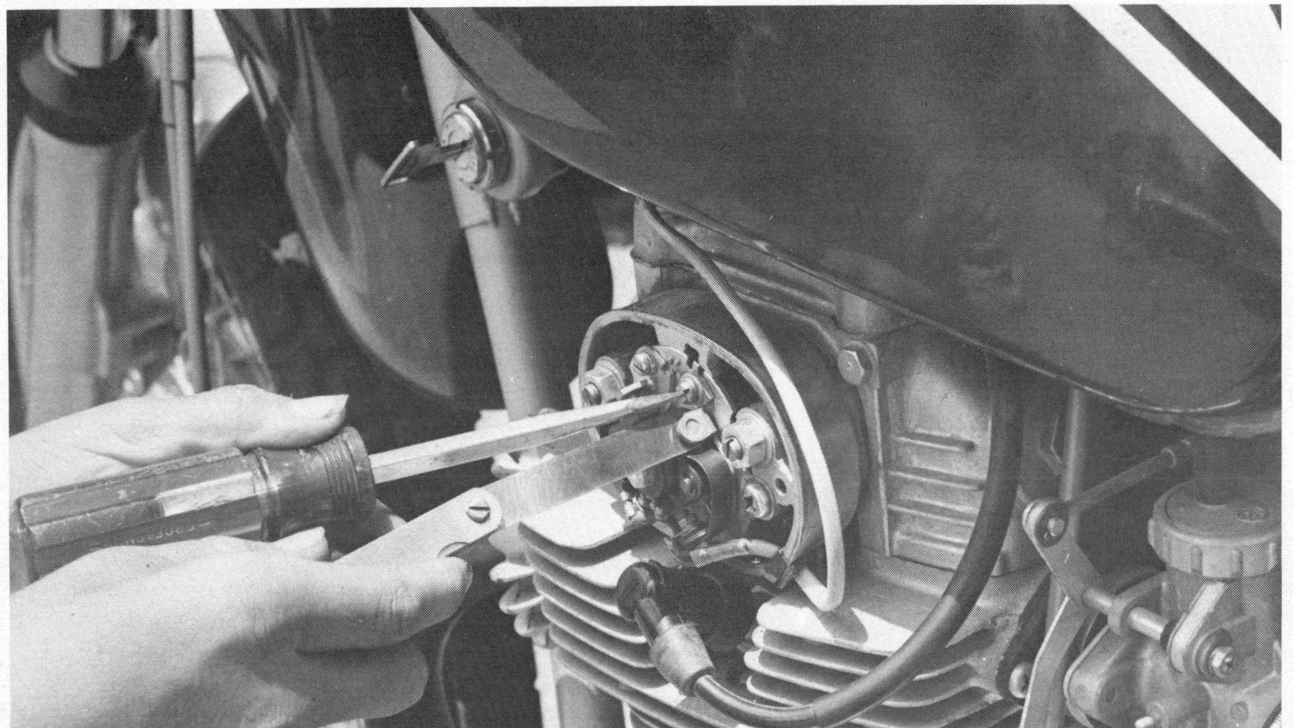

It's expensive, but the torque wrench is a very valuable tool, and one that most mechanics couldn't work without. Using a torque wrench is the only way to get accurate torque values when tightening parts.

A hand tool not generally required for minor tune-up work but one that should be in every motorcycle owner's toolbox is the torque wrench. Torque is a measure of the force required to tighten a bolt or stud so that it won't come loose under normal use conditions. Applying the correct amount of torque to any fastener on your motorcycle is important, but torque is normally measured only on certain critical parts of the engine and suspension.

The proper torque values are called out in the shop manual for your bike, and you should always take care to tighten such things as head bolts, case bolts or studs and any other items called out in the shop manual to the specified torque. If too little torque is applied to a fastener, it can loosen up while you are riding the bike and damage the engine or suspension or even result in injury. If too much torque is applied to a fastener, it or the material it's screwed into can be strained to the failure point. The fastener can also simply break off under too much tightening strain, and then you have the extra work and expense of attempting to remove a broken bolt or stud and buying new parts.

There are three basic types of torque wrench. The deflecting beam style is probably the oldest. It and the dial indicator type of torque wrench (below) both require that you position yourself or the item you are working on so that you can see the scale to read the torque values.

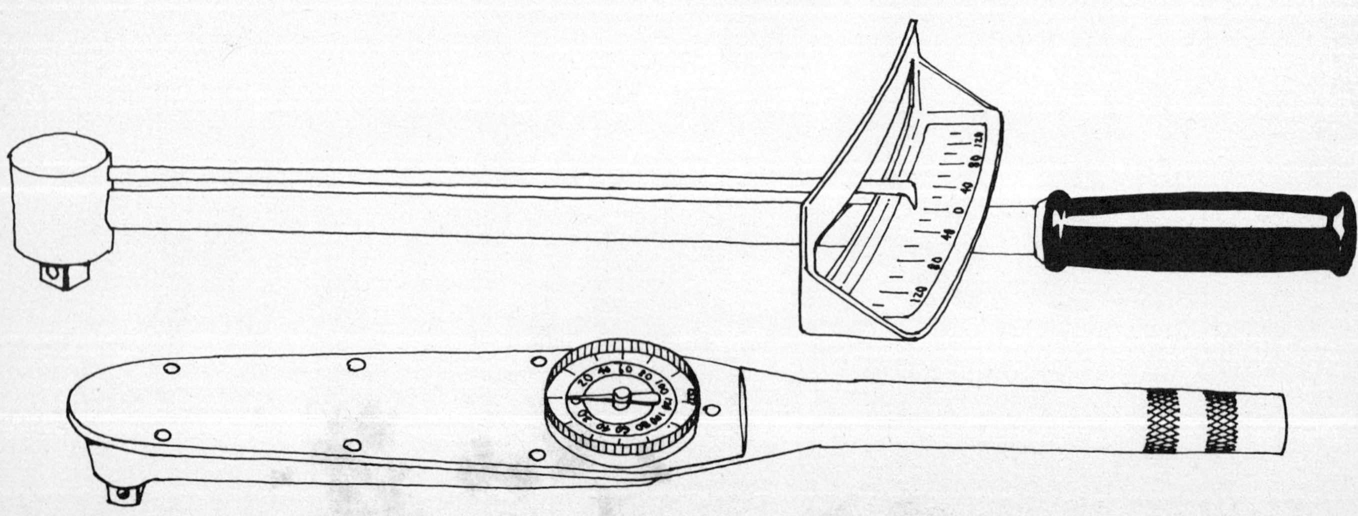

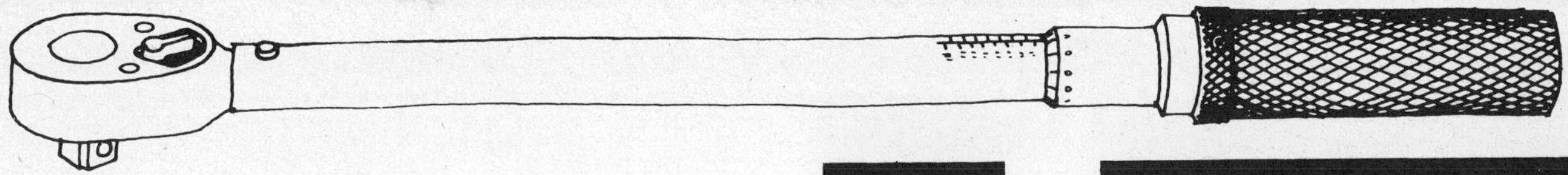

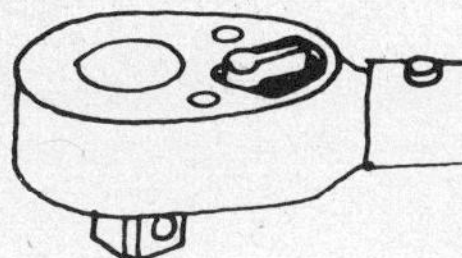

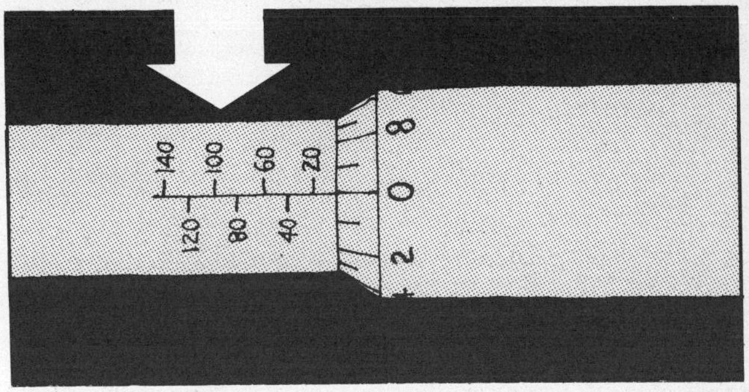

A better type of torque wrench is the audible click torque wrench. With this type of torque wrench, you adjust the handle to preset the required torque value. Then all you have to do is tighten the fastener slowly until the wrench responds with a slight "give" and an audible clicking sound to signal that the correct torque value has been reached. The great advantage of this type of torque wrench is that you don't have to look at it while you are using it, and once it is preset to a certain value, you can tighten several bolts or studs that require the same torque value without stopping.

Gears and alternator rotors are usually pressed on a shaft and held in place with a machined key. These parts are removed with a variety of pullers designed to take them off without damage to the shaft or the key. Pullers of this type are a necessary addition to your toolbox, but rather than purchase so-called "universal" pullers to start with, it's a good idea to consult your shop manual or a mechanic at your dealership to see if pullers of a special size or design are required for your motorcycle.

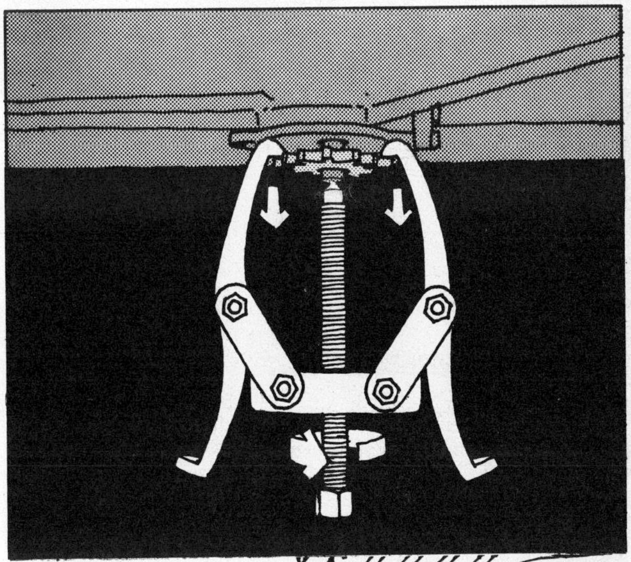

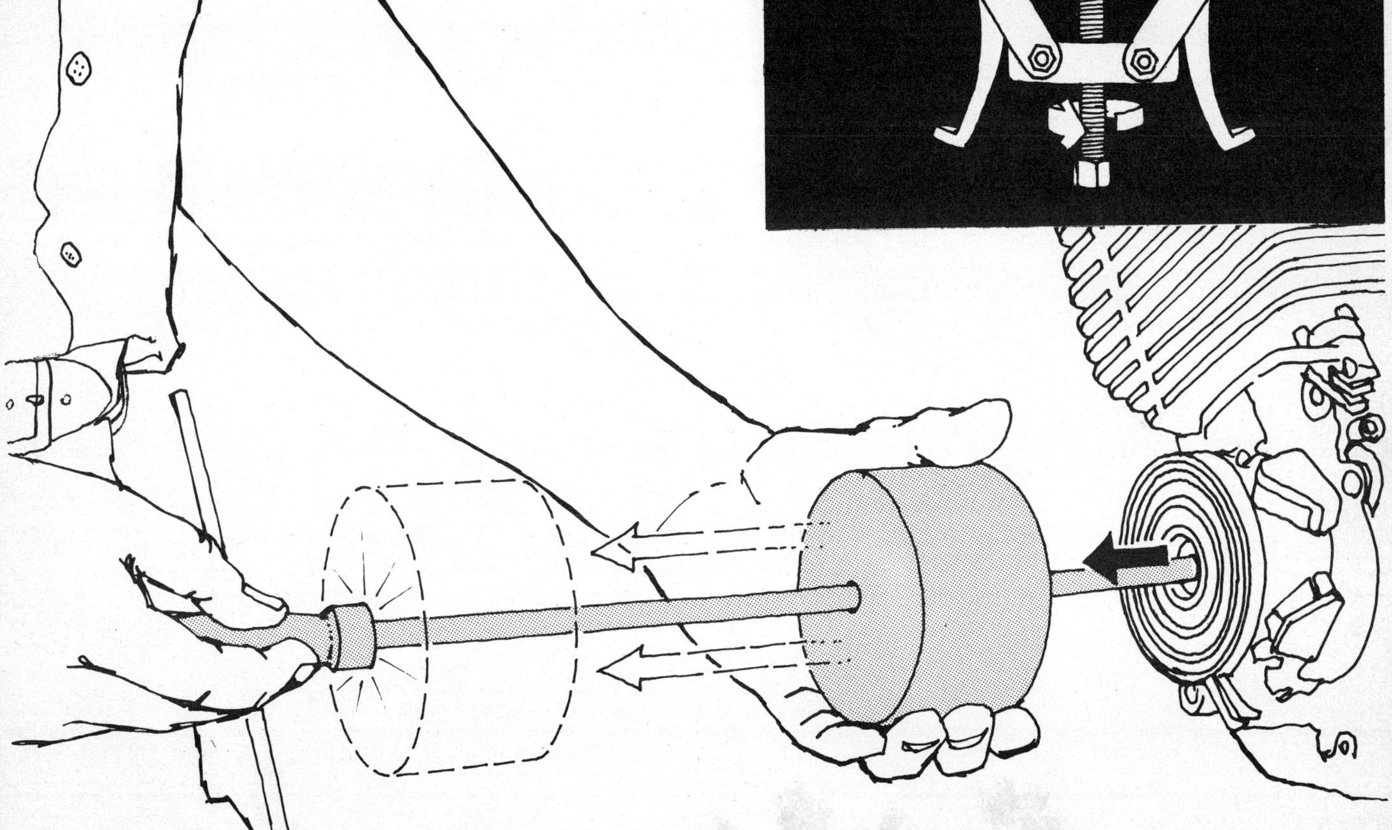

A gear puller and a slap hammer puller for removing the alternator and flywheels are often necessary for tune-up work.

1/Test Equipment and Gauges

There are several rather specialized tools in this category. Some are a required part of any tune-up. Others simply make it easier to do certain jobs, but are not strictly necessary for the average tune-up.

One of the most common test tools is the compression gauge. This gauge can tell you a lot about the internal condition of your engine. To use it, remove the spark plug from the cylinder head on your engine and insert the compression gauge. Then crank the engine over, either by electric starter or kick starter, and read the engine compression.

Many gauges have a device—similar to the valve core in a tire—that prevents the compression reading from dropping until you release the trapped air inside the gauge. This feature is very handy on bikes where it's difficult to read the gauge while it is in place.

A compression gauge can be used on both two-stroke and four-stroke engines and should be in your toolbox for both preventive maintenance and tune-up. There are two styles of this gauge. One has a cone-shaped rubber tip that is forced into the spark plug hole, while the other has a threaded tip that screws into the spark plug hole. The screw-in type is preferable. It makes a better seal, gives more accurate readings and often comes with a long rubber hose that connects the gauge and screw-in tip, so that you can position the gauge where it is easy to see while testing the compression.

A compression gauge is not an expensive piece of test equipment. You should have one in your toolbox.

A compression gauge with a screw-in adapter (below) is preferable to the rubber cone type. The adapter gives a better seal, and the long hose lets you see the gauge easily even if you are cranking the engine with the kick starter.

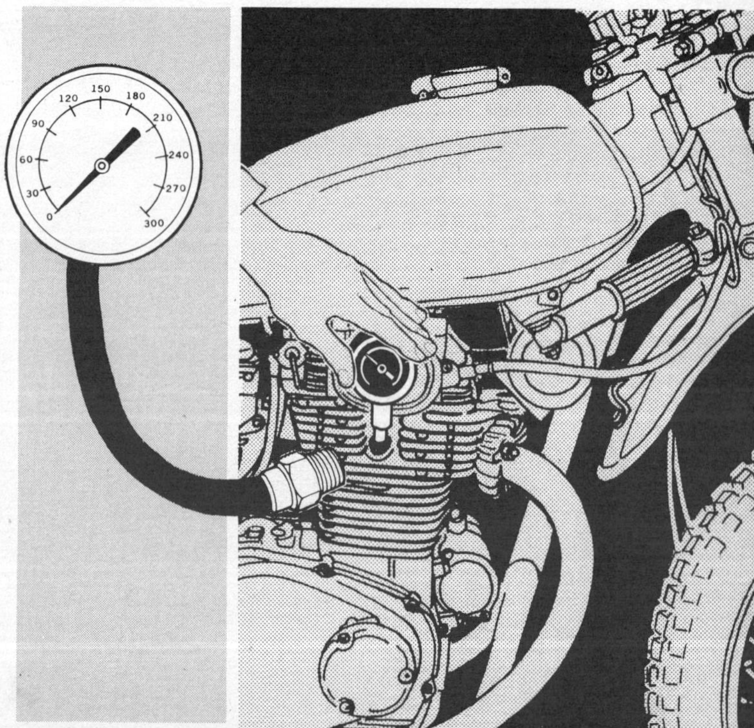

Two-stroke engines require a second type of compression tester to completely check out compression leaks. Because of their design, two-stroke engines pass the air/fuel mixture through the engine crankcase before it goes to the cylinder for burning. This requires the crankcase portion of the engine to hold pressure at certain times during each cycle of operation, just as the cylinder does.

To pressure-test the crankcase for leaks, you need a special compression testing kit. The kit includes a compression gauge, a hand pump for pressurizing the crankcase and blocking plates to close off the intake and exhaust sides of the cylinder. With this kit both engine crankcase and cylinder compression can be checked. While we hesitate to recommend this kit because of the additional expense, it is often the *only* way of detecting certain two-stroke engine problems.

Two-stroke engines require a sophisticated type of compression tester in order to check crankcase pressure as well as combustion chamber pressure. A kit like this is expensive, so you may want to consider having a shop mechanic do this kind of testing on your bike.

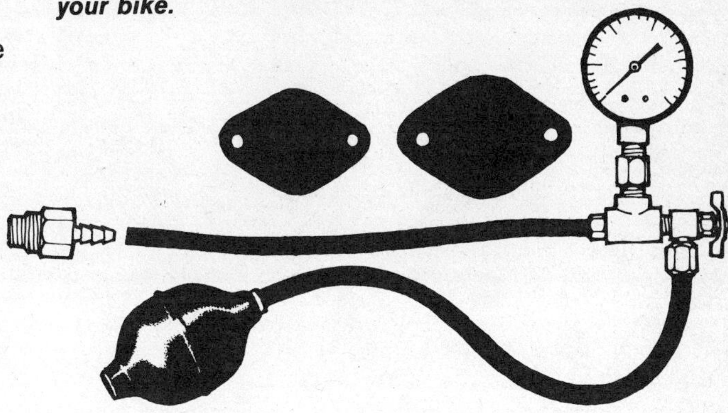

In two-stroke engines, the air/fuel mixture goes from the carburetor into the crankcase to be compressed before it passes through a port into the combustion chamber. Therefore the crankcase as well as the combustion chamber must be perfectly sealed during part of each cycle of operation. A leak in the crankcase is just as bad as a leak above the piston.

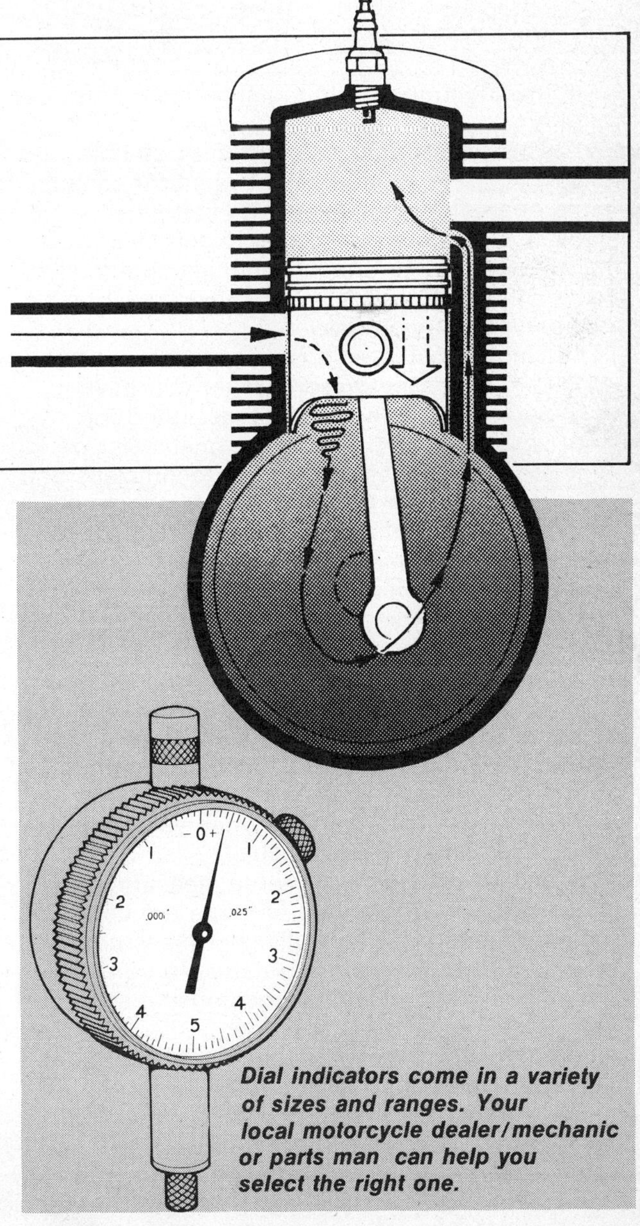

Dial indicators come in a variety of sizes and ranges. Your local motorcycle dealer/mechanic or parts man can help you select the right one.

Another useful tool is the dial indicator. It has many applications, but perhaps the most common is for measuring the position of the piston in the cylinder as part of the process of ignition timing. A good dial indicator is not cheap, and it should be taken care of carefully. When not in use, store it in a cushioned box (most come in a suitable container), along with the various attachments that may be used with the basic indicator.

On many engines, piston TDC (Top Dead Center) can be checked by inserting the dial indicator probe through the spark plug hole in the head. On some models it is necessary to remove the head.

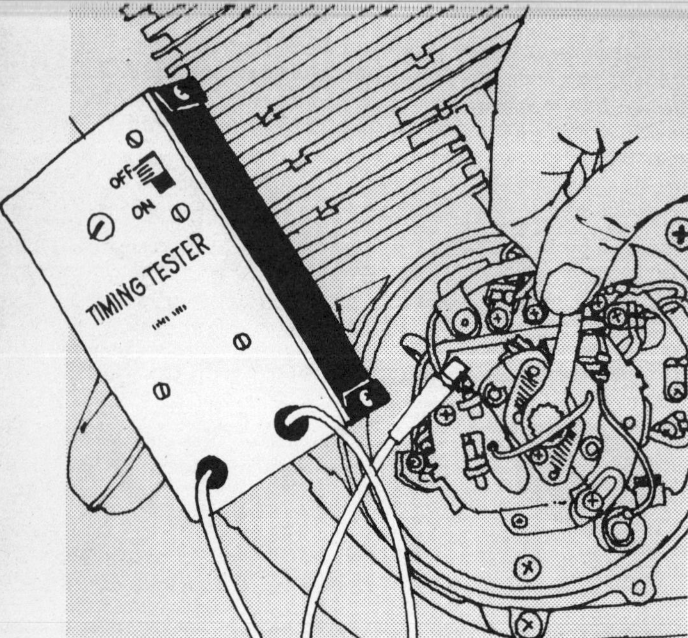

With its test leads connected across the ignition points, a buzz box will sound off when the point surfaces open or break contact. This is a more exact method of determining point opening than by eye.

Another item used in the ignition timing process is the timing tester, often referred to as the "buzz box." This tester provides a visual or audible indication of the exact moment when the ignition points open. In combination with the dial indicator, it is more often used to set timing on motorcycles than is the conventional automobile timing light, though the timing light is used on several types of motorcycles.

The single most useful piece of test equipment any mechanic or motorcycle owner can have in his toolbox is an item not really designed for motorcycle use at all. This is the multimeter or ohmmeter, with which electronics technicians and television repairmen troubleshoot electrical components. This is one piece of test equipment we strongly recommend that you purchase and learn to use. A multimeter can substitute for a buzz box as an indicator of ignition point opening. What's more, you can check the condition of your battery, troubleshoot ignition problems, find shorted or broken wires and check the condition of any electrical component on the motorcycle with a multimeter. Also, these units are not expensive. A toolbox-sized multimeter generally costs less than $20. Once you learn to use it, you'll find it indispensable.

The multimeter combines three measuring functions into a single unit. All three are common electrical functions. The multimeter measures voltage, current flow and resistance to current flow in wiring and electrical components such as lights, switches, starters and alternators. Two test leads connect the meter to the item being tested, making the meter part of the circuit. The multimeter displays information on a meter face that has several scales. There are function switches on the front of the meter so you can choose what kind of measurements you want to take. Once you have operated a multimeter for a short time, you will find there is nothing imposing about its scales and functions. It's really a simple, easy-to-use piece of test equipment.

On some motorcycles, a timing light can be used (see below). The light operates on what is called the "stroboscopic" effect. That is, a fast-blinking light appears to freeze a moving mark in relation to an unmoving mark. The light flashes at the same time as the spark plug fires.

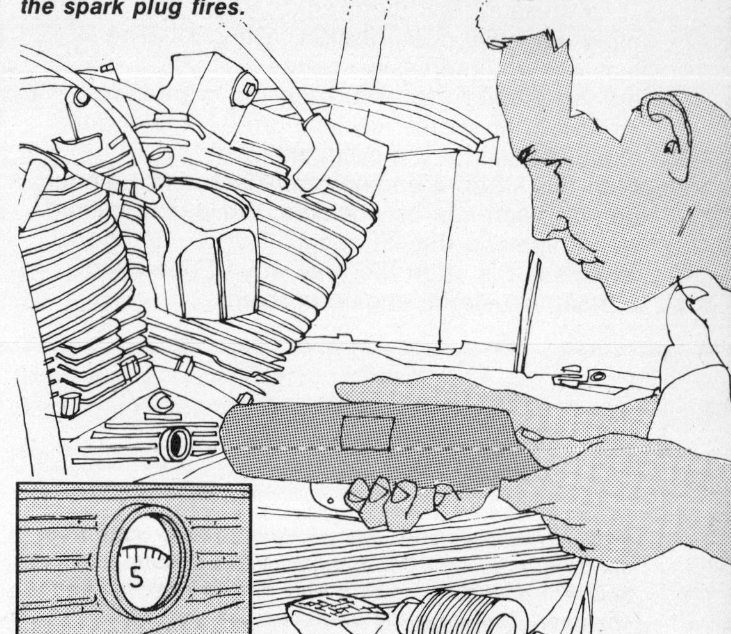

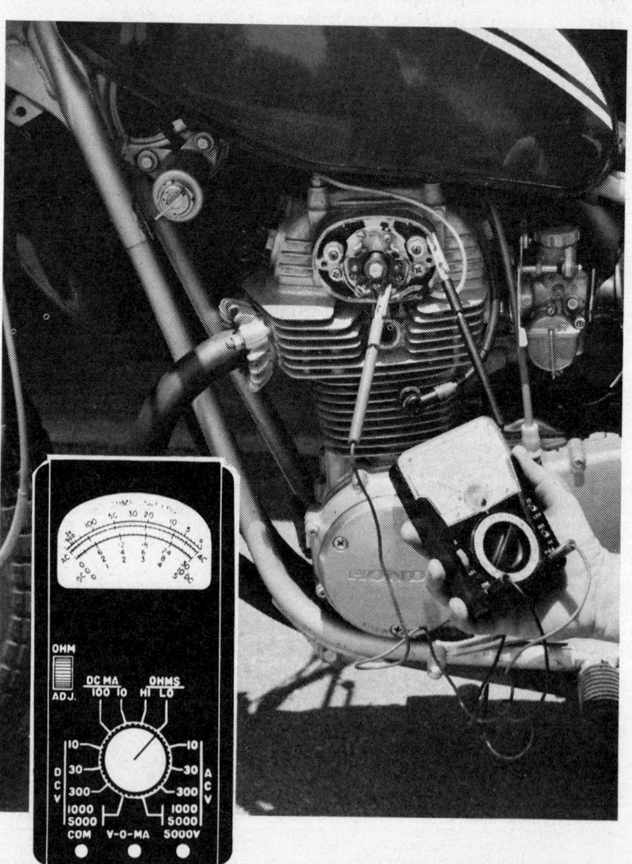

The multimeter can be used to troubleshoot the various parts of the ignition system. Although the meter face looks complex with its many scales, you can easily learn to use one in an afternoon.

One other piece of exotic test equipment adapted from the world of electronics is the oscilloscope. Anyone who watches television has seen this machine on medical shows, tracing out the heartbeat of patients in the operating room. It also serves in troubleshooting and repair of electronics equipment. Most important from a mechanical viewpoint, the oscilloscope has become the chief tool for rapid troubleshooting at automotive and motorcycle dealerships.

An oscilloscope combines a picture tube with a sensitive amplifier, which picks up electrical signals and displays them on the screen in the form of a thin, bright line. The line on the screen records for the eye what is happening inside electronics equipment, your heart or the ignition system of your motorcycle.

The picture tube of the oscilloscope is a big vacuum tube which operates on the same principles as a TV picture tube. A high-velocity beam of electrons formed inside the tube sweeps across the inside of the tube face at speeds of thousands of miles an hour. When this beam of electrons strikes the material covering the inside of the tube face, the material glows briefly. This glow traces the path of the electron beam so that you can see it.

In a television set, the beam is altered or modified as it moves to correspond with the brightness or darkness of the picture that the camera is taking. In the "O-scope," however, instead of making the line brighter or darker at intervals to form a picture, the line moves up and down on the face of the scope to form a momentary graph of what the electrical signal we are interested in is doing.

When the test leads of the O-scope are connected to the ignition system of a motorcycle, we get to see exactly what's going on inside the ignition system while it is working. The changing patterns displayed on the tube tell the experienced mechanic or tuner if there is anything wrong with the ignition system. Usually they even pinpoint the exact cause of the problem.

While the oscilloscope is an expensive item, not one generally found in the home garage, some oscilloscopes are within reach of the average pocketbook, including one that comes in a do-it-yourself kit. The next time you are at your bike dealership, stop by the service area. If they have an O-scope, ask if you can watch the mechanic use it to tune a bike. You'll find it interesting and informative.

One piece of test equipment that is outside the price range of most home tuners is the shop oscilloscope. This machine reduces troubleshooting time on customers' motorcycles at many dealerships.

The main component of the oscilloscope is a large picture tube, much like the one in your television set. A beam of high-velocity electrons is generated at the back of the tube. The beam, directed by magnetic fields, paints a picture in light on the tube, showing the signals received by the scope from the ignition.

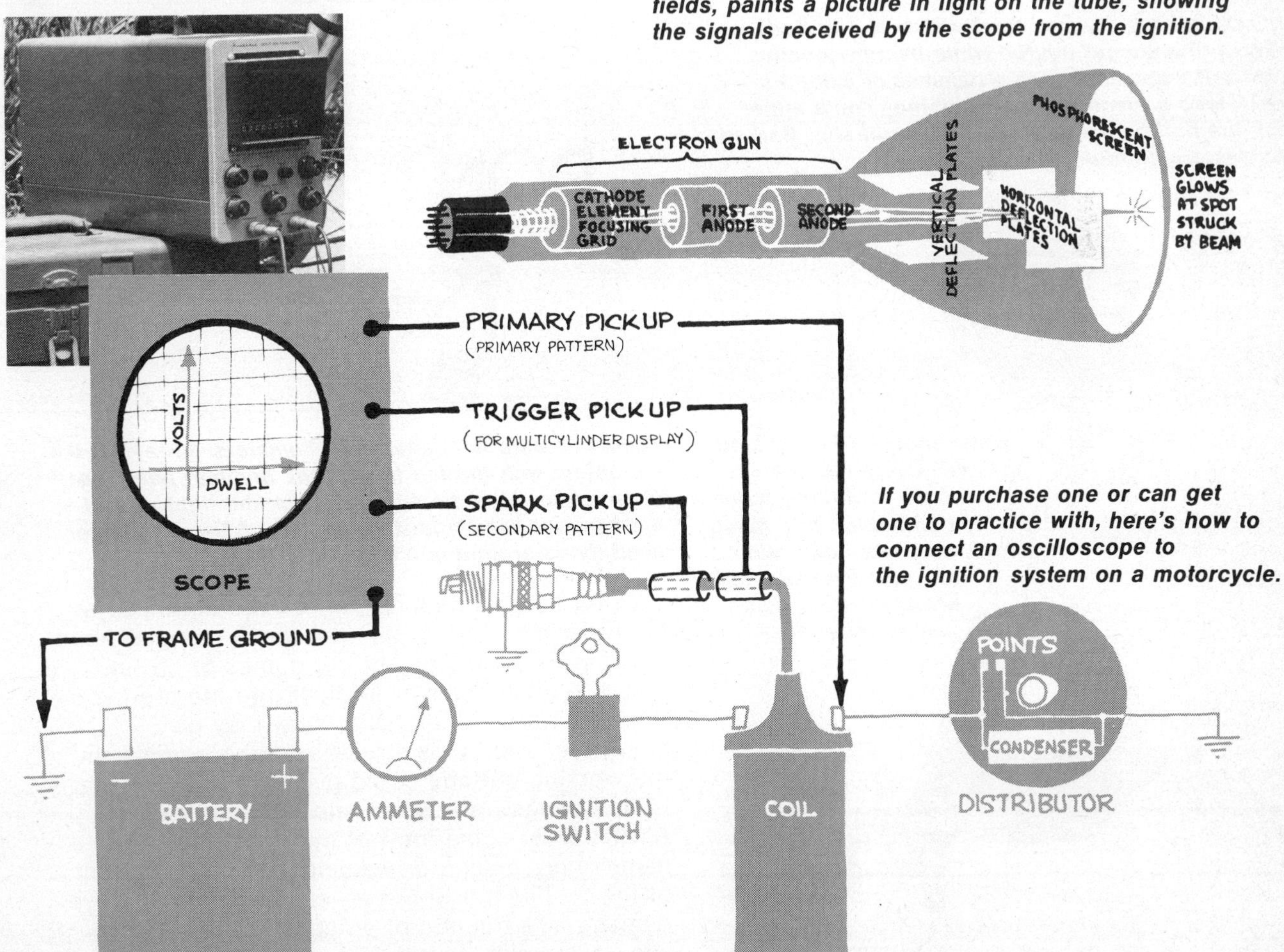

If you purchase one or can get one to practice with, here's how to connect an oscilloscope to the ignition system on a motorcycle.

I/ Using Tools Safely

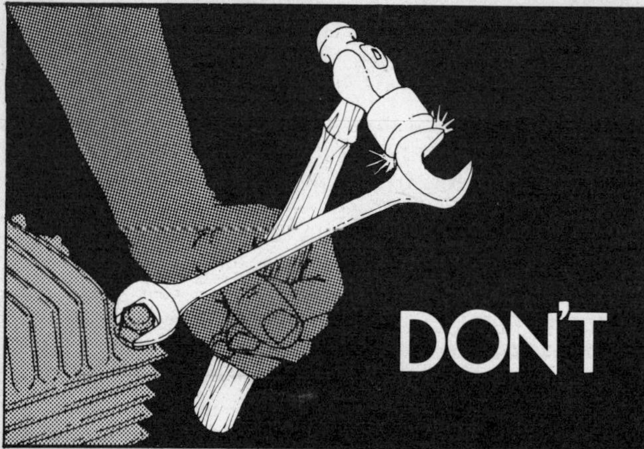

Illustrated above are two common ways that parts get broken or hands get injured while using wrenches. Never strike a wrench with a hammer or extend a wrench with a piece of pipe or tubing. You'll either break the bolt by overtorqueing or you'll slip. Barked knuckles are painful!

Don't become a statistic in your own garage! Safe handling of tools while working on your motorcycle may seem like a subject so elementary it's not worth mentioning, but it's a sad fact that a lot of people get hurt using just simple hand tools each year.

There aren't many tools simpler than a combination wrench, for example, but using it incorrectly can hurt. There are two simple lessons here. First, don't use a pipe to extend a wrench to apply more torque. The result is usually a broken wrench, a broken bolthead or broken knuckles when the whole flimsy affair slips and smashes your hand into the engine or frame. Second, always pull the wrench toward you if possible. Pushing the wrench away from you can end in bloody knuckles if the wrench slips.

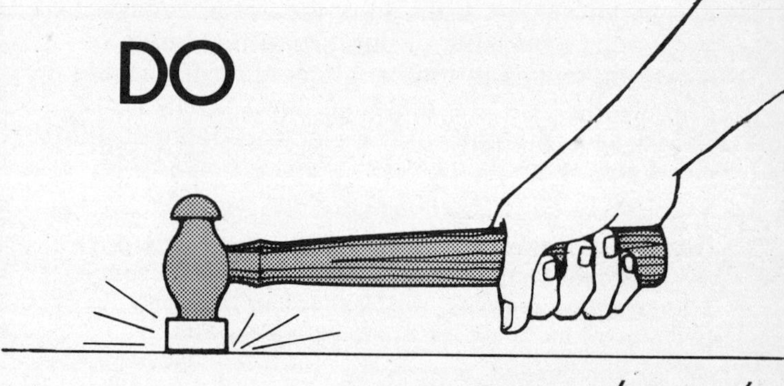

The same care is needed with hammers. Always strike the object with the full face of the hammer head, not at an angle. Also, be sure to check the tightness of the hammer head from time to time. A loose hammer head flying around is a lethal missile.

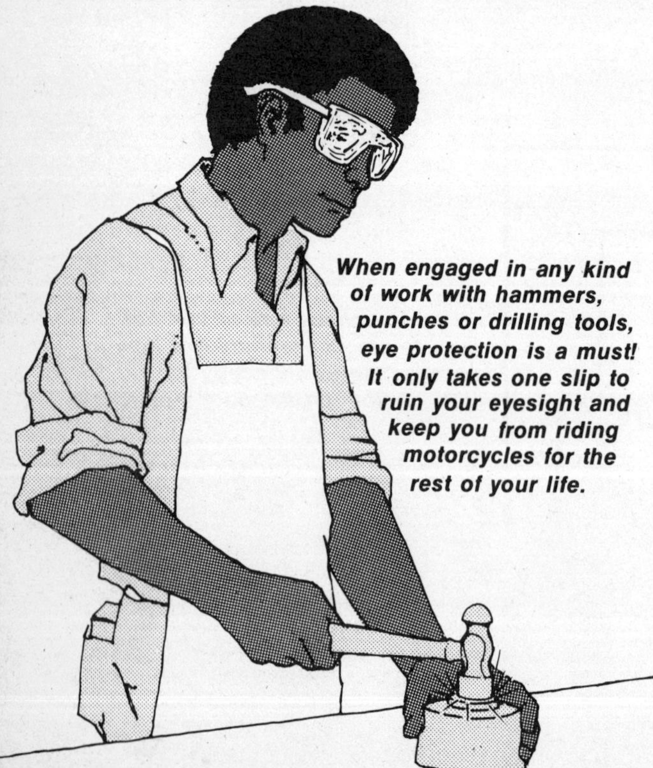

When engaged in any kind of work with hammers, punches or drilling tools, eye protection is a must! It only takes one slip to ruin your eyesight and keep you from riding motorcycles for the rest of your life.

When using a hammer, check the tightness of the head from time to time. A loose hammer head becomes a deadly object if it comes off in full swing. Always hammer straight into the area you are working on. A glancing blow may go anywhere, and chips struck from the hammer or the working surface could go flying about.

This brings up another important subject. Always wear some form of eye protection when hammering, drilling or welding. A loose fragment of the tool or the work can cause permanent eye damage in a fraction of a second. Then it's too late to do anything about it.

One of the most common forms of tool misuse is grabbing the nearest screwdriver instead of going to the box for a suitable punch to remove a stud or broken rivet. In a word, DON'T! Screwdrivers were not made for this kind of abuse.

Good working conditions in the shop are just as important as how you use your tools. Wherever your "shop" is, whether the garage or the driveway on a sunny day, it's important to have good lighting, adequate ventilation and a safe, practical layout of tools and parts. Any experienced mechanic will tell you that a clean, well-organized shop is a safe shop. It does no good to handle a tool safely on your motorcycle if you haphazardly leave it on the floor afterward, then slip on it later and break your leg!

When working on your motorcycle, it's always a good idea to take off jewelry such as watches, rings, ID bracelets, etc. These items can get caught on protruding parts of the bike and injure you. Also, if anything metallic you are wearing comes in contact with "hot" parts of the bike's electrical system, you can suffer a severe shock and burns. Finally, if the battery is not necessary to the work you are doing, disconnect it while working.

The fact that your motorcycle only has two wheels is another thing that can cause trouble. Side kickstands and even centerstands can fold up if you put a lot of pressure on them, and the bike can fall over. This usually damages the bike, and if you are in the way, it can hurt! To prevent this, block up the bike securely with wooden blocks or axle stands of the type used on automobiles. Also, never work on your bike on the lawn or other soft surface. This is inviting the bike to fall on you.

If you take a few moments to think over what you are doing and what conditions you need to work on your bike safely, you run much less risk of injury while performing a tune-up.

This is definitely a no-no! A screwdriver is not a punch and should not be used in place of one. It's a sure path to broken knuckles or worse.

When working on your motorcycle, it's always smart to put a secure foundation under it before moving the front forks or applying a lot of pressure to a wrench.

I/Riding Safety

There are over three million motorcycles now registered in the United States, and the number could double by 1980. However, there are more than 10 times that many registered cars and trucks traveling our roads. It is therefore essential to form good riding habits in the beginning. This means knowing your bike, how it functions and how to ride safely under any conditions.

University studies show that 70% of all motorcycle accidents involve riders with less than six months of riding experience. This "experience" is the ability to ride in traffic, make proper turns and use good judgment about speed and braking. Remember that the motorcycle you ride is only as safe as the guy operating it. So make and keep good riding habits. They will help ensure that you get the fullest enjoyment of motorcycle riding through the years.

The following safety tips should be reviewed frequently by every bike rider, regardless of how long he has been riding. Memorize them—they could save your life.

1. *Always wear protective gear.* This includes:

- A good motorcycle helmet.
- Clothing that is visible at long distances, like bright jackets or strips of fluorescent material that attach to outer garments. A good bike shop carries all these accessories.
- Gloves.
- Good boots or sturdy shoes.
- A pair of motorcycle goggles or face shield to protect you from rocks, bugs and flying debris.

2. *Stay alert.* Be prepared for sudden stops by the vehicles ahead of you and for cars pulling away from the curb. Many motorcycle accidents occur at intersections.

3. *Be seen.* Keep your headlight on at all times, day and night. Many collisions occur simply because the other vehicle did not see the bike.

4. *Use mirrors.* Use rearview mirrors on the left and right sides of your handlebars. They are a cheap investment but let you see what's going on behind you before changing lanes. Without them you have to turn your head to look behind you. This split second with your eyes off the road could make a big difference in your health.

5. *Keep your distance.* When following another vehicle, keep at least 50 feet away at a speed of 20 mph, 100 feet at 30 mph and more than 300 feet at 50 mph. You cannot drive defensively when following too closely.

6. *If you can't see it, don't try it.* This means passing on hills and curves. Sure, you've got more quick power than most cars and trucks, but the obstacle that can hurt you is the one you don't see in time.

7. *Turn left carefully.* Always enter the left traffic lane well in advance of turning left, and be sure you signal your intent. Do not continue your left turn until oncoming traffic is past and it is safe to proceed.

8. *Use your brakes wisely.* Combined braking delivers the safest stops. Since the front brake is more powerful, apply the rear brake first, then ease down gently on the front brake. Always brake *gently* on slippery surfaces. Also, use your brakes before rounding a turn, not while in it. Be sure that both brakes are always in proper adjustment.

9. *Watch those slick surfaces.* Always reduce your speed when riding on wet roads or roads strewn with sand or loose gravel. The first few hours of a rainstorm, when roads first become wet, are the most dangerous. All the oil deposits from passing traffic rise to the surface of the water, making roads one massive oil slick. Use extreme caution.

Always ride defensively to protect yourself, especially in traffic. Automobile drivers usually don't pay too much attention to a bike rider. Courtesy is a part of good defensive driving. When you consider the other person first *regardless* of who has the right of way, you will probably enjoy years of safe riding.

Never be "Mr. Cool" and try to show off for your girlfriend or anyone else. You could end up "Mr. Dead." Always obey the traffic laws. They apply to bike riders as well as to cars. The laws were made to *protect* you and all people who use the roads.

Be familiar with the bike you are riding. Know where the controls are and how they operate. Study that owner's manual.

I/Math for Tuners

WHITWORTH SIZES

Unless you own or work with British motorcycles, you won't be concerned with this information on Whitworth wrench sizes, but if you do, it should prove quite helpful. For many years the British have used a Whitworth thread on nuts, screws and bolts, thus creating the Whitworth wrench size.

This screw thread form is used for the British Standard Whitworth (BSW) and the British Standard Five (BSF). Over the years, many thousands of these popular British motorcycles have been imported into this country. Until just the last few years, the majority of the fasteners on these bikes were Whitworth.

Since British manufacturers have now almost completed the changeover to the metric system, the Whitworth thread form should only be used for replacements or spare parts. The chart gives you the U.S., metric and British Whitworth sizes and a comparison in decimal inches.

COMPARISON OF U.S., METRIC AND WHITWORTH WRENCH SIZES

U.S.	METRIC	WHITWORTH	DECIMAL INCHES	OPEN-END WRENCH		BOX-END OR SOCKET WRENCH	
NOMINAL NUT SIZE				MIN.	MAX.	MIN.	MAX.
5/32			.156	.158	.161	.158	.163
	4mm		.157	.159	.162	.159	.164
		7BA	.172	.174	.177	.174	.179
3/16			.187	.190	.193	.190	.195
		6BA	.193	.195	.198	.195	.200
	5mm		.197	.199	.202	.199	.204
13/64			.203	.205	.208	.205	.210
7/32			.218	.221	.224	.221	.226
		5BA	.220	.222	.225	.222	.227
15/64			.234	.236	.239	.236	.241
	6mm		.236	.238	.241	.238	.243
		4BA	.248	.250	.253	.250	.255
1/4			.250	.252	.255	.252	.257
17/64			.265	.268	.271	.268	.273
	7mm		.276	.278	.281	.278	.283
9/32			.281	.284	.288	.284	.290
		3BA	.282	.284	.288	.284	.289
5/16			.312	.316	.320	.316	.322
	8mm		.315	.317	.321	.317	.322
		2BA	.324	.327	.331	.327	.333
		1/8W	.338	.341	.345	.341	.347
11/32			.343	.347	.351	.347	.353
	9mm		.354	.357	.361	.357	.363
		1BA	.365	.368	.372	.368	.374
3/8			.375	.378	.382	.378	.384
	10mm		.393	.396	.400	.396	.402
		0BA	.413	.416	.420	.416	.422
	11mm		.433	.436	.440	.436	.442
7/16			.437	.440	.444	.440	.446
		3/16W	.448	.451	.455	.451	.457
15/32			.468	.472	.476	.472	.478
	12mm		.472	.475	.479	.475	.481
1/2			.500	.504	.508	.504	.510
	13mm		.512	.516	.520	.516	.522
		1/4W	.525	.529	.533	.529	.535
17/32			.531	.535	.539	.535	.541
	14mm		.551	.555	.559	.555	.561
9/16			.562	.566	.570	.566	.573
	15mm		.591	.595	.599	.595	.601
19/32			.593	.598	.602	.598	.604
		5/16W	.600	.604	.608	.604	.612
5/8			.625	.629	.633	.629	.636
	16mm		.630	.634	.638	.634	.642
21/32			.656	.661	.665	.661	.668
	17mm		.669	.673	.677	.673	.681
11/16			.687	.692	.696	.692	.699
	18mm		.709	.715	.720	.715	.723
		3/8W	.710	.715	.720	.715	.723
	19mm		.748	.753	.758	.758	.761
3/4			.750	.755	.760	.755	.763
25/32			.781	.786	.791	.786	.794
	20mm		.787	.792	.797	.792	.800
13/16			.812	.818	.823	.818	.826
		7/16W	.820	.825	.830	.825	.833
	21mm		.827	.832	.837	.832	.840
	22mm		.866	.871	.876	.871	.879
7/8			.875	.880	.885	.880	.888
	23mm		.906	.911	.916	.911	.920
29/32			906	.911	.916	.911	.920
		1/2W	.920	.925	.930	.925	.934
15/16			.937	.944	.949	.944	.953
	24mm		.945	.950	.955	.950	.959
31/32			.968	.975	.981	.975	.984
	25mm		.984	.990	.996	.990	.999
1			1.000	1.006	1.012	1.006	1.015
		9/16W	1.010	1.016	1.022	1.016	1.025
	26mm		1.024	1.030	1.036	1.030	1.039
1-1/16			1.062	1.068	1.074	1.068	1.077
	27mm		1.063	1.069	1.075	1.069	1.078
		5/8W	1.100	1.107	1.113	1.107	1.117
	28mm		1.102	1.109	1.115	1.109	1.119
1-1/8			1.125	1.132	1.139	1.132	1.142
	29mm		1.142	1.149	1.156	1.149	1.159
	30mm		1.181	1.188	1.195	1.188	1.198
1-3/16			1.187	1.195	1.202	1.195	1.205
		11/16W	1.200	1.207	1.214	1.207	1.217
	31mm		1.220	1.227	1.234	1.227	1.237
1-1/4			1.250	1.258	1.266	1.258	1.269
	32mm		1.260	1.267	1.275	1.267	1.277
	33mm		1.299	1.306	1.314	1.306	1.316

CONVERSION FROM FRACTIONAL INCHES TO MILLIMETERS

inch		mm	inch		mm
1/64	0.015 625	0.396 875	33/64	0.515 625	13.096 875
1/32	0.031 250	0.793 750	17/32	0.531 250	13.493 750
3/64	0.046 875	1.190 625	35/64	0.546 875	13.890 625
1/16	0.062 500	1.587 500	9/16	0.562 500	14.287 500
5/64	0.078 125	1.984 375	37/64	0.578 125	14.684 375
3/32	0.093 750	2.381 250	19/32	0.593 750	15.081 250
7/64	0.109 375	2.778 125	39/64	0.609 375	15.478 125
1/8	0.125 000	3.175 000	5/8	0.625 000	15.875 000
9/64	0.140 625	3.571 875	41/64	0.640 625	16.271 875
5/32	0.156 250	3.968 750	21/32	0.656 250	16.668 750
11/64	0.171 875	4.365 625	43/64	0.671 875	17.065 625
3/16	0.187 500	4.762 500	11/16	0.687 500	17.462 500
13/64	0.203 125	5.159 375	45/64	0.703 125	17.859 375
7/32	0.218 750	5.556 250	23/32	0.718 750	18.256 250
15/64	0.234 375	5.953 125	47/64	0.734 375	18.653 125
1/4	0.250 000	6.350 000	3/4	0.750 000	19.050 000
17/64	0.265 625	6.746 875	49/64	0.765 625	19.446 875
9/32	0.281 250	7.143 750	25/32	0.781 250	19.843 750
19/64	0.296 875	7.540 625	51/64	0.796 875	20.240 625
5/16	0.312 500	7.937 500	13/16	0.812 500	20.637 500
21/64	0.328 125	8.334 375	53/64	0.828 125	21.034 375
11/32	0.343 750	8.731 250	27/32	0.843 750	21.431 250
23/64	0.359 375	9.128 125	55/64	0.859 375	21.828 125
3/8	0.375 000	9.525 000	7/8	0.875 000	22.225 000
25/64	0.390 625	9.921 875	57/64	0.890 625	22.621 875
13/32	0.406 250	10.318 750	29/32	0.906 250	23.018 750
27/64	0.421 875	10.715 625	59/64	0.921 875	23.415 625
7/16	0.437 500	11.112 500	15/16	0.937 500	23.812 500
29/64	0.453 125	11.509 375	61/64	0.953 125	24.209 375
15/32	0.468 750	11.906 250	31/32	0.968 750	24.606 250
31/64	0.484 375	12.303 125	63/64	0.984 375	25.003 125
1/2	0.500 000	12.700 000	1	1.000 000	25.400 000

NOTE: All values in table are exact.

The chart below can be used to convert foot-pounds to meter-kilograms. The foot-pound column at the left increases in 10 ft.-lb. increments from 0 to 110 ft.-lbs. For each additional ft.-lb., read the top row of numbers. Example: If you desire 45 ft.-lbs., you would look to the number 40 in the left column and the number 5 in the top row. The conversion to meter-kilograms would be 6.22 mkgs. For your use, the conversion formula is:

FT.-LBS. X .1383 = METER-KILOGRAMS

Ft. Lbs.	0	1	2	3	4	5	6	7	8	9
	Mkgs	Mkgs	Mkgs	Mkgs	Mkgs	Mkgs	Mkgs	Mkgs	Mkgs	Mkgs
0	0	.14	.28	.42	.55	.69	.83	.97	1.11	1.25
10	1.38	1.52	1.66	1.80	1.94	2.07	2.21	2.35	2.49	2.63
20	2.77	2.90	3.04	3.18	3.32	3.46	3.60	3.73	3.87	4.01
30	4.15	4.29	4.43	4.56	4.70	4.84	4.98	5.12	5.26	5.39
40	5.53	5.67	5.81	5.95	6.09	6.22	6.36	6.50	6.64	6.78
50	6.92	7.05	7.19	7.33	7.47	7.61	7.75	7.88	8.02	8.16
60	8.30	8.44	8.57	8.71	8.85	8.90	9.13	9.27	9.40	9.54
70	9.68	9.82	9.96	10.09	10.23	10.37	10.51	10.65	10.79	10.92
80	11.01	11.20	11.34	11.48	11.62	11.75	11.89	12.03	12.17	12.31
90	12.45	12.59	12.73	12.86	13.00	13.14	13.28	13.42	13.55	13.69
100	13.83	13.97	14.11	14.25	14.38	14.52	14.66	14.80	14.94	15.08
110	15.21	15.35	15.49	15.63	15.76	15.90	16.04	16.18	16.32	16.46

CONVERSION FROM MILLIMETERS TO INCHES

mm	inch	mm	inch	mm	inch
1	0.039 370 08	36	1.417 322 8	71	2.795 275 6
2	0.078 740 16	37	1.456 692 9	72	2.834 645 7
3	0.118 110 24	38	1.496 063 0	73	2.874 015 7
4	0.157 480 31	39	1.535 433 1	74	2.913 385 8
5	0.196 850 39	40	1.574 803 1	75	2.952 755 9
6	0.236 220 47	41	1.614 173 2	76	2.992 126 0
7	0.275 590 55	42	1.653 543 3	77	3.031 496 1
8	0.314 960 63	43	1.692 913 4	78	3.070 866 1
9	0.354 330 71	44	1.732 283 5	79	3.110 236 2
10	0.393 700 8	45	1.771 653 5	80	3.149 606 3
11	0.433 070 9	46	1.811 023 6	81	3.188 976 4
12	0.472 440 9	47	1.850 393 7	82	3.228 346 5
13	0.511 811 0	48	1.889 763 8	83	3.267 716 5
14	0.551 181 1	49	1.929 133 9	84	3.307 086 6
15	0.590 551 2	50	1.968 503 9	85	3.346 456 7
16	0.629 921 3	51	2.007 874 0	86	3.385 826 8
17	0.669 291 3	52	2.047 244 1	87	3.425 196 8
18	0.708 661 4	53	2.086 614 2	88	3.464 566 9
19	0.748 031 5	54	2.125 984 2	89	3.503 937 0
20	0.787 401 6	55	2.165 354 3	90	3.543 307 1
21	0.826 771 7	56	2.204 724 4	91	3.582 677 2
22	0.866 141 7	57	2.244 094 5	92	3.622 047 2
23	0.905 511 8	58	2.283 464 6	93	3.661 417 3
24	0.944 881 9	59	2.322 834 6	94	3.700 787 4
25	0.984 252 0	60	2.362 204 7	95	3.740 157 5
26	1.023 622 0	61	2.401 574 8	96	3.779 527 6
27	1.062 992 1	62	2.440 944 9	97	3.818 897 6
28	1.102 362 2	63	2.480 315 0	98	3.858 267 7
29	1.141 732 3	64	2.519 685 0	99	3.897 637 8
30	1.181 102 4	65	2.559 055 1	100	3.937 008
31	1.220 472 4	66	2.598 425 2		
32	1.259 842 5	67	2.637 795 3		
33	1.299 212 6	68	2.677 165 4		
34	1.338 582 7	69	2.716 535 4		
35	1.377 952 8	70	2.755 905 5		

FORMULA TO CONVERT mm TO INCHES: Divide 25.4 into known mm.

NOTE: The inch values in this table are rounded off.

CONVERSION FROM DECIMAL INCHES TO MILLIMETERS

inch	mm	inch	mm	inch	mm
1	25.4	36	914.4	71	1 803.4
2	50.8	37	939.8	72	1 828.8
3	76.2	38	965.2	73	1 854.2
4	101.6	39	990.6	74	1 879.6
5	127.0	40	1 016.0	75	1 905.0
6	152.4	41	1 041.4	76	1 930.4
7	177.8	42	1 066.8	77	1 955.8
8	203.2	43	1 092.2	78	1 981.2
9	228.6	44	1 117.6	79	2 006.6
10	254.0	45	1 143.0	80	2 032.0
11	279.4	46	1 168.4	81	2 057.4
12	304.8	47	1 193.8	82	2 082.8
13	330.2	48	1 219.2	83	2 108.2
14	355.6	49	1 244.6	84	2 133.6
15	381.0	50	1 270.0	85	2 159.0
16	406.4	51	1 295.4	86	2 184.4
17	431.8	52	1 320.8	87	2 209.8
18	457.2	53	1 346.2	88	2 235.2
19	482.6	54	1 371.6	89	2 260.6
20	508.0	55	1 397.0	90	2 286.0
21	533.4	56	1 422.4	91	2 311.4
22	558.8	57	1 447.8	92	2 336.8
23	584.2	58	1 473.2	93	2 362.2
24	609.6	59	1 498.6	94	2 387.6
25	635.0	60	1 524.0	95	2 413.0
26	660.4	61	1 549.4	96	2 438.4
27	685.8	62	1 574.8	97	2 463.8
28	711.2	63	1 600.2	98	2 489.2
29	736.6	64	1 625.6	99	2 514.6
30	762.0	65	1 651.0	100	2 540.0
31	787.4	66	1 676.4		
32	812.8	67	1 701.8		
33	838.2	68	1 727.2		
34	863.6	69	1 752.6		
35	889.0	70	1 778.0		

NOTE: All values in this table are exact.

Since every major nation in the world except the United States uses the metric system of measurement, your bike may well be made up of metric-sized parts. With the following tables you can convert metric tool and part sizes to American sizes (and vice versa). Also, the formulas given can teach you a lot about your bike and help you improve its performance and/or economy.

U.S. STANDARD

GRADE OF BOLT		SAE 1 & 2	SAE 5	SAE 6	SAE 8		
MIN. TENSILE STRENGTH		64,000 P.S.I.	105,000 P.S.I.	133,000 P.S.I.	150,000 P.S.I.		
GRADE MARKINGS ON HEAD						SOCKET OR WRENCH SIZE	
U.S. STANDARD		TORQUE (IN FOOT POUNDS)				U.S. REGULAR	
BOLT DIA.	U.S. DEC. EQUIV.					BOLT HEAD	NUT
1/4	.250	5	7	10	10.5	3/8	7/16
5/16	.3125	9	14	19	22	1/2	9/16
3/8	.375	15	25	34	37	9/16	5/8
7/16	.4375	24	40	55	60	5/8	3/4
1/2	.500	37	60	85	92	3/4	13/16
9/16	.5625	53	88	120	132	7/8	7/8
5/8	.625	74	120	167	180	15/16	1.
3/4	.750	120	200	280	296	1-1/8	1-1/8
7/8	.875	190	302	440	473	1-5/16	1-5/16
1.	1.000	282	466	660	714	1-1/2	1-1/2

MULTIPLY READINGS BY 12 FOR INCH POUND VALUES

METRIC STANDARD

GRADE OF BOLT		5D	8G	10K	12K		
MIN. TENSILE STRENGTH		71,160 P.S.I.	113,800 P.S.I.	142,200 P.S.I.	170,679 P.S.I.		
GRADE MARKINGS ON HEAD		5D	8G	10K	12K	SOCKET OR WRENCH SIZE	
METRIC		TORQUE (IN FOOT POUNDS)				METRIC	
BOLT DIA.	U.S. DEC. EQUIV.					BOLT HEAD	NUT
6mm	.2362	5	6	8	10	10mm	10mm
8mm	.3150	10	16	22	27	14mm	14mm
10mm	.3937	19	31	40	49	17mm	17mm
12mm	.4720	34	54	70	86	19mm	19mm
14mm	.5512	55	89	117	137	22mm	22mm
16mm	.6299	83	132	175	208	24mm	24mm
18mm	.709	111	182	236	283	27mm	27mm
22mm	.8661	182	284	394	464	32mm	32mm
24mm	.945	261	419	570	689	36mm	36mm

WHITWORTH STANDARD

GRADE OF BOLT		A & B	S	T	V		
MIN. TENSILE STRENGTH		62,720 P.S.I.	112,000 P.S.I.	123,200 P.S.I.	145,600 P.S.I.		
GRADE MARKINGS ON HEAD			S	T	V	SOCKET OR WRENCH SIZE	
WHITWORTH		TORQUE (IN FOOT POUNDS)				WHITWORTH	
BOLT DIA.	U.S. DEC. EQUIV.					BOLT HEAD	NUT
1/4	.250	5	7	9	10	* 1/4	* 1/4
5/16	.3125	9	15	18	21	*5/16	*5/16
3/8	.375	15	27	31	36	* 3/8	* 3/8
7/16	.4375	24	43	51	58	*7/16	*7/16
1/2	.500	36	64	79	89	* 1/2	* 1/2
9/16	.5625	52	94	111	128	*9/16	*9/16
5/8	.625	73	128	155	175	* 5/8	* 5/8
3/4	.750	118	213	259	287	* 3/4	* 3/4
7/8	.875	186	322	407	459	*7/8	*7/8
1.	1.000	276	497	611	693	* 1.	* 1.

*Dimensions given on handles of U.S. wrenches refer to actual size of bolt head or nut. Dimension given on Whitworth wrenches refer to the shank or body diameter of the bolt, NOT THE BOLT HEAD OR NUT SIZE.

FORMULAS

ENGINE FORMULAS

PISTON DISPLACEMENT=bore diameter² (squared) x .7854 x stroke length.

Example: An engine has a bore diameter of 70mm and a stroke length of 64mm; find piston displacement.

piston displacement=70mm x 70mm x .7854 x 64mm

piston displacement=246301 cubic millimeters; divide answer by 1000 to get cubic centimeters. 246301 divided by 1000 =246.301 cubic centimeters.

ENGINE DISPLACEMENT=piston displacement x number of cylinders.

Example: An engine has a piston displacement of 246.3 cubic centimeters and two cylinders; find engine displacement.

engine displacement=246.3cc x 2 cylinders

engine displacement=492.6 cubic centimeters

$$\textbf{COMPRESSION RATIO}=\frac{\text{piston displacement + combustion chamber vol.}}{\text{combustion chamber volume}}$$

Example: Piston displacement is 246cc and the combustion chamber volume is 36cc; what is the compression ratio?

$$\text{compression ratio}=\frac{246\text{cc} + 36\text{cc}}{36\text{cc}}$$

compression ratio=7.833 (to one)

$$\textbf{PISTON SPEED}=\frac{\text{2 x stroke length (in inches) x rpm}}{12}$$

Example: An engine has a stroke length of 2.31 inches; what's the piston speed at 7500 rpm?

$$\text{piston speed}=\frac{\text{2 x 2.31 inches x 7500 rpm}}{12}$$

piston speed=2887.5 feet per minute

$$\textbf{HORSEPOWER}=\frac{\text{torque x rpm}}{5252}$$

Example: An engine produces 40 foot-pounds of torque at 6500 rpm; what's the horsepower?

$$\text{horsepower}=\frac{\text{40 foot-pounds x 6500 rpm}}{5252}$$

horsepower=49.5

$$\textbf{TORQUE}=\frac{\text{horsepower x 5252}}{\text{rpm}}$$

Example: An engine churns out 37 horsepower at 8700 rpm; how much torque is generated?

$$\text{torque}=\frac{\text{37 hp x 5252}}{\text{8700 rpm}}$$

torque=22.3 foot-pounds

$$\textbf{PRIMARY REDUCTION RATIO}=\frac{\text{no. of teeth on clutch driven sprocket or gear}}{\text{no. of teeth on engine drive sprocket or gear}}$$

Example: Find primary reduction ratio if the machine has a 27 tooth engine sprocket and a 65 tooth clutch sprocket.

$$\text{primary reduction ratio}=\frac{65}{27}$$

primary reduction ratio=2.41 (to one)

This means there are 2.41 engine revolutions to each complete turn of the clutch.

$$\textbf{FINAL REDUCTION RATIO}=\frac{\text{no. of teeth on rear wheel sprocket}}{\text{no. of teeth on gearbox output sprocket}}$$

Example: There are 15 teeth on the gearbox output sprocket and 45 teeth on the rear wheel sprocket; what is the final reduction ratio?

$$\text{final reduction ratio}=\frac{45}{15}$$

final reduction ratio=3.0 (to one)

This means there are 3.0 gearbox output shaft revolutions to each complete turn of the rear wheel.

FIXED DRIVE RATIO=primary reduction ratio x final reduction ratio.

Example: Primary reduction ratio is 2.41 and the final reduction ratio is 3.0; calculate the fixed drive ratio.

fixed drive ratio=2.41 x 3.

fixed drive ratio=7.23 (to one)

$$\text{INTERNAL GEAR RATIO} = \frac{\text{no. of teeth on specific driven gear}}{\text{no. of teeth on specific drive gear}}$$

Example: Find 5th gear internal ratio if 5th drive gear has 26 teeth and 5th driven gear has 21.

$$\text{5th internal gear ratio} = \frac{21}{26}$$

5th internal gear ratio = .81 (to one)

(Note: In some transmissions, particularly British, two pairs of gears are used per each internal gear ratio. When this is the case, use the following internal gear ratio formula.)

$$\text{INTERNAL GEAR RATIO} = \frac{\text{no. of teeth on specific layshaft gear}}{\text{no. of teeth on specific mainshaft gear}} \times \frac{\text{no. of teeth on mainshaft top gear}}{\text{no. of teeth on layshaft top gear}}$$

Example: Layshaft 3rd gear has 22 teeth, mainshaft 3rd gear has 26 teeth, mainshaft top gear has 23 teeth and layshaft top gear has 17 teeth; find 3rd internal gear ratio.

$$\text{3rd internal gear ratio} = \frac{22}{26} \times \frac{23}{17}$$

3rd internal gear ratio = 1.144 (to one)

These give you the number of drive gear revolutions (clutch revolutions if mounted on transmission) for each turn of the output shaft.

OVERALL DRIVE RATIO = fixed drive ratio x specific internal gear ratio.

Example: A motorcycle has a fixed drive ratio of 7.23 and internal gearbox ratios as follows:

Internal Ratio	X	Fixed Ratio	=	Overall Drive Ratio
Low 2.06		7.23		14.89
2nd 1.42		7.23		10.26
3rd 1.14		7.23		8.24
4th 0.96		7.23		6.94
Top 0.84		7.23		6.07

This gives you the number of engine revolutions for each turn of the rear wheel.

The following four formulas are used to compute motorcycle speed in MPH, engine speed in RPM, effective rear wheel radius in INCHES and overall drive ratio REQUIRED to attain the related velocity. These formulas are interrelated; where three factors are known, besides the 168 constant, the fourth may be determined mathematically. A word about accurately measuring effective rear wheel radius is due here; measure the radius distance in inches from the road surface-tire contact point, perpendicularly to the center of the rear axle with the tires properly inflated and the rider seated.

The four formulas are:

$$\text{MPH} = \frac{\text{rpm x effective rear wheel radius}}{\text{overall drive ratio x 168}}$$

$$\text{RPM} = \frac{\text{mph x overall drive ratio x 168}}{\text{effective rear wheel radius}}$$

$$\text{OVERALL DRIVE RATIO} = \frac{\text{rpm x effective rear wheel radius}}{\text{mph x 168}}$$

$$\text{EFFECTIVE REAR WHEEL RADIUS} = \frac{\text{mph x overall drive ratio x 168}}{\text{rpm}}$$

Example: A motorcycle has a speed of 96.7 mph at 5000 engine rpm; the overall drive ratio (in third gear) is 4.00 to 1 and the rear wheel tire radius is 13 inches. These numerical values setup to solve for the ( ) unknown would look like this:

$$\text{(96.7) MPH} = \frac{\text{5000 rpm x 13-inch radius}}{\text{4.0 x 168}}$$

$$\text{(5000) RPM} = \frac{\text{96.7 mph x 4.0 x 168}}{\text{13-inch radius}}$$

$$\text{(4.0) OVERALL DRIVE RATIO} = \frac{\text{5000 rpm x 13-inch radius}}{\text{96.7 mph x 168}}$$

$$\text{(13-INCH) EFFECTIVE REAR WHEEL RADIUS} = \frac{\text{96.7 mph x 4.0 x 168}}{\text{5000 rpm}}$$

METRIC - AMERICAN CONVERSION TABLE

MULTIPLY	BY	TO OBTAIN
LINEAR		
Millimeters (mm)	.03937	Inches
Millimeters (mm)	.00328	Feet
Centimeters (cm)	.3937	Inches
Centimeters (cm)	.0328	Feet
DISTANCE		
Meters (m)	39.37	Inches
Meters (m)	3.28	Feet
Kilometers (km)	3281	Feet
Kilometers (km)	.6214	Miles
AREA		
Square Centimeters	.155	Square Inches
Square Centimeters	.001076	Square Feet
Square Meters (m^2)	10.76	Square Feet
VOLUME		
Cubic Centimeters (cc)	.06102	Cubic Inches
Liters (l)	61.02	Cubic Inches
LIQUID CAPACITY		
Liters (l)	2.113	Pints
Liters (l)	1.057	Quarts
Liters (l)	.2642	Gallons
Cubic Centimeters (cc)	.0338	Fluid Ounces
WEIGHT		
Grams (gm)	.03527	Ounces
Kilograms (kg)	2.205	Pounds
OTHER		
Kilogram-Meters (kg-m)	7.233	Foot-Pounds
Kilometers/Liters (km/l)	2.352	Miles/Gallon
Metric Horsepower (ps)	1.014	Brake Horsepower

AMERICAN - METRIC CONVERSION TABLE

MULTIPLY	BY	TO OBTAIN
LINEAR		
Inches (in.)	25.4	Millimeters
Inches (in.)	2.54	Centimeters
Feet (ft.)	304.8	Millimeters
Feet (ft.)	30.48	Centimeters
DISTANCE		
Inches (in.)	.0254	Meters
Feet (ft.)	.3048	Meters
Miles (mi.)	1.609	Kilometers
AREA		
Square Inches (in^2)	6.452	Sq.Centimeters
Square Feet (sq. ft.)	929	Sq.Centimeters
VOLUME		
Cubic Inches (cu. in.)	16.39	Cu.Centimeters
Cubic Inches (cu. in.)	.01639	Liters
LIQUID CAPACITY		
Pints (pt.)	.4732	Liters
Quarts (qt.)	.9463	Liters
Gallons (gal.)	3.785	Liters
Fluid Ounces (fl. oz.)	29.58	Cu.Centimeters
WEIGHT		
Ounces (oz.)	28.35	Grams
Pounds (lb.)	.4536	Kilograms
OTHER		
Foot-Pounds (Ft.-Lbs.)	.1383	Kilogram-Meters
Miles/Gallon (mpg)	.4252	Kilometers/Liter
Brake Horsepower (bhp)	.9862	Metric Horsepower (ps)

Decimal Equivalents
of 8ths, 16ths, 32nds, 64ths

8ths	32nds	64ths	64ths
1/8 = .125	1/32 = .03125	1/64 = .015625	33/64 = .515625
1/4 = .250	3/32 = .09375	3/64 = .046875	35/64 = .546875
3/8 = .375	5/32 = .15625	5/64 = .078125	37/64 = .578125
1/2 = .500	7/32 = .21875	7/64 = .109375	39/64 = .609375
5/8 = .625	9/32 = .28125	9/64 = .140625	41/64 = .640625
3/4 = .750	11/32 = .34375	11/64 = .171875	43/64 = .671875
7/8 = .875	13/32 = .40625	13/64 = .203125	45/64 = .703125
16ths	15/32 = .46875	15/64 = .234370	47/64 = .734375
1/16 = .0625	17/32 = .53125	17/64 = .265625	49/64 = .765625
3/16 = .1875	19/32 = .59375	19/64 = .296875	51/64 = .796875
5/16 = .3125	21/32 = .65625	21/64 = .328125	53/64 = .828125
7/16 = .4375	23/32 = .71875	23/64 = .359375	55/64 = .859375
9/16 = .5625	25/32 = .78125	25/64 = .390625	57/64 = .890625
11/16 = .6875	27/32 = .84375	27/64 = .421875	59/64 = .921875
13/16 = .8125	29/32 = .90625	29/64 = .453125	61/64 = .953125
15/16 = .9375	31/32 = .96875	31/64 = .484375	63/64 = .984375

Letter Size Drills

Letter	Size of Drill in Inches
A	.234
B	.238
C	.242
D	.246
E	.250
F	.257
G	.261
H	.266
I	.272
J	.277
K	.281
L	.290
M	.295
N	.302
O	.316
P	.323
Q	.332
R	.339
S	.348
T	.358
U	.368
V	.377
W	.386
X	.397
Y	.404
Z	.413

Number Size Drills

No.	Size of Drill in Inches	No.	Size of Drill in Inches	No.	Size of Drill in Inches	No.	Size of Drill in Inches
1	.2280	21	.1590	41	.0960	61	.0390
2	.2210	22	.1570	42	.0935	62	.0380
3	.2130	23	.1540	43	.0890	63	.0370
4	.2090	24	.1520	44	.0860	64	.0360
5	.2055	25	.1495	45	.0820	65	.0350
6	.2040	26	.1470	46	.0810	66	.0330
7	.2010	27	.1440	47	.0785	67	.0320
8	.1990	28	.1405	48	.0760	68	.0310
9	.1960	29	.1360	49	.0730	69	.0292
10	.1935	30	.1285	50	.0700	70	.0280
11	.1910	31	.1200	51	.0670	71	.0260
12	.1890	32	.1160	52	.0635	72	.0250
13	.1850	33	.1130	53	.0595	73	.0240
14	.1820	34	.1110	54	.0550	74	.0225
15	.1800	35	.1100	55	.0520	75	.0210
16	.1770	36	.1065	56	.0465	76	.0200
17	.1730	37	.1040	57	.0430	77	.0180
18	.1695	38	.1015	58	.0420	78	.0160
19	.1660	39	.0995	59	.0410	79	.0145
20	.1610	40	.0980	60	.0400	80	.0135

Decimal Equivalents of Millimeters

mm.	Inches	mm.	Inches	mm.	Inches	mm.	Inches	mm.	Inches
.01	.00039	.41	.01614	.81	.03189	21	.82677	61	2.40157
.02	.00079	.42	.01654	.82	.03228	22	.86614	62	2.44094
.03	.00118	.43	.01693	.83	.03268	23	.90551	63	2.48031
.04	.00157	.44	.01732	.84	.03307	24	.94488	64	2.51968
.05	.00197	.45	.01772	.85	.03346	25	.98425	65	2.55905
.06	.00236	.46	.01811	.86	.03386	26	1.02362	66	2.59842
.07	.00276	.47	.01850	.87	.03425	27	1.06299	67	2.63779
.08	.00315	.48	.01890	.88	.03465	28	1.10236	68	2.67716
.09	.00354	.49	.01929	.89	.03504	29	1.14173	69	2.71653
.10	.00394	.50	.01969	.90	.03543	30	1.18110	70	2.75590
.11	.00433	.51	.02008	.91	.03583	31	1.22047	71	2.79527
.12	.00472	.52	.02047	.92	.03622	32	1.25984	72	2.83464
.13	.00512	.53	.02087	.93	.03661	33	1.29921	73	2.87401
.14	.00551	.54	.02126	.94	.03701	34	1.33858	74	2.91338
.15	.00591	.55	.02165	.95	.03740	35	1.37795	75	2.95275
.16	.00630	.56	.02205	.96	.03780	36	1.41732	76	2.99212
.17	.00669	.57	.02244	.97	.03819	37	1.45669	77	3.03149
.18	.00709	.58	.02283	.98	.03858	38	1.49606	78	3.07086
.19	.00748	.59	.02323	.99	.03898	39	1.53543	79	3.11023
.20	.00787	.60	.02362	1.00	.03937	40	1.57480	80	3.14960
.21	.00827	.61	.02402	1	.03937	41	1.61417	81	3.18897
.22	.00866	.62	.02441	2	.07874	42	1.65354	82	3.22834
.23	.00906	.63	.02480	3	.11811	43	1.69291	83	3.26771
.24	.00945	.64	.02520	4	.15748	44	1.73228	84	3.30708
.25	.00984	.65	.02559	5	.19685	45	1.77165	85	3.34645
.26	.01024	.66	.02598	6	.23622	46	1.81102	86	3.38582
.27	.01063	.67	.02638	7	.27559	47	1.85039	87	3.42519
.28	.01102	.68	.02677	8	.31496	48	1.88976	88	3.46456
.29	.01142	.69	.02717	9	.35433	49	1.92913	89	3.50393
.30	.01181	.70	.02756	10	.39370	50	1.96850	90	3.54330
.31	.01220	.71	.02795	11	.43307	51	2.00787	91	3.58267
.32	.01260	.72	.02835	12	.47244	52	2.04724	92	3.62204
.33	.01299	.73	.02874	13	.51181	53	2.08661	93	3.66141
.34	.01339	.74	.02913	14	.55118	54	2.12598	94	3.70078
.35	.01378	.75	.02953	15	.59055	55	2.16535	95	3.74015
.36	.01417	.76	.02992	16	.62992	56	2.20472	96	3.77952
.37	.01457	.77	.03032	17	.66929	57	2.24409	97	3.81889
.38	.01496	.78	.03071	18	.70866	58	2.28346	98	3.85826
.39	.01535	.79	.03110	19	.74803	59	2.32283	99	3.89763
.40	.01575	.80	.03150	20	.78740	60	2.36220	100	3.93700

STANDARD TORQUE VALUES

FASTENER	TYPE	MINIMUM TENSILE STRENGTH	MATERIAL	BODY SIZE OR OUTSIDE DIAMETER OF FASTENER										
				2	3	4	5	6	8	10	1/4	5/16	3/8	7/16
	SAE 0-1-2	74,000 PSI	LOW CARBON STEEL								6	12	20	32
	SAE 3	100,000 PSI	MEDIUM CARBON STEEL								9	17	30	47
	SAE 5	120,000 PSI	MEDIUM CARBON HEAT TREAT STEEL								10	19	33	54
	SAE 6	133,000 PSI	MED. CARBON STEEL QUENCHED TEMPERED								12.5	24	43	69
	SAE 7	133,000 PSI	MEDIUM CARBON ALLOY STEEL								13	25	44	71
	SAE 8	150,000 PSI	MEDIUM CARBON ALLOY STEEL								14	29	47	78
	SOCKET HEAD CAP SCREW	160,000 PSI	HIGH CARBON CASE HARDENED STEEL	TORQUE VALUES: All figures are foot-pounds except those marked with an asterisk (*), which are inch-pounds.							16	33	54	84
	SOCKET SET SCREW	212,000 PSI	HIGH CARBON CASE HARDENED STEEL					9*	16*	30*	70*	140*	18	29
	MACHINE SCREW YELLOW BRASS	60,000 PSI	COPPER (CU) 63% ZINC (ZU) 37%	2*	3.3*	4.4*	6.4*	8*	16*	20*	65*	110*	17	27
	SILICONE BRONZE TYPE "B"	70,000 PSI	COPPER (CU) 96% ZINC (ZNI) 2% SILICON (SI) 2%)	2.3*	3.7*	4.9*	7.2*	10*	19*	22*	70*	125*	20	30
	STUDS	Use SAE 2, 5 or 8 values when grade is known, with a nut of sufficient strength.												

In the above chart, there is no difference in torque figures between fine threads and coarse threads. The torque figures for a finely-threaded fastener as compared to a coarsely-threaded fastener of the same diameter may be slightly higher, but so slightly that they are hardly worth mentioning.

BODY SIZE OR OUTSIDE DIAMETER OF FASTENER																	
1/2	9/16	5/8	3/4	7/8	1	1-1/8	1-1/4	1-3/8	1-1/2	1-5/8	1-3/4	1-7/8	2	2-1/4	2-1/2	2-3/4	3
47	69	96	155	206	310	480	675	900	1100	1470	1900	2360	2750	3450	4400	7350	9500
69	103	145	234	372	551	872	1211	1624	1943	2660	3463	4695	5427	7226	8049	13450	17548
78	114	154	257	382	587	794	1105	1500	1775	2425	3150	4200	4550	6550	7175	13000	16000
106	150	209	350	550	825	1304	1815	2434	2913	3985	5189	6980	7491	10825	14983	20151	26286
110	154	215	360	570	840	1325	1825	2500	3000	4000	5300	7000	7500	11000	15500	21000	27000
119	169	230	380	600	700	1430	1975	2650	3200	4400	5650	7600	8200	12000	17000	23000	29000
125	180	250	400	640	970	1520	2130	2850	3450	4700	6100	8200	8800	13000	18000	24000	31000
43	63	100	146														
37	49	78	104	160	215	325	400		595								
41	53	88	117	180	250	365	450		655								

CAUTION: THERE ARE MANY VARIABLE FACTORS WHICH AFFECT TORQUE. THE FIGURES IN THIS CHART ARE SAFE FIGURES FOR STANDARD TORQUE APPLICATIONS ONLY.

11. How Your Motorcycle

How a Four-stroke Engine Works

A four-stroke engine requires two complete revolutions of the crankshaft to complete one full cycle of operation. During these two revolutions, the piston makes two upward movements and two downward movements. This is how the four-stroke engine gets its name—a total of four piston movements (strokes) are necessary to complete one full cycle of operation.

The four-part drawing here represents a simplified four-stroke engine. It can be used to trace the four stages of a complete cycle of operation. The drawing shows only a single cylinder for clarity, but large motorcycle engines with two or more cylinders operate in exactly the same manner. Let's follow our simple four-stroke engine through one complete cycle of operation and learn how it works.

The four-stroke cycle of operation begins with the INTAKE VALVE open, allowing a fresh air/fuel mixture to enter the COMBUSTION CHAMBER. The PISTON is just below TDC and moving down. (TDC or Top Dead Center is the piston's highest point of travel in the cylinder.) As the piston moves down, it creates suction, which pulls the air/fuel mixture into the cylinder. When the piston reaches the bottom of its travel, the intake valve closes, trapping the air/fuel mixture inside the cylinder. This is the first of the four separate operations, and it is known as the INTAKE STROKE.

On the second stroke, both VALVES are closed as the piston moves up, compressing the mixture in the cylinder. The mixture, which once filled the whole cylinder, is now squeezed into the small space of the combustion chamber. This is known as the COMPRESSION STROKE.

Now the SPARK PLUG fires, igniting the air/fuel mixture. The mixture burns rapidly, creating a powerful pressure that forces the piston down in the cylinder. This rotates the CRANKSHAFT. This downward movement is the third stroke in the sequence and is known as the POWER STROKE. (It is the only time the engine is actually producing power.)

As the piston reaches the bottom of its travel in the cylinder, known as BDC (Bottom Dead Center), the EXHAUST VALVE opens. When the piston begins moving up on the exhaust stroke, the burned gases are forced out of the cylinder, through the open exhaust valve and into the exhaust pipe. When the piston reaches the point of TDC (Top Dead Center) once more, the exhaust valve closes and the intake valve opens. With one full cycle of operation complete, the engine is ready to start over again with the entry of more air/fuel mixture. This final stroke of the piston is the EXHAUST STROKE.

How a Two-stroke Engine Works

The two-stroke engine is much simpler mechanically than the four-stroke engine described elsewhere. The four-stroke engine uses a system of valves operated by a cam to control the four parts of the cycle of operation. The two-stroke engine has no valves or cam. The piston-port two-stroke engine (shown in this example) uses a series of openings (ports) in the cylinder walls which are covered and uncovered by the piston as it moves up and down in the cylinder. Let's follow a simple, single-cylinder piston-port engine through one complete cycle of operation to show how this works.

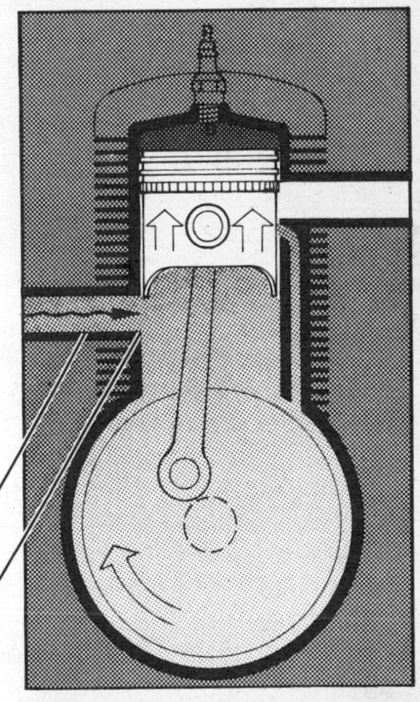

In the two-stroke engine, a mixture of air and fuel is compressed and burned to produce power. But instead of passing this mixture directly to the combustion chamber through a valve, as in the four-stroke engine, the AIR/FUEL MIXTURE first enters the crankcase below the piston. Let's start the sequence of operation just as the piston nears TDC (Top Dead Center) in the cylinder to compress the air/fuel mixture from the previous cycle. In the first drawing, the piston is moving up. Notice that the INTAKE PORT is not covered by the side of the piston, and the port is open to the crankcase. This allows the air/fuel charge to enter the crankcase beneath the piston.

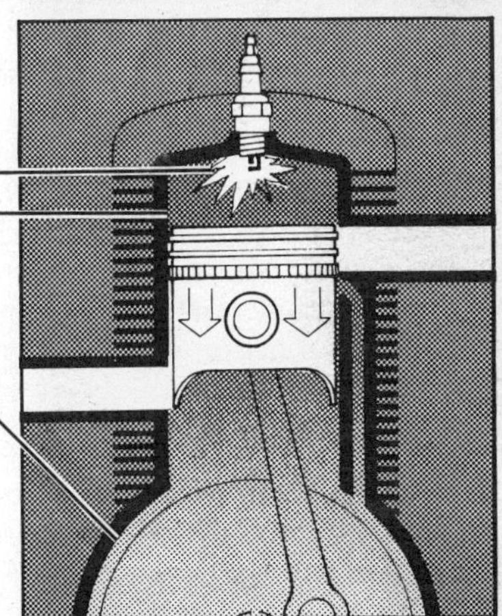

Now the SPARK PLUG has fired, igniting the air/fuel mixture from the previous cycle. The EXPANDING GASES are forcing the piston down in the powered portion of the stroke, and the downward movement is compressing the trapped air/fuel mixture in the CRANKCASE. Remember, the piston is being forced down in the cylinder by the burning gases from the previous cycle of operation.

The piston's downward movement has uncovered two ports. One, the EXHAUST PORT, allows the burned gases from the previous cycle of operation to escape by way of the exhaust pipe. The other, the TRANSFER PORT, connects the crankcase and the combustion chamber. With the transfer port opened, the compressed air/fuel mixture in the crankcase flows through the opening and into the cylinder above the piston. A small amount of this gas follows the burned gases out of the exhaust port, but most of it is trapped in the combustion chamber during the next sequence.

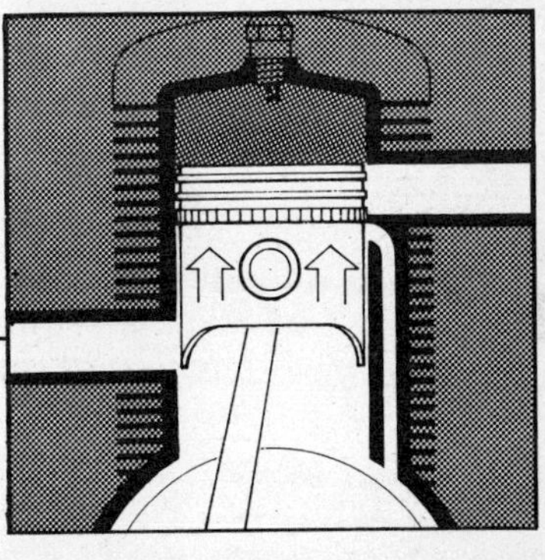

When the air/fuel mixture from the crankcase has filled the combustion chamber completely, the piston, which has traveled to the bottom (BDC—Bottom Dead Center) of its stroke, begins to move up, sealing off both the transfer port and the exhaust port. This seals the combustion chamber. The air/fuel mixture can then be compressed and, when ignited by the spark plug, provide power for the engine. As the piston moves up to complete the compression of the air/fuel mixture, it again uncovers the INTAKE PORT, which allows an air/fuel charge to enter the crankcase, bringing the engine back to the condition shown in the first drawing. This is how the two-stroke engine got its name. Only two movements of the piston are required to complete a full cycle of operation.

THE ROTARY-VALVE TWO-STROKE ENGINE

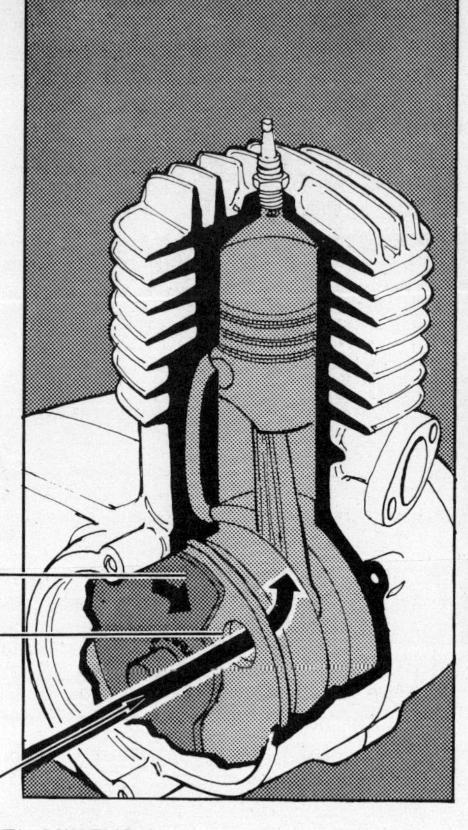

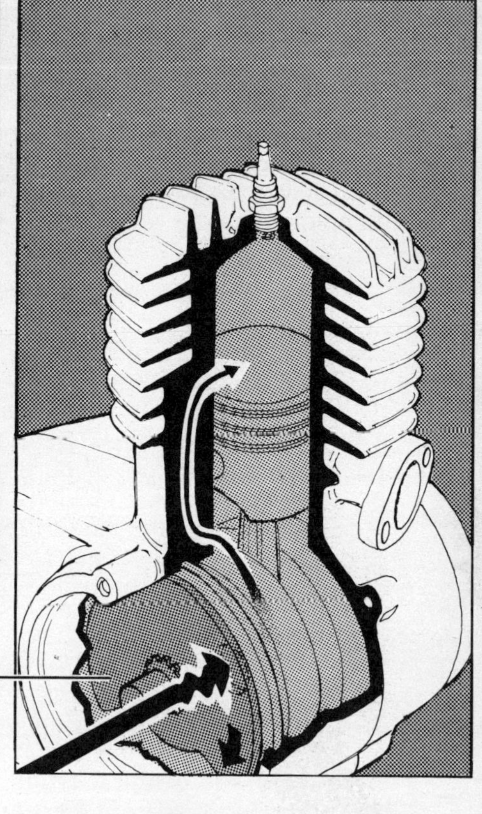

In a rotary-valve two-stroke engine, the intake is not controlled by a port that is covered and uncovered by the side of the piston as it moves up and down in the cylinder. Instead, the opening and closing of the port are controlled by a METAL or FIBER DISC attached to the end of the crankshaft. This disc has an opening in it which lets the air/fuel mixture enter the crankcase each time the disc rotates one full circle.

When the intake port in the crankcase and the opening in the disc are lined up, the AIR/FUEL MIXTURE can enter the crankcase. When the crankshaft rotates the opening in the disc enough to close the port, the crankcase is closed until the transfer port opens. The transfer and exhaust ports in the rotary-valve two-stroke engine work exactly like those in the piston-port engine. Only the intake port is different.

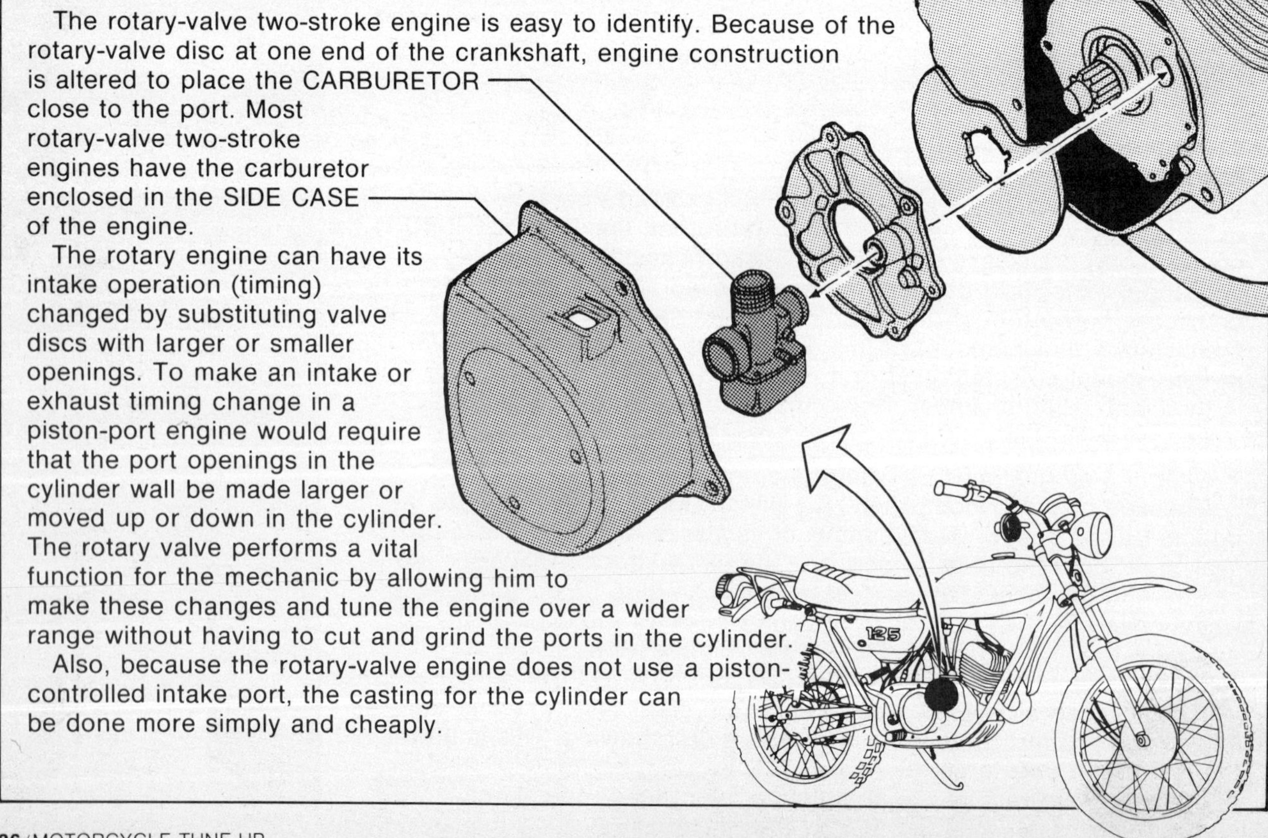

The rotary-valve two-stroke engine is easy to identify. Because of the rotary-valve disc at one end of the crankshaft, engine construction is altered to place the CARBURETOR close to the port. Most rotary-valve two-stroke engines have the carburetor enclosed in the SIDE CASE of the engine.

The rotary engine can have its intake operation (timing) changed by substituting valve discs with larger or smaller openings. To make an intake or exhaust timing change in a piston-port engine would require that the port openings in the cylinder wall be made larger or moved up or down in the cylinder. The rotary valve performs a vital function for the mechanic by allowing him to make these changes and tune the engine over a wider range without having to cut and grind the ports in the cylinder.

Also, because the rotary-valve engine does not use a piston-controlled intake port, the casting for the cylinder can be done more simply and cheaply.

THE REED-VALVE TWO-STROKE ENGINE

Another means of controlling the intake of air and fuel into the two-stroke engine is the reed valve. The reed valve is also found in many industrial two-stroke power units, such as chain saws, and is common on two-stroke engines used in go-karts.

Just as in the rotary-valve engine, the reed-valve engine uses something other than the piston to control the intake of air and fuel into the crankcase. A METAL or PLASTIC FLAP is placed across the intake opening just behind the CARBURETOR. When the piston is moving up in the cylinder, it creates a low pressure (suction) in the crankcase. This suction pulls the reed valve open, allowing the air/fuel mixture to enter the crankcase. As the piston starts down to compress the mixture in the crankcase, the pressure in the crankcase is greater than the outside air, and the reed valve closes. It remains closed while the transfer port is open and does not open again until the next intake stroke.

Some new two-stroke engines use this method in factory-built motorcycles, and the reed valve is a common modification on piston-port engines for off-road and road-racing motorcycles.

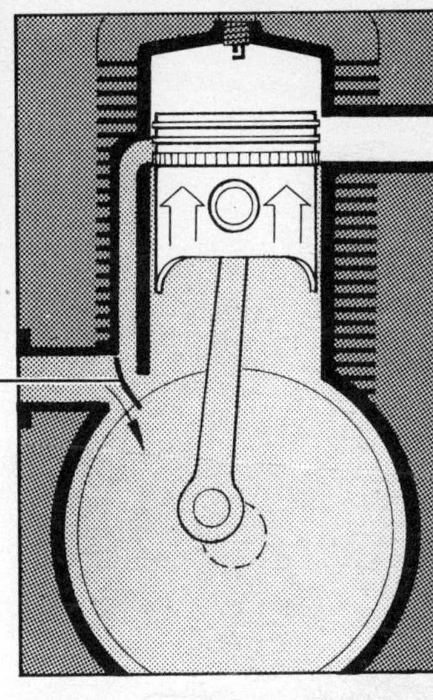

EFFICIENT STROKE

Unlike the four-stroke engine, which uses a valve to control the exhaust port and gets usable power from the burning gases until the valve is opened by the cam, the two-stroke engine's power stroke stops the moment the exhaust port opens and the burned exhaust gases escape to the exhaust pipe and into the outside atmosphere.

That part of the downstroke of the piston between the time the spark plug fires and the exhaust port opens is the total amount of travel under power. This is called the *efficient stroke.*

You can see in the drawing that the EFFICIENT STROKE is much shorter than the total travel of the piston, because the efficient stroke is limited. Port placement is critical to the amount of power that can be obtained from the two-stroke engine. A well-designed two-stroke gets the maximum travel under power possible before the exhaust port opens.

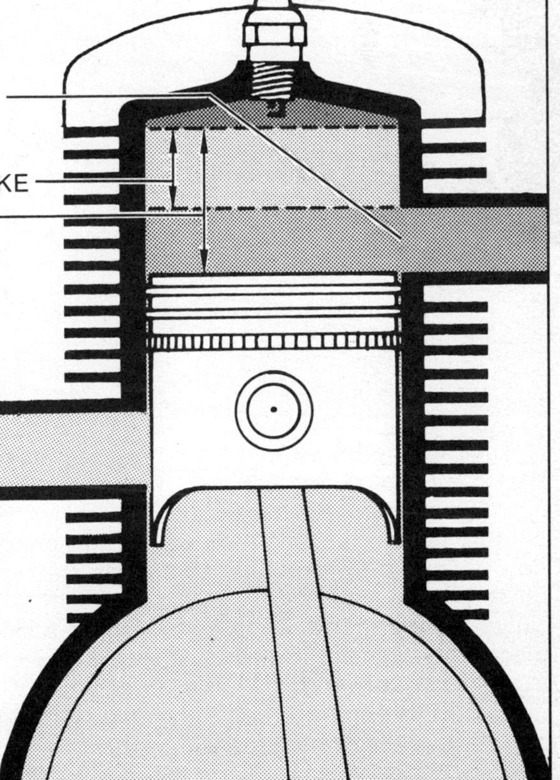

II/Carburetion

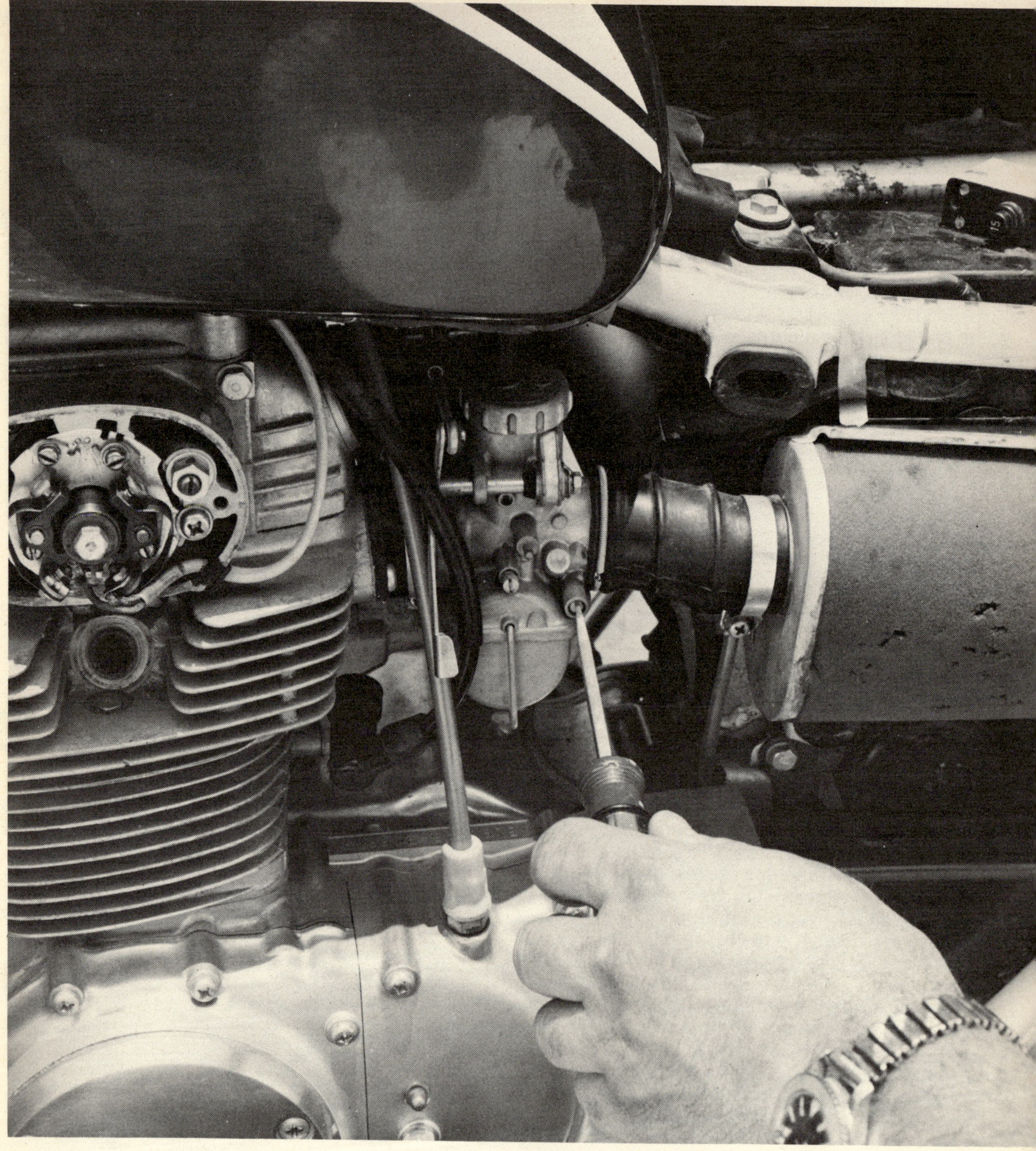

__It really isn't complicated, but before you take a screwdriver and start adjusting things on your carburetor, do a little reading about the way they function. It can save you a lot of trouble.__

While the carburetor on your motorcycle may look complicated, it really isn't. It's *so* simple that it confuses many tuners, who try to make the carburetor do things it really wasn't designed to do or blame it for problems that originate in some other engine system.

Despite the fact that the carburetor is a simple piece of equipment, however, it has a very complicated job to do. What's more, it must perform it through the complete range of engine operation, from starting to full throttle, without a miss.

The carburetor mixes air and fuel together for the engine to burn. Since the engine demands greater or lesser amounts of air and fuel depending on throttle position and engine speed, the carburetor must constantly adjust its mixing action to provide the engine with the correct amount of air and fuel.

The first thing the carburetor must do is ensure a ready supply of fuel for the engine at all times. This is the job of the FLOAT CHAMBER.

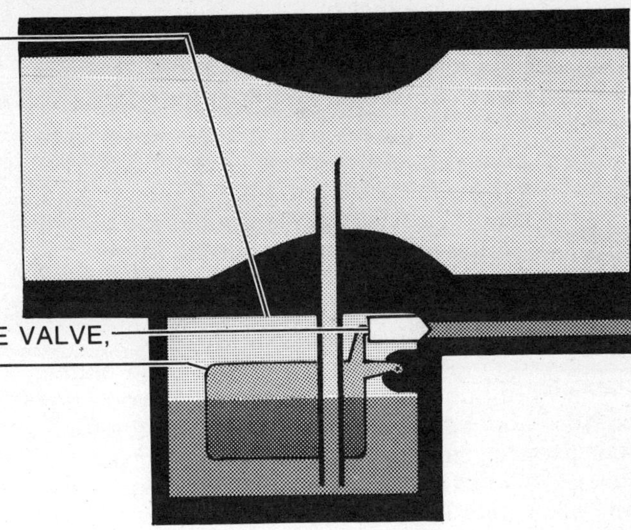

NOTE: THERE ARE SPECIALIZED TYPES OF CARBURETORS WHICH DO NOT HAVE A FLOAT CHAMBER. THEY ARE COVERED LATER ON IN THIS SECTION.

Gas coming from the fuel tank enters the carburetor through a valve located inside the float chamber. The opening of the valve, called a NEEDLE VALVE, is controlled by the FLOAT.

If the engine is not using as much fuel as the gas tank can supply, the float chamber fills up, and the rising float cuts off the fuel supply by shutting the needle valve.

Now the engine is operating only on the gasoline in the float bowl. As this gas is used, the level in the float bowl drops (right), letting the float move downward and opening the needle valve to admit more gasoline from the tank.

Regulating the amount of gas in the float bowl this way is a constant operation when the engine is running. What actually happens is that some gas is always entering the float bowl from the gas tank *in proportion* to the amount of gas being withdrawn from the float bowl and burned.

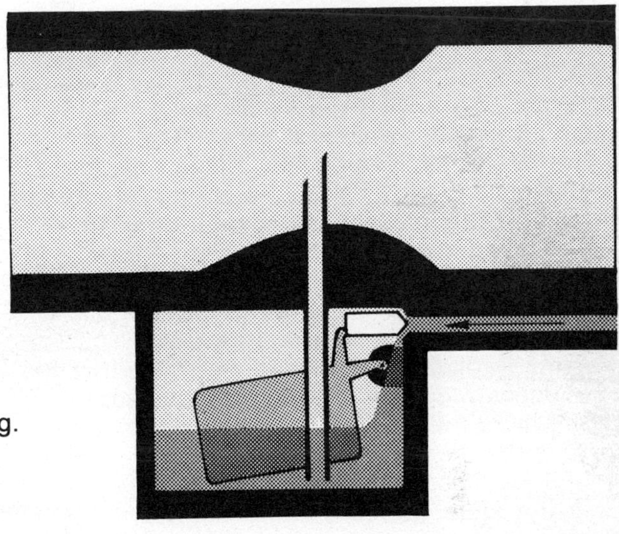

What the float bowl and float do is regulate the flow of fuel and provide a reservoir of fuel so that the carburetor can meet a sudden increase in engine demand. When the engine is shut off, the float bowl fills with fuel and the float closes the needle valve. This prevents the fuel from overflowing the chamber and flooding the engine. For further protection, it is wise to turn the fuel valve to the OFF position when the bike is not running.

The air/fuel mixture burned by the engine enters the engine because of engine vacuum. This vacuum develops each time the piston moves downward in the cylinder on the intake stroke.

NOTE: SINCE THE OPERATION OF TWO- AND FOUR-STROKE ENGINES DIFFERS, A QUICK REVIEW OF THE SECTIONS "HOW A FOUR-STROKE ENGINE WORKS" AND "HOW A TWO-STROKE ENGINE WORKS" MAY BE HELPFUL HERE.

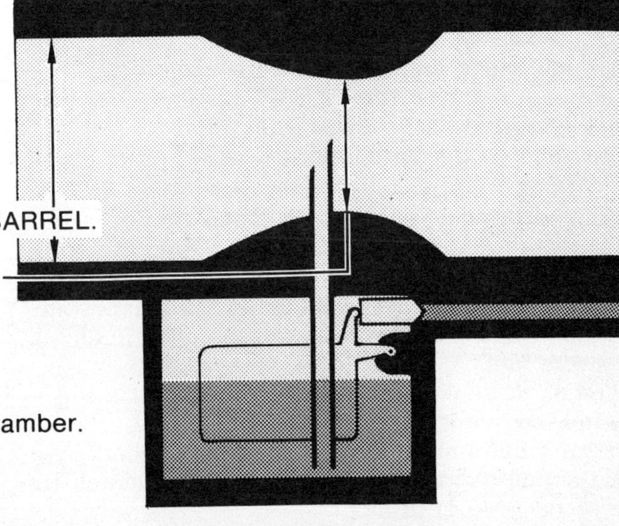

The suction created by this downward movement draws air through the carburetor and into the engine. The passageway the air travels through in the carburetor is called the THROAT or BARREL. At one point in the throat there is a slight constriction (reduction in diameter) called the VENTURI.

The carburetor operates on the simple physical principle that a stream of air pulled through a restricted opening *gains velocity* and *drops in pressure.* This drop in pressure creates a mild vacuum, which is used to draw fuel from the float chamber.

The float bowl has a vent (an air hole) to sense outside air pressure, and it has a tube or passageway going to the throat of the carburetor near the venturi. When the air pressure inside the throat drops below that of the normal outside air, the pressure difference pulls fuel from the float bowl into the airstream inside the throat. It works the same way you suck a soft drink through a straw.

The opening through which the gas flows from the float chamber is sometimes called the SPRAY TUBE. It delivers the gas so that as it hits the airstream, it vaporizes into a fine mist, saturating the air with fuel. This is the mixture that is burned in the combustion chamber of the engine to produce power. Unless the fuel is vaporized and well mixed with the air, it will not burn readily.

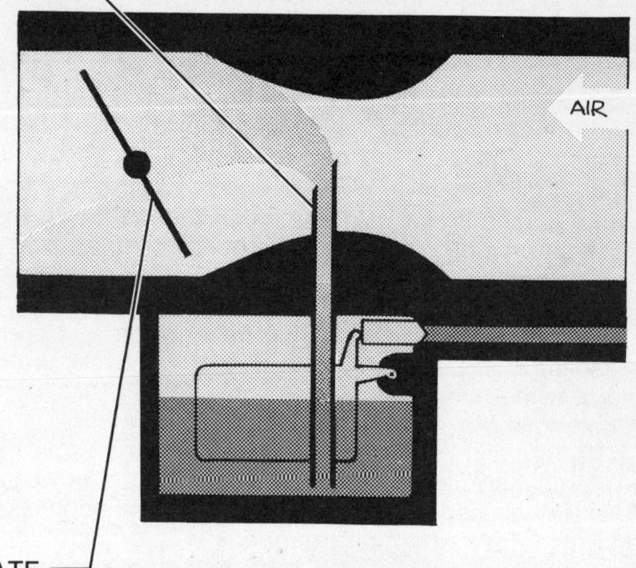

When too much raw gasoline enters the engine, it's called a rich mixture or flooding. As you know from experience, when you flood the engine on your motorcycle, you sometimes have to wait several minutes before trying to start it again. The wait allows the extra gas coating the inside of the carburetor and intake surfaces to evaporate.

So far we've shown a simplified carburetor in the accompanying drawings in order to concentrate on the float chamber. Now, as we talk about each of the remaining parts of a carburetor, we'll add that part to the drawing.

Just beyond the venturi on our sample carburetor, we've added a metal plate, called the THROTTLE PLATE, which pivots when you twist the throttle grip. When the throttle is open only a little way, the throttle plate is nearly closed, blocking off most of the throat. This reduces the amount of air that can be drawn into the engine, which in turn reduces the vacuum available at the venturi. Less vacuum means less fuel is drawn into the throat to mix with the air.

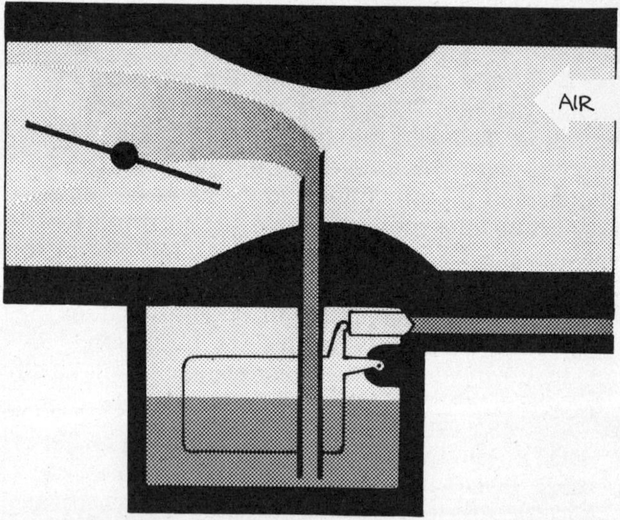

As the throttle grip is twisted more, the throttle plate opens wider and the airflow increases, pulling more fuel from the float bowl. This is the second way the carburetor regulates the flow of air and fuel into the engine. The amount of air/fuel mixture delivered to the engine determines the amount of power the engine produces.

Now that we've seen how the main fuel circuit of our basic carburetor works, let's take a look at how the carburetor operates when the bike is idling. Since the nearly-closed throttle plate almost stops the flow of air through the carburetor, we must add another path through which fuel can enter the engine. This path is called the IDLE CIRCUIT. It is a second passageway from the float bowl to the carburetor throat.

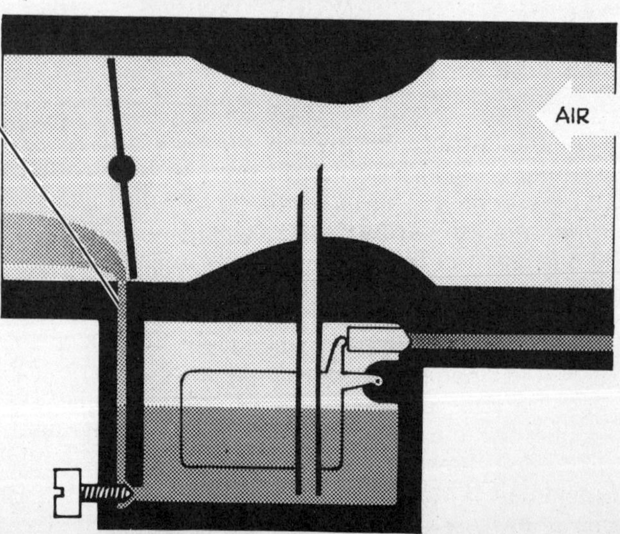

Although the closed throttle plate has reduced the flow of air through the venturi to the point where no fuel is being pulled from the spray tube, a strong vacuum is still being developed by piston movement. This vacuum is felt behind the throttle plate, and this is where the idle circuit delivers fuel.

When you take your hand off the throttle and let the engine idle, just enough air passes through the carburetor to sustain idle speed. The idle circuit supplies only enough fuel to match the reduced amount of air.

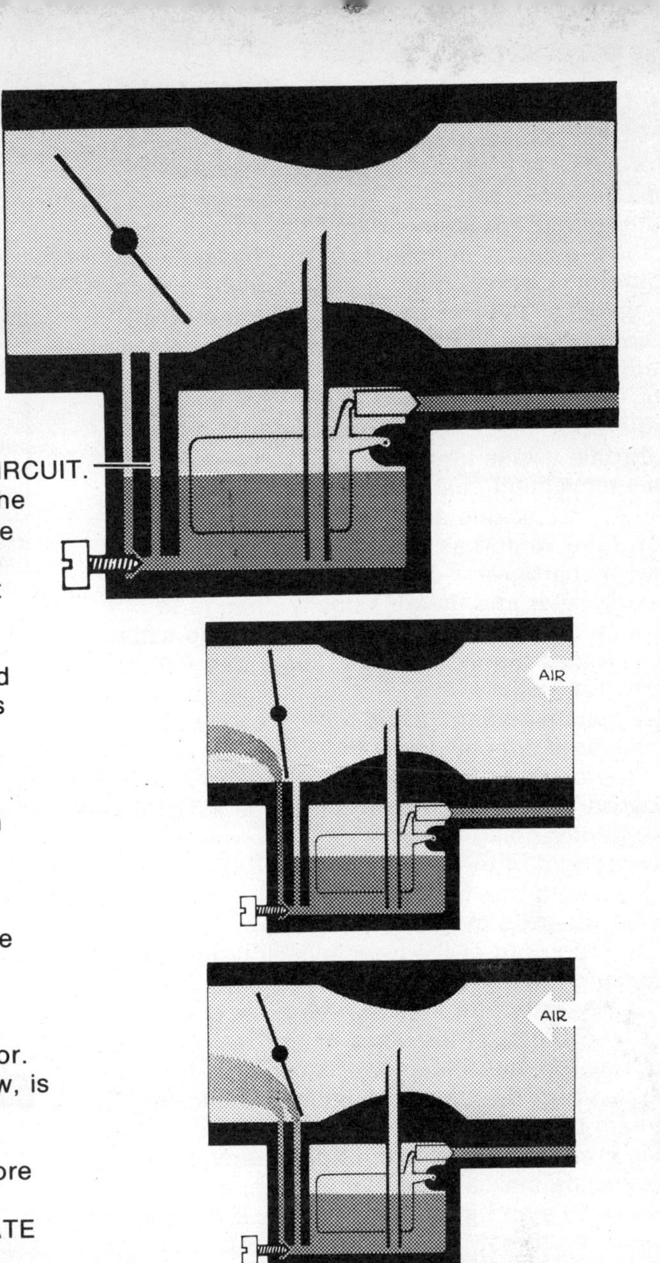

Now we have a carburetor which both idles and runs at different throttle settings. One other fuel circuit should be added to this basic carburetor: the INTERMEDIATE CIRCUIT. This is a third pathway from the float bowl to the throat of the carburetor. When the throttle plate opens (as the rider twists the throttle grip) and the idle circuit cuts off, the intermediate circuit opens and starts flowing fuel.

As the throttle plate opens, air starts to flow through the carburetor in greater amounts, and the vacuum built up behind the throttle plate is quickly reduced. Soon the vacuum behind the plate is so low that the idle circuit stops delivering fuel, but there is not yet sufficent vacuum at the venturi to pull enough fuel from the spray tube. If there were no intermediate circuit, you would experience a "flat spot" in engine acceleration. The intermediate circuit takes over at the right moment and delivers the right amount of fuel to match the engine's requirements.

To help start the engine, let's add a second plate in the throttle bore of the basic carburetor. This plate, which blocks off some of the airflow, is the choke. A cold engine starts better with a slightly richer air/fuel mixture than is normally required for engine operation. (Rich means more fuel than air in the air/fuel mix.)

By moving the choke lever, the CHOKE PLATE closes off most of the throat of the carburetor, and airflow is reduced. At the same time, a considerable vacuum builds up behind the plate from engine suction. The throttle plate works the same way.

At this point, the throttle plate is nearly closed and the vacuum behind it is drawing fuel from the idle circuit. There is also vacuum behind the choke plate, and here *additional* fuel is drawn from the spray tube or a special choke circuit. In this way, the ratio of fuel to air is altered to produce a rich mixture to aid starting. After the engine starts and warms up for a few minutes, return the choke lever to the normal running position.

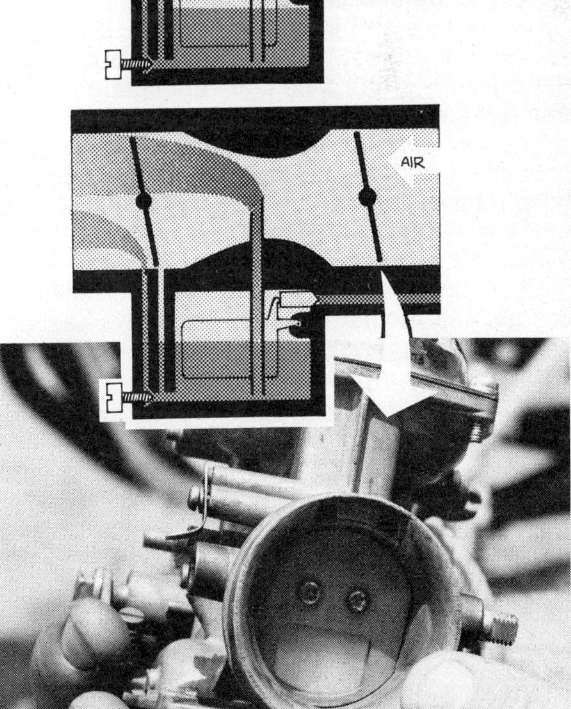

NOTE: THERE ARE MANY DIFFERENT KINDS OF MOTORCYCLE CARBURETORS. NOT ALL HAVE A CHOKE PLATE, OR EVEN A THROTTLE PLATE AS SHOWN IN OUR EXAMPLE, BUT ALL WORK ON THE SAME PRINCIPLE. ALL USE DIFFERENCES IN AIR PRESSURE TO PULL GASOLINE OUT OF A "RESERVOIR" TO MIX WITH AIR.

SLIDE VALVE CARBURETORS

The most common kind of carburetor used on motorcycles is the slide valve, manufactured by Amal, Bing, Dellorto, IRZ, Keihin, Mikuni and several others. While this carburetor functions on the same physical principles as our basic carburetor, it differs quite a bit in looks.

A typical slide valve carburetor like the one shown here has no throttle plate. Instead, there is a cylindrical or round SLIDE, which moves up and down at right angles to the throttle bore, blocking or unblocking the bore as the throttle grip is turned.

This movement changes the size of the venturi, rather than blocking and unblocking the throat beyond the venturi as the throttle plate does in our basic carburetor. The amount of air entering the carburetor and the air velocity change in response to changes in the position of the slide. This changes the amount of vacuum and varies the flow of fuel.

The main metering device for the slide valve carburetor is directly below the slide. The float bowl is at the bottom of the carburetor, and the path for fuel is a TUBE in the center going upwards. At the bottom of the slide is a TAPERED NEEDLE which fits into this tube or hole.

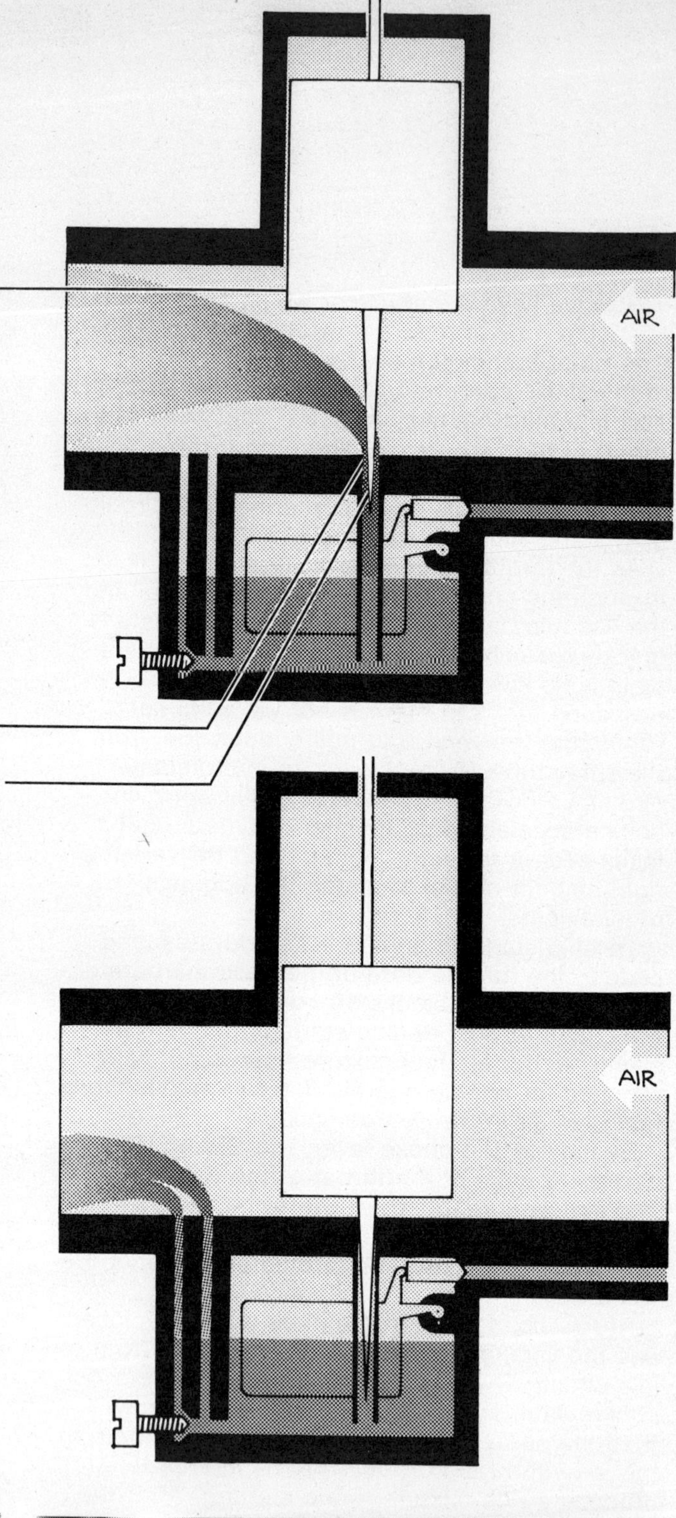

When the slide moves up and down, the needle moves in and out of the hole, blocking and unblocking it according to slide position. The tip of the tube sticks into the throttle bore or throat of the carburetor at the place where the vacuum is strongest. When the engine is running, fuel is drawn up past the tapered needle and into the airstream to be vaporized. If the slide is high, the needle is withdrawn from the hole nearly all the way, and the maximum amount of fuel can pass by the needle and into the airstream. If the slide is low in the throat, the needle shuts off most of the opening of the tube and very little gasoline can get past to enter the airstream.

You can see that both the amount of slide movement and the shape of the taper on the needle have a great deal to do with the flow of fuel and air inside the carburetor. That's what makes the slide valve carburetor so good for motorcycle use. By changing to a shorter needle or one with a different taper, you can change the whole metering system of the carburetor to conform with any requirement.

CAUTION: BEFORE MAKING ANY CARBURETOR CHANGES FROM THE ORIGINAL EQUIPMENT, CHECK WITH YOUR SHOP MANUAL OR YOUR LOCAL MECHANIC. ALL CARBURETORS ARE FACTORY-SET, AND THE WRONG CHANGE COULD HARM YOUR BIKE'S ENGINE.

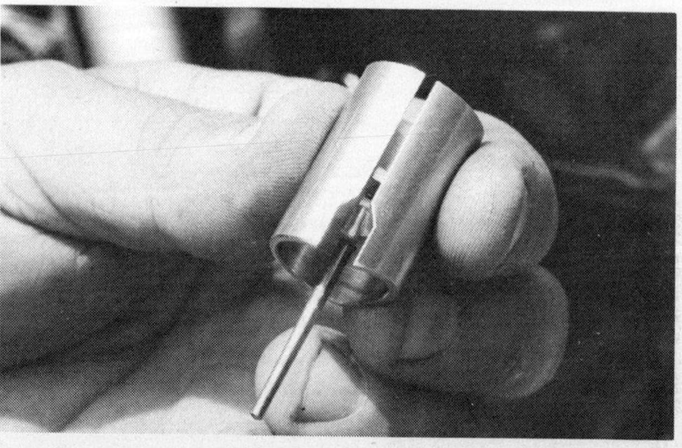

This is the slide and needle from a typical carburetor. The slot in the side of the slide body keeps the slide aligned with a pin inside the slide bore of the carburetor. The shape and length of the tapered needle strongly affect tuning. Many sizes and shapes are available.

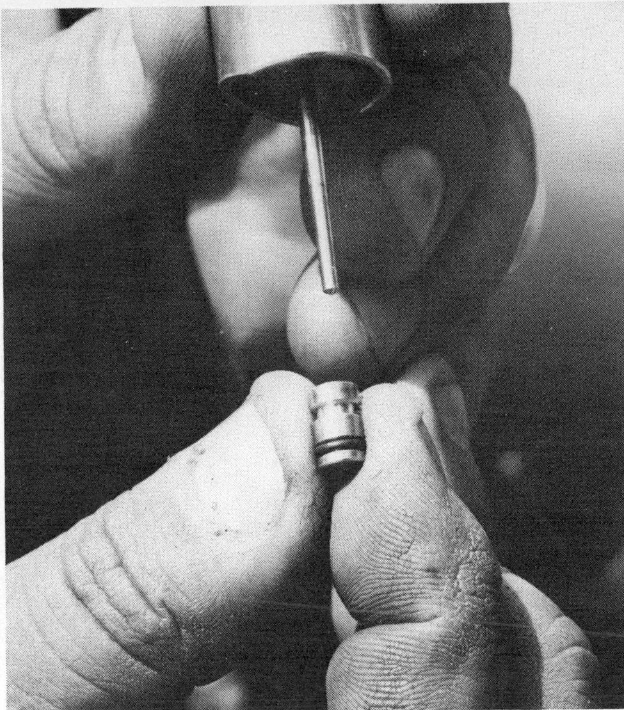

The main jet, here shown removed from the carburetor body, is the final control on the amount of fuel that flows from the float bowl. When the throttle is completely opened and the needle is withdrawn all the way, then—and only then—the diameter of the main jet becomes critical to tuning. Too many beginning tuners start changing jets before they try adjusting other changeable parts.

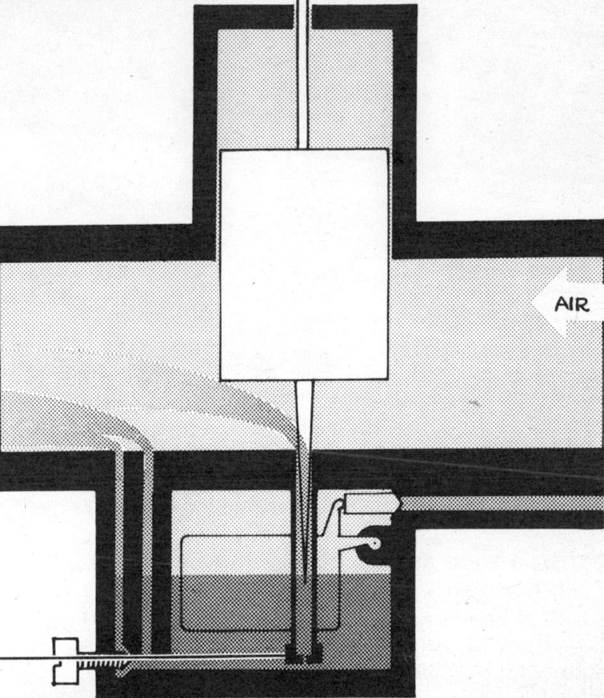

At the bottom of the draw tube is another part that affects the way the carburetor supplies fuel to the engine. This has an adjustable opening or "jet" and is called the MAIN JET, because the majority of the fuel used by the engine passes through it. The jet determines the total amount of fuel that can pass up the tube and into the throat of the carburetor. When the engine is being run at full throttle and the tapered needle has withdrawn all the way from the draw tube, it is the size of the hole in the main jet which limits the amount of fuel. Many carburetors are designed so that the main jet size can be changed without disassembling the carburetor. This is a great help when tuning the bike, especially if you like to make changes to compensate for altitude while riding in the mountains.

Main jets come in several sizes for any carburetor, with the size of the jet measured either in thousandths of an inch or in millimeters.

The slide valve carburetor is a very simple device, with few moving parts. The biggest problem is with dirt and dust that get inside the carburetor and make the slide stick. Buildup of varnish and other deposits from gasoline can also collect in the throat, on the slide and needle or in the jet, and this buildup can cause sticking or dirt-collecting problems too. For this reason, the carburetor should be cleaned at regular intervals (during tune-up) to keep it in peak operating condition.

When it does become necessary to change main jets, a carburetor with a fitting that allows you to change the main jet without taking the carburetor apart is a blessing. This type of carburetor is normally found on racing bikes, where tuning the full throttle action is critical to winning races. Main jets come in a wide variety of sizes, available at your dealership.

VACUUM-CONTROLLED VENTURI CARBURETORS

Variable-venturi carburetors like this Keihin unit for Hondas are recognizable by their large top housing for the diaphragm. These are excellent carburetors, if somewhat sensitive to dirt. Good air filters are the best medicine for them.

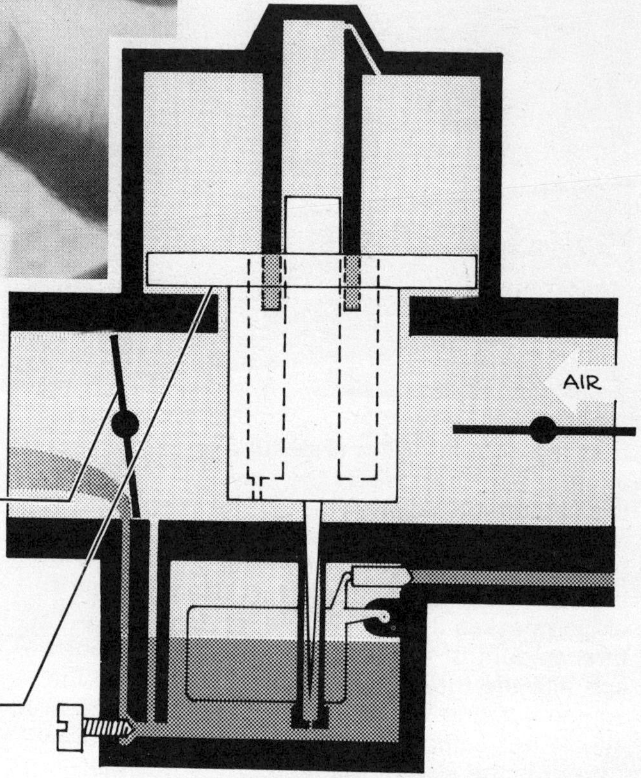

AIR

These carburetors mix the operating principles of both automotive-type carburetors (with a throttle plate like our basic carburetor) and slide valve carburetors. They not only use a slide and needle to control the flow of fuel, but also have a THROTTLE PLATE to control the overall operation of the carburetor. This throttle plate is linked to the throttle cable, while the slide and needle are operated only by changes in internal air pressure.

A vacuum-controlled venturi carburetor is easily recognizable by the large air chamber on top of the carburetor body. Inside this chamber is a PISTON that is a part of the slide. One side of the chamber is vented to the outside air, while the other side is exposed to the air pressure present in the throttle bore of the carburetor. Behind the slide in the bore is the throttle plate.

It's easier to understand how this carburetor works if we imagine it on an engine that is running at idle. At this point, the throttle plate is closed nearly all the way, creating a strong vacuum behind it. This vacuum draws fuel from the idle circuit of the carburetor to feed the engine. Note that the air pressure in front of the throttle plate is nearly the same as that of the outside air. This equal pressure is felt in the chamber housing the carburetor's piston/slide and does not affect its position.

If the throttle is twisted slightly to open the throttle plate, the air flowing through the throttle bore and the venturi will cause a pressure drop with respect to the outside air. This pressure change is felt inside the carburetor chamber and by the piston/slide. The piston then moves to open the venturi slightly, until the air pressure is equalized. In this case, the piston moves upward, enlarging the venturi area and permitting more air to enter the engine.

At the same time, the needle withdraws slightly from the draw tube and some fuel starts flowing up from the float bowl to add to that already entering the airstream from the idle circuits.

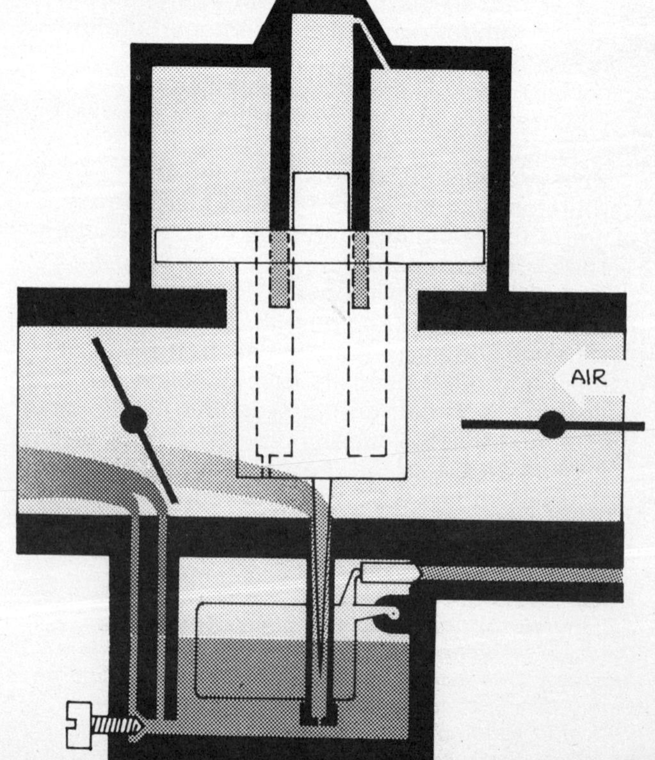

> **NOTE:** AS THE THROTTLE OPENING INCREASES, THE IDLE CIRCUIT BEGINS TO SHUT DOWN AND THE INTERMEDIATE JET OPENING STARTS DISCHARGING FUEL. THEN, AS THE INTERMEDIATE CIRCUIT BEGINS TO SHUT DOWN, THE MAIN JET STARTS DISCHARGING FUEL. THIS PROCESS MAINTAINS THE BALANCE OR RATIO OF FUEL TO AIR FOR THE ENGINE.

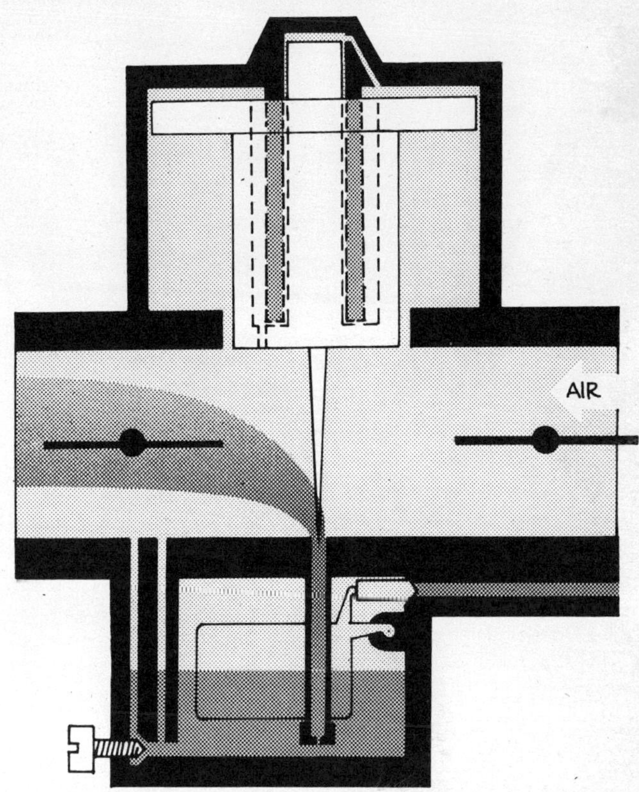

By moving the piston to change the size of the venturi opening, the velocity of the airstream is held almost constant. With the throttle plate all the way open, the change in internal air pressure forces the piston to the top of the chamber, opening the venturi all the way and withdrawing the needle from the draw tube. Now the carburetor is getting all its fuel from the drawtube, and the amount is controlled by the size of the main jet at the bottom of the tube.

As you can see, the vacuum-controlled venturi carburetor is an extremely sensitive piece of equipment. The rider's slightest change in the throttle position brings about a corresponding change in piston position and a change in the airflow through the carburetor. This change in airflow is reflected in a change in pressure, which moves the piston up and down in the chamber to balance the pressure. In doing this, the piston constantly varies the amount of air and fuel available to exactly match engine demand.

Mechanical problems associated with the vacuum-controlled venturi carburetor are much the same as those with the slide-valve carburetor. The vacuum-controlled carburetor is slightly more sensitive to dirt, because the movement of the slide is controlled by small changes in air pressure rather than a cable. It doesn't take much to put one out of action if it is not properly cared for and kept free of dirt and dust. For this reason, these carburetors are seldom used on off-road motorcycles.

AUTOMOTIVE-TYPE CARBURETORS

While these carburetors are not used on the majority of motorcycles, you will find them on some large road models. This carburetor operates much like the basic carburetor we showed in the first part of this section.

An automotive-type carburetor has a float bowl with a float controlling the flow of fuel from the gas tank. It has the same type of needle and seat, main jet, and secondary fuel delivery circuits as any other carburetor. One circuit found on these carburetors that is *not* found on other types, though, is the ACCELERATOR PUMP.

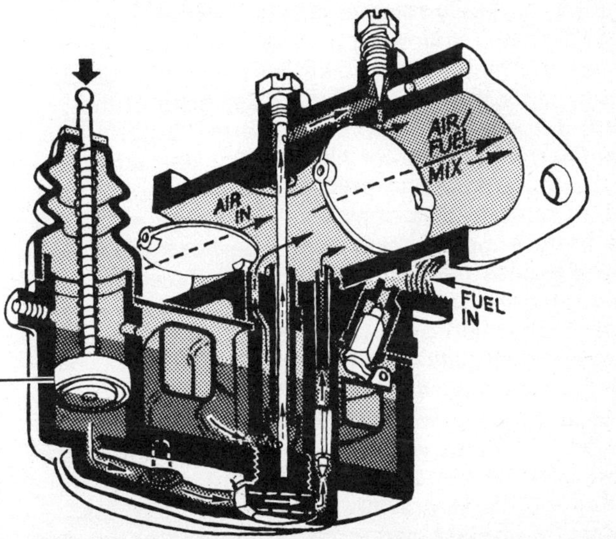

The accelerator pump adds extra fuel under pressure in response to a sudden demand by the rider. This is a one-shot supply of extra fuel given when the throttle is suddenly opened wide, such as in passing or sudden starts. The accelerator pump is mechanically connected to the throttle by an external linkage. Any sudden opening of the throttle actuates the accelerator pump, which provides additional fuel to the engine until the main circuits of the carburetor can begin supplying fuel at a faster rate to match the increased engine demand. This does much to eliminate flat spots or "bogging" when the throttle is opened too quickly.

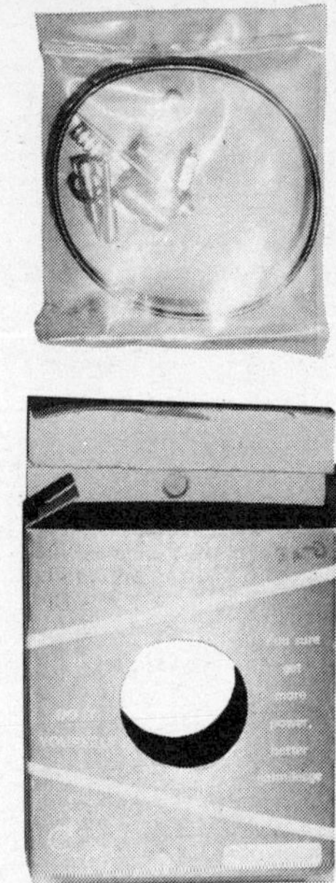

The rebuilding kit for a carburetor contains needle and seat, main jet and various air screws, springs, gaskets and other small parts.

Before installing new parts, clean the disassembled carburetor with carburetor cleaner. The basket which comes with the can of cleaner prevents small parts from becoming lost in the cleaner fluid.

There are many minor differences among motorcycle carburetors, so consult the shop manual for specific information on adjustments or rebuilding. Most such information is beyond the scope of this chapter, but some general tips on carburetor maintenance apply to all types of carburetors. Most manufacturers sell a carburetor rebuilding kit separate from other tune-up parts. These kits generally consist of parts that wear out, such as the gaskets, jets, springs, small clips and fasteners and the needle and seat for the float bowl.

First, carefully remove and disassemble the carburetor(s), following a shop manual or other reference material. Examine all parts for wear, particularly the slide and the slide bore of the carburetor body. Next, clean the metal parts in a commercial carburetor cleaner or *clean* solvent.

It's a good idea to dry the carburetor parts with an air hose from a compressor after removing the parts from the cleaning fluid. The hose will blow away excess fluid and any small particles which might otherwise clog the tiny passageways and openings which pass fuel to the idle, intermediate and main circuits. Then reassemble the carburetor, following the directions in the shop manual *exactly,* with new parts substituted as required. Unless you are making a jet change for a reason, take special care that the new parts (jets) you install are the same as the old ones.

Most manufacturers number jets and needles, and you should compare numbers between old and new parts. The parts man at your dealership may not always give you what you need. There are many different carburetors in his stocklists and mistakes can be made. Know the number of your carburetor.

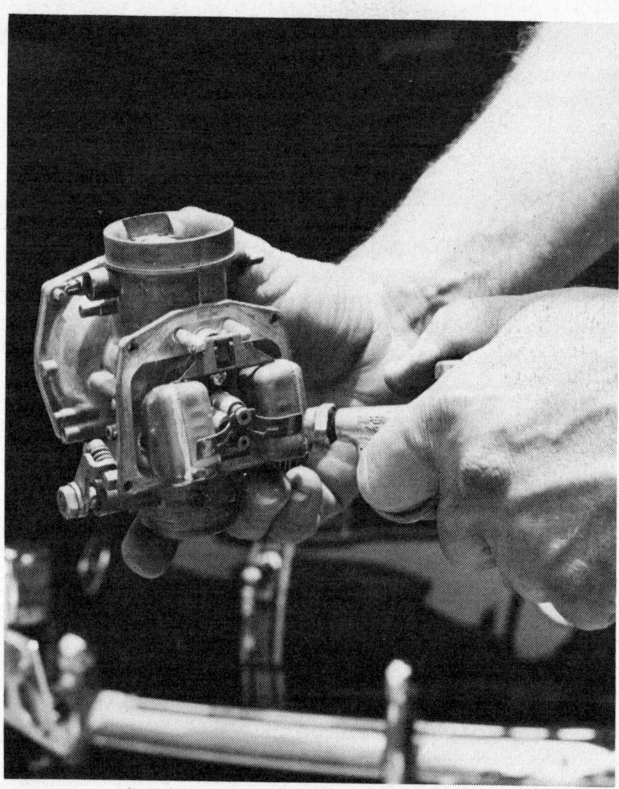

After removing the carburetor from the cleaner, you can further clean out small passageways and dry the carburetor by using an air compressor. Don't use extremely high pressure—just enough to remove the residue of the cleaner and any small bits of material left behind.

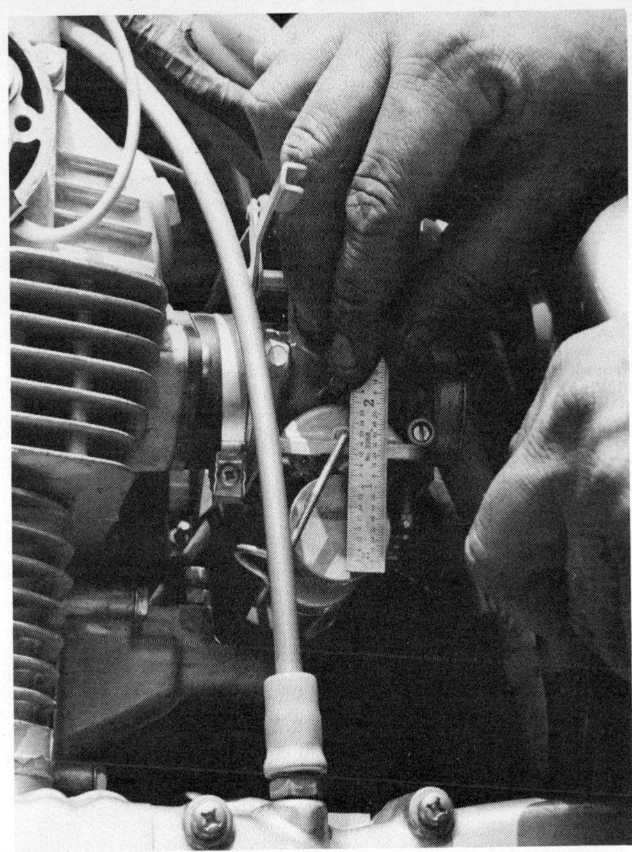

Your shop manual or owner's manual tells the measurement for setting float level. Most carburetor floats are adjusted by bending the tang. Pivot the tang against the needle and seat. Don't bend the tang too much; it may break.

One critical carburetor adjustment is setting the float level. If this is not correct, you may starve the engine by not allowing the float bowl to fill to the proper level. If set too far the other way, the float bowl may overfill and flood the engine, since the needle and seat valve never quite shut off the flow of fuel. Many carburetors have dual floats inside the float bowl. Correct adjustment requires that the adjusting tang (metal stop) be adjusted properly for *both* floats.

Once you have the carburetor back together and installed on the engine, make all necessary minor adjustments to external linkage, idle screws, etc. Check the mechanical operation of the carburetor to see that the slide functions normally and does not bind or stick. Then start the engine to check for fuel leaks and make the rest of the required adjustments for proper operation.

CAUTION: WHEN ADJUSTING IDLE AIR OR IDLE SPEED SCREWS OR ANY JET SETTING, BE CAREFUL NOT TO BOTTOM THE SCREW OUT FORCIBLY. THIS CAN DAMAGE THE NEEDLE OR ITS SEAT AND CAUSE ERRATIC RUNNING OR HARD STARTING. CRITICAL PARTS IN CARBURETORS ARE GENERALLY MADE OUT OF BRASS, AND IT DOESN'T TAKE MUCH PRESSURE TO RUIN THEM. EXCESSIVE FORCE CAN ALSO STRIP OUT THREADS, ALLOWING SMALL METAL CHIPS TO ENTER THE FUEL OR AIR AND, FROM THERE, THE ENGINE.

The final step, after all other rebuilding and setting the float level, is to adjust idle speed and idle air mixture on the outside of the reassembled carburetor. The technical manual gives the proper starting point for adjustment.

One problem often encountered by tuners is a leak at the base of the carburetor, where it attaches to the engine. Bolt-mounted carburetors have an O-ring seal which should be replaced during a carburetor rebuild. When the carburetor is reinstalled, watch the O-ring carefully to see that a good seal is maintained. An air leak here upsets the air/fuel balance of the engine and causes a wide variety of problems, from erratic running to an engine that will not start at all.

Some carburetors do not mount directly to the engine, but have a phenolic or fiberboard block between carburetor and engine. This block prevents engine heat from transferring to the carburetor and causing the gasoline in the float bowl to boil. Examine the block to see that it is not cracked or warped. This prevents air leaks. There may also be O-rings or paper gaskets on both sides of the phenolic block; always check and/or change these during the carburetor tune-up process.

Another mounting variation is the spigot-mounted carburetor. This carburetor is connected to the engine by a section of tubing, usually made of rubber or plastic, which isolates the carburetor from engine heat and also from vibration. Always look closely at this tubing to be sure it's not cracked or rotted. The method of fastening is usually clamps, but some motorcycles use hooked springs to hold the tubing in place. These springs tend to stretch and destroy the seal between the engine and the carburetor, so check them well.

The tubing connecting the carburetor with the aircleaner box needs examination for similar reasons. A cracked, rotted piece of tubing or a bad clamp or spring here can undo all your cleaning and replacement of parts in a hurry. It doesn't take long for dirt to start affecting the inside of a carburetor.

Fuel line connections from the fuel tank and/or remote float bowls should be carefully checked. A leak here could cause an engine fire. Fuel lines of the clear plastic type age and become brittle after a few months, so they require frequent attention. Rubber hoses can grow soft and collapse internally or shed particles which stop up the jets and passageways inside the carburetor.

When installing carburetors that mount solidly against the engine mount or against a phenolic block, it's important to check the condition of the O-ring gasket (below left) at the base of the carburetor. If it's damaged or worn, replace it.

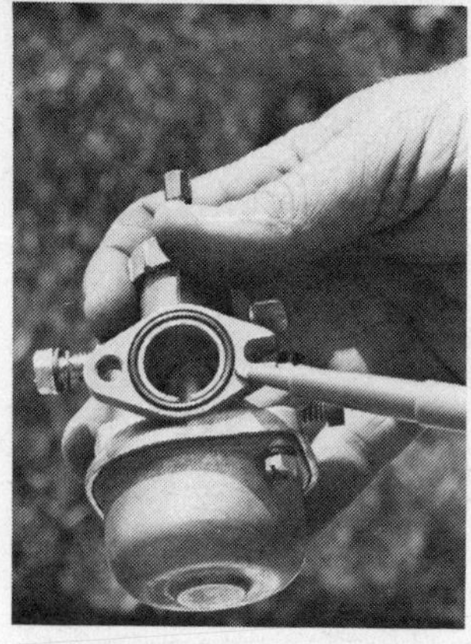

The phenolic block (above right) should be checked for cracks too. If cracked, it may allow air to enter the engine and upset the air/fuel ratio, creating a lean mixture. This and other air leaks from O-rings or rubber tubes connecting carburetors to the engine are often hard to find.

Carburetors which mount on a flexible rubber or plastic tube are called "spigot mounted." Be sure the groove (above) at the base of the carburetor is well inside the tube before tightening the hose clamp or installing the spring which holds the carburetor.

The little clips (left) that secure the fuel lines to the carb on most bikes are prone to failure after they have been removed and reinstalled a time or two. Check and replace them with hose clamps of the screw-down type to prevent fuel leaks.

One of the hardest problems to troubleshoot is a fuel line that is collapsing internally when the engine is running, shutting off part of the fuel flow and starving the engine. When you stop the engine to look for the source of the problem, the line will appear normal. Another thing to watch is line routing. A sharply curved fuel line may develop a kink which will partly block the flow of fuel from the tank to the carburetor.

The only sure way to finish off a carburetor rebuild or any other tuning operation is a test ride. Choose a riding place which allows you to ride the bike as it will be ridden in normal operation. For instance, a quick turn around the block may suffice for a street bike, but it won't show up a problem that a dirt bike would encounter while going over a jump or undergoing the up-and-down movements of riding in rough terrain.

Be sure to check out the bike in all gears and at sufficent rpm to get a good reading of power output. This is an individual thing. You have to develop a feel for how the bike is running compared to before you started tuning, but it will come naturally after you've been at it for a few months.

Always check the routing of fuel lines to make sure they don't crimp the hose. Check also for soft spots or inner rotting, which indicate the hose is about to fail.

CAUTION: WHEN TESTING, ALWAYS WEAR ALL THE SAFETY EQUIPMENT YOU WOULD FOR NORMAL RIDING. WEAR EYE PROTECTION AND A HELMET. DON'T RIDE BAREFOOT OR WITH STREET SHOES IF YOU HAVE GOOD RIDING BOOTS. IT MAY TAKE A LITTLE LONGER TO DRESS PROPERLY FOR A RIDE THAT MAY ONLY LAST A FEW MINUTES, BUT THIS IS WHERE MANY RIDERS GET HURT. WHEN TESTING, YOUR ATTENTION WILL BE ON HOW THE BIKE SOUNDS AND WORKS, NOT ON YOUR SURROUNDINGS. ALSO, CHOOSE AN AREA THAT IS FREE OF TRAFFIC AND OTHER POSSIBLE DANGERS.

For a complete, step-by-step photo guide to rebuilding carburetors, see "Your First Four-stroke Tune-up" or "Your First Two-stroke Tune-up."

Test riding after a tune-up requires proper clothing for safety. Minimum includes helmet, eye protection and good shoes or boots. This rider has added a long-sleeved shirt and gloves for extra safety.

II/Ignition

The ignition system on your motorcycle is called on to perform a very tough job. It must deliver a high voltage potential to the spark plug to fire the air/fuel mixture in the combustion chamber, and it must do this at *exactly* the right moment. Each time the piston comes up to the top of the cylinder in the compression stroke, the spark plug must be fired within a very short time, in order to create a flame front which will move across the combustion chamber and completely burn the compressed air and fuel, producing maximum power. When you consider that at normal speeds, this operation must take place thousands of times in an hour, it is easy to see how critical the proper operation of the ignition system is to motorcycle tuning.

The electrical system is one of the hardest things for most motorcycle tuners to understand. Yet it doesn't take a degree in electronics—just willingness to learn and to follow the book.

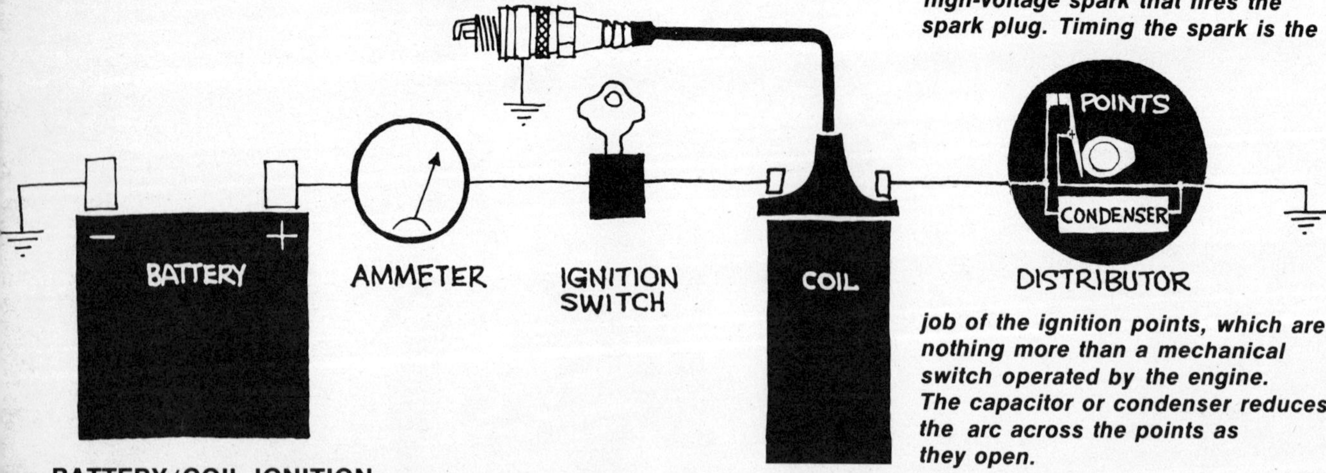

This simplified diagram (below) of a typical battery/coil ignition circuit should help you understand how it works. The ignition coil creates the high-voltage spark that fires the spark plug. Timing the spark is the job of the ignition points, which are nothing more than a mechanical switch operated by the engine. The capacitor or condenser reduces the arc across the points as they open.

BATTERY/COIL IGNITION

Let's take as an example the simplest form of motorcycle ignition system, *battery/coil* ignition, and follow its cycle of operation to learn how it works before going on to tuning tips and the various other types of ignition systems used on motorcycles.

The main components of battery/coil ignition are: the battery, ignition switch, coil, ignition points and the spark plug. The battery supplies the basic electrical current that powers the starting system, ignition system and all other electrical components.

The battery is a chemical generator of electrical energy. Plates composed of a lead compound which are suspended in an acid mixture undergo a chemical reaction, producing a strong voltage potential between the terminals of the battery. Contrary to popular belief, the battery does not *store* electricity; it manufactures electricity by this chemical process.

When a complete circuit is established between the two battery terminals, current (amperage) flows through the circuit from one terminal to the other. When this electrical current is flowing in the circuit and passes through electrical components, it performs useful work.

NOTE: MOST ELECTRICAL SYSTEMS IN THIS COUNTRY ARE NEGATIVE GROUND (−), WHICH INDICATES THAT THE DIRECTION OF CURRENT FLOW IS FROM THE NEGATIVE TERMINAL TO THE POSITIVE TERMINAL. SOME MOTORCYCLES, PRIMARILY THOSE OF ENGLISH ORIGIN, ARE POSITIVE GROUND (+), AND IN THEM THE DIRECTION OF CURRENT FLOW IS REVERSED. THIS DOES NOT AFFECT THE OPERATION OF THE ELECTRICAL SYSTEM, BUT YOU MUST USE DIFFERENT METHODS OF CONNECTING TEST EQUIPMENT AND INSTALLING THE WIRES ON REPLACEMENT PARTS.

After passing through the ignition switch, the first component in the circuit is the COIL. The coil is the device that changes the low-voltage, high-current output of the battery to the high-voltage, low-current flow used by the spark plug.

There are actually two coils of wire inside the molded body of the coil. The side through which battery current flows, composed of a few turns of heavy wire, is called the PRIMARY WINDING. The other side is called the SECONDARY WINDING, and it's made of many turns of fine wire.

The coil is a transformer, just like the one on the power pole outside your house. The power transformer steps high voltage down to low voltage to run your household appliances and lights. The motorcycle ignition coil steps up voltage from the battery for use by the spark plugs. Both types of transformer work by using magnetic fields to transfer energy from one winding of the coil to the other. There is no direct electrical connection between the coils of wire.

This energy transfer process is called *induction.* It is easier to understand if we examine how another piece of electrical equipment on the bike, the GENERATOR or ALTERNATOR, works to produce electrical energy.

In the generator are many coils of wire, which are rotated past magnets. As these coils move in and out of the magnetic field, an electrical potential builds up in them. It is not just the presence of the magnetic field that does the job; there must be a rapid change in the *strength* of the field. With the coils moving rapidly through the magnetic field, the electrical potential induced rises and falls, producing pulses of electrical current and voltage.

The battery, usually located under the seat, generates electricity by chemical means. Check the fluid level by looking at the marks on the side of the clear plastic shell or by removing the filler caps. Good preventive maintenance requires a regular check of the battery fluid level.

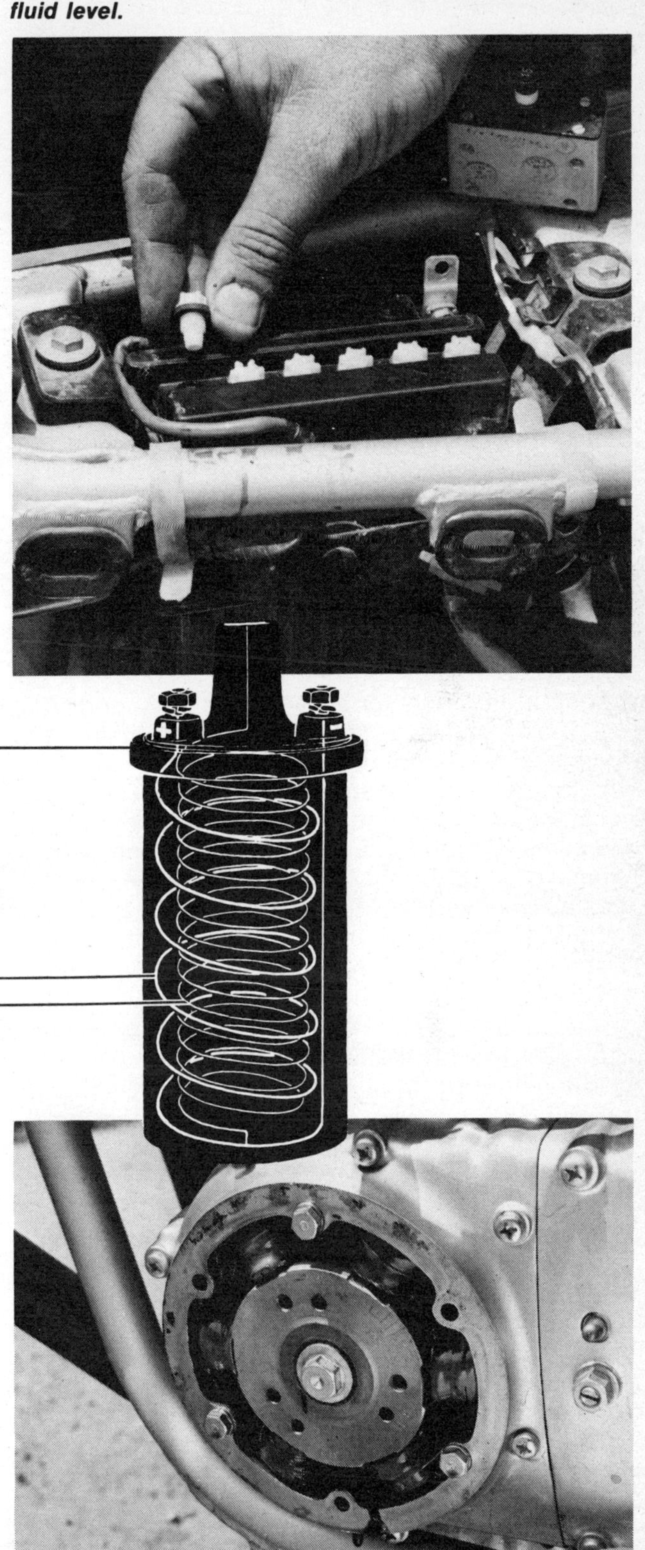

Another part of the electrical system that makes use of magnetic fields to transfer power or create electricity is the generator or alternator. This unit is a series of fixed coils with a magnet rotating in the center (or coils rotating around a fixed magnet) to produce electricity for running the engine and charging the battery.

The ignition points are a switch held shut by spring tension. The engine opens and closes these points to create the high-voltage surge in the coil secondary winding that fires the air/fuel mixture. The timing of this action is critical. Note that the motorcycle in the background has dual points.

Now, the coils in the ignition coil do not move in relation to the magnetic field built up in the primary winding, so some way must be found to quickly change the strength of the field at the right time to produce a strong pulse of electricity in the secondary winding. This is done by opening a switch that breaks the circuit at the precise moment required. The switch is called the ignition points.

When the flow of current first starts in the primary winding, it builds up gradually to full strength, without inducing any significant amount of energy in the secondary winding. But if we break the circuit after the full magnetic field is built up, the abrupt stop of the current flow in the primary winding collapses the magnetic field almost instantly. This quick collapse induces a powerful burst of electrical energy in the secondary winding.

While the current flowing in the primary was low-voltage (12 volts battery supply), high-current energy, the voltage induced in the secondary, though it only lasts for a fraction of a second, may reach 10,000 to 20,000 volts! Such high voltage is necessary to get a strong spark across the gap between the spark plug electrodes.

Let's go through one cycle of operation of the basic ignition system to see how it operates. When you turn on the IGNITION KEY, it establishes a complete primary circuit, and current starts to flow in the PRIMARY WINDING of the ignition coil. This builds up a strong magnetic field, which spreads and also covers the SECONDARY WINDING of wire.

The IGNITION POINTS are a pair of metal contacts held together by spring tension. A small CAM LOBE, rotated by the engine crankshaft or the camshaft, forces the points open as it turns at exactly the right time to stop the flow of current in the primary winding.

When the primary circuit is interrupted by the opening of the ignition points, a strong electrical pulse is induced in the secondary winding of the coil. This pulse of electricity is so strong that it bridges the gap between the electrodes of the spark plug (see above). The flash of current or spark then ignites the air/fuel mixture inside the combustion chamber.

The two most important elements of a good ignition system are a strong spark and proper timing. A strong spark is produced by a coil and spark plugs that are in good condition, with the plug correctly gapped. The timing of the spark is determined by the rotation of the point cam that opens and closes the points.

The points are adjustable within certain limits. Setting them is one of the most essential parts of a tune-up, because the spark plug must be fired at or very close to the time the piston reaches top dead center (TDC) on the compression stroke.

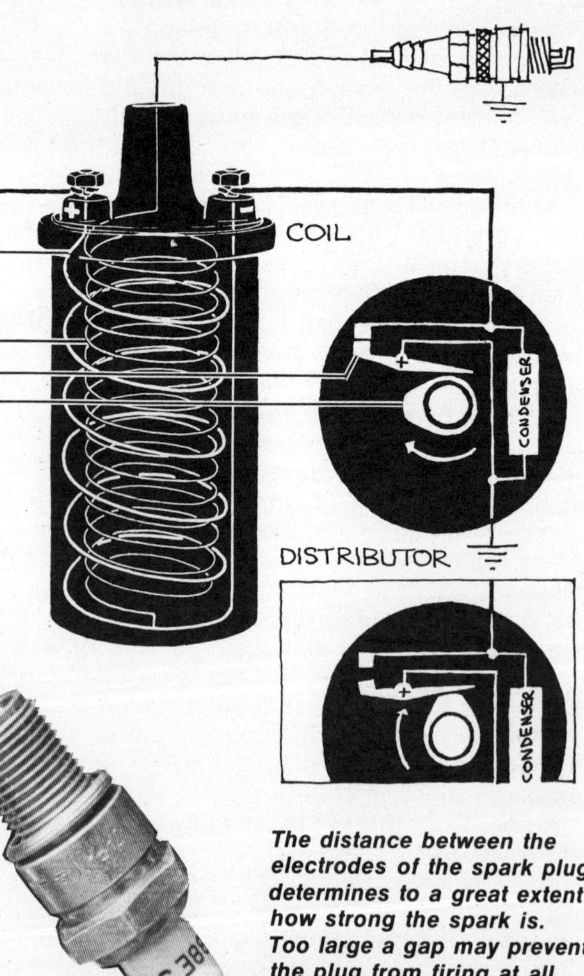

The distance between the electrodes of the spark plug determines to a great extent how strong the spark is. Too large a gap may prevent the plug from firing at all, while too small a gap may not produce a wide enough flame front inside the combustion chamber.

> **NOTE:** THE SPARK IS ACTUALLY REQUIRED JUST BEFORE PISTON TDC FOR PROPER ENGINE OPERATION, AND THE TIMING MUST CHANGE AS ENGINE SPEED INCREASES AND DECREASES.

A spark plug with the gap closed like this could mean the plug is too long in reach. That closed gap may have been caused by the piston hitting the plug.

The spark plug is a very important part of the electrical system. If it is the wrong type or is gapped incorrectly, it will not fire properly and engine horsepower will be lost. Spark plugs need to be checked and cleaned at frequent intervals, especially on two-stroke bikes.

The fact that a two-stroke engine burns oil along with gasoline alerts you to the fact that its plug will get much rougher treatment from the buildup of deposits than the plug in a four-stroke bike. If you found a plug in your four-stroke engine that looked like the average used plug from a two-stroke engine, you would worry that the rings or valve guides were worn out and the engine needed an overhaul!

The type of ignition system we have described is a very simplified, basic ignition. You won't find any motorcycle that uses *exactly* this system. However, the main parts of this ignition system are present in all modern motorcycles.

CAPACITOR DISCHARGE IGNITION

The capacitor is a device that stores electricity. Most electrical ignition systems have a small capacitor to tone down the spark across the ignition points, but capacitors can also create a much stronger spark plug spark.

When a complete circuit for current flow is established, with a capacitor in the circuit, the capacitor will charge up to the value of the circuit voltage. In the case of the battery circuit, it will charge up to the voltage of the battery (six or 12 volts). The amount of resistance in the circuit determines the charging time, but it is very fast.

Once the capacitor takes a full charge, it will maintain the charge as long as the circuit is in operation. If the circuit is broken, then quickly switched to provide a low-resistance path for the capacitor to discharge through, the capacitor will discharge its stored electricity at a very high rate.

The capacitor that operates the ignition points may not be physically close to the points. That's one of the things that makes electrical wiring confusing to some; things are not always what they seem. On many bikes, the capacitor is located under the fuel tank along with the ignition coils.

Two different types of CDI (Capacitor Discharge Ignition) are shown in this schematic drawing (below). Both have a signal generator, a separate coil in the generator housing and an SCR or thyristor as a switch to replace the ignition points used in a battery/coil ignition system.

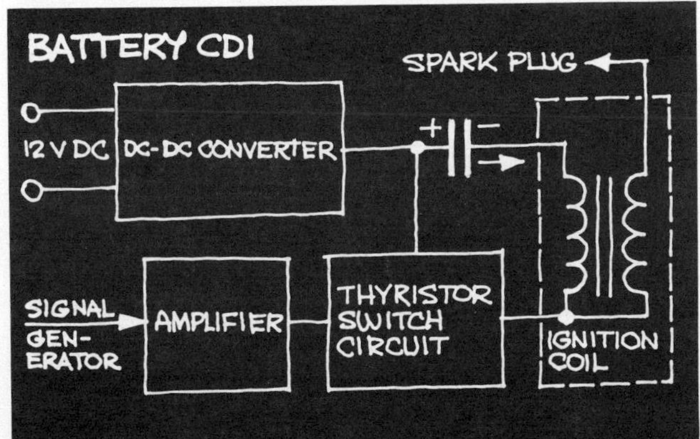

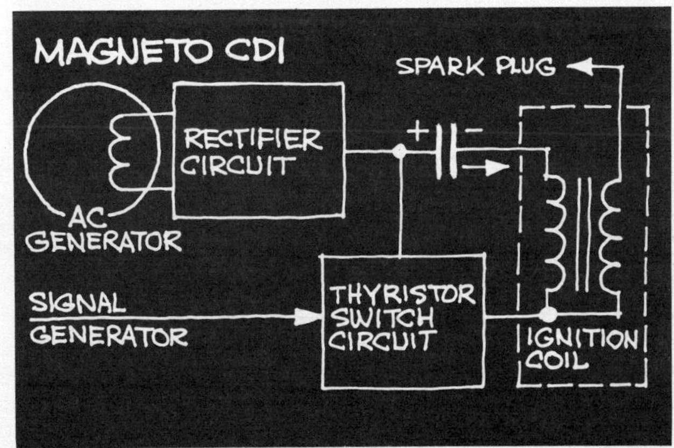

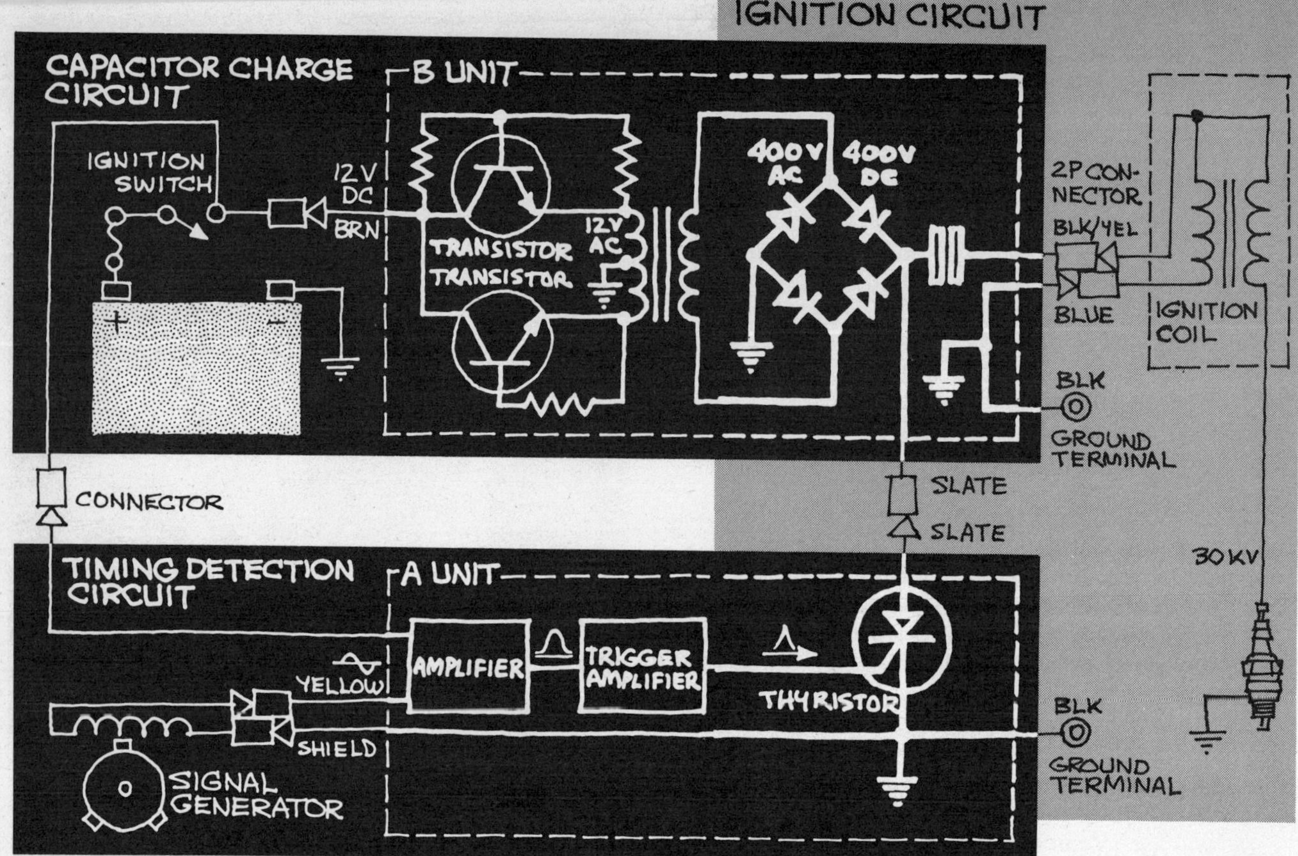

A more detailed look at the workings of a CDI system shows the electronic components. These are normally sealed units and are replaced rather than repaired.

By allowing the capacitor to charge, then switching the circuit so that it discharges quickly through the primary winding, the capacitor can deliver a strong, quick pulse of electricity to the primary winding of an ignition coil. The reason this works so well is that the primary winding (which is a few turns of heavy wire), has a much lower resistance to current flow than the circuit which charges the capacitor.

Still, this offers no real advantage over the standard battery ignition. Some means had to be found to raise the battery voltage. Engineers designed several ways to do this. One way is to add a converter, which delivers a higher DC voltage from battery power. Another way is to change the output of the AC alternator or magneto on a bike to DC through a rectifier. (A rectifier modifies alternating current to produce direct current of the same value.) By either method, a high voltage, around 400 volts in most systems, can be developed for the capacitor.

This means that the capacitor, now charging to this higher voltage, can discharge through the primary winding of the coil with great force. The short, sharp pulse of high voltage creates a strong magnetic field, and because the coils of the ignition are wound like a step-up transformer, the voltage leaving the coil and going to the spark plug is very high—about 30,000 to 40,000 volts.

That much voltage will fire the spark plugs under almost any conditions. There's just one problem. Normal ignition points can't handle such a strong spark. The voltage is so high that the spark simply jumps the gap between the open points.

A new type of switching device then had to be found to handle the higher primary voltage. For motorcycle use, a solid-state device called the *thyristor* was used. This is a transistor switch that can handle high voltages easily. It presents an open circuit until it is triggered by a small input voltage on one connection. It then switches and becomes a complete circuit switch to the high voltage. Another name for the thyristor is the SCR, or silicon-controlled rectifier.

The thyristor can be triggered by battery voltage sent through conventional ignition points. Some bolt-on capacitor discharge systems do exactly this, but it amounts to using one switch (the ignition points) to control another switch (the thyristor). Even though the voltage is reduced across the ignition points, they can still wear and pit and they must still be adjusted.

A better way was needed. Since the thyristor needed only a small trigger pulse to activate it, why not create another small generator with only one magnet and one coil of wire? This generator could be positioned so that the magnet produced a small pulse of electricity each time the engine needed it to fire a spark plug, and the small pulse could act as a switching trigger for the thyristor. The idea worked. It's called the *Capacitor Discharge Ignition* system.

The small generator is usually mounted on the crankshaft, along with the alternator, and is adjustable to provide a means of timing the spark. Included in this design is an amplifier to boost the tiny output of the trigger coil to a level where the thyristor can make use of it. The CDI type of ignition system is becoming standard on almost all motorcycles, especially smaller-displacement bikes and those used for off-road riding and racing.

Since there are no ignition points to clean or adjust, minor tuning of a CDI system is limited to cleaning and gapping the spark plug and checking the timing. The timing on most CDI systems is set by aligning two marks, one on the alternator rotor, the other on the case. The timing is set at the factory and nothing much in the system can change the timing from wear, so a quick check is usually all that's necessary.

If a check shows an out-of-adjustment condition, you can perform a simple adjustment as outlined in the owner's manual, or go a step further and adjust and time the engine with a timing light.

That's the beauty of these newer types of ignition systems—most of the time they don't require any tune-up or preventive maintenance. The drawback is that when something does go bad, it often takes specialized test equipment to find the problem. Most of the parts in a CDI system are solid-state units which are replaceable but not fixable. You simply throw away the old unit and install a new one.

For a step-by step tune-up of a battery/coil ignition, see "Your First Four-stroke Tune-up," and for the same treatment of a CDI system, see "Your First Two-stroke Tune-up."

The signal that triggers the SCR in the CDI system is developed in this coil. It uses the same principles of magnetic induction as an ignition coil or alternator. The pulse is so weak it must be amplified for use by the SCR part of the circuit.

A timing light is the most effective way of setting exact timing, including advance, on CDI units. The stroboscopic (fast-blinking) light makes the timing marks "freeze" in relation to each other during each engine revolution.

III. Preventive Maintenance

What Is Preventive Maintenance?

A thorough cleanup and inspection of your motorcycle at regular intervals is the best medicine.

If a tune-up consists of restoring your bike to the way it was when it left the factory, then preventive maintenance can be defined as the day-to-day work required to keep it that way. This is true for the whole motorcycle, not just the engine.

A few hours a week spent going over your bike can reduce costly repair bills and increase both your riding enjoyment and safety. All motorcycles, especially those used off-road, need a little attention before and after riding to keep them in a state of top tune. Letting things go can result in poor performance, loss of economy and sometimes a dangerous loosening or wear of vital parts. It's a good idea to establish a regular program of inspection and routine maintenance for your motorcycle to keep it in the best possible shape.

A before and after riding check or a weekly going-over is good practice. It needn't be a complete checkup, but it should include checking
GAS and OIL LEVELS
(including injection oil in two-stroke engines equipped with a separate oil tank),
BATTERY FLUID LEVEL,
BRAKE FLUID LEVEL on bikes equipped with hydraulic brakes
and a general look around at
NUTS and BOLTS.

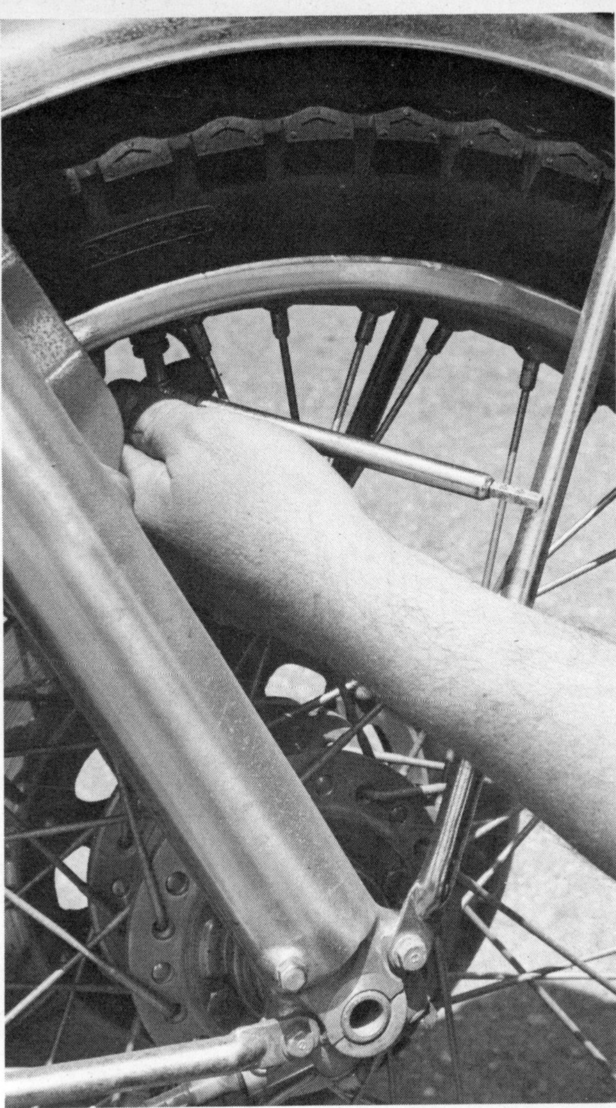

It's important to check the nuts or bolts holding the front and rear axles in place (see above). If these loosen up, you could be in big trouble. Also remember to check wheel spokes for tightness.

Make a regular check of tire pressures (right). This is especially important if you lower pressures for increased traction while riding off-road. A tire gauge is cheap insurance against tire problems.

Pay special attention to
FRONT and REAR AXLE NUTS and
WHEEL SPOKES. Tighten them if necessary. Sit on the bike and test all controls such as
THROTTLE, CLUTCH and both
BRAKES for ease of operation. Then start the bike and give all the electrical components a quick check-out.

This last part will not only make riding safer but may prevent a traffic ticket. Motorcycles vibrate, and it is not uncommon to find a broken tail or headlight bulb. Check the
HEADLIGHT,
TAILLIGHT,
TURN INDICATORS (if so equipped)
and the performance of
GAUGES and WARNING LIGHTS.

Check tire pressures before and after riding. This will also give you a chance to look at the condition of your tires. You should be on the lookout for wear, damage to the sidewalls and foreign objects, such as nails or thorns, stuck into the tire. This is most important on bikes used off-road, since hazards such as cactus are often not seen while riding, but those long spines can cause plenty of problems later on.

An after-riding inspection should cover the same general areas as the before-riding once-over. In addition, off-road riders should start with a cleanup of the bike. A thick covering of dirt or mud can hide potential trouble. Hosing the bike off with water or cleaning it with a good solvent is the first step in preventive maintenance.

WARNING: DO NOT CLEAN YOUR BIKE WITH GASOLINE OR OTHER INFLAMMABLE SOLVENTS. HOT ENGINE PARTS OR THE IGNITION CAN SET THESE LIQUIDS ON FIRE, RESULTING IN SERIOUS DAMAGE AND INJURY.

A more complete check of all parts of your motorcycle should be made at regular intervals. If you bought your bike new and have the operator's manual and a shop manual, then you should follow the recommended inspection times given in the factory books. If you want to set up your own inspections, 30-day intervals are just about right for most uses. The following 30-day checklist is only a guide. You can alter it to suit your needs. However, it covers all the items you should be looking at.

III/Monthly Inspection Checklist

BATTERY

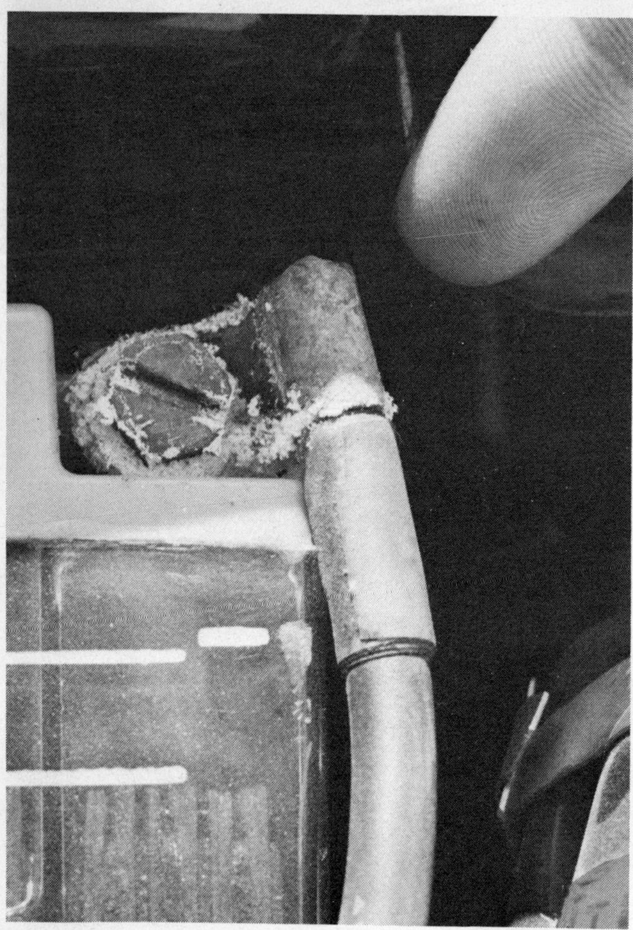

Take a close look at battery connections for evidence of a whitish buildup. This is corrosion, which can increase the resistance of connections to current flow. It will also destroy the metal connection if it is allowed to remain.

Check the fluid level in the battery. If it is low, add a little distilled water. Do not use regular tap water; the minerals in it will eventually harm the battery.

While the battery is a simple, self-contained device, it can fail. You should inspect the battery to satisfy yourself that it is in good condition and that the charging circuit is working. Most motorcycle batteries are constructed of clear plastic so you can see the fluid level from the side without having to remove caps. While you are checking the fluid level, examine the outside of the battery for cracks or signs of fluid leakage. Battery acid is highly corrosive and may damage paint or soft materials such as rubber or leather. Dried battery acid deposits can be seen as whitish material. These deposits usually form around terminals on the battery or at the bottom of the battery box or bracket.

WARNING: BATTERY ACID IS DANGEROUS TO SKIN AND EYES. IF YOU GET ACID ON YOUR SKIN, REMOVE IT RIGHT AWAY BY WASHING WITH COOL WATER. IF YOU GET ACID IN YOUR EYES, WASH THEM OUT IMMEDIATELY WITH WATER. SEE A DOCTOR IF THE BURNING SENSATION CONTINUES.

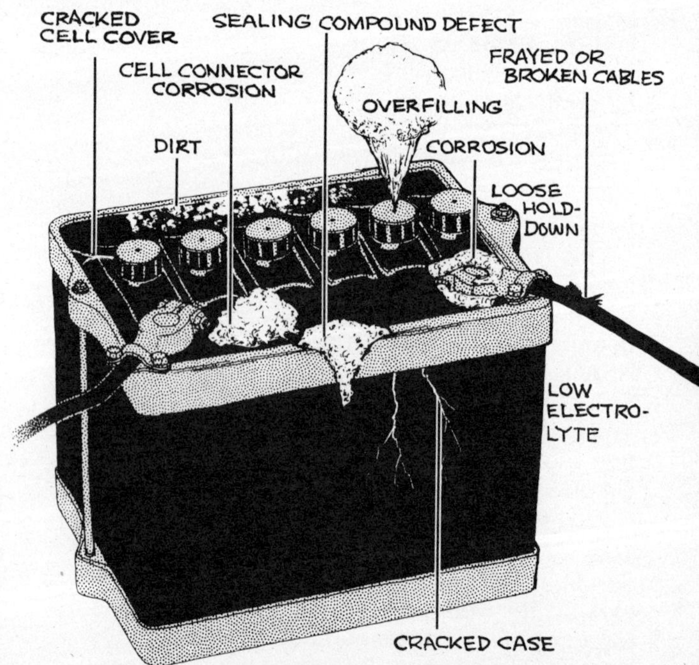

Batteries are subject to all kinds of problems, as illustrated here. Keeping the battery clean and charged will prolong its life.

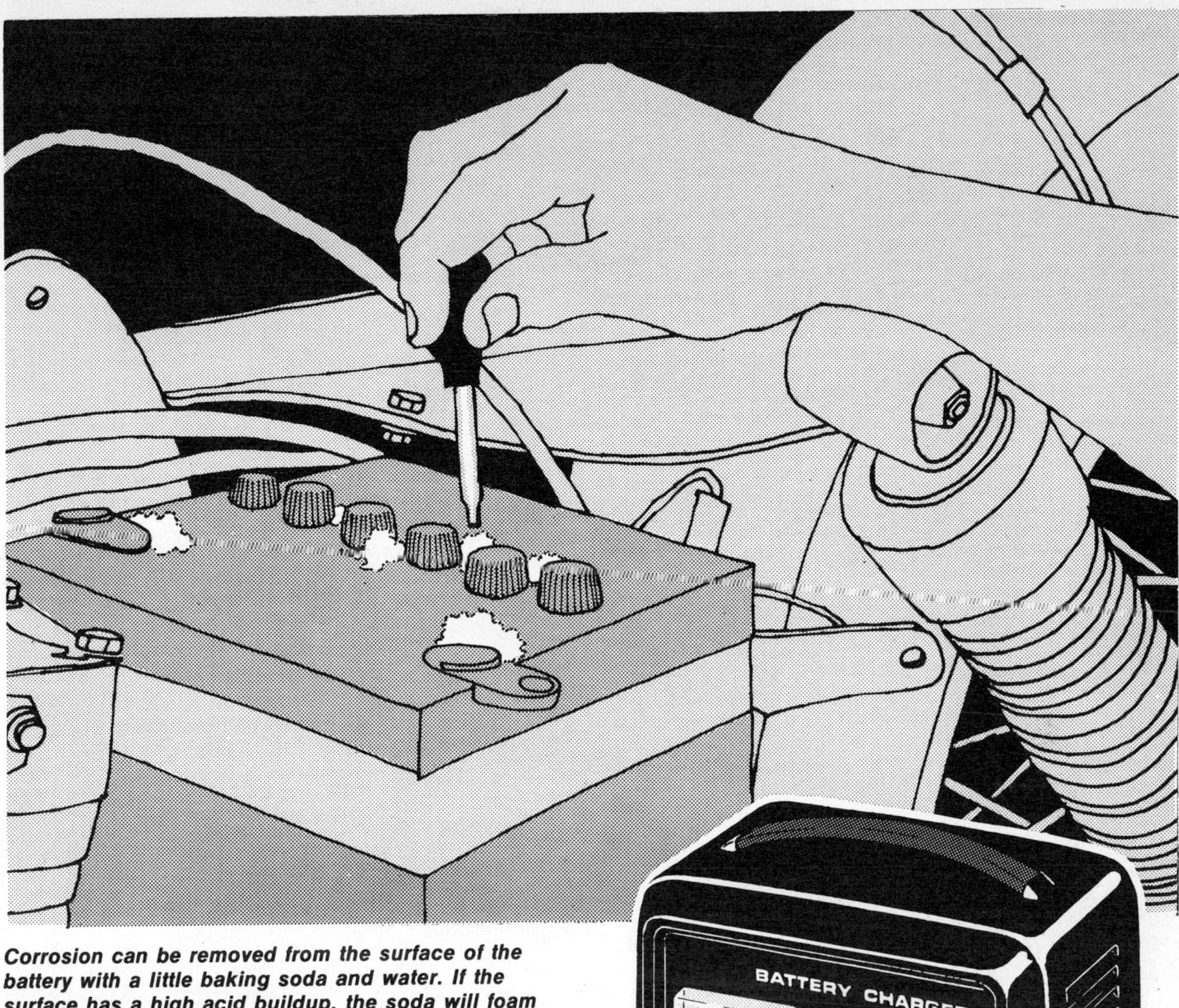

Corrosion can be removed from the surface of the battery with a little baking soda and water. If the surface has a high acid buildup, the soda will foam when applied. Scrub clean and repeat until the soda does not react to the surface of the battery.

Battery acid can have another bad effect. The buildup of acid corrosion on the wires running from the battery can increase the resistance of the connection to the point where it affects the operation of the electrical system. Battery acid buildup is best removed by cleaning the area with a mixture of water and baking soda. This neutralizes the acid and removes it from most surfaces.

If there is a heavy buildup of corrosion on battery terminals, disconnect the terminals and clean them completely before riding the bike. Be sure to tighten them well when you are finished; a loose connection can cause all sorts of problems and is difficult to troubleshoot.

Once you are satisfied with the battery's external condition, try the lights, horn or electric starter to get an indication of how fully charged the battery is. If you don't ride your bike every day, the battery can discharge.

You might want to consider purchasing a small battery charger of the type known as a "trickle charger." This charger can be plugged into any outlet in the garage, and it will keep the battery charged while you are not riding the bike.

A small battery charger can keep your battery in top shape during those intervals when you're not riding. If not kept on the charger, the battery will go dead when the bike sits idle.

CAUTION: MOTORCYCLE BATTERIES CANNOT STAND THE RATE OF CHARGING USED FOR AUTOMOBILE BATTERIES. DON'T CHARGE YOUR MOTORCYCLE BATTERY ON A SERVICE STATION CHARGER. IF YOU DON'T HAVE A TRICKLE CHARGER, TAKE YOUR BATTERY TO A QUALIFIED MOTORCYCLE SHOP.

AIR CLEANER

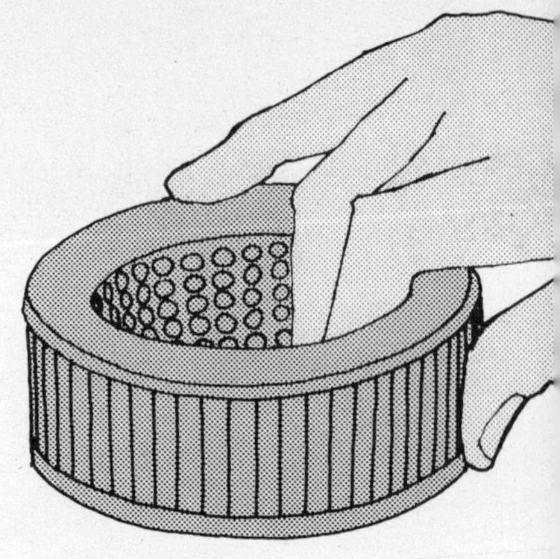

Air filters should be looked at and serviced regularly, as running dirt and grit through your engine shortens its life. Remember to check the condition of the foam element for cracking or rot.

Foam filter elements (see below) are most common on dirt bikes. These types can be cleaned with solvent, reoiled and put back in place many times before they wear out.

This is a must item. A clogged or damaged air cleaner can cause loss of power or even engine impairment. The air cleaner should be removed and inspected, then either cleaned and reinstalled or replaced.

Most motorcycle air cleaners can be cleaned. A great number have a foam element, which uses oil to trap dust and dirt particles. This type of air cleaner should be cleaned in a solvent, then re-oiled and replaced on the engine. There are a number of commercial spray oils for foam element air cleaners, but one simple way to re-oil a clean filter is to add some two-stroke engine oil (which dissolves readily in gasoline) to a small container of gas, then immerse the filter in the mixture. Allow the mixture to completely penetrate the foam. Wring out the filter element and hang it outside to dry. As the gasoline evaporates, it leaves behind a light coating of oil throughout the foam.

Paper elements are even simpler. They can either be vacuumed out with an ordinary house vacuum cleaner or blown out with an air hose. If you don't have a compressor in your garage, a quick trip to the gas station will do the trick.

Most paper elements even clean up fairly well by simply shaking them or rapping them sharply on something to knock dirt and dust loose. Paper elements provide good filtration unless they get wet, so if you ride through streams or wash your bike at the local carwash, it's advisable to inspect a paper filter more often than once a month.

Don't clean or replace the filter element and forget to clean the inside of the filter box. A handful of sand or dirt inside the box might get

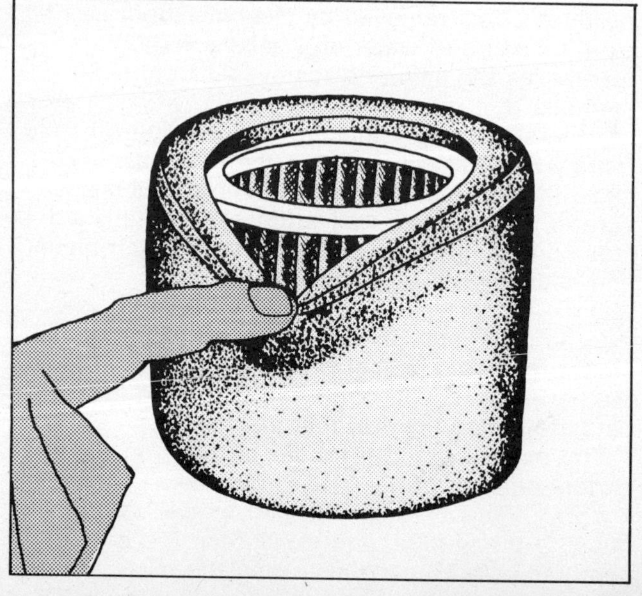

around the filter element and pass through to the engine. Off-road riders should check how tightly the filter element fits inside the housing. Any gaps should be filled either with a larger filter or extra foam (available at most cycle shops). A good practice is to smear a coat of grease on the top and bottom of the element to give a dustproof seal between the ends of the filter and the box. This will prevent collected dust from slipping by the filter and getting into the engine.

Don't forget to clean the inside of the airbox or cover over the filter. It doesn't do a bit of good to clean the filter, then reinstall it in a dirty box. The dirt from the cover will get right into the clean filter.

It's good practice to put a little grease on the edges of the filter where it comes in contact with the air box. This prevents dirt from sliding around the filter element and into the carburetor and engine.

NOTE: OFF-ROAD RIDERS WHO RIDE EVERY WEEKEND SHOULD INSPECT THE AIR FILTER WEEKLY RATHER THAN MONTHLY.

NUTS AND BOLTS

Vibration is a constant problem in motorcycles. Any inspection should include testing all the nuts and bolts on the bike for tightness. This doesn't mean just the ones that are easy to get to. It's the nut or bolt you skip over because it's hard to get at that will fall out on the road. Look for loose fasteners and missing lock washers and cotter keys. Lock washers and cotter keys are your best friends where safety is concerned.

Lock washers (above) and cotter keys (below) are necessary for safety. Never reinstall nuts and bolts without using the proper lock washers or keys. If you do, parts can loosen up due to vibration and cause an accident.

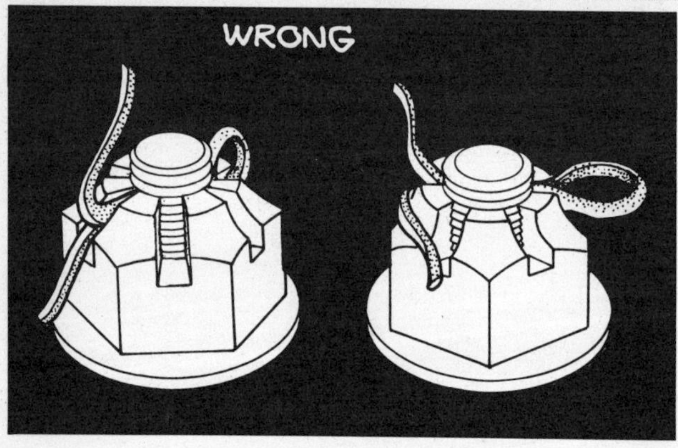

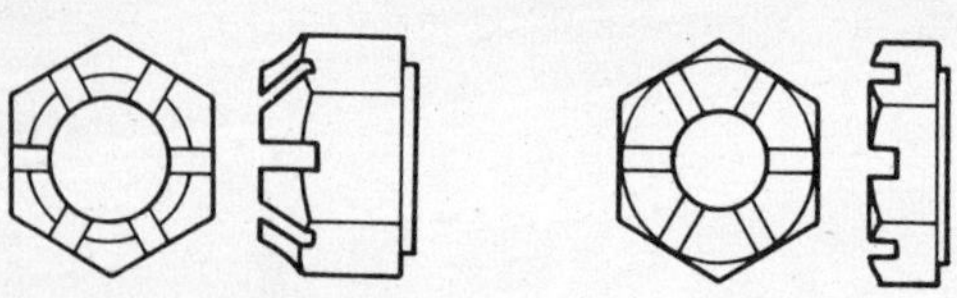

Some types of fasteners are special. Castellated nuts (above) are designed to be used with cotter keys. The various types of lock nuts (below) hold very securely, but can only be retightened a certain number of times before they must be discarded.

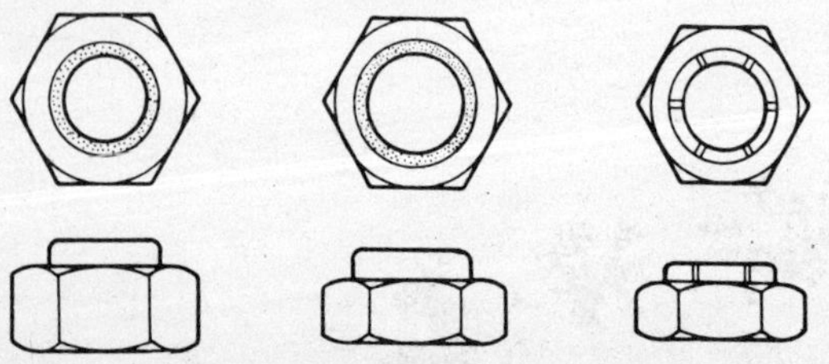

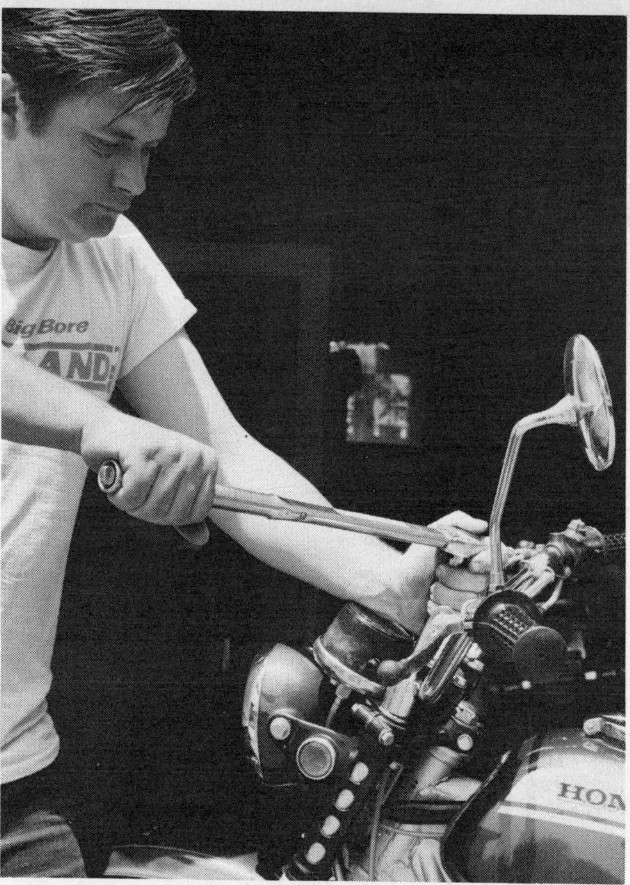

Going over all nuts and bolts with wrenches is a good idea. On fasteners where torque values are called out in the manual, use a torque wrench.

In addition to common nuts that are held tight by lock washers, you may find special nuts on your motorcycle. These include castellated nuts (for use with cotter keys), steel lock nuts and fiber lock nuts of the type developed for aircraft use. The fiber and steel lock nuts are perhaps the best-locking fasteners in use today, but they are designed to fasten parts that are not removed very often. After you loosen and tighten a fiber nut a few times, it loses its holding power and should be replaced.

When tightening nuts and bolts on your bike, don't overdo it. It is easy to get too rough on a small fastener and strain it by tightening it beyond its capacity. On most fasteners, you can do a satisfactory job of tightening by feel. You will develop a sense of just how much pressure you can apply to a nut or bolt.

There are many fasteners on your motorcycle, however, that must be torqued to specific settings. Consult your owner's manual or the shop manual for information on this. Also see the "Standard Torque Values" chart in the math section.

The final part of any 30-day inspection is setting the ignition timing, carburetor adjustment, points setting (not all motorcycles have ignition points) and valve adjustment on four-stroke engines. Since this constitutes a tune-up, see the chapters on tuning two-strokes and four-strokes and the specific tune-up information contained elsewhere in this book.

ENGINE AND GEARBOX OIL

Always check the oil level at least once a month, or even more often if you are riding a lot.

Of all the things vital to the good health of your motorcycle engine, oil is probably the most important. Without it, your engine will run only minutes, and the resulting damage often finishes the engine for good. The oil level should always be checked at least every 30 days.

Engine oiling systems differ between two and four-stroke engines. Two-stroke engines, because they pass the air/fuel mixture to be burned in the combustion chamber through the crankcase first, require that lubrication be supplied as part of this mixture.

Most modern two-stroke engines have a separate oil pump, which adds a predetermined amount of oil to the gasoline as it passes from the carburetor to the engine. On some older bikes, a specified amount of oil must be poured by hand into the gasoline tank. The pump, controlled by a cable from the throttle, meters the flow of oil at a rate consistent with the requirements of the engine. As the throttle is opened and more gas is used, the quantity of oil introduced is increased to match.

Engine oil is contained in a small external tank, usually located under the seat. The level of oil in this tank should be checked before riding, but it is also important to check it on the 30-day list. Most two-stroke motorcycles that use this type of tank have a small inspection window in the side of the tank so that you need not remove the filler cap to check the oil level.

While you are looking at the oil level (and adding oil if necessary), check the condition of the oil line and connections running to the pump. If the hose looks as if it might be leaking, repair or replace it.

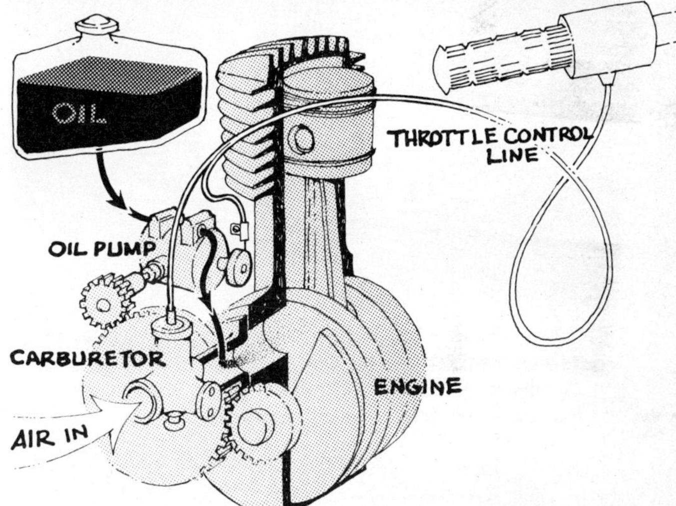

Since a two-stroke engine passes fuel through the crankcase, oil must be mixed with the fuel to lubricate the inside of the engine. On most two-stroke motorcycles this is done by a separate oil tank and a pump controlled by the throttle cable. The correct amount of oil is automatically injected into the engine along with the fuel.

Most motorcycles have a view window for greater convenience in checking the oil level.

Remove the cover over the oil pump and inspect it for signs of leaking, too, and at the 30-day interval, adjust the pump for proper operation. Look at the pump output line going to the intake manifold or carburetor to make sure it's secure and free from cracks or loose fittings.

NOTE: SOME SPECIALIZED RACING TWO-STROKE MOTORCYCLES AND SOME OLDER BIKES DO NOT HAVE AN OIL PUMP. INSTEAD, LUBRICATING OIL IS ADDED DIRECTLY TO THE GAS IN THE TANK. IF YOU HAVE ONE OF THESE MACHINES, FOLLOW THE FACTORY-RECOMMENDED PROCEDURE FOR ADDING OIL.

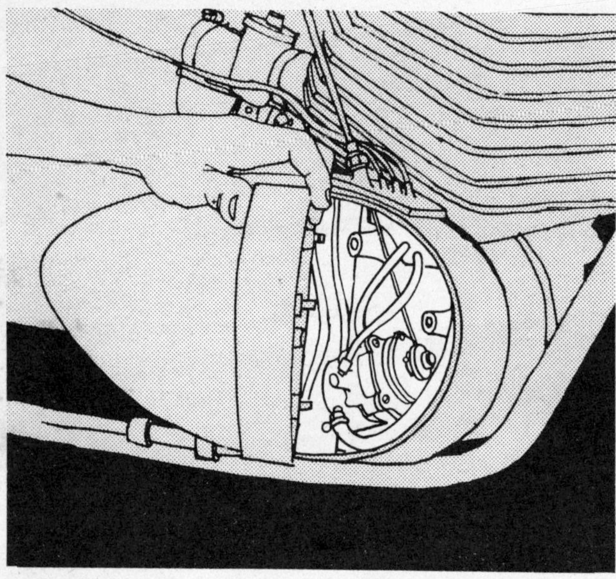

The oil pump on a two-stroke engine is normally located under one of the small covers on the side of the engine. It should be checked and adjusted on a regular basis to ensure good lubrication.

Four-stroke motorcycles do not mix oil with the gasoline to lubricate the engine. They have an internal pump that circulates oil to various parts of the engine from a supply inside the engine.

NOTE: SOME OLDER MOTORCYCLES AND ENGLISH FOUR-STROKES MAY HAVE A SEPARATE OIL SUPPLY. SUCH BIKES ARE SAID TO HAVE "DRY SUMP" ENGINES, BECAUSE THE CRANKCASE OR "SUMP" OF THE ENGINE DOES NOT CONTAIN THE ENTIRE OIL SUPPLY.

Bikes with a separate oil supply or dry sump type of oiling system require a little extra attention because of the number of lines running between the engine and the remote oil tank. Examine these lines carefully for signs of wear and leaking, and look at the tank for signs of split seams or broken mounting brackets.

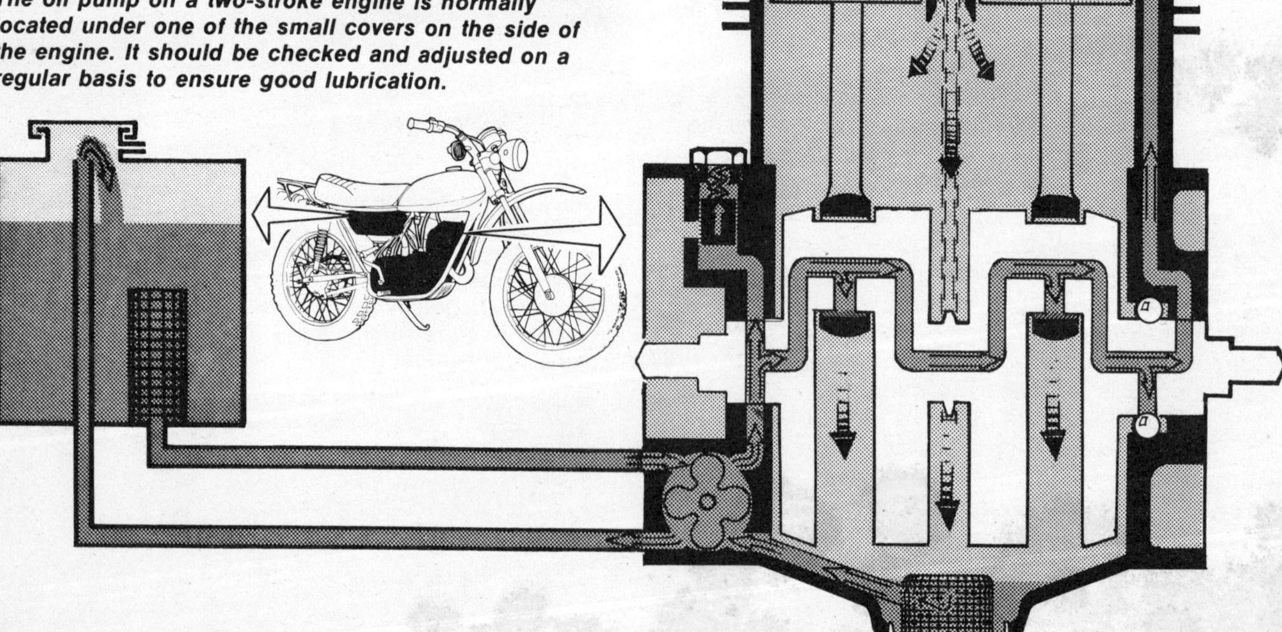

Some motorcycles use a separate oil tank to lubricate four-stroke engines. This is called the "dry sump" method, because the oil is not kept in the lower engine cases or "sump." Instead, oil is pumped through external lines to the engine and back to the oil tank.

Some large motorcycles have a removable filter element, just like the one on an automobile engine. It's usually contained in a finned cover to help oil cooling. This one on a Honda 500 is a bit hard to see, as it is between the front frame rails.

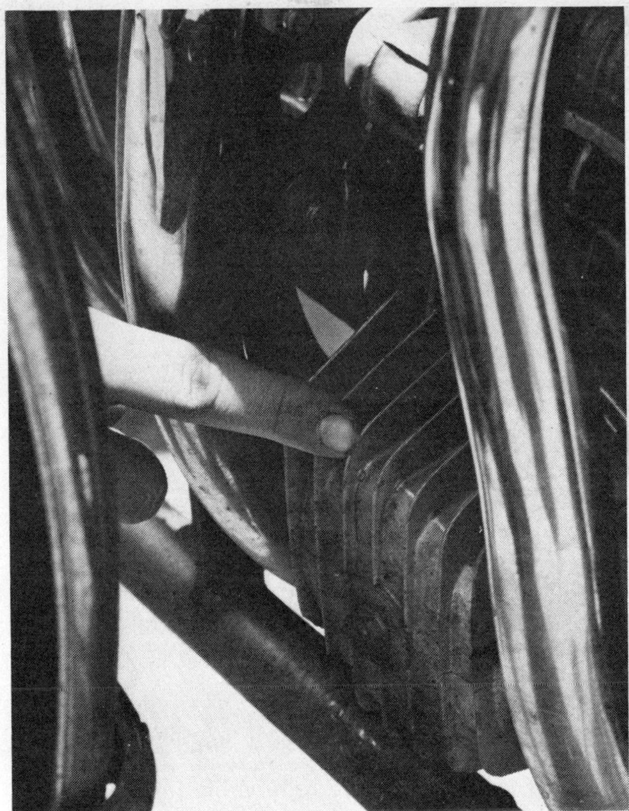

Wet sump engines maintain the oil supply as part of the engine. While this reduces the external complexity, it does add to the wear and tear on the oil, because engine oil lubricates the entire engine *and* the transmission in most bikes.

For both wet and dry sump oiling systems, regular oil change intervals are indicated in the owner's manual. It is sound practice to follow those instructions *faithfully.* Accumulated metal particles in the oil are a major cause of engine wear. What's more, oil breaks down after prolonged use, and can no longer protect the engine as it was designed to do. If you ride your bike a lot in severe dust or dirt conditions, you may want to consider shortening the time between oil changes.

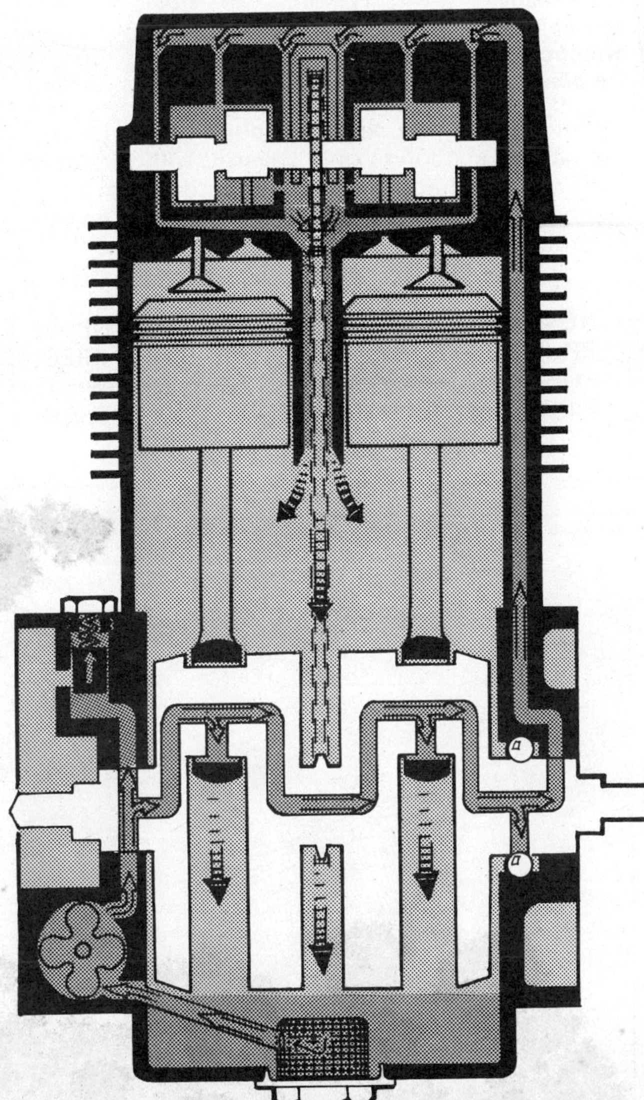

The majority of modern motorcycles use a "wet sump" system, where the oil is contained in the lower engine cases. From there, oil is circulated through the engine by a pump, then returned to the sump.

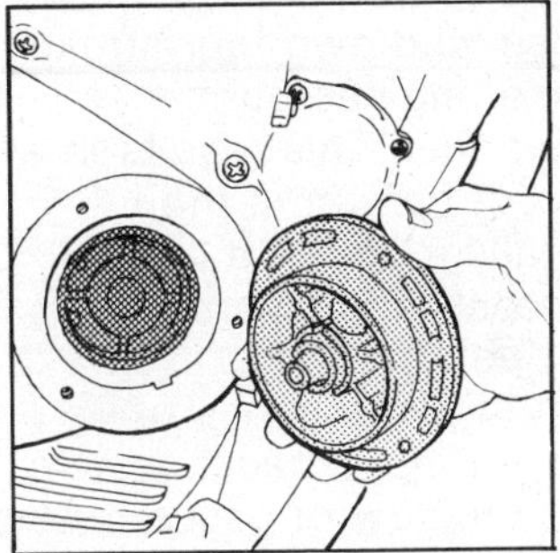

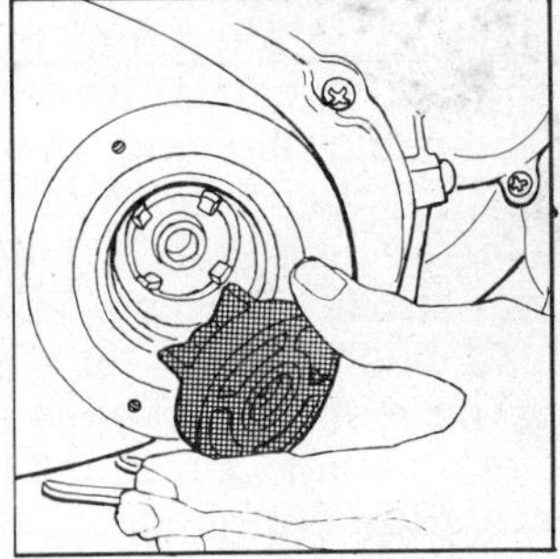

Many motorcycles use a strainer like this one instead of a filter. The strainer should be removed and cleaned whenever the oil is changed.

All four-stroke motorcycles use some form of oil screens or filters to remove harmful materials from the oil before it reaches engine parts. These should be removed and cleaned or a new filter element installed on a regular basis. The location of these screens and filters varies widely with different models of motorcycles, so you will have to refer to the shop or owner's manual for their location on your bike. There may be more than one oil filter on your engine, so be sure you know the location of *all* oil filters and screens.

An important point to remember when servicing the oil system on your motorcycle is to follow the manufacturer's recommendations on oil type and weight unless you have a specific reason for changing to a different oil. There *are* times when you might want to change from the oil listed in the owner's manual, mostly to suit extremely hot or cold weather operating conditions. Before you do, however, it's best to take the question up with an experienced mechanic.

EXHAUST SYSTEM

This is generally one of the most reliable systems on any motorcycle. Most exhaust systems never give any trouble, requiring only a general cleanup once a year or so. If regular inspections of the exhaust system on your bike show a buildup of carbon is taking place more rapidly than you think is right, look to the engine as the probable source of the trouble. The exhaust system is a very good indicator of internal engine condition.

Most motorcycle exhaust systems, with the exception of straight through pipes on bikes intended for racing, have removable muffler sections which can be cleaned and reinstalled. Two-stroke owners will have to do this much more often than those who own four-stroke engines, because two-stroke engines burn lubricating oil along with the fuel. This results in a much higher concentration of carbon in the exhaust pipe than is generally found in a four-stroke. The time lapse between cleanings is also much shorter for best performance.

The exhaust system needs scrutiny, especially on two-strokes. Small cracks or dents in the pipe can rob the engine of power.

The muffler section is often just a series of metal baffles. These baffles in the exhaust system serve to control and direct the flow of gases out of the exhaust pipe and help cut down noise. If the muffler section is only covered with a coat of fluffy carbon that hasn't gotten hard, it can be cleaned in a can of carburetor cleaner or solvent or brushed out with a wire brush.

NOTE: A SHOTGUN BARREL CLEANING BRUSH IS JUST ABOUT THE RIGHT SIZE FOR CLEANING MOTORCYCLE EXHAUST PIPES AND IS HANDY FOR MANY OTHER JOBS AS WELL.

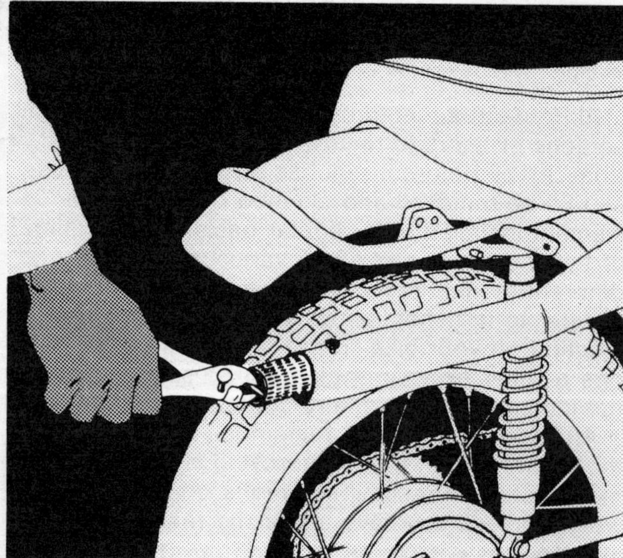

Exhaust baffles (mufflers) should be removed and checked from time to time to see if carbon buildup is bad enough to require cleaning. This carbon buildup can choke the engine, which creates backpressure and engine missing or overheating.

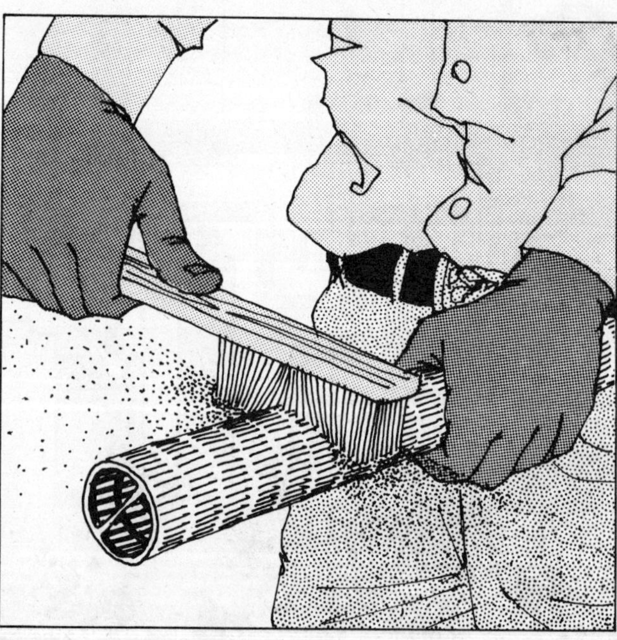

The best method of cleaning baffles is with solvent and a stiff brush. Soaking softens hard carbon so that the majority of it can be brushed away.

If the carbon is really caked on the baffles and is too hard to get off by soaking, it may be necessary to heat the baffles to remove the carbon. This is best done with a butane bottle or acetylene torch. Once the carbon buildup has been loosened by the heat of the torch, you can knock most of the carbon out of the baffles by tapping it on the concrete or scrubbing it out with a wire brush.

WARNING: NEVER USE ANY KIND OF TORCH TO CLEAN EXHAUST PIPES OR BAFFLES IF YOU'VE BEEN WORKING WITH SOLVENT OR GASOLINE. DO NOT TRY TO BURN CARBON OUT OF A BAFFLE THAT HAS RECENTLY BEEN SOAKED IN A SOLVENT. AN EXPLOSION AND SERIOUS INJURY COULD RESULT. ALSO, WHEN USING A TORCH, ALWAYS WEAR EYE PROTECTION AND GLOVES, AVOID BURNS FROM HOT METAL AND WORK IN A CLEAN, WELL-VENTILATED AREA. IF YOU DON'T HAVE THE RIGHT EQUIPMENT, TAKE THE PIECES TO A GARAGE FOR CLEANING.

While you are reassembling the exhaust system, check the mounting brackets and the outside of the pipes for cracks or dents. A good-sized dent in an exhaust pipe can reduce the power output of your engine considerably. Many exhaust pipes have rubber mounts to minimize vibration. These mounts should be examined for cracking or rotting caused by heat and smog.

On motorcycles there are three methods of fastening the exhaust pipe to the engine. The first method is the screw-on flange. This is probably the most rigid of the three, but it can be very hard to remove after the bike has a few hundred miles on it. The second is a flange secured by bolts, which may also be tough to remove. The third method is a pair of springs that hold the pipe in place. These are easy to take off, but have the annoying habit of rattling.

When inspecting the exhaust system, you should always check its mounting to the engine to make sure it is not loose. Leaks in an exhaust system can cause erratic running, backfiring and the possibility of overheating and valve or piston damage. On most engines, there is also a gasket between the pipe and the engine. Take a look at this and replace it if necessary.

Always test exhaust flanges where they fasten to the engine. A loose flange bolt can allow exhaust to escape, causing all sorts of problems, from overheating to burned valves on four-stroke engines.

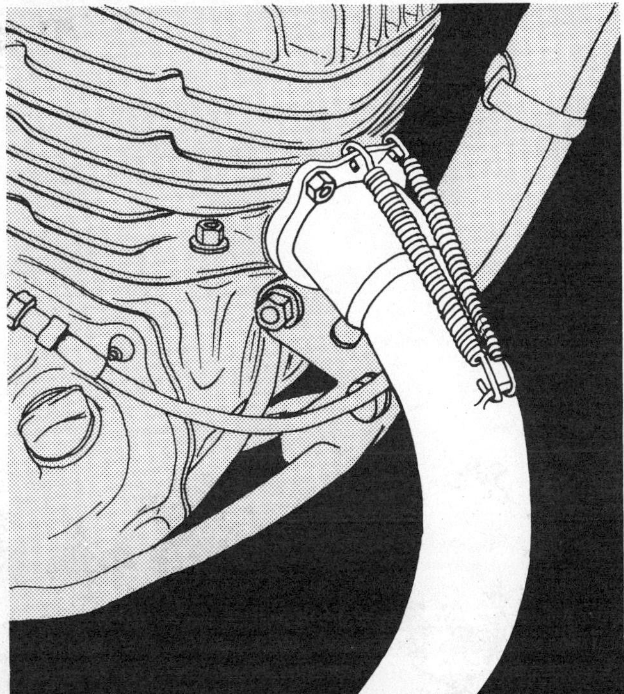

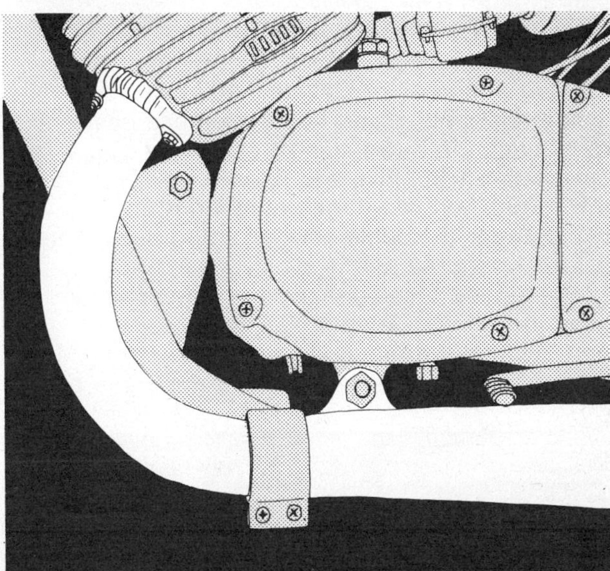

There are several types of exhaust flanges. Four-stroke engines usually have bolted types, but a majority of two-strokes use springs to hold the pipe tightly to the cylinder head. Proper spring tension and fit are a must.

BRAKES, CABLES AND CONTROLS

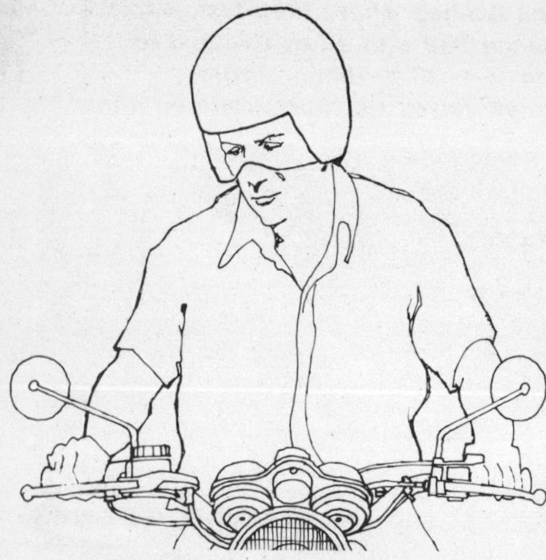

Part of the preventive maintenance inspection should be a careful survey of the condition of controls and cables. Levers with cracks are ready to break.

Checking controls and cables is part of the general exterior inspection your bike needs both before and after riding. The 30-day check is a good time for a complete, detailed inspection, combined with a liberal application of lubricant for preventive maintenance.

Control cables really suffer, especially in off-road riding. It's a good idea to examine closely the ends of all cables (where they attach to levers) for signs of loose tips or broken strands of wire. A broken cable can really let you down far from home. A valuable tip to remember is that the front brake cable can often be removed and substituted for either the throttle or clutch cables in an emergency. This allows you to ride home—slowly, using the rear brake to stop.

Cables should be oiled at regular intervals by running a little oil or powered graphite down inside the cable cover. It is sometimes easier to get lubrication down along the cable if you take the cable off the bike and hang it up. That way the oil can run down the entire length of the cable under the cable cover. Letting cables hang overnight should do the trick.

If you have a cable that binds consistently, even though you keep it well lubricated, the problem may be that it is routed incorrectly. Too tight a bend in a cable will make the cable bind

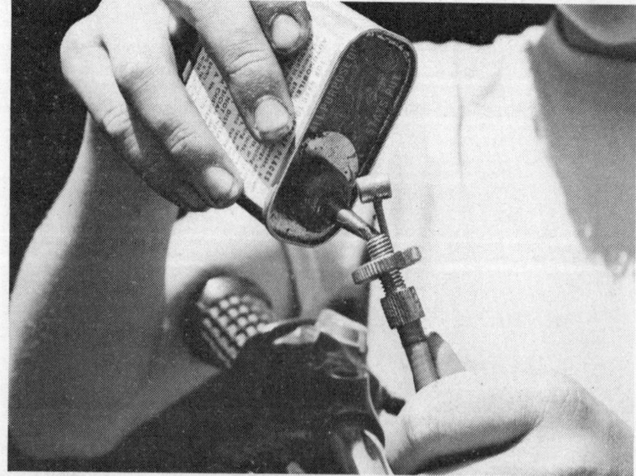

Cable ends take terrific punishment, so examine them carefully for signs of wear or broken strands.

A liberal dose of oil (above) helps cables. Another good medicine is silicone-based lubricant, but getting this stuff down inside the cable cover usually requires a little patience.

Cables should be routed without any sharp bends. A frequent problem area is at the neck, where cables flex with each movement of the handlebars.

on the inside of the cable cover. You should also check the cable cover itself for signs of cuts or kinks that can cause friction. This is especially true of cables that hang down close to the underside of the bike. You can damage a cable while riding without noticing it at first, but sooner or later it will cause problems.

A further problem area occurs where the cables pass close to the neck of the front forks. In this spot they flex and bend more than any other place on the bike.

Other cables that deserve special attention are the throttle cables, especially those on multicylinder motorcycles. On these larger bikes, there is an octopus-like clump of cables going to the individual carburetors, and they are all operated by a single throttle cable. If any *one* of these cables hangs up, it can cause *all* of them to hang up, with the result that you might unexpectedly find yourself in serious trouble.

There is one other throttle problem to watch for. If the hand control moves inward on the handlebar (toward the center of the bike) to the point where the tip of the handlebar begins rubbing on the inside of the grip, it can cause the throttle to bind, with about the same results as a cable that hangs up.

On brake and clutch levers, you should check for proper adjustment at the time you check the cable ends. The owner's manual usually tells how much clearance or "play" there should be in the lever action. Don't forget to set the adjustment at the other end of the cable as prescribed in the manual. A slipping clutch or a brake that never quite releases can cause considerable trouble, and the results can be expensive.

While you are testing control levers and cables, check the levers, both hand and foot, for signs of stress or cracking. Most motorcycle levers are designed to bend rather than break if you fall, and many riders who do a lot of off-road riding will have pounded out their bent levers several times. Each time a piece of metal is bent back to its original shape, though, it loses some of its strength. At some point, the lever will finally begin to crack, and ultimately it will fail.

The final step in checking brakes is to remove the wheels and take a look at the brake linings, but this need not be done at a 30-day inspection; once or twice a year should be enough.

Once you are satisfied that the bike's brakes and controls are adjusted properly, go for a short test ride to check everything out. A word of caution here—don't forget to wear your helmet and other safety gear, such as eye protection and boots, when taking even an around-the-block ride. You'll probably be paying a lot of attention to how the bike sounds and handles, and it's not impossible to have an accident even though you're only gone for a minute.

Adjustment of excess play or slack in brake and clutch cables is necessary, as cables stretch with use. The owner's manual will tell you the amount of play required for your motorcycle.

FUEL SYSTEM

Always look at the fuel system during your 30-day check. The first step is to look into the gas tank itself for signs of dirt, rust or any other contamination that might block fuel flow or damage the engine. This is especially important on motorcycles that sit for long periods of time in the garage. Gasoline can go bad after sitting for a period of weeks, so it's a good idea to drain the tank and refill it with fresh gas after a period of inactivity. If you don't, the varnish or sludge that builds up inside the tank can clog fuel lines and make gasoline burn poorly.

Another problem is water buildup inside the gas tank due to condensation. Condensation takes place when a gas (in this case water vapor) is changed into a liquid (in this case water). This certainly doesn't do the engine any good, and in time the inside of the tank will rust out.

Take a good look inside the gas tank for signs of rust, dirt or other contaminants that might clog the fuel system. If you can see much loose foreign material inside the tank, drain and clean it.

WARNING: DO NOT SMOKE OR ALLOW OPEN FLAMES OR SPARKS NEAR THE MOTORCYCLE WHILE WORKING ON THE FUEL SYSTEM OR FILLING THE TANK WITH GASOLINE. ALSO, BE SURE THAT THE ENGINE AND EXHAUST SYSTEM ARE COOL ENOUGH NOT TO IGNITE GASOLINE.

Gasoline can go bad if it sits for awhile. The more volatile components vaporize away, leaving behind a sticky residue which can gum up the carburetor and fuel strainer. Add a fresh load of gas after the bike has been in the garage for awhile.

All motorcycles have a fuel shutoff valve. In most cases this valve incorporates a small wire screen strainer. Always inspect this valve and clean any dirt off the screen. To do this, turn the valve to the OFF position and remove the cup at the bottom which holds the strainer. Position a rag under the valve, because a small amount of gas will escape when you take the cup off. Check the strainer and clean it with a brush or blow it out with an air hose. If there is a lot of dirt or rust in the strainer screen, you may want to drain the tank completely, remove it and give it a more careful inspection and cleaning.

The fuel strainer screen on the bottom of the shutoff valve should be removed and checked. Particles of rust and sludge can be washed off with gasoline.

Just blow through the gas cap vent to check it. If this vent becomes plugged, a vacuum will build up inside the tank and fuel flow will stop. To restart the flow, open the cap so air can enter the tank. Use a rag to prevent gas from dripping on the engine.

While you are working on the fuel system, don't overlook the vent system for the fuel tank. On most bikes, this vent is a small hole in the gas cap. The vent is necessary so that air can enter the gas tank to replace the fuel being consumed. If this vent is clogged, the engine will suck fuel from the tank until a vacuum builds up inside the tank and prevents any more fuel from flowing.

The easiest way to test the cap vent is to hold it up to your mouth and blow through it. On some off-road models, the vent has a piece of tubing extending from it which runs away from the tank (usually to the neck area of the frame). The purpose of the tubing is to keep gas from sloshing out onto the tank surface while riding in rough terrain. You should always inspect this type of vent to see that the hose is not pinched shut or clogged with dirt.

After checking the tank, strainer and vent, replace everything and disconnect the fuel line at the carburetor. Again, use a rag to catch any fuel that might be in the line itself, so the gas won't get on the paint or the engine. Holding up a cup or can to catch the fuel as it flows out, turn the shutoff valve for a moment to both MAIN and RESERVE positions. This should give you an indication of the normal flow in both positions.

At this time, inspect the carburetor(s) for loose nuts and bolts and adjust it/them. For specific adjustment instructions, see the owner's manual or shop manual for your bike, and the special section on tune-ups in this book.

A fuel flow check is a good method of determining if the fuel system is sending gas to the carburetor and the shutoff valve is working properly.

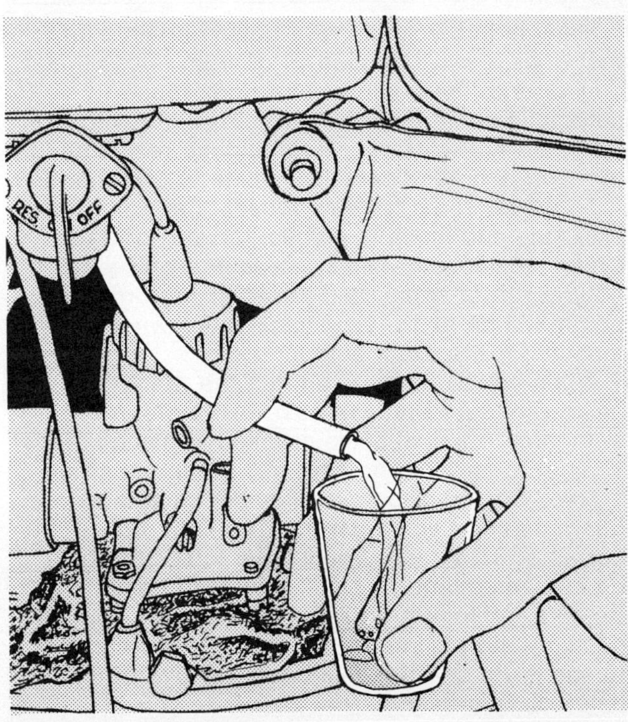

SUSPENSION, CHAINS AND WHEELS

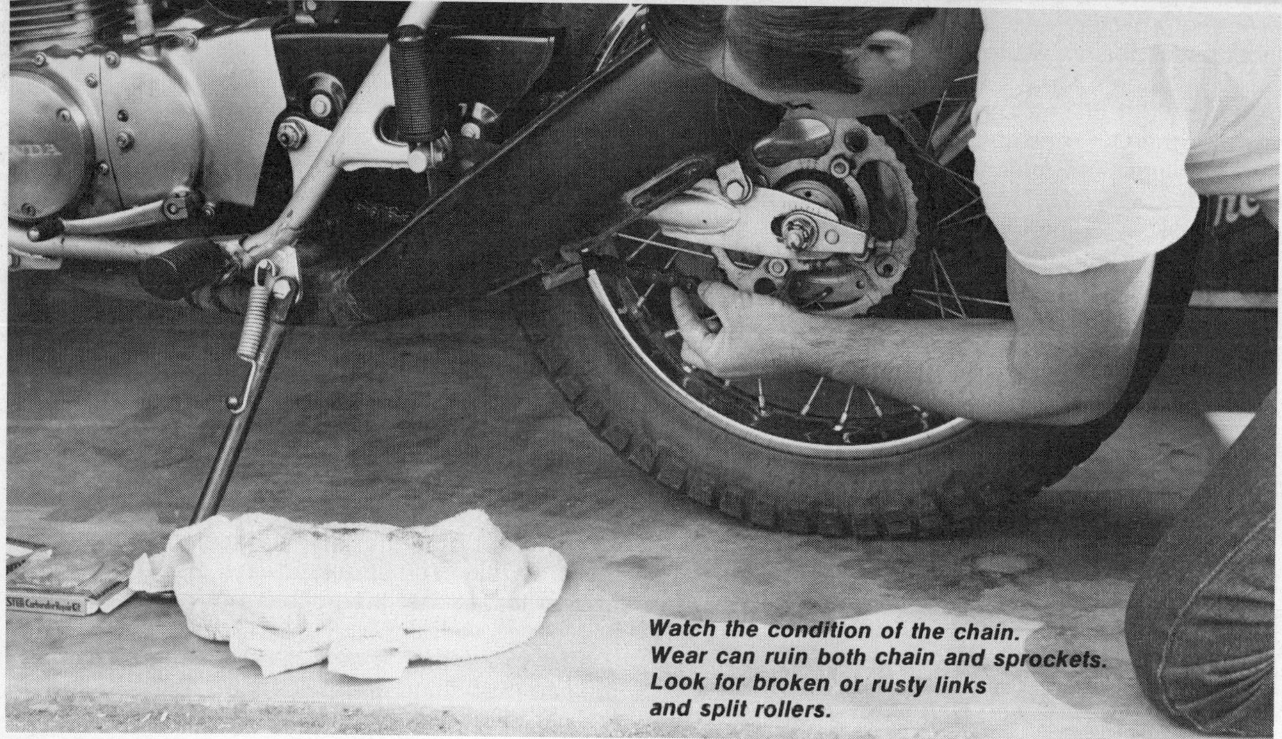

Watch the condition of the chain. Wear can ruin both chain and sprockets. Look for broken or rusty links and split rollers.

The final drive chain on your motorcycle has a difficult job. It must transmit all the power of the engine to the rear wheel, and it is always completely exposed to the elements. This requires that the chain be kept in good condition, adjusted properly and lubricated. There are a number of good chain lubes on the market, and you can use any of them on your bike.

> **NOTE:** CHECK THE OWNER'S MANUAL FOR SPECIFIC RECOMMENDATIONS ON CHAIN LUBRICATION FOR YOUR BIKE.

Many motorcycles have a built-in chain oiler that drips a small amount of oil from inside the engine onto the chain as you ride. These automatic chain oilers should also be looked at. Some do not work very well, and we recommend that you add additional lubrication to the chain.

To adjust chain tension, loosen the rear wheel axle nuts and move the wheel forward or back. Chain tension is generally measured on the bottom run of chain, and the slack is normally about ¾ inch to 1 inch. Check your owner's manual for the exact amount.

When you're ready to tighten the rear wheel, make very sure that you have it straight in the swingarm. If the wheel is crooked, it places the chain in a terrific bind and may break the chain.

Most motorcycles have alignment marks to guarantee that you'll get the axle lined up correctly. To do this, you'll have to put the bike on its centerstand or block it up with something. Be sure to block it up securely, because you'll be pushing and pulling on the rear wheel quite a bit to line it up, and the bike could fall over if it isn't held solidly in place.

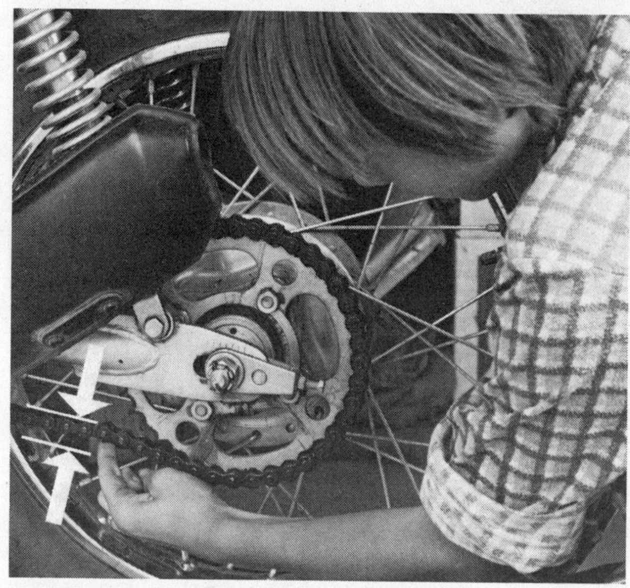

Chain tension is critical to proper operation. Slack should be about ¾ inch to 1 inch, measured on the lower run of the chain.

While you're inspecting the chain, also take a look at the front and back sprockets. Check the teeth for signs of wear. A worn-out chain is very hard on sprockets, and if the sprockets are worn badly, they will damage a new chain, so you must inspect both as if they were one unit.

> **NOTE:** MOTORCYCLE MODELS WITH A SHAFT DRIVE HAVE INSPECTION AND PREVENTIVE MAINTENANCE REQUIREMENTS TOO COMPLEX TO COVER HERE. CONSULT THE SHOP MANUAL OR TAKE YOUR BIKE TO A QUALIFIED MECHANIC.

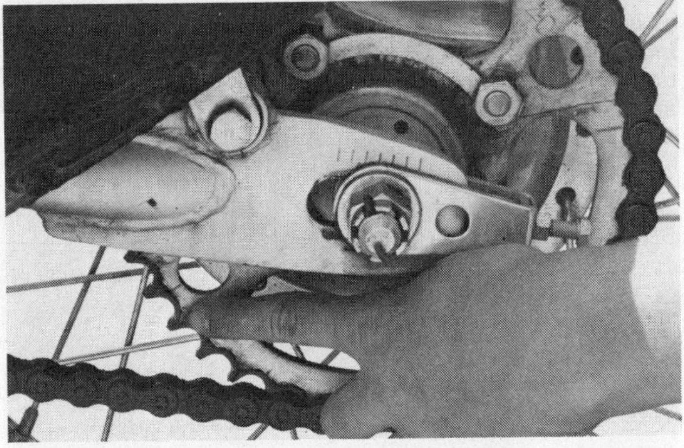

Broken or chipped sprocket teeth mean that the chain is probably in bad shape also. Badly worn teeth will eventually destroy the chain, so you should keep an eye on sprockets.

On motorcycles which have a primary drive chain between engine and transmission, remove the cover to check the chain and drive sprockets.

Some motorcycles have more than one drive chain. Examples are the American-made Harley-Davidson V-twins and the majority of English motorcycles. These motorcycles have a transmission that is separate from the engine and enclosed in its own case. The clutch is located on the transmission, and the engine is linked to the clutch and transmission by a drive chain. On these motorcycles, the chain between the engine and transmission is called the *primary chain.*

These primary chains need constant lubrication. The oil is supplied by the engine. On some models, the clutch is bathed in oil, while in others the clutch is inside an oil-tight shield. The primary chain is adjustable just like the chain that goes to the rear wheel, and it should be checked and adjusted once or twice a year (more often if you ride a lot, especially off-road). Getting at the primary chain is a bit troublesome, as it is usually inside a sealed case that must be removed to gain access. If you have one of these bikes, though, you'll be an old hand at it after a few months.

On motorcycles with primary chain drives, inspect the sprocket teeth on the primary drive and clutch sprockets just as you do the rear sprocket. Pay attention to wear on the teeth, which could cause a tooth to break or wear the chain rapidly.

The front suspension should be checked for excessive play in the bearings at the neck. To do this, block up the bike so that the front wheel is off the ground. Then try to shake the front forks back and forth in a straight line with the bike. If there is very much play at all, the bearings in the neck (steering head) may be going bad, or the large stem nut at the top of the neck may be coming loose. Also check the bolts that hold the forks in the triple clamps (front yoke) to make sure that they are tight. Test the bolts holding the handlebars, too. If your handlebars are mounted in rubber to absorb shock (as some larger road bikes' bars are), inspect these mounts and lubricate them with a high quality rubber lubricant.

At the top of the lower section of each fork leg is a seal to keep dirt and dust from getting into the oil contained in the fork. This seal should be inspected to see if it is in good condition. If it looks chewed up or split, replace it. There should be a very small amount of oil on the upper portion of the fork leg where the seal slides, but if there is more than a couple of drops of oil, the seal is leaking too much and should be changed.

The oil contained inside the lower forks must be changed at regular intervals; consult your shop manual on this. The weight of oil used has a lot to do with the riding and handling qualities of your motorcycle, so if you consider changing the oil from the factory recommendation, talk things over with a good mechanic first. He will be able to advise you properly.

Raising the front forks off the ground and shaking them (see left) is a good way to determine if neck bearings are bad.

Worn front fork seals allow dirt to enter the lower legs. Watch these seals to see that they don't crack or rot. If you find excessive amounts of oil on upper legs, the seals are leaking.

Check spokes for tightness. If you do not have a spoke wrench, a small crescent wrench will work, but be careful not to overtighten spokes.

Spokes in both wheels need to be checked at least every 30 days, and it doesn't hurt to check them on a weekly basis. Go over each wheel carefully and look at each spoke, tugging at it by hand to make sure that it is tight. If it is loose, tighten it with either a spoke wrench designed for the job or a small crescent wrench.

Do not overtighten any spoke to the point where you distort the wheel. You'll have to develop a feel for the right amount of tightening. If you have a dial indicator, you can remove the wheel and mount it on an old axle stub. Then check the roundness (called runout) of the wheel and tighten spokes on one side or the other to bring the wheel to a true round shape.

Motorcycles ridden in the dirt frequently end up with a bent rim. Sometimes this looks worse than it really is, and the wheel can be satisfactorily straightened with a plastic-faced mallet, followed by a check of the results with a dial indicator. Be careful, however—this method only works well on steel rims. Aluminum alloy rims resist bending to a much greater degree, but once bent, they are difficult to straighten. Leave alloy rims to the wheel repairman at the local motorcycle shop or dealer.

While you have the front end of the bike up in the air to check the bearings in the neck, grab the wheel and try to move it from *side to side* to check for wheel bearings that are becoming loose. If you can detect much side-to-side movement of the wheel in the forks, it's time to take things apart for a more complete investigation. Make absolutely sure that the bolts holding the front axle in the forks are tight. That's one piece of hardware you don't want to lose!

Spokes can be adjusted and the wheel trued by mounting wheel on an old axle in a vise and using a dial indicator to check runout. This is really a job for an expert wheel lacer, but you might try it if you work carefully and don't overtighten any of the spokes. You have to develop a sense of touch for this.

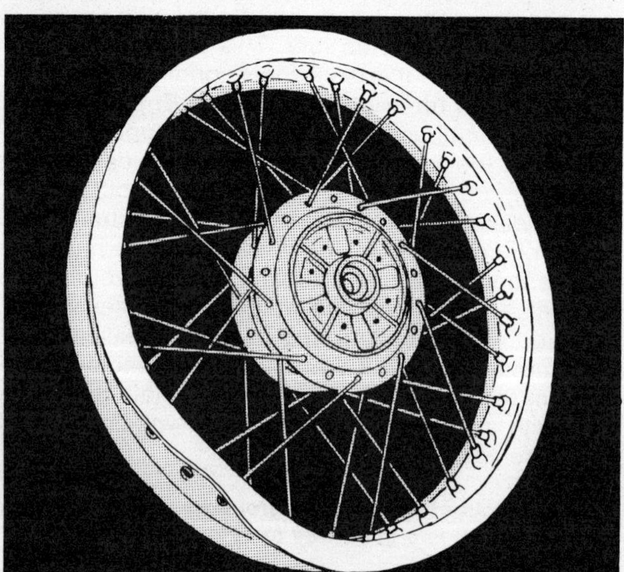

A bent steel rim can be straightened by pounding it into shape with a soft-faced mallet. You may not get perfect results the first time you try this, but then, the wheel was a total loss anyhow, wasn't it?

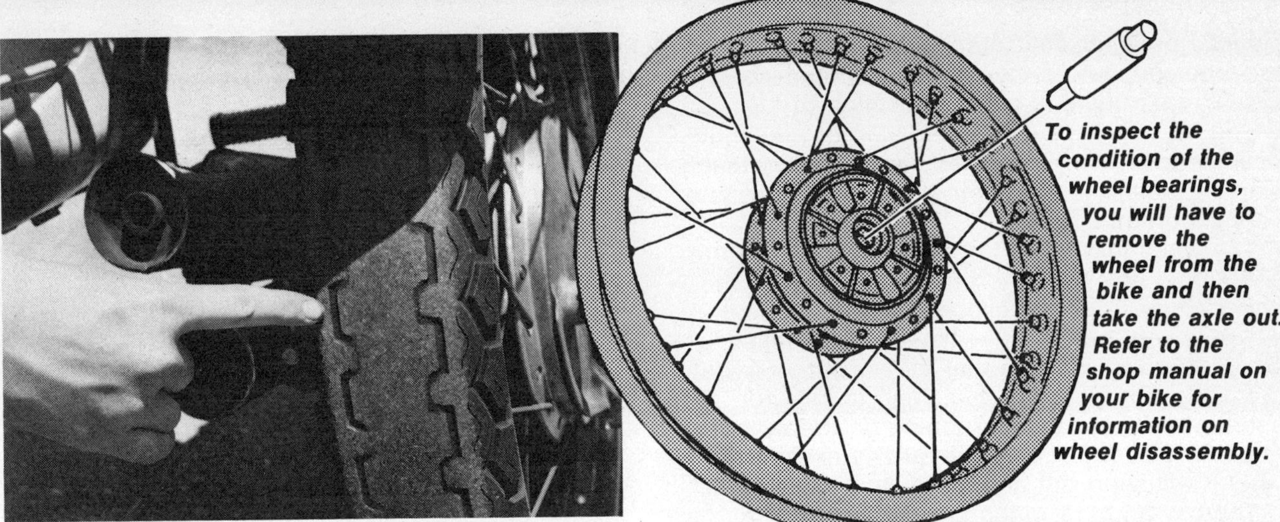

To inspect the condition of the wheel bearings, you will have to remove the wheel from the bike and then take the axle out. Refer to the shop manual on your bike for information on wheel disassembly.

This tire is worn out! Inspection of tires should include sidewalls and valve stems for signs of rotting or cracking rubber. A tire in this condition is unsafe and should be replaced.

When looking at rear shocks (below), don't forget to remove the nut and large washer to check the condition of the rubber bushings. These bushings can wear out or rot, causing all sorts of strange riding sensations. Also check shocks for signs of leaking.

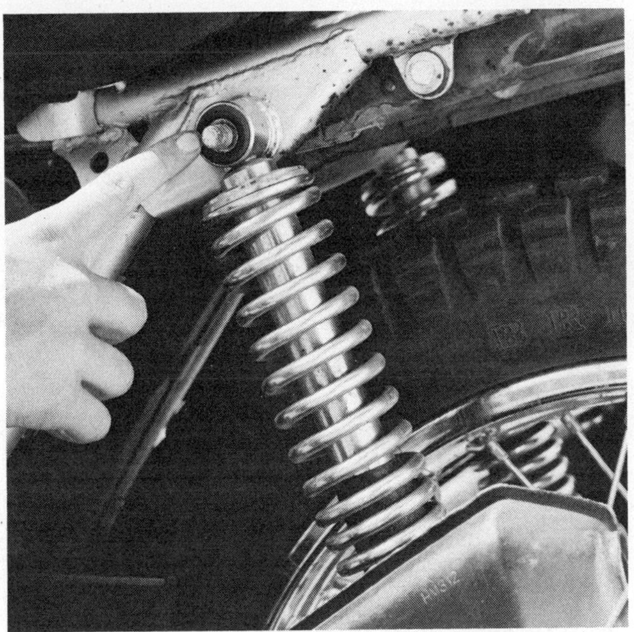

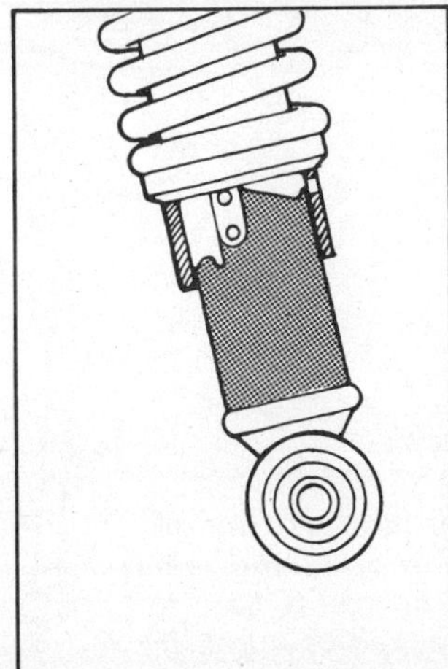

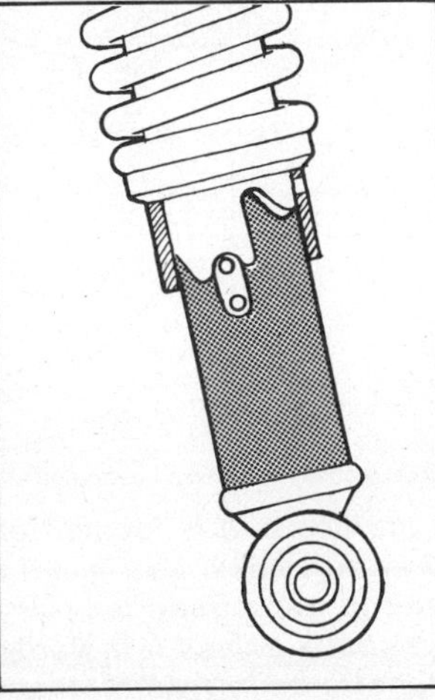

CAUTION: TIGHTENING SPOKES AND TRUING WHEELS CALL FOR AN EXPERT. CERTAIN STEP-BY-STEP PROCEDURES MUST BE FOLLOWED WHEN TRUING ANY SPOKED WHEEL. IF IN DOUBT, TAKE THE WHEEL TO YOUR MOTORCYCLE DEALER.

Examine the rear wheel and spokes in the same manner as the front. On both wheels, check the tire tread and the sidewalls for signs of wear or damage, and don't forget to take a look at the valve stems on both tires.

Watch out for cracked or worn valve stems. If they are leaning over in the hole in the rim, you can guess that the tube is being pinched by the tire sliding on the rim. This is not uncommon on bikes ridden off-road, where the rider lowers tire pressures to get a better bite in loose soil. If the tire slips far enough, though, it will pinch the valve stem off and you'll have a long walk home. Replace any faulty valve stems.

With the rear wheel off the ground (on a centerstand if your bike has one, or up on wood blocks), grasp the swingarm and try to move it back and forth, just as you did with the front forks. If it has a lot of slop, inspect the bearings and the bolt that holds it to the frame.

Look at the rear shocks, too, to see that they don't leak or have bent shafts. Check the rubber bushings at the top and bottom of the shocks and replace them if they are worn or cracking. Also check the bolts for tigntness.

You can bounce the rear end up and down to check the shocks, but this won't tell you nearly as much about their condition as a short ride over the kind of terrain you intend to use the bike on. Most motorcycles have adjustable shocks which can be set to give several different riding qualities. You may find that you want to set the shocks to a harder position for dirt use. Similarly, you might set the shocks one notch softer for street use.

Rear shocks may be adjusted to suit your individual riding needs. The owner's manual will show you how to make a change in the shock action.

ELECTRICAL WIRING

Since preventive maintenance means looking for problems before they get bad enough to cause real trouble, a good inspection of the wiring on your bike is the best kind of preventive maintenance. Wiring problems seldom give much warning before leaving you stranded, so this is a very important check.

The wires that take the greatest abuse are the spark plug wires, which run from the coil to the spark plugs. They are exposed to engine heat, which is very hard on the insulation. Examine spark plug wires to see that the insulation is not cracked or burned. Another thing to look for is spark plug wiring that is rubbing on the cylinder head fins. Such rubbing will quickly expose the wire, it will short out and the engine will misfire.

The coil and the wiring around it call for a check from time to time, but this generally means removing the gas tank, since most bikes have the coil(s) mounted on the frame rail up under the tank. You may not want to do this on a 30-day inspection, but get to it once or twice a year. Most gas tanks are mounted on rubber mounts and can move slightly to dampen vibration. This is good for the tank, but if a wire is pinched between the tank and the frame, sooner or later it will short out or break in two.

One problem area in wiring is the spark plug wires. They're directly over the hottest part of the engine.

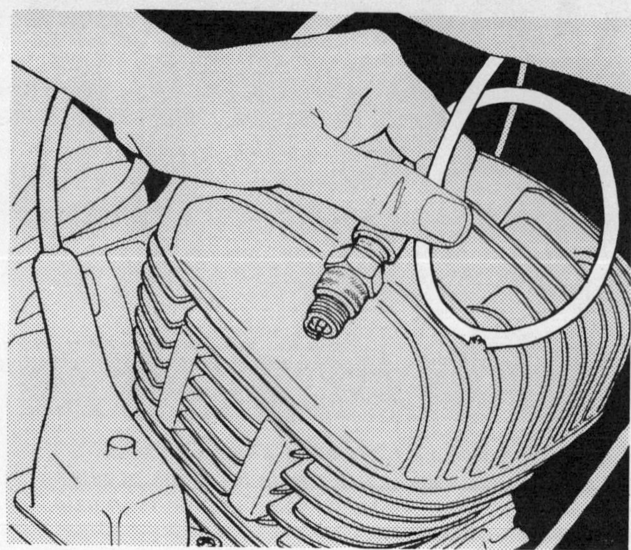

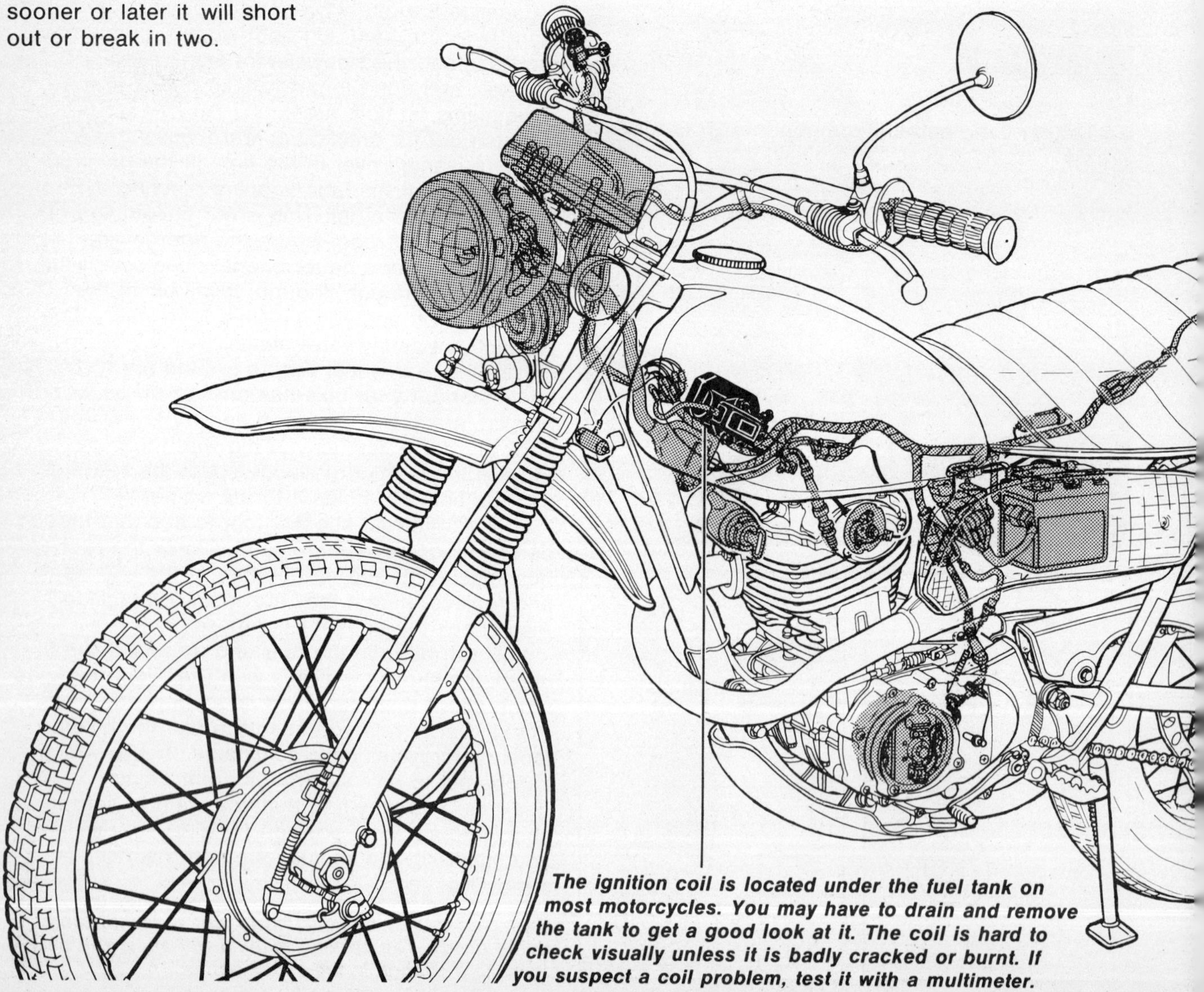

The ignition coil is located under the fuel tank on most motorcycles. You may have to drain and remove the tank to get a good look at it. The coil is hard to check visually unless it is badly cracked or burnt. If you suspect a coil problem, test it with a multimeter.

Wiring that passes from handlebars to frame gets flexed more than other wires and is usually a trouble spot. Chafing on frame is the problem, causing bare wires to short out.

Another bad area for wiring is where the wire bundle leaves the front forks and goes to the main frame of the motorcycle. This wiring gets bent back and forth every time the handlebars are turned, so almost every motorcycle rider experiences trouble here at one time or another.

The wiring in the front forks region is hard to inspect, unfortunately, because wiring there is generally covered with heavy plastic insulation tubing. Having a multimeter and knowing how to use it can be a great help here, as you can often locate the trouble by taking resistance measurements from connection points at either end of the covered wiring without having to strip out wiring and check it visually.

NOTE: EVEN IF YOU HAVE A MULTIMETER, GO AHEAD AND INSPECT WIRING BY EYE. MORE WIRING PROBLEMS HAVE BEEN FOUND BY A CAREFUL EYEBALL EXAMINATION THAN WITH ALL THE FANCY TEST EQUIPMENT EVER BUILT.

Take a look at the wiring under the seat as well. Your motorcycle should have a fuse protecting the electrical components. This fuse is normally located close to the battery inside a fuse holder. Open the fuse holder and visually inspect the fuse for corrosion. Next, look at the contacts inside the fuse holder. If the fuse on your bike does not have a clear glass section that allows you to inspect the fine wire inside, check the fuse with a multimeter.

NOTE: IF THE FUSE IS ACTUALLY BAD, YOU WON'T BE ABLE TO START YOUR BIKE IN THE FIRST PLACE, BUT IT'S SURPRISING HOW OFTEN YOU'LL DISCOVER THAT THE FUSE IS COVERED WITH A BUILDUP OF ACID CORROSION.

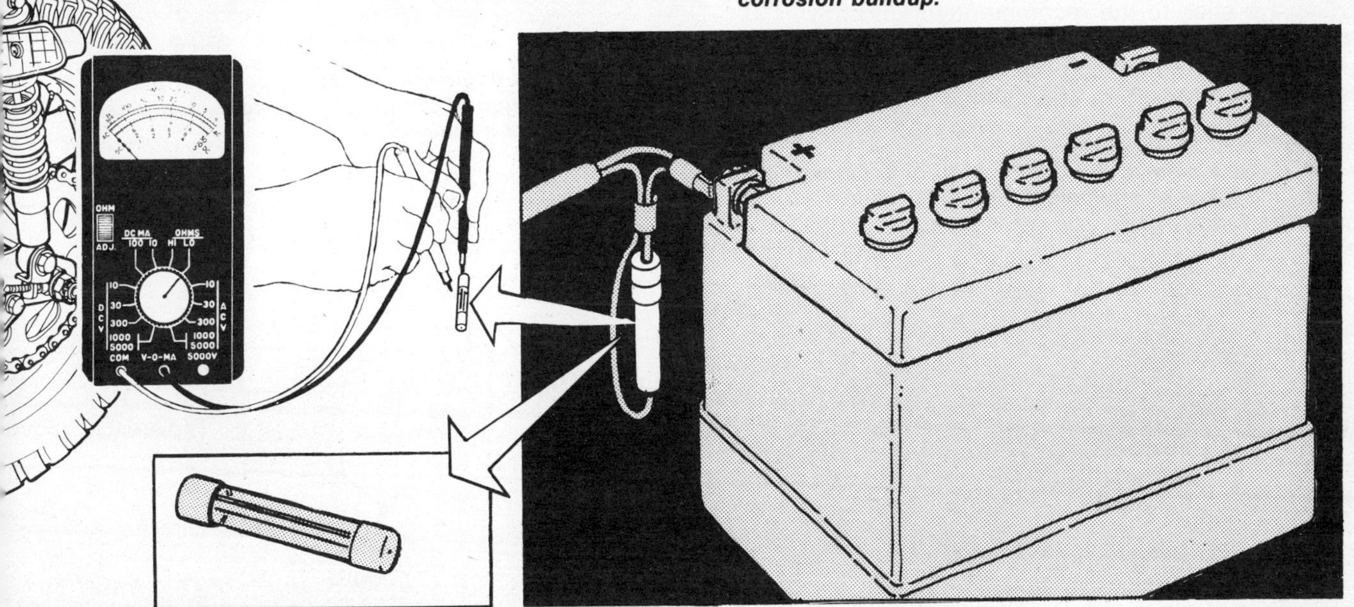

If the fuse goes bad, the electrical system will not work. Examine the fuse from time to time for signs of corrosion buildup.

IV. Troubleshooting Your Motorcycle

Reading Spark Plugs

The spark plug in your engine has only one adjustment and no moving parts. It may seem simple and not very interesting to a tuner, but that's far from true. The spark plug(s) can be one of the most important items in a tune-up. Why? Because the spark plug is a kind of window that lets you see what's going on inside your engine while it's running.

When you remove a spark plug and look it over during a tune-up, it gives you an exact reading of the state of tune of the engine and tells you a lot about engine wear and the way the carburetor is working.

The spark plug does not *create* a spark; it simply provides a place for the electrical pulse from the ignition system to make the spark. At the bottom of the plug are two electrodes, which stick out into the combustion chamber. When the high-voltage pulse from the ignition system jumps between these two electrodes, it creates a very hot spark. The spark fires the compressed air/fuel mixture inside the combustion chamber. One electrode (the center one) is connected by a wire to the secondary winding of the ignition coil. The other (the L-shaped arm over the center electrode) is the ground electrode. The ground electrode is connected to the return path for electricity.

Each type of spark plug is designed to work best under certain conditions of temperature and pressure. That's why the manufacturer recommends a specific type of spark plug, by number, for your motorcycle for average use.

Your shop manual or owner's manual may list other types of plug to substitute if you are racing your bike or riding in extreme weather conditions, but always stick to the recommended kind of plug. You can choose among different brands of spark plugs by consulting the cross-reference chart at the motorcycle shop where you buy your tune-up parts.

Your "window" on engine condition is the spark plug. A careful examination of the plugs from your engine is a very basic part of a tune-up.

Below: It looks simple, but there's a lot of engineering in this little piece of equipment. The illustration shows the various parts of a spark plug.

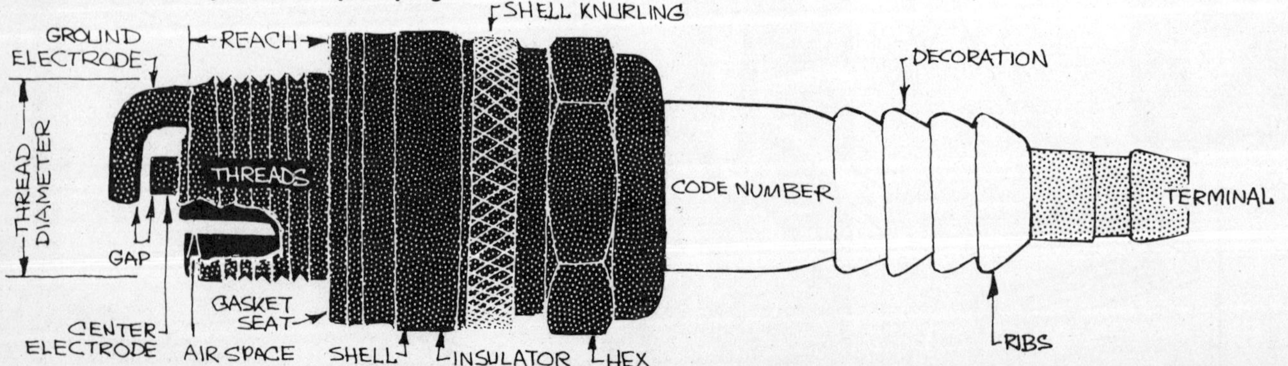

The most important part of a new plug destined for your engine is the distance between those two electrodes. This gap, measured in thousandths of an inch, is critical to proper spark plug performance.

A new spark plug has a clean, white insulator and unblemished electrodes. Compare a brand new plug with the plug just removed from your engine. You can see that the spark plug undergoes quite a change after it has been running in the engine for awhile.

A spark plug from an engine that is in a good state of tune has a definite color that sets it apart from plugs taken out of engines *not* in good tune. On the plug from the well-tuned engine, the insulator tip will be a chocolate brown. The color will be lighter for four-stroke engines, darker brown or grayish for two-stroke engines, because the oil that a two-stroke engine burns along with the fuel affects the coloration of the plug.

The electrodes on a good plug will be clean, free of built-up crust and carbon. The ground electrode, which is part of the outside portion of the metal shell, is usually cleaner and shows the effects of heat more than the center electrode. Neither electrode should be pitted or cracked.

A spark plug from a correctly-tuned engine has a light chocolate color on the porcelain and no carbon buildup. Two-stroke engines may show a slight burned oil residue and a somewhat darker color.

One of the most important things about a plug is the correct heat range of that plug. The heat range of a plug depends on its construction. Each plug is designed to operate most effectively under specific riding conditions.

For example, a spark plug on a street bike must perform a different job than a plug in a racing motorcycle. In the racing motorcycle, much higher heat builds up in the combustion chamber. The spark plug would not function effectively if it could not absorb some of this heat, then radiate it away from the tip of the plug to keep temperatures down. (If the tip of the plug got hot enough, it would prematurely ignite the air/fuel mixture, like the glow-plug in a model airplane engine.) A plug that helps cool high operating temperatures is called a cold plug.

A too-hot plug (below) won't show much color on the porcelain, but the outer shell will be dark. These are indications that a colder plug may be required.

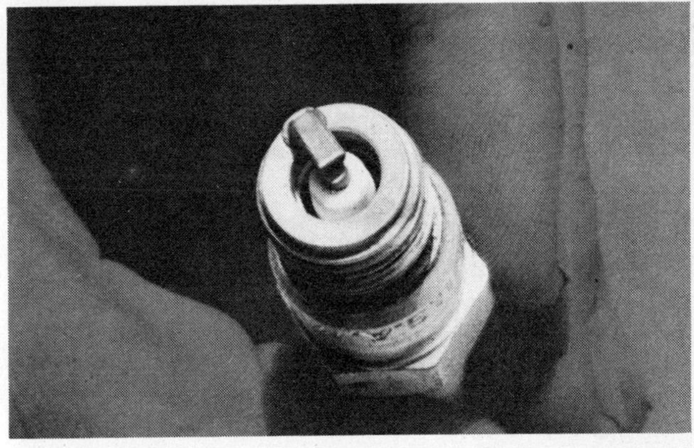

On the other hand, a plug for street use may have to maintain a hotter temperature in order to burn cleanly and not foul from unburned fuel and oil. Such a plug is called a hot plug.

A plug that is too hot for engine operating conditions looks similar to a new plug when removed from the engine except for some discoloration on the outer shell. The insulator will be quite white. If the ground electrode is colored a light silver-brown, the air/fuel mixture is all right; it's just the heat range of the plug that is wrong. Change to a colder plug.

A cold plug will be heavily discolored with deposits of unburned fuel and oil. The black carbon on the insulator shows that your engine is not developing enough heat to keep the plug clean. Switch to a hotter plug.

If the porcelain and center electrode of the plug are covered with a fine carbon soot and the outer shell is dark, the plug is probably too cold for the engine. Switching to a hotter plug will burn away such deposits.

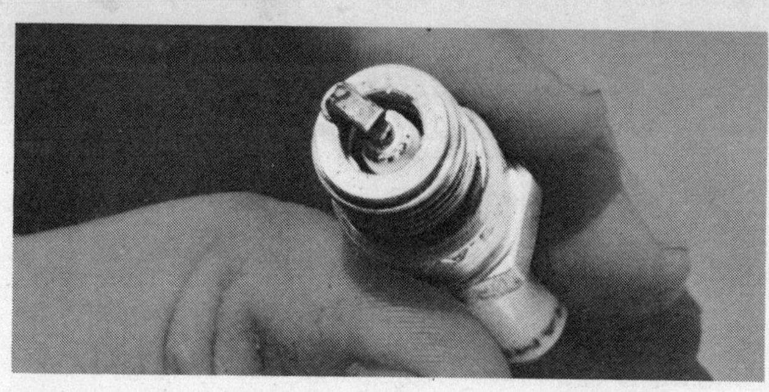

A too-hot plug combined with a lean mixture can spell trouble. The plug will show little color, except possibly specks of oil burned onto the electrodes and insulator. Switching to a colder plug and richening the mixture will cure the problem.

A plug that is too hot combined with a lean mixture (too much air for the amount of fuel being burned) will have the same no-color indications, but may also have spots of carbon buildup on the electrodes and insulator.

This ugly mess is the result of too much engine heat buildup in the combustion chamber. A loss of lubrication effectiveness results in the condition known as "black death" by racers.

To take the point one step further, this is the result of high-speed leanout in a racing motorcycle engine. Excessive heat buildup in the combustion chamber actually melted this piston! Evidence of the start of this process can often be detected by finding small bits of metal adhering to the electrodes of the spark plug.

If you detect small bits of a material that looks like melted metal on the surface of the plug, engine temperatures are getting high enough to melt parts of the inside of the combustion chamber and the top of the piston. This could also indicate loss of lubricating efficiency, rings that are scuffing or a piston that is sticking to the cylinder wall.

If this high-temperature condition is allowed to continue, the top of the piston can actually melt! This severely damages the engine. Racers refer to piston skirt scuffing as "black death." The results of high-speed leanout, as shown in the photo of the high-compression racing piston from a Harley-Davidson salt flats racing bike, are awesome to behold. A lean condition can be more trouble in a two-stroke engine than in a four-stroke, but high temperatures can make any motorcycle engine stick or "seize."

A hot plug running with a rich mixture will show a clean insulator, but soot on the shell. The ground electrode will be dark gray.

A too-hot plug combined with a rich condition (too much fuel for the air intake) is not as big a problem. In cases of extreme richness, though, unburned fuel can wash down cylinder walls and destroy lubrication to the point where rings and cylinders wear out quickly.

The plug in a hot and rich cylinder will show a clean insulator but will have a discolored shell coated with black carbon soot. Such signs indicate that a colder plug should be installed. Carburetor rejetting to correct the lean condition is also necessary. Do the same to correct a lean condition and too-hot plug.

If the condition persists despite jet corrections, examine the intake system for leaks which would allow extra air into the system. In the case of a too-rich condition, a check of the air filter is a good idea. A clogged air filter produces signs of a rich condition even when the carburetor is adjusted and jetted correctly.

A lean condition can often be traced to an air leak behind the carburetor. The plastic tubing that connects the carb to the engine can break or rot, permitting extra air to get into the engine and upsetting the air/fuel ratio.

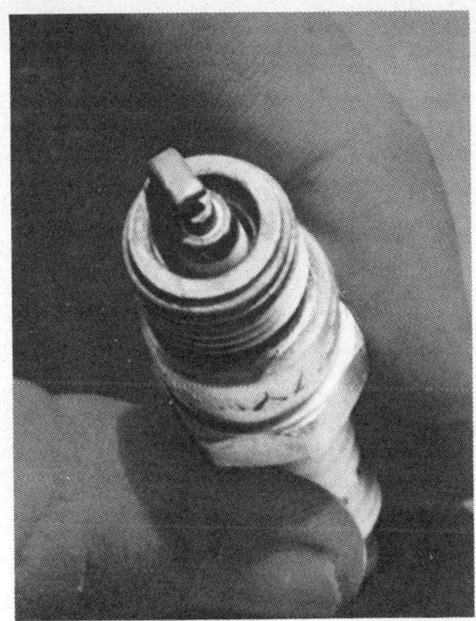

Here's a cold plug/lean mixture combination. The outer shell of the plug will be clean, but the center electrode and insulator will show soot. Switch to a hotter plug and enrich the mixture.

A cold plug and a lean mixture show up as a clean shell with black soot buildup on the insulator and center electrode. On some plugs the ground electrode will also have a generous coating of soot and carbon. Correct this condition by going to a hotter plug. In addition, rejet and adjust the carburetor for a slightly richer mixture.

If you have a cold plug and a too-rich condition, the plug will show heavy black soot deposits all over. You may have experienced some hard starting and missing as well. Lean out the carburetor and go to a hotter plug.

NOTE: A BAD PLUG OR FAULTY WIRING THAT PREVENTS THE PLUG FROM FIRING NORMALLY MAY RESEMBLE A COLD PLUG/TOO RICH CONDITION, BUT THERE WILL USUALLY BE TRACES OF UNBURNED FUEL ON THE PLUG. A PLUG THAT IS NOT FIRING AT ALL WILL BE WET WITH FUEL IF REMOVED SOON AFTER YOU ATTEMPT TO START THE ENGINE.

Professional tuners and racing mechanics often use a magnifying glass to look closely at the condition of the spark plug. This procedure can help you with your spark plug reading problems. Careful examination of spark plugs is a troubleshooting technique that enables you to do a much better job of fine-tuning your engine.

A cold plug matched with a rich mixture (below) will show soot on the entire tip. A loaded-up plug like this is a sign that you need a hotter plug for your around-town riding and some readjustment of the fuel mixture.

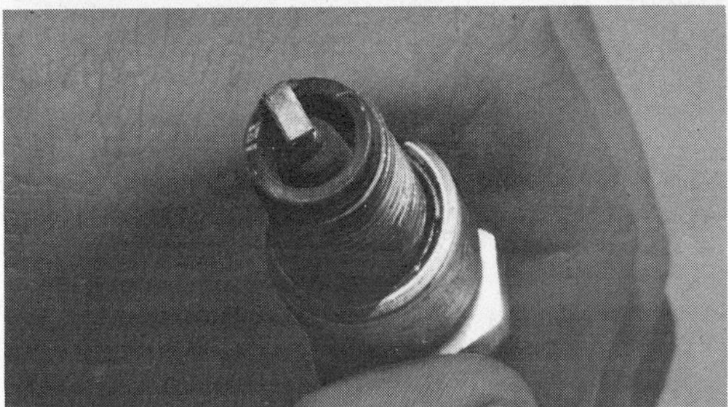

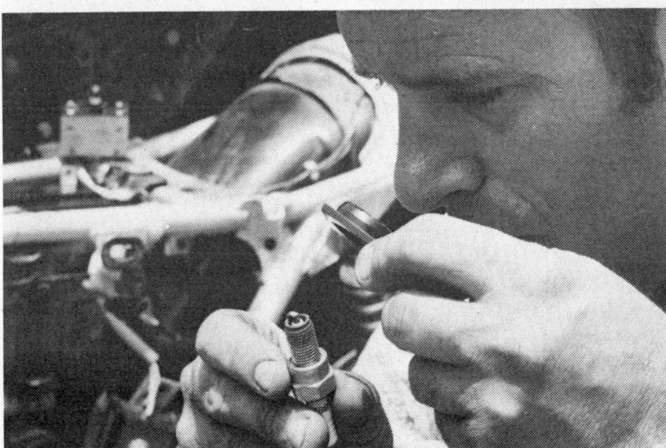

Don't laugh! Examining the plug with a magnifying glass is an old racer's trick. It sometimes requires this kind of close look at the plug to solve tricky tuning problems.

While you're at it, a careful check of the external condition of the spark plug is a good idea. They can break or develop carbon tracks down the insulator that short-circuit the voltage pulse from the coil.

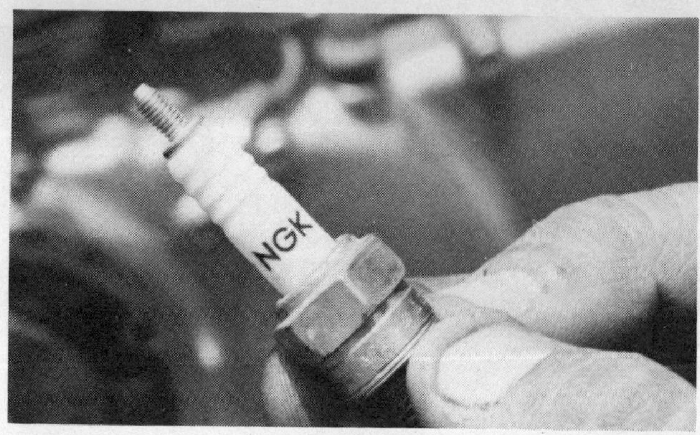

The tip of the plug isn't the only part to look at. The outside of the plug is also important. Check the external insulator and connection as a part of the tune-up process. Look for signs of cracked porcelain or discoloration on the side of the plug. A track of carbon down the side of the plug can indicate an arc-over from the spark plug wire to ground, robbing the spark plug of much or all of the high voltage it needs to fire the air/fuel mix.

If your motorcycle has washers under the plug, always replace the washer with a new one when changing plugs.

CAUTION: DON'T APPLY TOO MUCH PRESSURE WHEN TIGHTENING A SPARK PLUG IN THE CYLINDER HEAD.

It's not strictly necessary to use a torque wrench when tightening a plug, but make sure you don't overtorque. The result can be a broken plug or stripped threads in the spark plug hole.

Most tuners do not use a torque wrench to install plugs, but you should develop a *feel* for the amount of pressure needed to obtain a good seal without damaging the plug or cylinder head. It isn't hard to overtorque a plug and either break the plug or strip the threads in the plug hole.

The best way to get a good reading on a spark plug is to test ride the bike, remove the plug and check it, then make any indicated tuning changes and test ride the bike again. To test correctly, get the engine up to normal operating temperature, run it fairly hard in the upper gears, then shut it off cleanly to keep the plug in the same condition it was in during the first ride.

Running the bike fairly hard, then cutting it off clean and checking the plug is a good way to get an accurate plug reading. Remember not to do this in residential neighborhoods; there's no sense in angering those who live around you.

CAUTION: ALWAYS WEAR THE PROPER RIDING CLOTHING, SUCH AS HELMET, EYE PROTECTION, BOOTS AND GLOVES, ETC., WHEN DOING ANY TEST RIDING.

Since higher engine rpm and speeds are involved in getting good plug readings, you may not be able to find a suitable place to do this type of tuning and still be able to get right back to your driveway or garage. Racing up and down the street where you live is not a good way to tune. It might be better to load up the bike and your tools and go someplace better suited to this kind of activity.

Whenever you clean and reinstall plugs during tuning or replace old plugs with new ones, proper gapping is a must. A good gapping tool uses a round wire gauge surface to set the gap, so that any wear or pitting on the underside of the ground electrode will be taken into account.

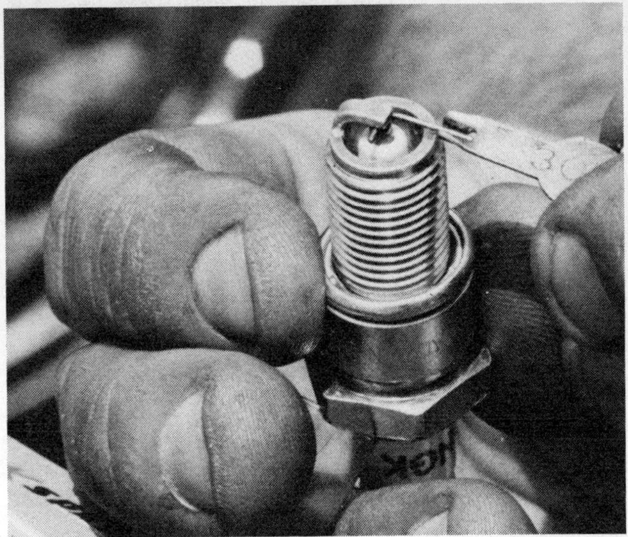

Gapping plugs is a most important part of tuning your bike. Use a good quality gauge, preferably of the round wire gauge variety.

A spark plug whose electrodes become bridged by foreign material (usually a bit of carbon) will not produce a spark. This is a common cause of engine failure when riding two-stroke bikes, because of carbon buildup from the oil mixed with the gasoline. Small, hard particles of carbon often break loose from the inside of the cylinder head and sometimes lodge between the electrodes.

Always examine a bridged plug carefully to satisfy yourself that the material is only carbon and not metal chips. Chips would indicate serious problems inside the engine. Off-road two-stroke riders often carry a spare plug for this very reason. It's easier to simply swap plugs than to clean and regap the plug.

Small bits of carbon that break off from the piston or cylinder head can sometimes become lodged between the electrodes (below), shorting out the gap. Carbon is an excellent conductor of electricity.

If you find a plug whose electrode is bent down, very probably the plug is the wrong type and reaches too deeply into the cylinder head. On many motorcycle engines, the distance between the spark plug tip and the top of the piston at TDC is only a few thousandths of an inch. If the tip of the plug is too long, the piston may touch the spark plug and beat the ground electrode down until the gap is too narrow for a good spark, or even break it off entirely.

When looking at a plug with a flattened electrode, it may turn out that you only forgot to put the copper gasket on the plug before you installed it. If this is the case, the plug can still be used if the electrode can be straightened and regapped properly.

Don't forget to check the center electrode on this kind of plug. It could easily have been broken by the pounding. Sometimes you can hear a broken center electrode by shaking the plug up and down near your ear. If the electrode is broken and is sliding back and forth in the insulation, it makes a distinct sound as you shake the plug.

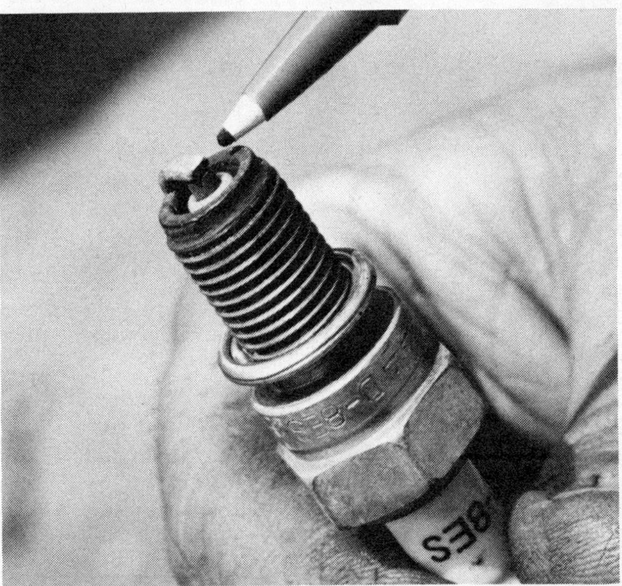

A bent electrode indicates that the piston is hitting the plug. This may be caused by using a plug with too long a reach or by leaving the washer off when installing the plug.

IV/ How To Troubleshoot

Before you start tearing things apart, you need a plan. Good troubleshooting means a methodical approach to finding and fixing problems.

If you've owned your motorcycle for a few months, chances are good that you've found and fixed a few minor problems. The steps you took to find the source of the problems are called troubleshooting. Any corrective measures that followed are not considered troubleshooting, only maintenance or repair. By this definition, troubleshooting is separate from normal tune-up procedures.

At first, troubleshooting may not seem like much. It can be as simple as finding a loose connection on the brake light wires or locating the loose bolt on the underside of the engine that made a funny noise when you were riding.

But suppose the time comes when the engine goes dead in the middle of nowhere? Or the entire electrical system refuses to operate, even though you know the battery is fully charged? Then troubleshooting takes on much more significance.

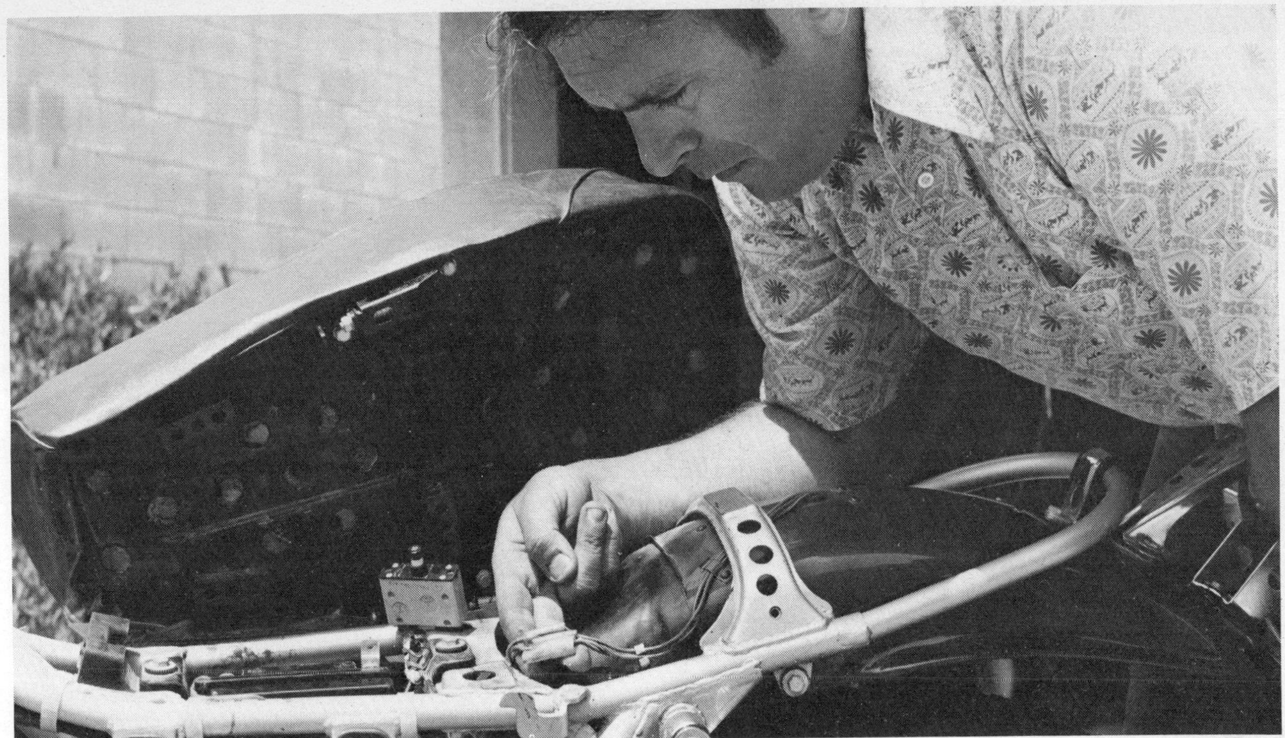

Good troubleshooting is an art. To troubleshoot is to use a process of elimination. Work methodically, dividing the parts of a problem until you have reduced it to a single, isolated area. If there is one rule to follow when troubleshooting a problem, it's: *Don't jump to conclusions!*

A second rule is: *Don't overlook the obvious.* You don't need fancy tools and test equipment for troubleshooting. Your eyes and brain are your best tools. More mechanical problems have been discovered by a good knowledge of the subject and a pair of sharp eyes than by all the sophisticated test equipment ever designed.

For example, in troubleshooting electrical problems (an area where even experienced mechanics seem to have their share of problems), the actual cause of a failure can often be found simply by looking closely at suspected problem areas. Such things as loose connections, broken wiring, corrosion, etc. are easy to see if the troubleshooter will just take a few seconds to examine things.

Once you have established a system for checking things, stick to it. Good troubleshooting helps the beginning troubleshooter (and the expert) approach each separate problem with an easy-to-follow method of determining just where the trouble lies. Following a practical system of faultfinding is not only a good way to find and fix problems right from the start, it's also a good way to learn more about the various parts of your motorcycle.

Rather than jump in feet first when you're looking for the source of a problem on your motorcycle, relax. Take a few minutes to go over the problem in your mind and get a clear idea of the way you want to troubleshoot it. Read the applicable parts of the shop or owner's manual for information on the system you suspect is at fault.

Confusing, isn't it? Electrical system troubles give most tuners the hardest time, yet by following the technical manual and using simple test equipment, most electrical problems are easy to locate and repair.

One point that can't be stressed enough is: Read the manual before you start, especially if it concerns electrical troubles. Spend a few minutes reading and save hours of work.

Gather together all tools and test equipment needed before you start. Lay things out in an orderly manner. It makes the job a lot easier if you don't have to stop and go looking for tools every few minutes.

If you are troubleshooting at home, gather up the tools and test equipment you feel you will need to solve the problem. It's asking for trouble to go hunting for tools several times while you are checking out a system.

If you wind up performing emergency troubleshooting away from home, you may not be able to do as much. A good inspection, however, will often get you going again. Having a good set of tools in the tool kit on your bike can make all the difference here. It doesn't do much good to successfully find the source of a minor problem by proper troubleshooting methods and then not be able to repair the problem.

If the part you suspect is bad is one that's easily replaced, substitution is often a good way to test the part. For instance, if you suspect a spark plug wire is bad, exchange it for a new one or one from another cylinder (on multicylinder models). If the wire is in fact faulty, the problem will then disappear or move to the cylinder where the suspected wire is now located.

Substitution is not always possible with more expensive parts that would have to be purchased before a swap could be made, but keep it in the back of your mind. Even when dealing with low-cost parts, though, refer to the troubleshooting sections of your shop and owner's manual for tips before making a final judgment on changing parts. Try to make sure that the part is really bad before changing it.

Next we include a short section on emergency troubleshooting and a one-page troubleshooting reference guide for the newer rider (you more expert riders may get something out of it also). It tells how to handle a "will not start" condition.

At right: For quick and simple troubleshooting, substitute parts. If a part is readily available or doesn't cost too much, this is a good technique for isolating troubles to a single part or system.

IV/Emergency Troubleshooting

If your motorcycle is difficult to start or won't start at all, by proper troubleshooting you can quickly isolate the probable cause of the difficulty to a specific area. All motorcycle engines, two-stroke or four-stroke, must have three things before they will run. These are: *fuel, ignition* and *compression.* If any one of the three is missing, the engine will not run. If any one is faulty, then even though all are present, the engine may start but it will not run well.

The first step is always to analyze the situation. Spend a few minutes reading the owner's manual for your motorcycle. On most motorcycles, it is packed under the seat or in the tool kit. Go over the starting procedure outlined in the book and follow the instructions carefully. As you read, touch each of the controls and make sure that they are in the correct position for starting. If the motorcycle still won't start, proceed to the checklist which follows.

Step one is to read the motorcycle owner's manual, usually packed under the bike's seat. Go over the starting procedure to make sure that you're doing all the things required to start the bike.

PRESTART CHECKLIST

The first rule when troubleshooting is: *Check the obvious first!* It's not uncommon for a beginning rider to spend hours looking for the source of a serious problem before discovering something as simple as a dead battery or a disconnected wire. Riders have been known to spend a long time trying to start their motorcycle only to find that they didn't have any gas in the tank.

Give the entire motorcycle a thorough visual inspection. Look for loose parts, disconnected wires, leaks of gas or oil or anything that might be causing your problem. If you don't discover anything that might be causing your particular problem, go on to the steps directly concerned with those three critical factors—*fuel, ignition* and *compression.*

A good first step is a visual examination of the bike. You might even remove a plug to see if it can tell you anything about engine condition.

IS THERE GAS IN THE GAS TANK?

Check by removing the filler cap and looking into the gas tank, or by rocking the motorcycle from side to side and listening for the sound of gas sloshing in the tank. Pushing a stick or ruler down inside the tank will help you determine the fuel level, if any. A flashlight may also come in handy for checking the fuel level.

WARNING: NEVER USE ANY OPEN FLAME, SUCH AS A MATCH OR CIGARETTE LIGHTER, TO LOOK INSIDE THE GAS TANK. FIRE OR EXPLOSION CAN RESULT.

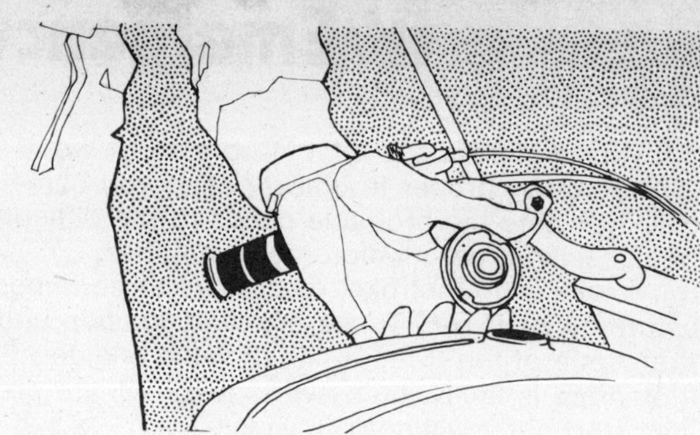

A quick look into the fuel tank is the first step in checking the fuel system. It's surprising how often the problem turns out to be lack of gas.

IS THE FUEL VALVE TURNED ON?

Motorcycles are equipped with a hand-operated valve to turn the fuel on and off. The valve usually has three positions: OFF, ON and RESERVE. In the OFF position, no gasoline can flow from the tank to the carburetor. This shutoff valve is necessary to prevent flooding the carburetor. Motorcycles use the pull of gravity to supply gas, which means that gas can continue to run into the carburetor and flood the engine if the fuel valve is left open when the engine is not running.

NOTE: THE NEEDLE-AND-SEAT CHECK VALVE AT THE ENTRANCE TO THE FLOAT BOWL IS SUPPOSED TO PREVENT FLOODING. SOMETIMES, THOUGH, IT STICKS OR FAILS TO CLOSE TIGHTLY, AND FLOODING CAN OCCUR.

In the ON position, gas can flow from the tank to the carburetor until the level of fuel in the tank falls below a certain level. Then, to get the rest of the fuel from the tank, the rider must switch the valve to the RESERVE position, which allows the rest of the fuel to flow to the carburetor.

This two-stage system is necessary because most motorcycles do not have a gas gauge to tell the rider when he is running low on gas. If he runs the tank dry in the ON position, switching to the RESERVE position usually supplies him with enough gas to reach a service station.

If the gas level in your tank appears low, switch the fuel valve to the RESERVE position instead of the ON position. This ensures that the carburetor will get a full supply of fuel, unless something is wrong with the valve or line.

Unlike automobiles, motorcycles have a shutoff valve. Forgetting to turn it on is a common failure, especially with beginning riders.

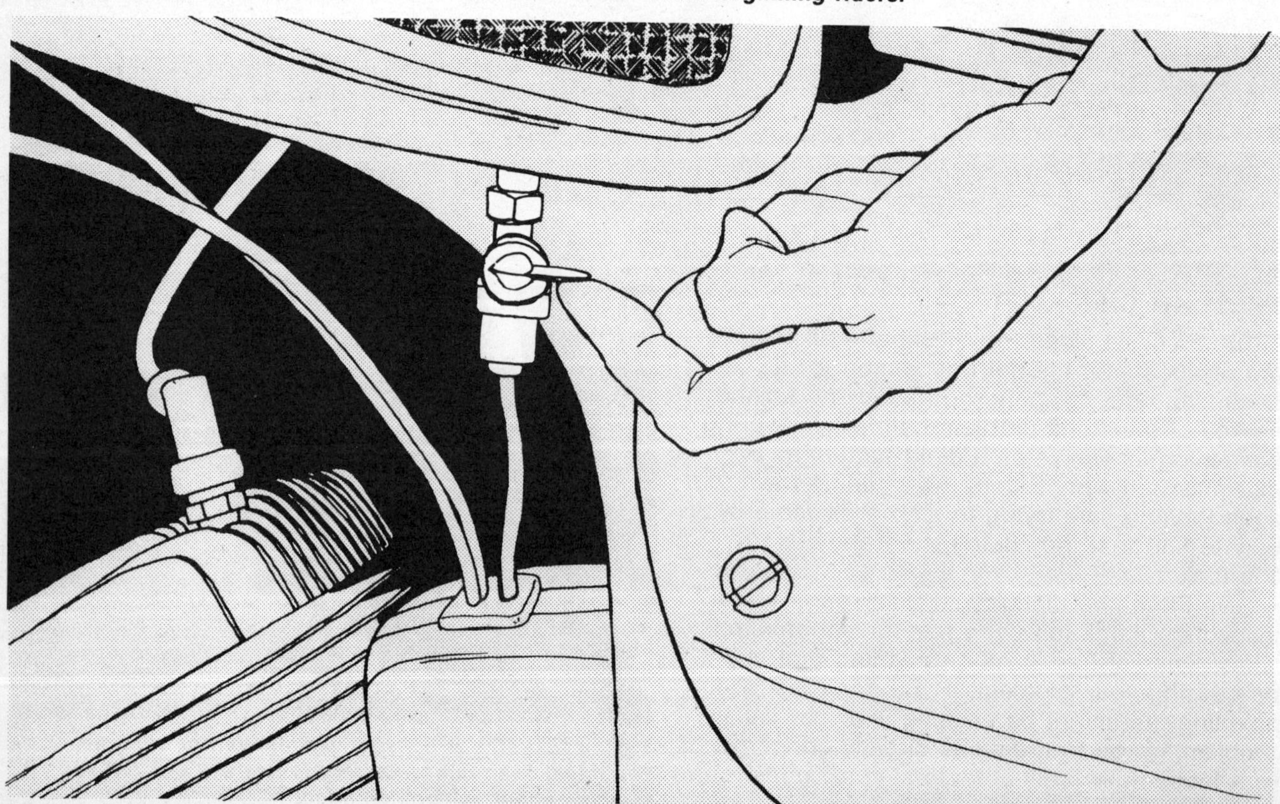

Bikes equipped with clear plastic fuel lines can be checked visually for signs of gas in the lines.

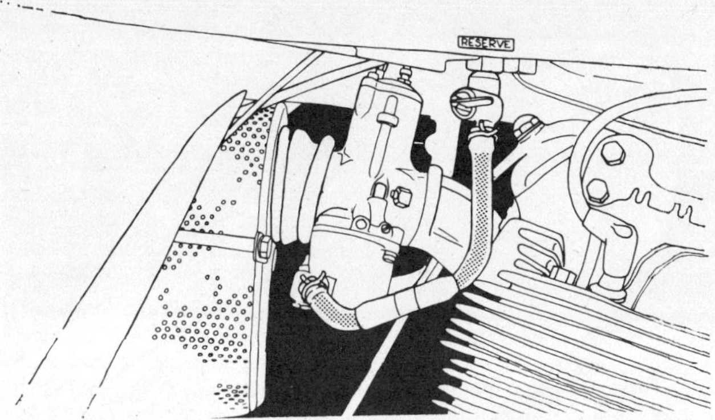

Another way to check for fuel is to look at the fuel line between the gas tank and the carburetor. This line is often made of clear plastic, so if fuel is present, it should be easy to see.

> **NOTE:** IF THERE IS GASOLINE IN THE TANK BUT NONE IN THE FUEL LINE REGARDLESS OF VALVE POSITION, PROBABLY THE FUEL STRAINER IS CLOGGED. REMOVE THE STRAINER CUP FROM THE VALVE, CHECK THE SCREEN AND CLEAN IT IF NECESSARY.

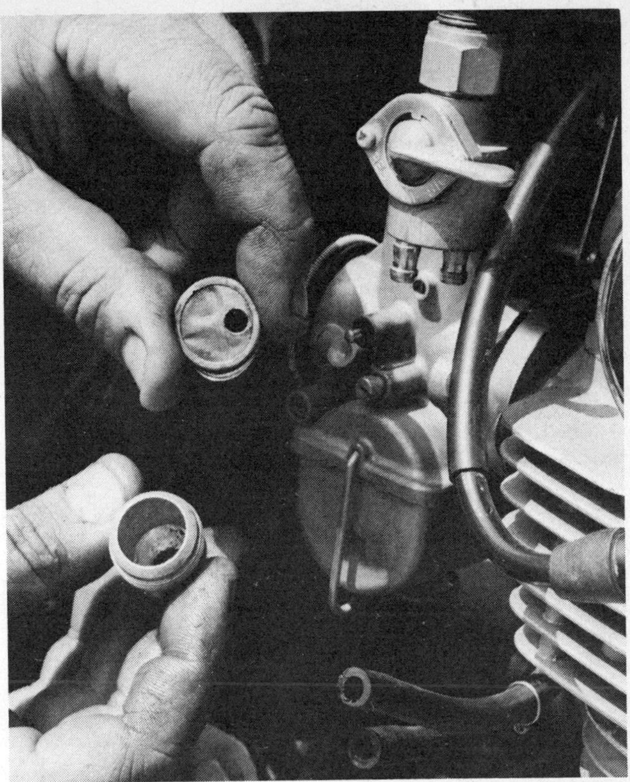

If there is gas in the tank but not in the line, the fuel strainer could be clogged. Remove it and check for rust or other foreign matter.

IS THE IGNITION ON?

Without ignition the engine will not run, and there are enough different ignition switch positions on various bikes to make it a bit confusing for some new riders. Your bike may have one of the two main types of ignition switch or a combination of the two.

The first kind of ignition is the key switch, like that on an automobile. It may be spring-loaded and feature a START position on the switch, or it may be a plain switch that powers a starter button located on the handlebars. Either way, it must be turned to the ON positon to provide electricity to the ignition system.

Along with the key, there should be a pushbutton and a switch marked OFF/RUN/OFF on the handlebars, usually near the throttle grip on the right side. The pushbutton is for the electric starter, if your bike is equipped with one.

The OFF/RUN/OFF switch is a safety device that allows you to shut the engine down without leaning over to look for the key switch or fumbling for it. If you used this switch to shut the ignition off the last time you rode the bike and forgot to reposition it to the RUN position this time, the ignition system will not get power, even though you have the key turned to ON, until you move the switch back to the RUN position.

Some off-road motorcycles don't have an ignition key switch—only a simple hand switch on the handlebars to turn the ignition on and off. This is the easiest type of ignition to operate, because there is only one switch and no pushbutton for an electric starter. To save weight,

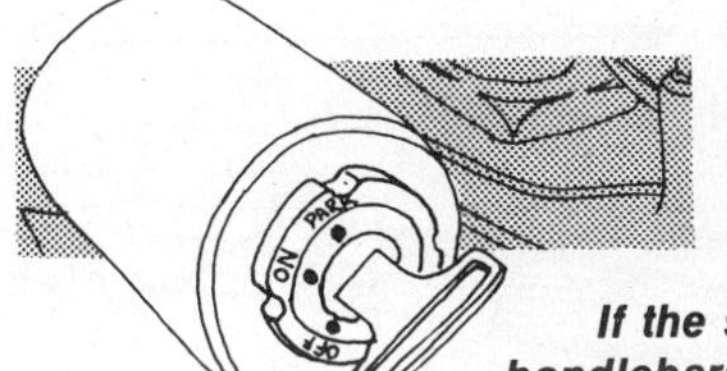

Most riders don't forget to turn on the ignition key switch, but it has been known to happen.

If the shutoff switch on the handlebars is not positioned correctly, the bike will not start even if the ignition key switch is in the ON position.

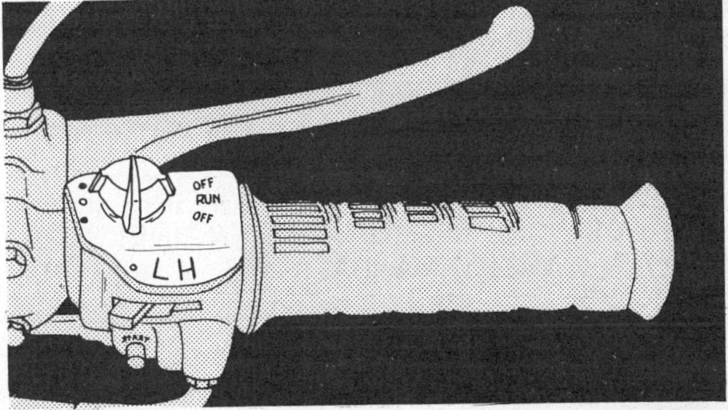

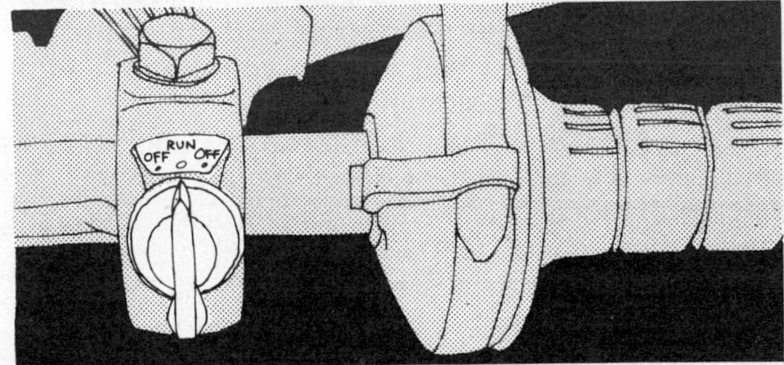

Some bikes have only a switch on the handlebars. This is most common on off-road and racing bikes.

most true dirt bikes and racing machines don't have an electric starter.

Always make sure that the ignition switches are positioned correctly. If you are not sure or the switch is poorly marked (many are), check the owner's manual.

Next, try turning on the headlight or sounding the horn to see if the electrical system is operating. Your ignition problem might be due to a total failure of the circuit, traceable to a blown fuse or a broken wire rather than a switch.

If headlights, turn signals or other electrical parts don't work, it's time to investigate the battery, fuse and wiring. The fuse is generally located near the battery. On most bikes, you reach both by raising the hinged seat.

Check the fuse (most fuses are clear glass so that you can inspect them by eye) and the battery connections. If the fuse appears good, remove the battery and take it to a shop for testing and, if necessary, recharging. It's suprising how often the reason a bike won't start turns out to be a dead battery.

NOTE: IF BATTERY FAILURE BECOMES FREQUENT, SUSPECT A MALFUNCTION IN THE WIRING OR THE CHARGING CIRCUIT. TROUBLESHOOT THE PROBLEM WITH THE SHOP MANUAL OR TAKE THE BIKE TO A GOOD MECHANIC.

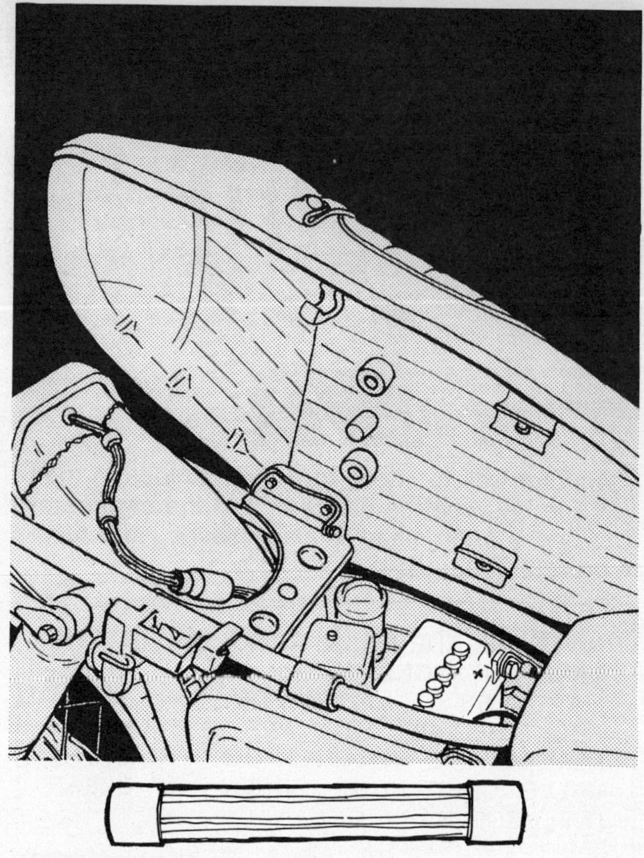

Don't forget to check the fuse. If it is blown, generally none of the electrical equipment will work.

IS THE TRANSMISSION IN NEUTRAL?

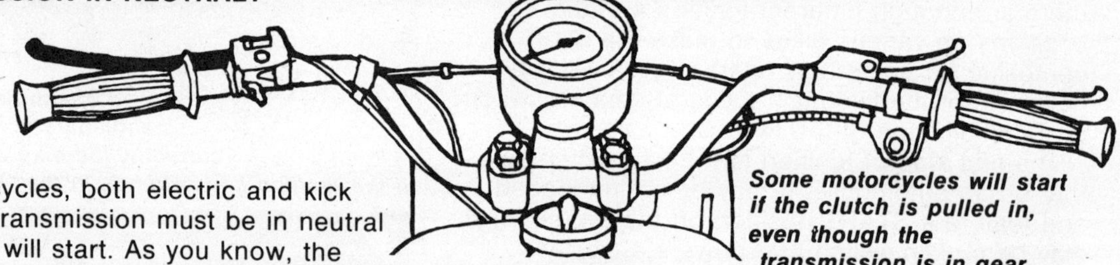

Some motorcycles will start if the clutch is pulled in, even though the transmission is in gear.

On most motorcycles, both electric and kick start models, the transmission must be in neutral before the engine will start. As you know, the transmission is operated by a foot lever. Since the shifting pattern differs from bike to bike, some having neutral between two gears, some between all gears and some at the top or bottom of the shifting sequence, it may be that you aren't shifting the transmission into neutral.

NOTE: SOME BIKES WILL START WITH THE TRANSMISSION IN GEAR IF THE CLUTCH LEVER IS PULLED IN, DISENGAGING THE TRANSMISSION FROM THE ENGINE. SEE YOUR OWNER'S MANUAL.

Check the owner's manual for information on your bike. It's a matter of developing a feel for placing the lever into neutral. Some bikes are just harder than others. On bikes with kick starters, you'll know instantly if you have the bike in gear when you try to start it, but electric starter bikes may have an interlock switch which prevents the electric starter from operating unless the gearshift is in neutral.

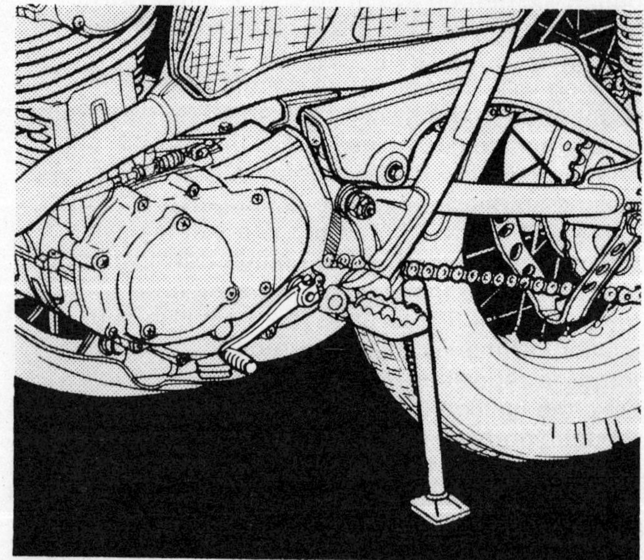

The foot shift lever on the transmission on your bike is sometimes hard to get into neutral. Double check it to make sure it's in the neutral position.

Motorcycles equipped with an instrument cluster often have a neutral light, which comes on if the transmission is in neutral. This light doesn't operate unless the ignition is on, but it can help you get the bike into neutral for starting.

If you find that you cannot get the bike to shift into neutral, something may be wrong with the clutch or transmission. Look into the section on clutches and transmissions in the shop manual for a little troubleshooting. Clutches and transmissions are complex, so you may wind up taking the bike to a shop. A good job of troubleshooting, however, may reveal a simple problem that can be fixed at home with your normal set of hand tools.

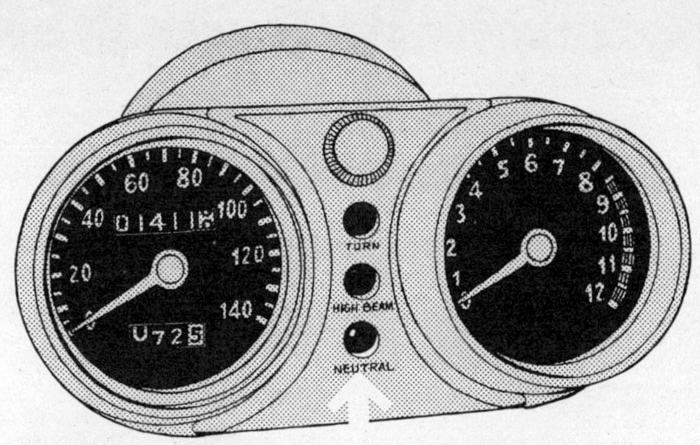

A helpful gadget for riders whose bikes have an instrument cluster is the neutral light, which glows when the transmission is in neutral.

IS THE CHOKE ON?

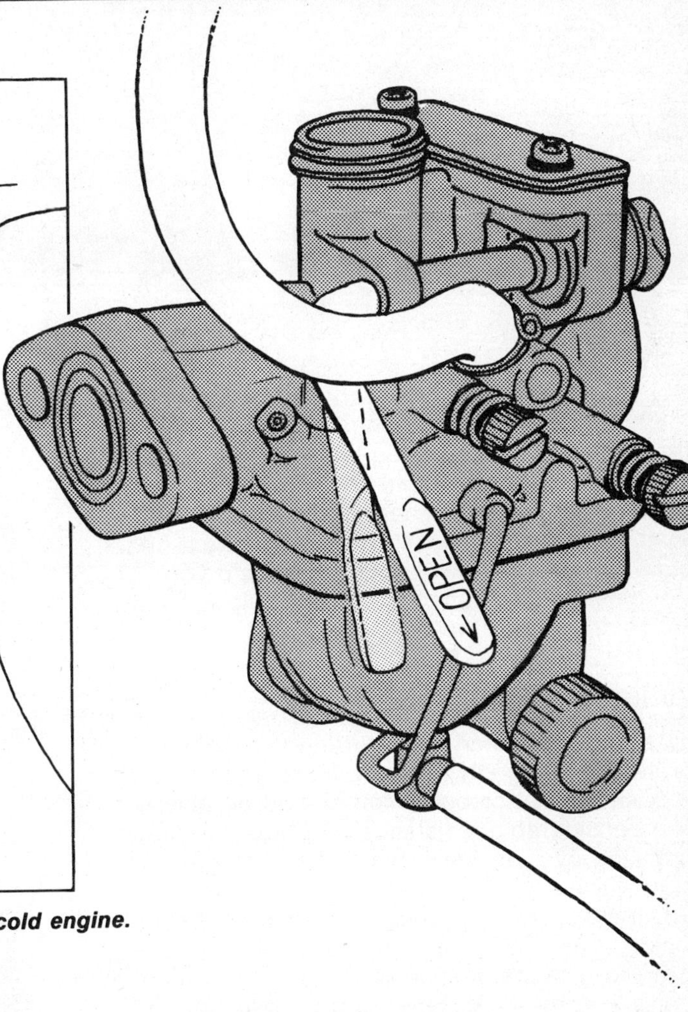

That little choke lever is a must item for starting a cold engine. The choke richens the air/fuel mixture to aid in starting the engine.

Motorcycles are equipped with a manual choke to enrich the air/fuel mixture for starting a cold engine. This choke is usually a lever mounted on or near the carburetor. When attempting to start a cold engine, put the choke lever in the ON position. On some motorcycles, this means pulling the lever up; on others it means pushing it down. See the owner's manual for specific information on the choke system for your motorcycle.

One thing you should remember: The choke is for starting a cold engine. If you turn on the choke to start an engine that is still warm from running, often the engine will flood and not start. If this happens, put the choke lever in the OFF position and crank the engine through several times without the ignition turned on to clear the engine of unburned fuel. After a short wait, it should start without using the choke.

After these preliminary questions about the proper positioning of controls have been answered to your satisfaction, you can go on to the "Basic Starting Checklist" which follows. With this simple checklist, the cause of a no-start condition can usually be traced to a single system. The faulty system can then be examined and repaired, using the shop manual as a guide. Another good source of information on troubleshooting and repair is Petersen's MOTORCYCLE REPAIR MANUAL, written by Bob Greene and the editors of *Motorcyclist* Magazine.

IV/Basic Starting Checklist

ELECTRIC STARTERS

To check the electric starter, turn the ignition key to ON and press the start button. Listen for the sound of the starter engaging and cranking the engine over. If nothing happens, or if the only sound you hear is a rapid clicking and the engine does not crank over, check the battery and fuse. Then read the section of the shop manual on starting systems for information to help you troubleshoot. If your bike is also equipped with a kick starter, read the next step.

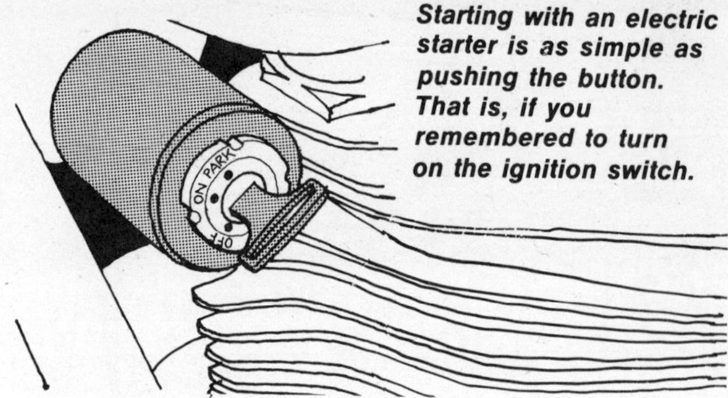

Starting with an electric starter is as simple as pushing the button. That is, if you remembered to turn on the ignition switch.

KICK STARTERS

Test the kick starter by putting the ignition key or switch in the ON position. Make your starting kick strong but smooth. You should be able to feel considerable resistance and hear the engine cranking over on the downstroke of the kick starter lever.

If there is no resistance to the movement of the kick starter lever or the engine does not crank over, turn to the section of the shop manual that deals with the kick starter and troubleshoot it. If the kick starter and/or the electric starter appear to be functioning normally but the engine will not start, go on to the next step to see if the engine is getting fuel.

WARNING: WHEN WORKING THE KICK STARTER, BE SURE THAT THE BIKE'S KICKSTAND IS ON A FIRM SURFACE. TRYING TO START THE BIKE ON SOFT DIRT OR GRASS CAN MAKE THE KICKSTAND SINK IN. THE BIKE MAY THEN FALL OVER WHEN THE RIDER PUTS HIS FULL WEIGHT ON THE KICK STARTER.

The old reliable method is muscle power delivered to the kick starter. Sometimes a weak battery prevents even the kick starter from firing the engine.

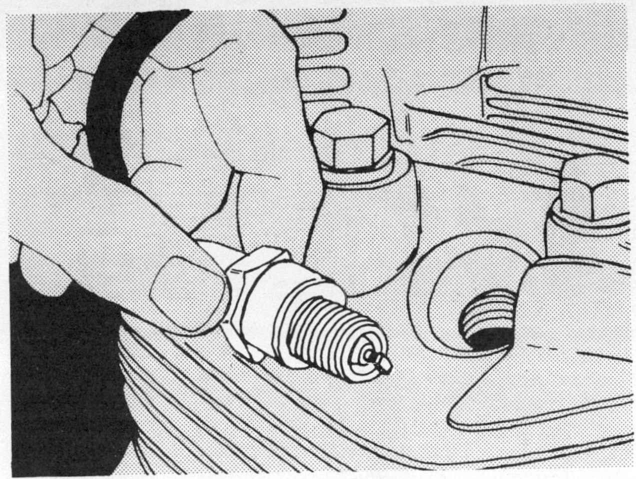

FUEL SYSTEM

The quickest way to determine if the engine is getting fuel is to remove a spark plug and examine it. If the spark plug is clean and dry even though you have been trying to start the engine, there is gas in the tank and all controls are positioned properly, a carburetor problem is the likeliest reason for the no-start condition.

Examine the carburetor for external evidence of a defect. Then read the chapter in this book on carburetors or the applicable section of the shop manual for further information to help you troubleshoot the carburetor and fuel system.

Checking the plug is the quickest way to determine if the engine is getting gas. A clean, dry plug after you've been cranking the engine usually means a lack of fuel for starting.

IGNITION SYSTEM

Again, the spark plug is the best indication of trouble. Remove the plug from the cylinder head. Place it so that the external metal portion of the plug is in contact with the cylinder head. Leaving the spark plug wire attached to the plug, crank the engine over.

> **NOTE:** THIS OFTEN REQUIRES TWO PEOPLE, ONE TO CRANK THE ENGINE OVER WITH THE KICK STARTER, THE OTHER TO HOLD THE SPARK PLUG IN PLACE AND WATCH IT.

Be careful to keep your fingers on the insulated ceramic part of the plug or the rubber insulation of the wire. Also make sure that the plug is in firm contact with the metal of the cylinder head. Operate the starter and watch the tip of the plug closely. If the ignition system is operating, you should see a strong spark across the electrodes of the spark plug.

> **NOTE:** FOR THE SAKE OF CLARITY, THIS BOOK GENERALLY USES SINGLE-CYLINDER ENGINES AS EXAMPLES. IF YOU HAVE A MULTICYLINDER BIKE, YOU CAN REMOVE ALL SPARK PLUGS AND EXAMINE THEM, BUT IT ISN'T STRICTLY NECESSARY FOR EITHER THE FUEL OR THE IGNITION CHECK.

If there is no spark, you probably have an ignition problem. Read the chapter on ignition and consult the shop manual on your bike for ways to find and fix the problem.

Recheck to make sure that you have all controls positioned correctly. Your first troubleshooting step should be a close visual examination of wiring. Often the problem is a bad connection or a burned-out fuse.

If you have both fuel entering the cylinder and a strong spark, but the bike will not start, proceed to the next check.

When making a spark check with the plug connected to the high tension lead, be sure to firmly ground the outside metal of the plug to the metal of the cylinder head. Save yourself a shock!

COMPRESSION CHECK

Even if you have a good ignition system and are getting fuel into the engine, the bike won't run unless the air/fuel mixture is being compressed by the upward movement of the piston in the cylinder. For a quick compression check that requires no test equipment, remove the spark plug from the cylinder head and lay it aside. Place your thumb or finger tightly over the spark plug hole and crank the engine over. As the piston comes up on the compression stroke, the rising pressure should force your finger off the plug hole.

If the pressure does push your finger off the hole, the compression is probably good. The reason we say "probably" is that without a compression gauge to get an accurate reading, you might still have a compression problem even though it seemed good with the thumb test.

> **NOTE:** TWO-STROKE ENGINES REQUIRE SPECIAL COMPRESSION TESTING METHODS. SEE BELOW.

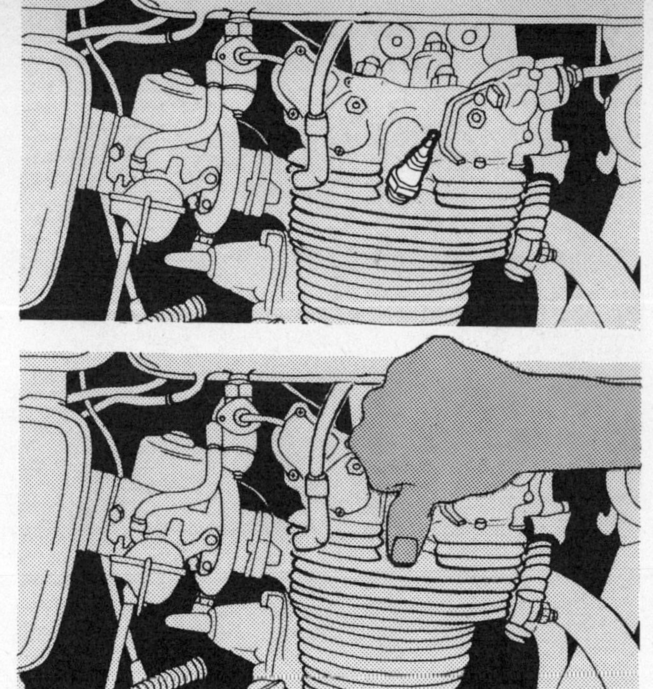

Removing the plug and using your thumb as a simple compression tester is a quick and dirty method, but it works just fine!

Below: A small amount of light oil added through the spark plug hole will seal bad rings and raise compression readings for a few moments if the rings are bad.

If you have the time and are at home, always use a compression gauge for this check. The shop manual will tell you what the compression reading on your bike should be. Usually the manual also includes a list of things to check if the compression is low.

A handy troubleshooting tip for four-stroke engines with a low compression reading is to add a small quantity of light oil to the combustion chamber through the spark plug hole. After adding the oil, repeat the compression check with the gauge.

A more accurate determination of compression problems is possible with a compression gauge. The type shown here, with a screw-in fitting, is the best. It allows precise readings and is easy to handle even if you are working alone.

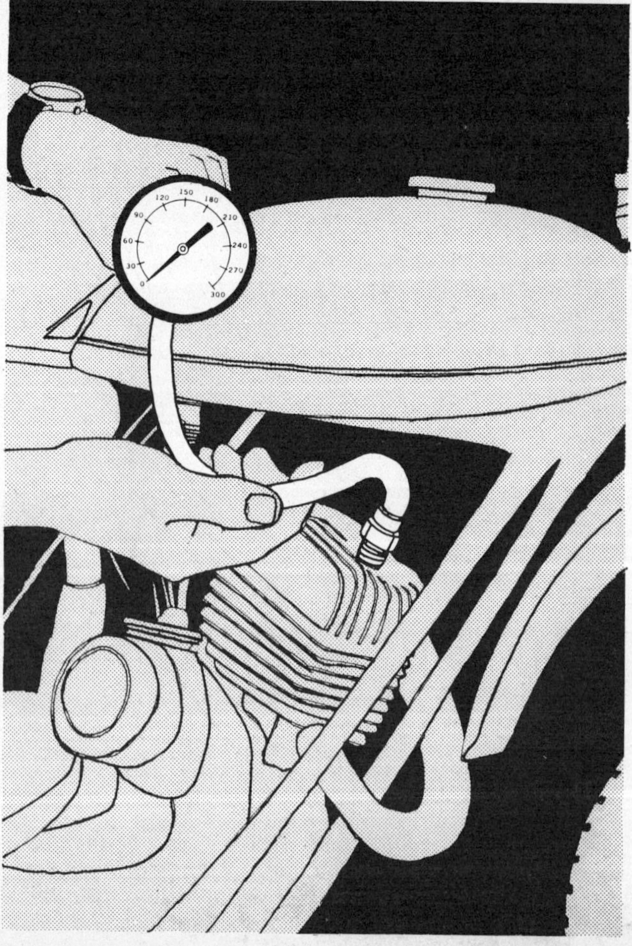

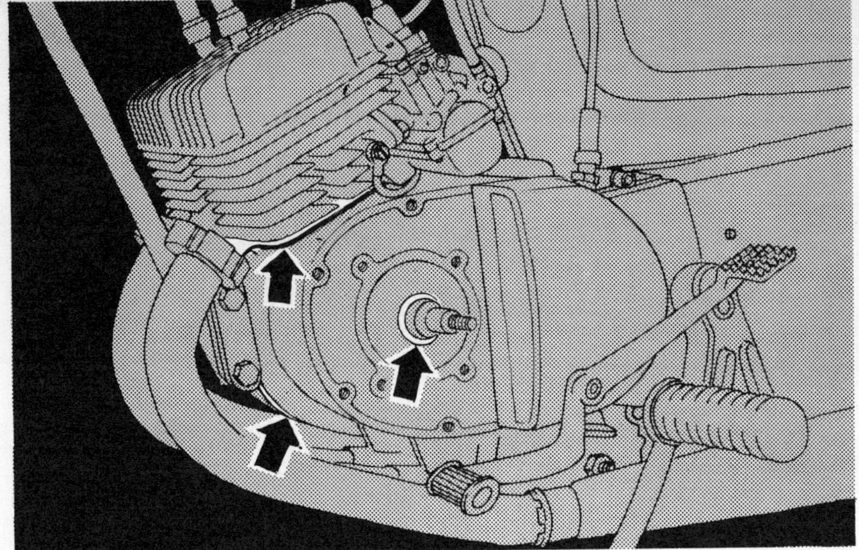

A two-stroke engine can develop leaks in several places other than the combustion chamber. A no-start condition will follow.

A more complicated compression tester is needed to check two-strokes. This kit uses a pressure pump and seals to check two-strokes for an airtight condition.

If the compression comes up to near normal, chances are the piston rings are bad. (The oil will seal them up for a few moments, giving a temporarily good compression reading.) If the reading stays low, the problem is more likely to be a blown head gasket or bad valves.

The same test procedure, using either your thumb or a compression gauge, will tell you something about cylinder compression in a two-stroke engine, but the information may be misleading. Air/fuel compression is complicated in a two-stroke engine because of the way the air-fuel mixture is passed through the engine crankcase before being routed to the combustion chamber.

This means that a leak at any point in the engine where fuel is routed could result in a no-start condition. Merely checking cylinder compression above the piston will not always tell you if there is a loss of compression at some other point.

To completely check the compression of a two-stroke engine, you need a special type of tester. This compression tester has a set of plates to block off the ports on the engine and a small pump to pressurize the engine. Compression readings are taken with a compression gauge that is more sensitive than a normal gauge (some gauges are dual-range), because crankcase pressures are much lower than cylinder pressures. Generally speaking, if a two-stroke engine will not hold a pressure of 5-6 psi (pounds per square inch) for about six minutes, there is a leak somewhere.

If you have gone all the way through the basic checklist and the starting checklist without finding a problem and the engine still won't start, even though you have fuel, a good spark and compression, faulty ignition timing may be the source of your no-start condition.

Ignition timing is critical to engine operation. If the timing is off far enough, the spark comes at a time when the engine is not ready to use the air/fuel mixture. It may not be compressed enough to ignite and burn properly, or a valve or port may still be open.

Backfiring through the carburetor is a good sign of ignition timing problems, but sometimes the ignition timing can slip so far away from normal that nothing happens, even though a cranking check shows a spark across the electrodes of the spark plug. If you suspect a timing problem, get into the shop manual and follow the procedures outlined to check out the timing of your engine.

As stated in the beginning of this section, the best tool you can use is your brain. Taking the problem one step at a time and following a well-thought-out plan of attack will quickly isolate most problems to a single system and then to a single component.

The next tool which should be used by the troubleshooter is technical books, in the form of shop manuals, owner's manuals and this and other Petersen motorcycle publications. Don't be afraid to admit that you need help. Use the tech manuals and ask more experienced friends for help. You'll learn a lot faster how your motorcycle works and how to keep it in good repair if you get and retain good advice and information.

Troubleshooting isn't magic, but it isn't an exact science, either. As you learn, you will develop methods that work for you, and one of these days, you'll be helping somebody else troubleshoot.

IV/Troubleshooting Review

IF ENGINE DOES NOT START OR IS HARD TO START:

(First check that the ignition is on and that there is enough fuel in the tank.)

CHECK THAT FUEL FLOWS INTO CARBURETOR.

IF FUEL DOES NOT ENTER THE CARBURETOR:

PROBLEM	SOLUTION
Fuel line clogged or damaged	Clean or replace.
Fuel strainer clogged	Remove and clean.
Fuel tank petcock clogged	Remove and clean.
Tank air vent clogged	Remove and clean.
Flow stopped at float needle	Remove and clean.
Float setting too high	Reset float level.

CHECK FOR SPARK AT THE PLUG AT KICK STARTER SPEED.

IF YOU HAVE A GOOD, HOT BLUE SPARK:

PROBLEM	SOLUTION
Faulty plug under compression	Replace plug.
Ignition timing off	Adjust timing correctly.
Carburetor float level incorrect	Adjust to factory specs.
Fuel mixture incorrect	Reset to factory specs.

IF SPARK IS WEAK:

PROBLEM	SOLUTION
Bad spark plug	Replace.
Incorrect spark plug gap	Adjust to factory specs.
Bad spark plug cap	Replace.
Damaged or cracked high-tension wire	Replace.
Dirty contact points	Clean and adjust.
Bad condenser	Replace.
Bad ignition coil	Replace.
Bad exciter coil in magneto	Replace.
Low charge in battery	Charge to full capacity.

IF THERE IS NO SPARK:

PROBLEM	SOLUTION
Shorted or fouled spark plug	Replace.
Dirty or wet contact points	Dry and clean with flexstone.
Blown fuse	Replace with new one.
Disconnected wire	Locate and reconnect.
Bad condenser	Replace.
Incorrect point gap	Adjust to correct gap.
Short in the wiring harness	Repair or replace.
Contact points installed wrong	Correct.
Kill button shorting out	Repair or replace.
Ignition coil failure	Replace.
Bad ignition switch	Repair or replace.
Magneto exciter coil failure	Replace.
No charge in battery	Charge to full capacity.
Battery will not hold charge	Replace.
CDI unit failure	Replace.

CHECK FOR PROPER ENGINE COMPRESSION (CHECK AT KICK STARTER SPEED WITH THE THROTTLE OPEN).

IF ENGINE COMPRESSION IS SUFFICIENT:

PROBLEM	SOLUTION
No fuel entering engine	Air leak between carburetor and engine.
Too much fuel entering engine	Float level too high; adjust.
Dirty air cleaner	Clean or replace.
Carburetor slide backwards or sideways	Install correctly.
Exhaust port or muffler carboned	Clean out.
Crankcase seals leaking	Replace.

IF ENGINE COMPRESSION IS INSUFFICIENT:

PROBLEM	SOLUTION
Loose spark plug	Tighten.
Loose head bolts	Tighten to correct torque specs.
Leaking head gasket	Replace.
Warped cylinder or head	Resurface or replace.
Worn piston rings	Deglaze cylinder and replace rings.
Rings stuck in lands on piston	Clean or replace.
Incorrect tappet clearance	Adjust to manufacturer's specs.
Bad valve seating	Regrind and reseat.
Bent valve	Replace.
Valve seized in valve guide	Replace both.
Incorrect valve timing	Retime correctly.
Badly worn cylinder	Rebore to next oversize.
Holed or burned-away piston	Replace.

IF ENGINE RUNS BUT DOES NOT RUN SMOOTHLY, TURN THROTTLE TO SEE IF ENGINE RPM INCREASE.

IF THE RPM INCREASE BUT THE SPEED DOES NOT:

PROBLEM	SOLUTION
Clutch slippage	Adjust or replace clutch plates.

IF ENGINE RPM WILL NOT INCREASE SMOOTHLY:

PROBLEM	SOLUTION
Bad spark plug	Replace.
Ignition timing incorrect	Adjust to correct timing.
Dirty air cleaner	Clean or replace.
Clogged gas cap breather	Clean.
Clogged fuel line	Clean.
Water in carburetor	Clean out entire fuel supply.
Improperly tuned carburetor	Rejet correctly.
Clogged exhaust pipe or muffler	Clean.
Improper tappet clearance	Reset clearances.
Leaking valves	Regrind and reseat.

IF ENGINE DOES NOT RUN SMOOTHLY AT LOW RPM:

PROBLEM	SOLUTION
Dirty or sooty spark plug	Replace
Improperly gapped spark plug	Regap.
Ignition timing advanced	Adjust to correct timing.
Dirty contact points	Clean and adjust.
Improper pilot air screw adjustment	Adjust.
Carburetor pilot jet plugged	Clean with compressed air.
Improper tappet clearances	Reset clearances.
Defective or discharged battery	Replace or recharge.

IF ENGINE DOES NOT RUN SMOOTHLY AT HIGH RPM:

PROBLEM	SOLUTION
Fouled spark plug	Replace.
Improper spark plug gap	Adjust to correct gap.
Pitted contact breakers	Replace.
Clogged fuel line or gas tank breather	Clean.
Dirty air cleaner	Clean or renew.
Ignition timing retarded	Adjust to correct timing.
Clogged main jet	Clean with compressed air.
Choke closed	Open it.
Carburetors not synchronized	Synchronize.
Carburetor float level incorrect	Reset to proper level.
Oversize main jet	Install correct main jet.
Jet needle positioned too high	Lower clip notch in needle.
Automatic advance stuck	Repair or replace.
Faulty condenser	Replace.
Faulty coil	Replace.
Charging system not operating	Repair or replace.
Bad crankcase seals (two-stroke)	Replace.
Incorrect tappet clearance	Reset clearance.
Weak or broken valve springs	Replace.
Broken rings	Replace.
Valve timing incorrect	Retime.

IF ENGINE OVERHEATS:

PROBLEM	SOLUTION
Spark plug too hot	Install colder plug.
Too-lean air/fuel mixture	Richen mixture.
Low-grade or stale gasoline	Change to fresh premium gasoline.
Improper ignition timing	Set to correct timing.
Carbon in combustion chamber	Clean out all carbon.
Oil level too low	Fill.
Automatic advance sticking	Repair or replace.
Brake dragging	Adjust.
Clutch slippage	Adjust or replace if necessary.
Drive chain too tight or dry	Adjust and lubricate.

IF ENGINE STOPS AS THOUGH KEY WERE TURNED OFF:

PROBLEM	SOLUTION
Out of fuel	Fill.
Spark plug bridged	Clean or replace.
Fuse blown	Replace.
Clogged fuel system	Clean.
Plug wire shorted or came off	Replace.
Broken or shorted contact point	Replace.

IF ENGINE STOPS AS THOUGH BRAKES WERE APPLIED:

PROBLEM	SOLUTION
Seized piston	Rebore and replace.
Seized crankshaft	Rebuild or replace.
Seized transmission gears	Replace.
Seized bearings	Replace.

IF ENGINE STOPS GRADUALLY:

PROBLEM	SOLUTION
Loose spark plug	Retighten.
Partially clogged fuel system	Remove and clean.
Blown head gasket	Replace.
Loose cylinder head	Tighten securely.
Bent or burnt valve	Replace.
Holed piston	Replace.

V. Tuning Your Motorcycle

Your First Four-stroke Tune-up

Getting through your first complete tune-up isn't difficult. It's apt to be more time-consuming than jobs you do thereafter because you're learning, but with care, the result will be a professional job you can be proud of. The basic ingredient is planning. Get the proper tools, parts and technical materials gathered together before you start work. One step we have stressed in previous chapters is worth repeating: Read the shop manual or owner's manual for your particular bike and get a good idea of all the tuning steps *before* you begin.

A basic tune-up kit is really several components which must be purchased separately: the carburetor kit(s) (two for our twin-cylinder bike), the various ignition parts and the spark plugs. You may add or delete parts, depending on what you plan for your bike.

A four-stroke motorcycle engine is mechanically more complex than a two-stroke engine, but that doesn't mean it is harder to tune. Since your four-stroke engine is exactly like the engine in an automobile except for being air cooled, it should be more familiar to you than a two-stroke. It works on the same physical principles and is tuned in the same manner as a car. In fact, tuning a motorcycle engine is simpler, because it does not have the complicated smog devices which affect tuning on automobile engines.

Your tune-up parts consist of spark plugs, ignition points (two sets in the case of our sample bike, a Honda 350), a condenser, and carburetor rebuilding kits. The parts contained in the carburetor kit vary according to the type of carburetor on your motorcycle, but basically they all contain gaskets, main jet and needle and seat for the float bowl. Other parts may be check valves, idle air metering screws, small springs and clips and other small parts that should be replaced when rebuilding the carburetor.

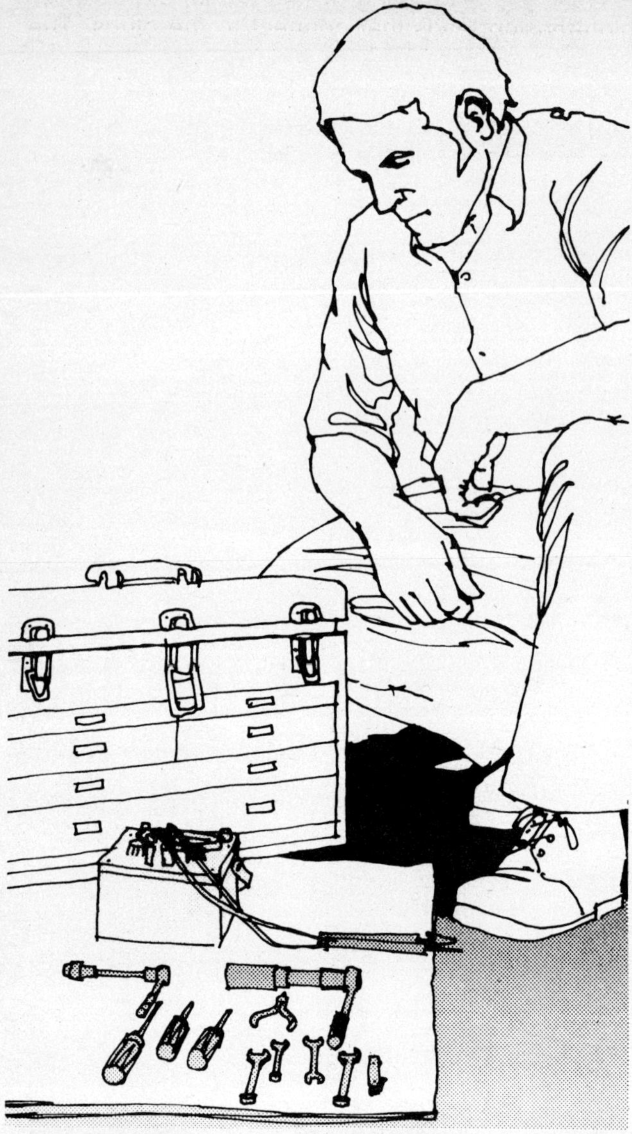

BEFORE YOU START . . .

Clean the motorcycle first, if necessary. Then position it in the place you have chosen as a work area and gather the tools and materials you will need.

The basic tools common to all tune-ups are hand tools such as open- and box-end wrenches, a spark plug socket and ratchet with extension, feeler gauges, spark plug gapping tool and a selection of screwdrivers. Most likely you'll need an impact driver and bits (screwdriver tips) to remove at least one cover on the engine, so you might as well get it out and put it with the rest of the tools.

To set timing, you'll need either a buzz box or a timing light. Some shop manuals give procedures for using both, but the timing light is more exact for overall operation.

Keep a supply of clean rags handy, and spread out some of the rags to position tools and parts on. That way small parts won't get lost. It also makes for a neater work area. The final step before actually picking up a tool is a last look at your work layout to make sure you haven't forgotten anything. It's better to discover it now rather than later. Having to stop in the middle of a complex task to go search for a tool or part leads to mistakes.

In general it's best to follow the tune-up procedure outlined in the shop manual or owner's manual for your motorcycle. All settings and clearances should be *exactly* as stated in the manual. In time, you can do certain portions of the tune-up out of sequence to make things easier for you, but beginners probably shouldn't attempt this. It's best to follow the book to the letter until you've done the job a few times.

SPARK PLUGS

The first step in any tune-up is a look at the spark plugs. They can tell you more about what's going on inside your engine than any other part of the engine. (Refer to the "Reading Spark Plugs" section of this book for more information about spark plugs.) Remove the plug, using the plug socket and ratchet, and examine it. Even if the plug looks fairly good and you can't detect any damage to the insulator or electrodes except for mild wear, you should replace the plugs with new ones. They are not expensive, and the old plugs can be saved for emergencies.

Cleaning and regapping used plugs is all right if you want to save a little money, but you really should replace the plugs if you are doing a regular tune-up and cleanup at the interval specified in the shop manual or owner's manual.

A round wire gapping gauge is best for gapping the plugs. It gives the truest readings. The correct plug gap setting for your engine can be found in the book on your bike.

Gap the plugs and install them in the engine, unless you'll be setting the timing with a dial indicator and buzz box. In that case, gap the plugs and then set them aside, out of the way, until it's time to reinstall them in the engine.

A round wire gauge like the one shown here is best for gapping spark plugs. It prevents any pitting on the underside of the electrode on a used plug from distorting the gap setting. On new plugs it doesn't make much difference, but you should still have a good wire gauge.

Going over ignition wires by hand or with a meter can be very helpful during a tune-up. Wiring is exposed to smog, heat and weather damage and it finally goes bad. Check for cracks in the insulation or indications of broken strands of wire inside.

POINT FACE ALIGNMENT

CORRECT

CONTACT AREA COVERED

MISALIGNMENT OF CENTERS

CONTACT AREA NOT CENTERED

MISALIGNMENT OF POINT CENTERS

CONTACT AREA NOT CENTERED

Off-center ignition point wear or metal transfer from one side to another is evidence of the need for corrective measures. Offset wear on points can sometimes be corrected by carefully bending the points with a pair of needle-nosed pliers. Excessive metal transfer from one side to the other generally means that the condenser is breaking down and should be replaced.

While you're working on the plugs, check the high-tension leads that connect to the plugs. The insulation should be in good shape, and the rubber boots that fit over the plug should be clean and intact. You can inspect the metal contacts inside the boots with a flashlight to see that they are clean and not corroded. Be sure the wire end snaps firmly onto the tip of the plug when the wire is installed. A loose spark plug wire makes the engine miss.

For a close look at the wires connected to the coils and plugs, you'll have to remove the gas tank from the frame. On bikes like our example, you'll have to do this in any event when it's time to install the condenser, since on these bikes the condenser is located under the gas tank.

To remove the gas tank, turn the fuel shutoff valve to OFF, disconnect the line or lines leading to the carburetor(s), then unfasten the tank. If there is a lot of gasoline in the tank, drain it into a suitable container before taking the tank off the frame.

CAUTION: BE VERY CAREFUL WHEN REMOVING THE GAS TANK. DON'T REMOVE THE TANK WHEN THE ENGINE IS STILL HOT. ALSO, DISCONNECT THE BATTERY BEFORE REMOVING THE TANK.

SETTING IGNITION POINT GAP

Methods of setting ignition point gap differ from bike to bike, but the basic technique is to rotate the engine until the point gap is at its widest, then set the gap as indicated in the shop manual. Since we plan to replace the ignition points as part of the tune-up, rotate the engine to the point of widest gap on the selected cylinder (usually the right-side cylinder on a twin-cylinder engine) and remove the points. Examine them for signs of wear and pitting, which could be the result of a bad condenser.

Replace the condenser whenever you replace the ignition points. A condenser that is leaking electrically can ruin new ignition points in a hurry.

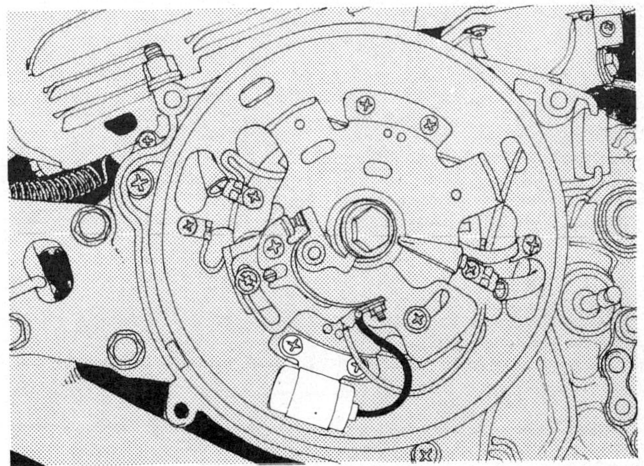

This tiny round part is the condenser. It is designed to reduce arcing across the points as they open. Many mechanics replace the condenser as often as the points are changed.

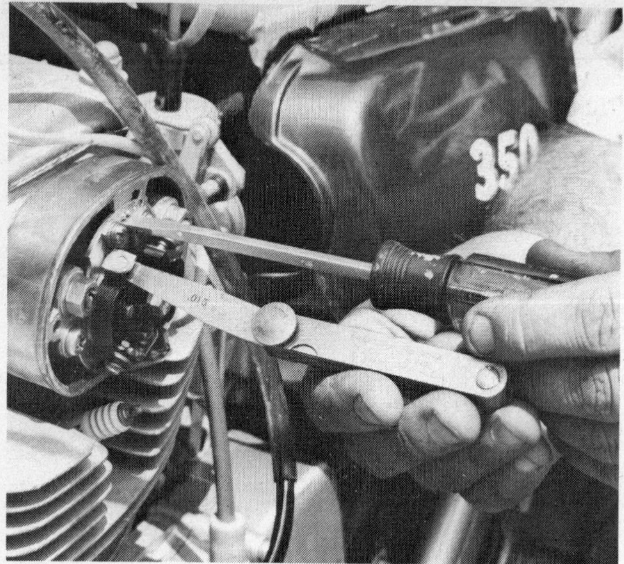

Setting ignition point gap with a feeler gauge calls for a blade that's clean and free of oil or dirt. When the gap is correct, you'll feel just a slight drag as you pull the blade between the opened ignition points. The angle must also be just right to avoid distorting the measurement.

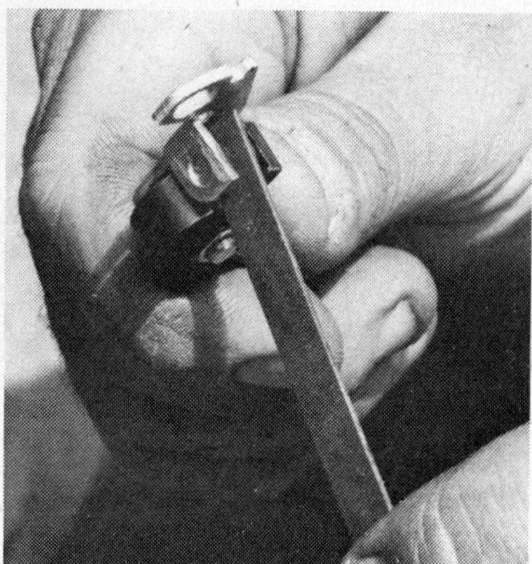

Old ignition points can be cleaned and reused. The proper technique for restoring them is to carefully smooth the inner surfaces with a point file or other gentle abrasive. If you have any doubts about the condition of a set of points, discard them and install new ones, since the cost isn't great.

Ignition timing marks are usually found on the generator rotor. Bringing them into alignment with marks on the case indicates when the points should open to deliver the spark to the cylinder being fired.

The feeler gauge you use to set the ignition points should be clean and free from any contaminating material such as oil. Many mechanics spray a little light oil on the feeler gauge blades to protect them from rusting while not being used, and this is a good idea. The only problem is that oil can harm the ignition points. Wipe the blade with a clean cloth before adjusting the points; you can re-oil the blades afterward.

When you insert the feeler gauge between the two contacts of the ignition points and tighten the adjusting screws, the blade should just pass through the gap, with a *slight* friction. If the blade sticks, the gap will be too narrow once the blade is withdrawn.

Also, be sure to hold the blade of the feeler gauge straight, directly in line with the gap between the points. If the blade is out of alignment with the surfaces of the points, the setting will be incorrect. You may have to adjust the points several times to get exactly the right gap. It's a good idea to rotate the engine through several revolutions after setting the points, then recheck them to make sure that the clearance hasn't changed.

On multicylinder engines there may be more than one set of ignition points. Because of design features of the ignition system, one set of points must always be adjusted first. Follow the shop manual exactly on this series of steps.

In some dual point units, final settings on the ignition points may not come out the same for both sets of points. This is all right as long as both sets fall within a specific range of variation.

Ignition points that are in good shape can be cleaned and regapped if you wish. To clean off any buildup of material on the inner surfaces, use an ignition file or an emery board—the kind ladies file their fingernails with. Don't use ordinary files to clean the contact surfaces of ignition points; they are much too rough and coarse.

SETTING IGNITION TIMING

After point gap comes setting the *timing* of the ignition points—the moment when they open. There are two methods of doing this. In one, the static method, you align timing marks on the rotor of the engine or on the points plate, using a buzz box or multimeter. With the other method, you use a timing light while the engine is running. When timing the engine statically, a dial indicator is sometimes necessary to establish piston TDC (Top Dead Center).

It is the exact moment of point opening that breaks the complete circuit in the primary winding of the ignition coil, collapsing the magnetic field and transferring to the secondary winding the high energy potential that arcs across the plug electrodes. Therefore the exact time that the points open is of critical interest. This is *not* something that can be judged visually. You need the aid of some mechanical test equipment to determine the moment of point opening. Only a buzz box, multimeter or timing light can give the tuner a *precise* reading of point opening.

The static method of setting point timing is so called because the engine is static, not running, when you do the timing. This method requires either a buzz box or a multimeter. Hook either of these pieces of test equipment into the points so that it forms a complete circuit as long as the points are closed.

Next, rotate the engine. It's easy to do with a large wrench on the nut which secures the engine alternator rotor to the crankshaft. Watch the meter or listen to the buzz box to find the exact time of ignition point *opening.*

When the test equipment signals that the points have opened, the timing marks ought to be aligned with each other. On some models, a special tool stops engine rotation at a specified place, at which time the points should be just opening.

To adjust timing, usually you loosen screws and move either the ignition point plate (on some models) or the alternator rotor. (See the section on specific tune-up procedure for your particular bike.) It often takes several tries to get everything just right. Take your time. Make sure you're following the instructions to the letter *and* getting the desired results.

Setting the timing with a timing light is probably the best overall method of setting timing, because it checks the actual firing pulse of the ignition circuit instead of just a mechanical position. Since the engine must be running before you can use the timing light, you may want to depart from the sequence of steps called for in the technical manual and go on to other parts of the tune-up until you have finished every step except timing.

The final method of checking and adjusting ignition point timing is the timing light. Since it displays timing under running conditions, it checks out the entire system. Static timing, on the other hand, may be misleading if you have an advance problem or wiring that is breaking down under load.

The basic piece of equipment for static timing is a multimeter or point checker. This tool indicates the exact moment of point opening, which cannot be judged accurately by eye. The buzz box, another type of point checker, buzzes to tell when points open.

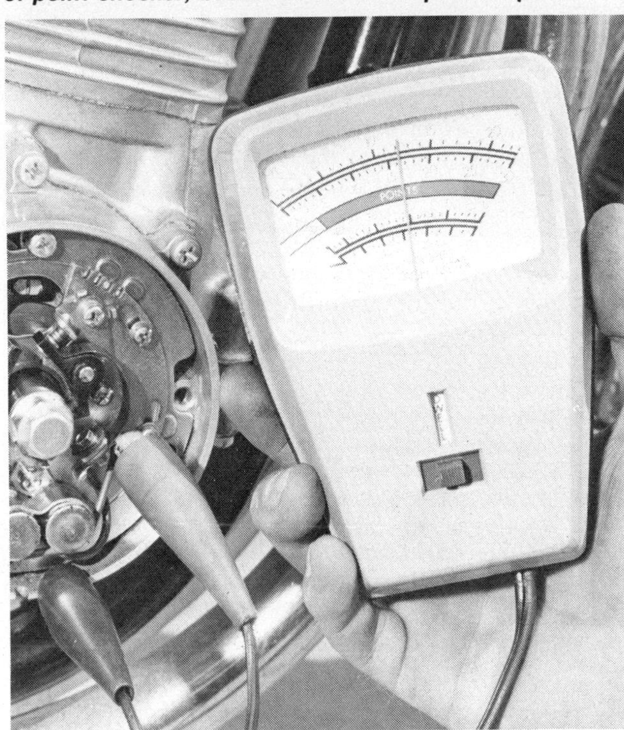

Because the engine must be running and because many bikes must be timed at a specific rpm (revolutions per minute), it often takes two people to time a motorcycle engine. One person operates the timing light while the other operates the engine and watches the tachometer. When running the engine, stand the bike firmly on the kickstand or prop it up so that it will not fall over. Make sure the transmission is in neutral and keep hands and feet away from the shift lever while timing the engine.

The timing light utilizes a stroboscopic (fast-blinking) light to make the timing mark on the rotor appear to "stand still" in relation to the fixed marks on the engine case. This feature also allows the tuner to see the firing action of the ignition system at different speeds and make sure it does what it is supposed to do.

Most tune-up instructions tell you to run the bike at a specific rpm when using the timing light. If your bike doesn't have a tachometer to tell you the rpm, accessory clip-on tachs are available.

IGNITION ADVANCE

As engine speed (rpm) increases, the timing must change. This is called *ignition advance*. The compression and ignition of the air/fuel mixture in the combustion chamber takes a fixed amount of time. As the mechanical speed of the piston and valves increases, there is less time for the air/fuel mixture to burn completely. You see, even though engine mechanical operations speed up, the burning time of the oxygen and gasoline remains essentially the same. So, to give the spark enough time to ignite the air/fuel mixture and let it burn sufficiently to create the required power, the spark must come a little earlier at high rpm. This is the function of the ignition advance circuit.

Ignition advance is accomplished by mechanically moving the ignition points slightly in relation to the engine-driven cam lobe, so that the points open earlier at high rpm than at low rpm.

The first step in rebuilding any carburetor is to get it clean. A painstaking washing in a good grade of solvent is one way. Dunking in a commerical carburetor cleaner is another. Whichever you choose, make sure the carburetor is clean and dry before starting to reassemble it.

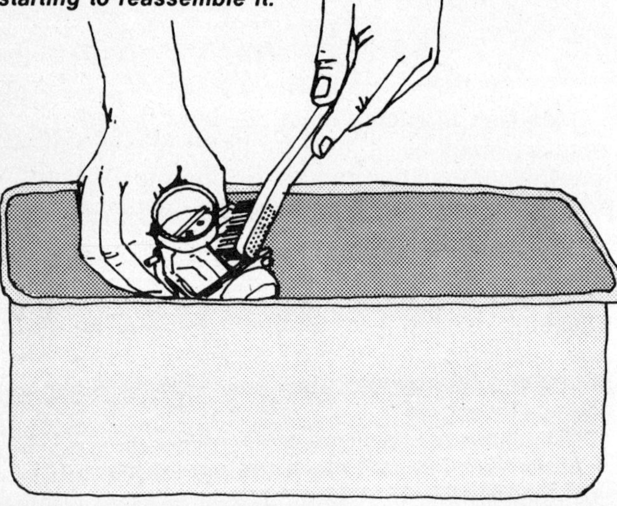

If you have one, an air compressor helps dry out internal passageways of the carburetor or other parts. Don't use high pressure and be careful not to blow solvent into your eyes.

Static timing, such as is done with a buzz box or multimeter, does not show the effect of ignition advance. This is why a timing light is better for complete timing.

On some bikes, the shop manual *forbids* you to power the timing light with the battery supply in the motorcycle. This is because ignition action on some motorcycles creates pulses in the rest of the electrical circuits which can cause false timing strobes or flashes. Study the pamphlet or book that comes with your timing light as well as the shop manual before using this tool to time your motorcycle.

CAUTION: BE SURE YOU WORK IN AN AREA WITH ADEQUATE VENTILATION. IF YOU'RE WORKING IN A GARAGE, KEEP THE DOOR OPEN WHILE THE ENGINE IS RUNNING.

CARBURETOR CLEANING & REBUILDING

Cleaning and rebuilding the carburetor is a major part of a tune-up. Small buildups of foreign material, such as dirt or varnish (left behind by evaporating gasoline), can clog passageways inside the carburetor or coat its walls, changing the internal settings of the carburetor.

The first step is to read through the section on rebuilding carburetors in the shop manual. Then remove the carburetor(s) from the engine and clean well in solvent or carburetor cleaner.

When taking the carburetor apart, lay each part aside in the same order you removed it, to help you reassemble the carb later on. Be sure to save all the little parts, even those you won't be using again. Pull all gaskets gently off the carburetor and set them aside. The most common problem faced by most beginning tuners—and quite a number of more experienced ones—is forgetting how the thing goes back together.

With a dual-carburetor motorcycle, it's a bit easier. You can do one carburetor at a time, using the other carburetor as a guide, For single-carburetor models, you'll just have to rely on the photos and description in the shop manual. You'll notice in the photos that our tuner didn't remove the carburetor bodies from the engine. This kind of on-bike rebuilding is possible with some slide-valve carburetors. Since the carburetor comes apart so easily, sometimes it's easier to do the job this way on motorcycles which have a complicated mounting or linkage system that connects the carbs to each other or to the engine.

Before reinstalling them, inspect and dry completely all parts of the carburetor. If you have an air compressor, use a little low-pressure air. You can use a soft rag, but it won't get into the smaller passageways. Be careful not to use a rag which sheds lint or threads. These can get into the jets and metering orifices and give you more trouble than the original dirty carburetor. Pipe cleaners can sometimes be a help in cleaning and drying the inside of the carburetor, but they tend to shed small fibers.

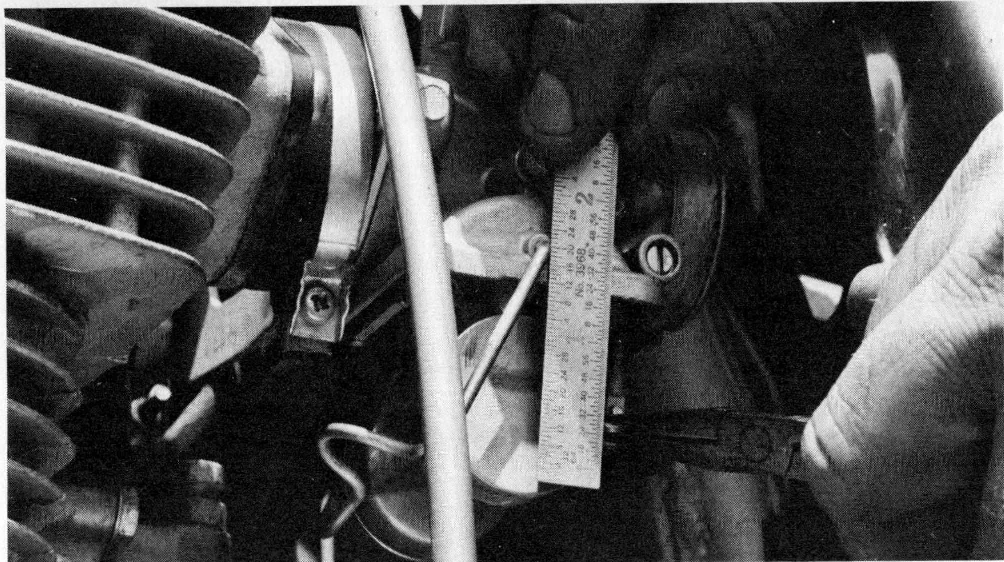

Setting the carb float level is easy, as long as you don't get too forceful in bending the tang. Positioning the float determines the level of fuel that will build up in the float bowl. Bending the tang to reposition the float adjusts the level to that recommended by the shop manual. This adjustment is critical to good carb operation, so approach it carefully.

When starting reassembly, lay out all parts on a clean cloth and follow instructions closely. Check the slide and the inside of the carburetor for signs of wear that might make the slide stick, and generally look the carburetor over for anything that might cause problems later on.

Unless you are making changes in the jetting on your carburetor at the time you rebuild (not recommended unless you have a specific reason), the major carburetor tune-up step is setting the float level. To do this, bend the tang which runs between the float and the needle of the needle-and-seat assembly. A pair of needle-nosed pliers and a measure of some kind are the best tools for the job.

NOTE: SOME CARBURETOR KITS INCLUDE A MEASURE TO HELP YOU SET THE FLOAT LEVEL.

Set the float level exactly as printed in the shop manual. On certain carburetor models with dual floats, you'll have to make the adjustment twice, once for each side. While you're at it, check the floats for signs of damage. A leaky float fills slowly with fuel, opens the valve and floods the engine. Make your float setting gently: The metal tang is fragile.

When putting the carburetor together again, replace all the parts for which the kit provides a replacement. You may look at some small part and be unable to detect a difference between the new part and the old one, so you may tempted to put the old part back in. Don't do it! The manufacturer supplies new parts in the kit for a reason; use them as outlined for best results.

Once you have the carburetor together and mounted on the engine again, with all cables and linkages hooked up, you can make the necessary external adjustments—the idle, the throttle control, etc.—and start the engine. Some manufacturers recommend making some of the adjustments after the engine has been running for a short time, and the idle speed must *always* be adjusted while the engine is running.

When adjusting parts such as the idle air needle, the shop manual usually tells you to bottom out the screw (screw it in all the way), then back it out one or more turns. Take it easy on this step. The metals are soft and the taper of the pin on the adjustment screw is critical. It doesn't take much pressure to ruin the screw and make accurate adjustment practically impossible. Turn the screw slowly and easily until it stops. Don't force it.

The final step in tuning the carburetor is making the external adjustments. One item often stressed and worth repeating here is: Don't force any adjustment. You can damage the needle and seat type of adjustment screws by forcing them. Work gently.

There are two sets of figures for setting valves given in the shop manual, depending on whether the engine is hot or cold. Do not confuse the two. Damage to the engine can result.

A typical valve train (shown here) has valves that are held closed by springs. The actuating mechanism is a rocker arm and follower assembly, which is raised and lowered by the action of the cam as it revolves.

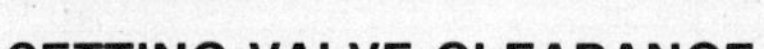

SETTING VALVE CLEARANCE

Setting the valves on a four-stroke motorcycle is critical to proper engine operation. Setting the valves means establishing a small clearance between the operating mechanism and the tip of the valve stem. This is done to prevent damage to the engine or poor performance due to improper valve action.

Just as with the ignition system, the valves are timed to operate in an exact relationship with piston movement. The small clearance set into the system is taken into account by the designer, so valve setting must be accurate.

The lock nut or screw must be loosened, usually with a ratchet and the correct-sized socket, to allow valve adjustment. However, some motorcycles have torsion bars to hold the valves closed, as on our sample bike, and the adjustment is not at the valve.

To set the valves properly, rotate the engine until the valve you are setting is fully closed. This means that no pressure is being applied to the

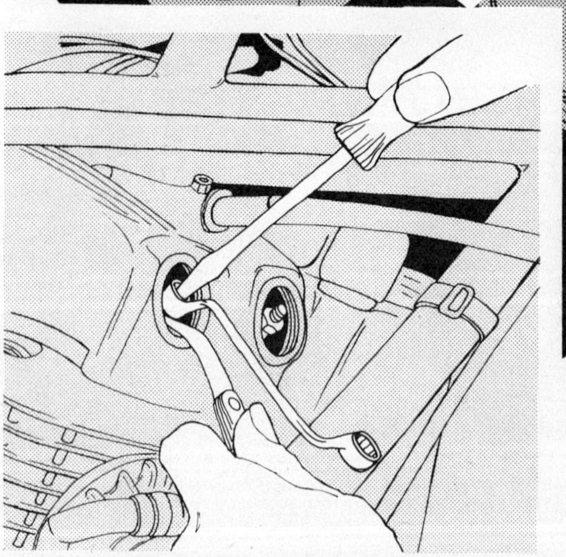

When adjusting valves, slide the feeler gauge between the stem of the valve and the tip of the rocker arm to set the required gap. This is much the same as setting ignition point gap.

The camshaft is a steel shaft with egg-shaped bumps on it to control the action of the valves. This illustration shows the overhead camshaft that is typical of most motorcycle engines. With the camshaft located near the valves on top of the cylinder head, there is less flex in the valve train and better timing of the valve action.

valves by the cam. Follow the procedure outlined in the owner's manual or shop manual, as this varies from bike to bike.

Once you have the engine set right, you can go ahead and loosen the hold-down nut. Then, using a feeler gauge, establish the proper clearance between the valve stem and the rocker arm or other actuating mechanism.

Just as in setting the ignition points, try to get just enough clearance so that the gauge blade barely fits between the valve stem and the rocker without binding, but also without being loose. This is often difficult to do the first time, so you may want to run through it more than once. After the valve is set to your satisfaction, tighten down the locking nut and set another valve.

NOTE: IF YOU POSITION THE ENGINE SO THAT IT IS ON THE COMPRESSION STROKE (FOR A GIVEN CYLINDER ON MULTICYLINDER BIKES), YOU CAN SET BOTH THE EXHAUST AND THE INTAKE VALVES FOR THAT CYLINDER AT THE SAME TIME. MAKE SURE YOU KNOW WHICH IS THE EXHAUST VALVE AND WHICH THE INTAKE VALVE BEFORE ADJUSTING THEM, HOWEVER, BECAUSE IT IS COMMON PRACTICE TO HAVE DIFFERENT CLEARANCES FOR INTAKE AND EXHAUST.

On multicylinder engines, each piston must be on its individual compression stroke and near or at TDC before setting the valves for that cylinder.

Another thing to remember about setting valves is that two settings are given in the shop manual—one for setting the valves when the engine is cold, the other for setting the valves when the engine is hot.

Cold and hot settings of the valve clearances differ because the metal parts expand (become larger) as the engine heats up. When the valves and other components become hot, they expand, which tightens the clearances. If you were to set the valves to the hot clearance while the engine was cold, the clearance would be reduced to nothing once the engine had warmed to operating temperature.

When you have finished the major steps of the tune-up on your motorcycle, it's time to go on to those things that are part of the normal maintenance, such as adjustment of the clutch and brakes and setting chain tension.

ADJUSTING CLUTCH, BRAKES AND CHAIN

After referring to the steps outlined in the shop manual, adjust the action of the clutch to take into account any wear on the clutch surfaces. Always set the clutch at the clutch end of the cable first, then adjust the cable to operate the correctly-set clutch. Setting the clutch is usually just a screwdriver adjustment; there's a lock nut on the bottom end and an adjusting wheel nut on the cable.

You'll develop a feel for proper operation of the clutch as you become more familiar with your motorcycle, and you'll be able to detect a slipping clutch instantly.

Setting the clutch starts with adjusting the clutch itself—at the engine casing. Most clutch adjustments are simple; they consist of bottoming out an adjusting screw or aligning it with the surface of the lock nut.

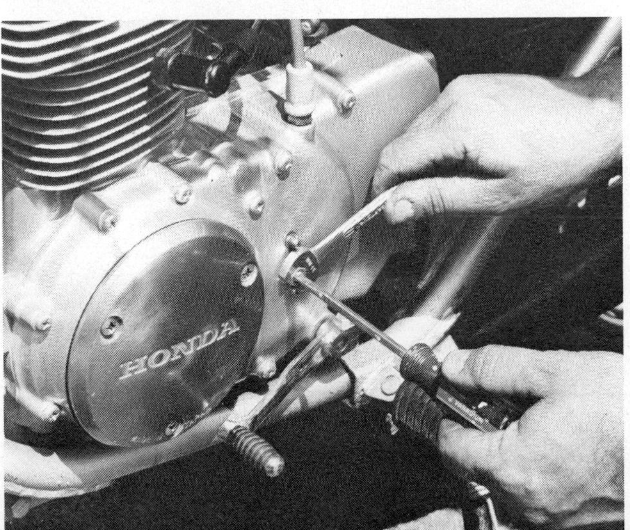

With the clutch set, the next step is to adjust the cable so that it also works properly.

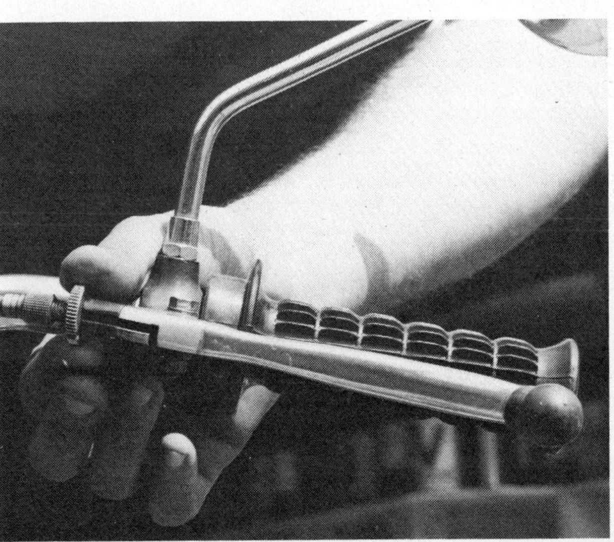

Setting the brake system is much the same as setting the clutch. The first step is to set the brake linkage at the wheel so that the brake works correctly. Then adjust the cable to provide a full range of braking action.

Adjusting the brakes on your motorcycle is much the same as the clutch. There is usually a linkage adjustment at the brake and a cable adjustment at the lever. You can deviate from the book a little here; brake action is partly a matter of individual judgment, especially for dirt riders. Many riders prefer not to have a strong front brake that might lock up in loose dirt and make them crash.

After you have set both front and rear brakes, ride the bike to check the action. For dirt riders, this means riding the bike on a dirt surface, not buzzing down the street. You can't tell much about how the bike will react to brake application in the dirt except in the dirt.

Adjust both the brake and clutch levers so that there is a certain amount of play in the lever movement. The owner's manual normally tells you the correct amount. This play is necessary to prevent preloading the brake or clutch. Again, dirt riders may want to adjust the front brake lever so that they do not get full front braking action.

Now set and clean the rear chain. The normal amount of slack in the chain is given in the owner's manual, generally about ½ to ¾ inch.

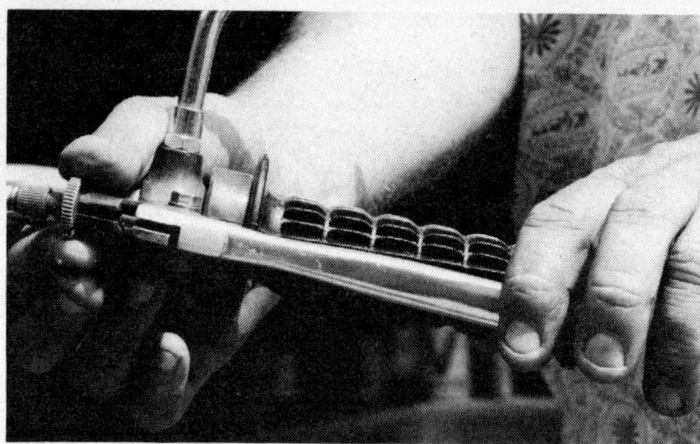

Setting the upper end of the brake cable on the front wheel can be done by the book, but many dirt riders prefer to leave the adjustment so that the front wheel brake doesn't fully apply. This is a protective measure for riding down hills in loose dirt, when too vigorous an application of the front brake can stand you on your head.

Check the drive chain and adjust it to compensate for wear. The book will tell you the proper amount of slack, which is usually ½ to 1 inch, measured at the bottom run of the chain.

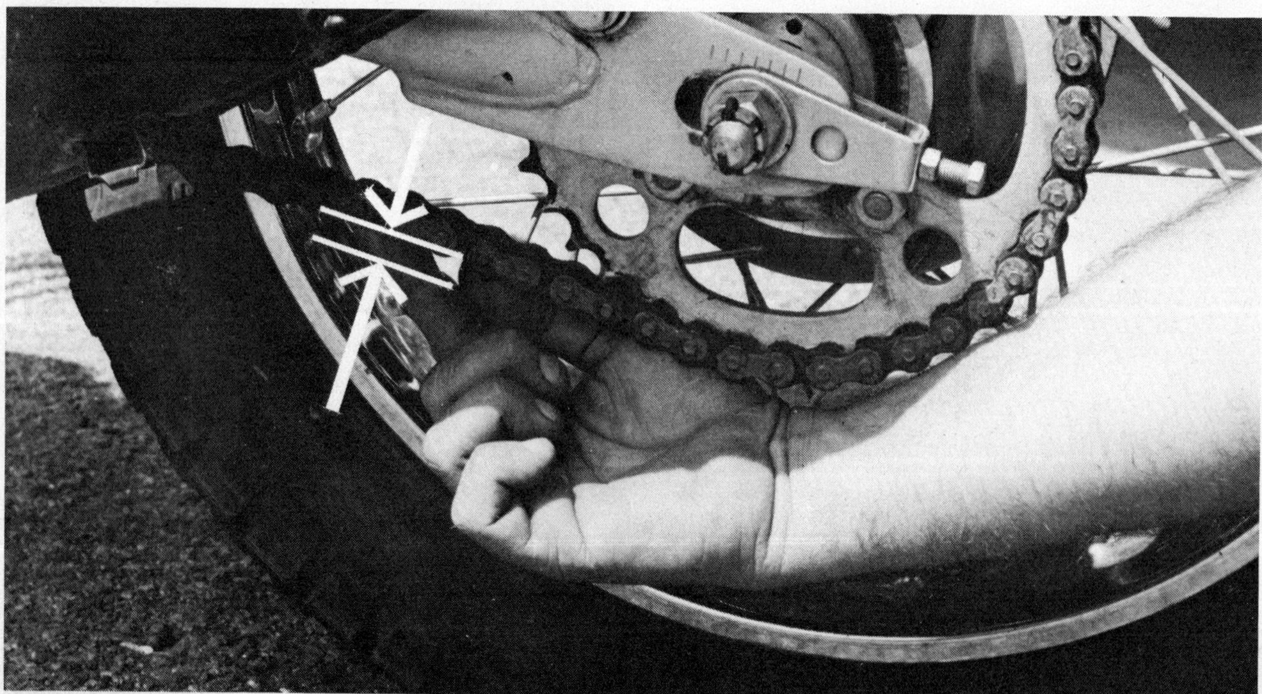

After adjusting the chain, lubricate it with a high-quality chain lubricant, making sure the lube penetrates all the links on the chain.

If you discover any rusty links or badly worn rollers, you might consider replacing the chain. It isn't nearly as expensive as letting the chain destroy the sprockets and then having to replace both chain and sprockets together.

After you have the bike tuned and running correctly, the final step is to put on your protective clothing and give the bike a good test ride. Dirt bikes should be ridden in the dirt, and street bikes should be given a good checkout on pavement. You may decide to alter certain adjustments after you have ridden the bike. This is the final stage of tuning. When everything is set to your satisfaction, you might as well spend the rest of the day riding. After all, that's what motorcycles are all about!

Hitting the chain with a good quality lube at regular intervals is a good preventive measure. Let the lube soak in well.

The final step, test riding, should be approached just like any other ride. Wear the proper safety clothing and conduct the testing in a safe riding area.

Kawasaki 900 Z1

KAWASAKI'S CONTRIBUTION TO MULTICYLINDER FOUR-STROKES STANDS ALONE AS A BRUTE WITH BEAUTY.

The 900 Z1 has two sets of ignition points. One set handles cylinders Nos. 1 and 4, the other fires cylinders Nos. 2 and 3 at 180° of crankshaft rotation later. To set the gap manually, rotate the crankshaft until the breaker points you are adjusting are at their widest gap. The measurement should be **.012 to .016 inch (0.3-0.4mm).** If not, loosen the screws and reset the points with a feeler gauge.

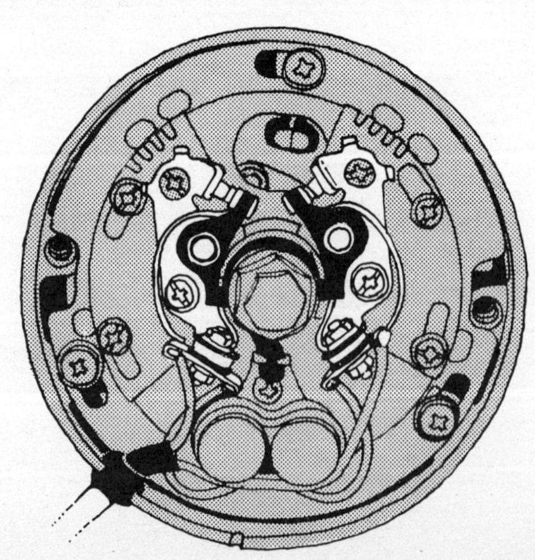

Another method of setting points is by dwell meter adjustment. With the dwell meter hooked across the points being adjusted at engine idle speed (800 to 1000 rpm), the meter should read 23 on the eight-cylinder scale, 46 on the four-cylinder scale.

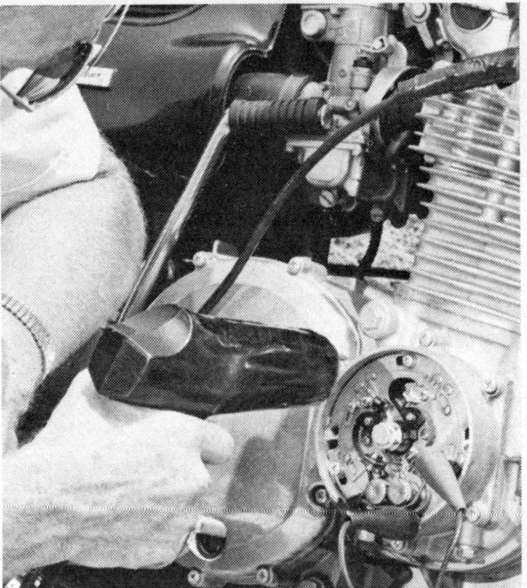

To set points with a timing light, align the timing mark on the housing with the "F" mark on the advancer when the engine is at idle speed. With engine speed at 2900 to 3100 rpm, the timing mark should now line up with the pin on the timing advancer. This indicates that ignition advance is taking place correctly.

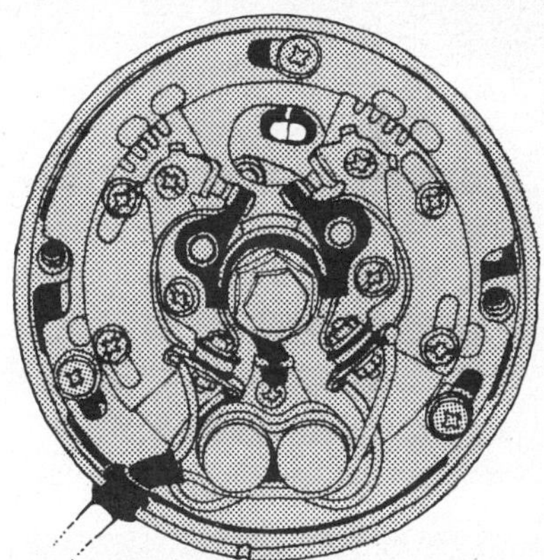

A single thumbscrew on the right side of the carburetor linkage sets the idle speed on this multicylinder engine. After starting the engine and allowing it to reach operating temperature, set the idle speed at 800 to 1000 rpm.

CAUTION: IF IDLE SPEED MUST BE SET HIGHER THAN 1000 RPM BY A SMALL AMOUNT TO OBTAIN SMOOTH RUNNING, CHECK THE PLUGS, POINTS AND TIMING.

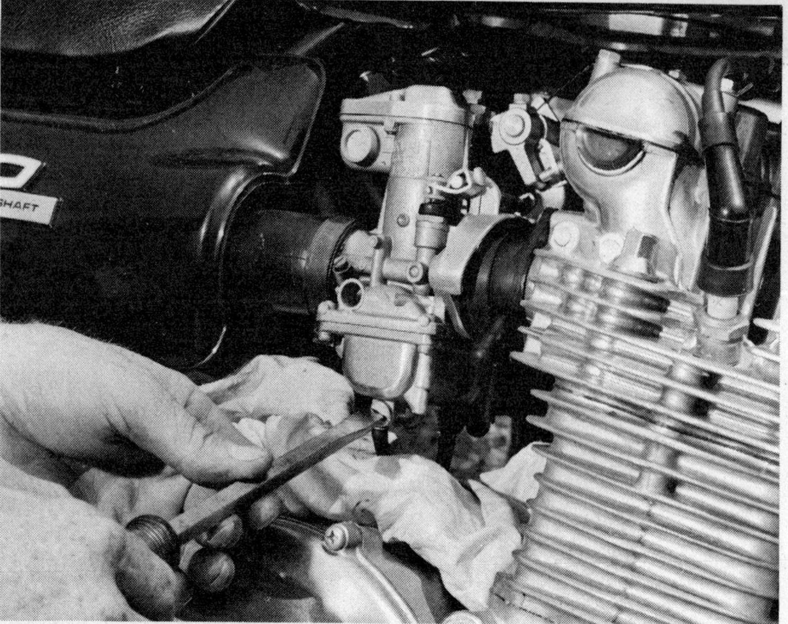

Separate carburetor adjustment on the 900 Z1 is not covered in the owner's manual. If this must be done, use factory vacuum gauges and tools and follow the shop manual procedure exactly. Having said that, we can give you a look at the process. The first step is removing the drain plug from the bottom of the float bowl on the carburetor.

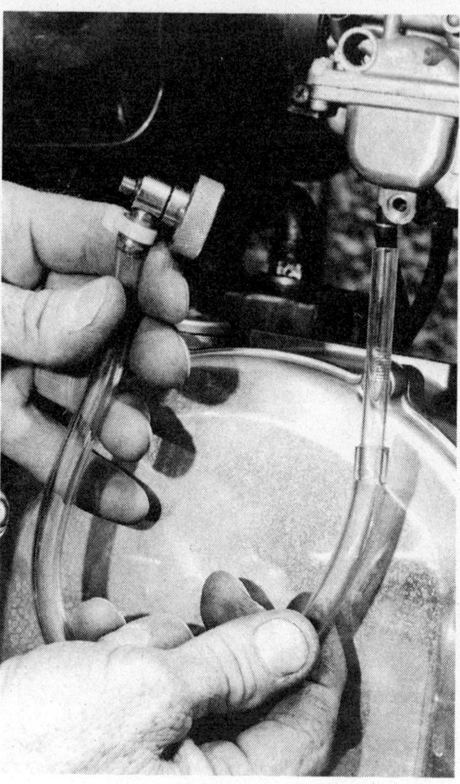

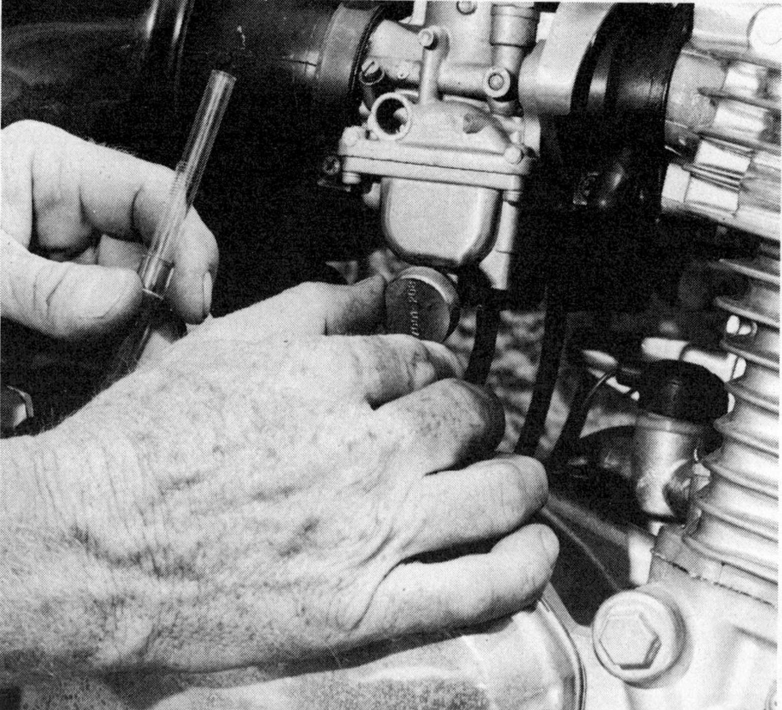

This fuel level gauge, Kawasaki part #57001-208, measures the level of the fuel in the float bowl as a guide to setting the float level.

Attach the gauge to the float bowl by screwing the adapter into the drain hole. Then turn the fuel shutoff to the ON position and let the bowl refill to measure the level.

If it is set correctly, the fuel level should be from **2.5 to 4.5mm** from the top edge of the float bowl. If everything checks, shut off the fuel again, remove the gauge and reinstall the drain plug. If not, refer to the shop manual for complete adjusting instructions.

NOTE: BECAUSE OF THE NEED FOR SPECIAL TOOLS, WE DO NOT RECOMMEND THAT THE AVERAGE HOME TUNER ATTEMPT THIS STEP AND THE NEXT, CARBURETOR SYNCHRONIZATION.

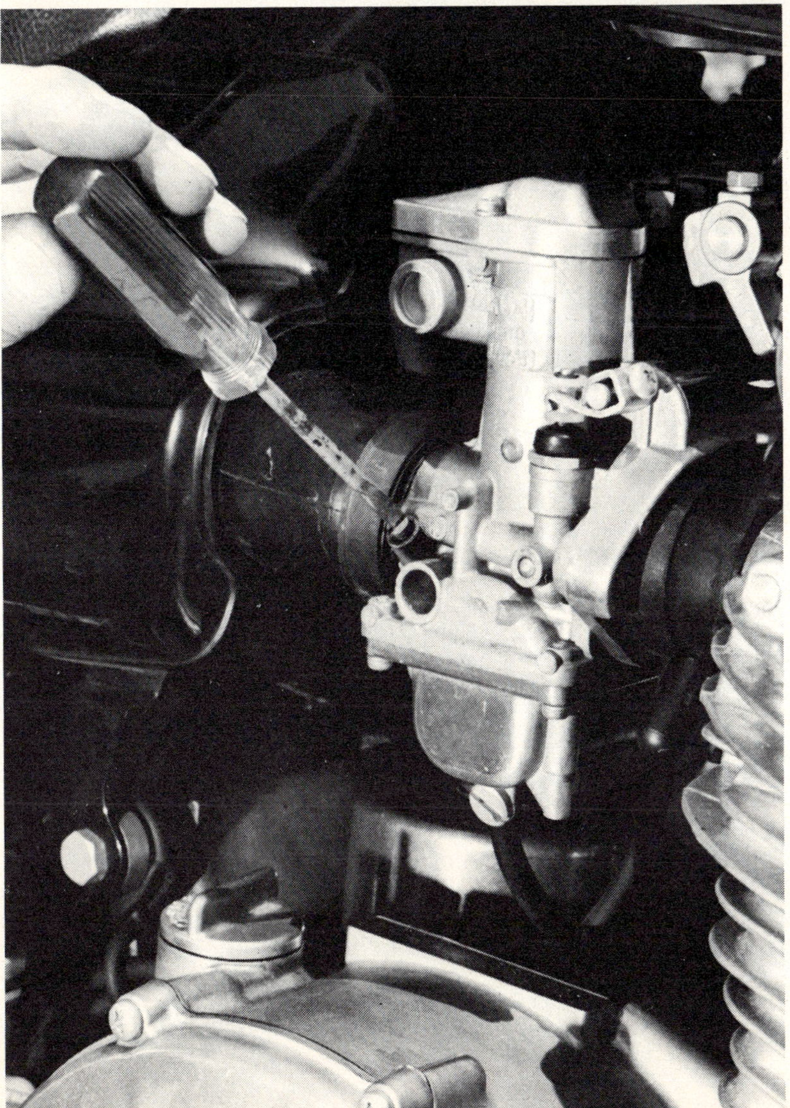

Synchronizing the four carburetors on the 900 Z1 requires two special Kawasaki tools. One is this adjusting tool (Kawasaki part #57001-120). The other is a vacuum gauge (Kawasaki part #T56019-031), shown in the next picture. The gauge, called Carb-Stix, measures individual intake vacuum through hoses connected to the intake runner tubes between the carburetors and the engine.

NOTE: WE DID NOT DO A VALVE ADJUSTMENT ON THE KAWASAKI 900 Z1. KAWASAKI DOES NOT RECOMMEND THAT THE HOME TUNER ATTEMPT THIS, AS IT REQUIRES SPECIAL TOOLS AND A MORE THAN ADEQUATE KNOWLEDGE OF TUNING PROCEDURES. TAKE THE BIKE TO THE DEALER FOR VALVE ADJUSTMENTS.

With the Carb-Stix gauge installed and the special tool inserted in the top of the carburetor being adjusted, start the engine. Adjust each carburetor in turn until the correct airflow balance between carburetors has been achieved.

Individual adjustment of the idle on the carburetors is also possible. Once you have all the carbs synchronized, you can go back and set the single idle speed thumbscrew on the linkage.

Yamaha XS 650B

THIS OVERHEAD-CAM TWIN IS A SUPERB ROAD BIKE, BUT NOT A GOOD TUNE-UP PROJECT FOR THE BEGINNER.

Before you can make the ignition timing adjustments on this single overhead cam engine, the tension of the cam chain must be adjusted to remove all slack. To do this, remove the cover over the adjuster, then rotate the engine in a counterclockwise direction (as viewed from the left side of the engine) to take chain slack to the tensioner. Loosen the tensioner lock nut. Then adjust the tensioner with a 22mm wrench until the tip of the pushrod inside the adjuster is flush with the end of the adjuster. Retighten the lock nut and install the cover.

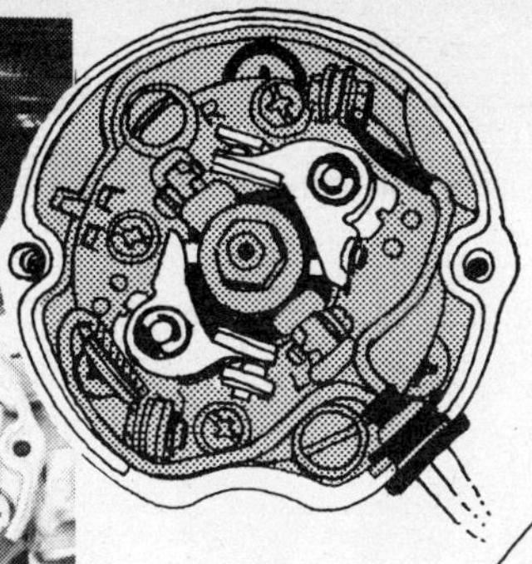

Before setting the timing, check and set the point gap. Rotate the engine until the set of points you are adjusting is fully open. Set them to **.012-.016 inch (0.3-0.4mm).**

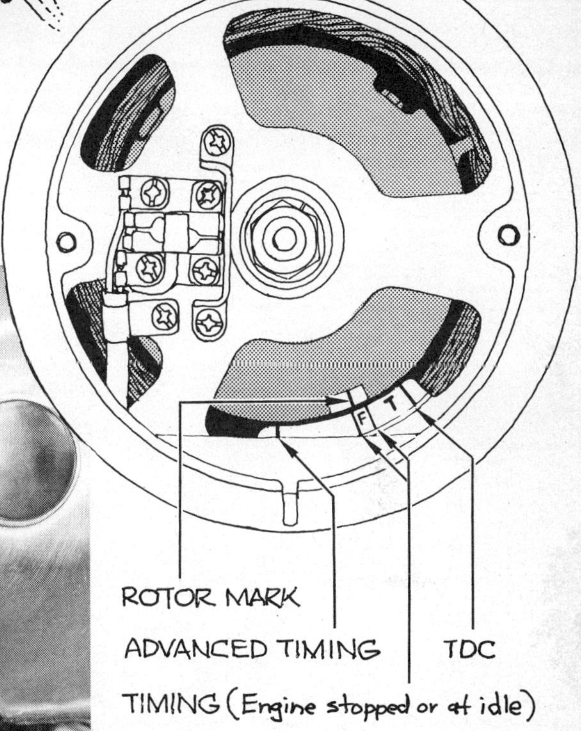

ROTOR MARK

ADVANCED TIMING

TDC

TIMING (Engine stopped or at idle)

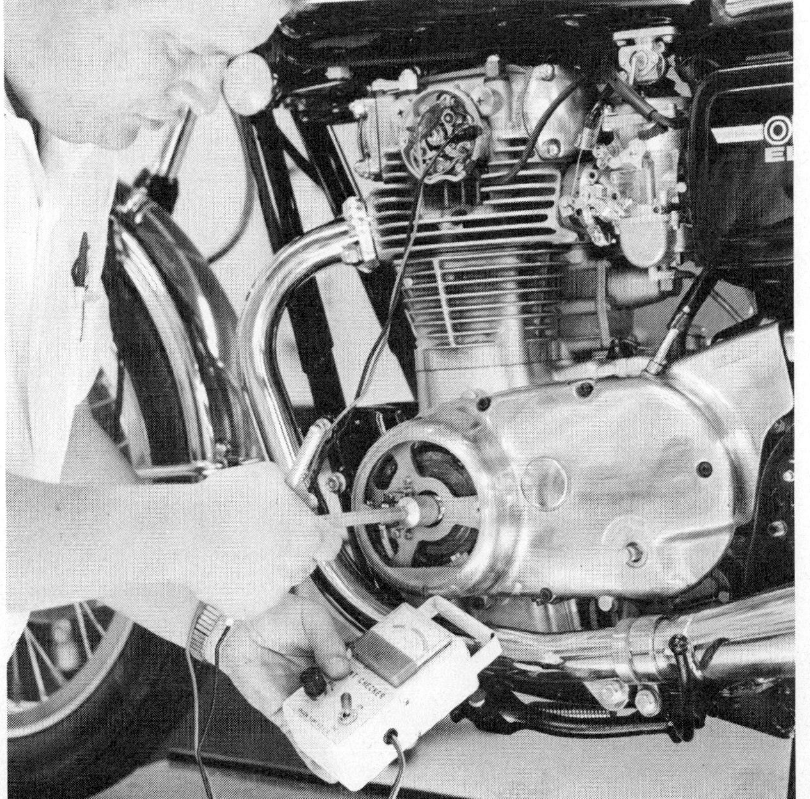

There is a single timing mark on the rotor. Align it with one of four marks, depending on which of four different steps in timing ignition and valves you are working on. The mark to the right of the letter "T" indicates TDC. The marks on either side of the letter "F" are ignition timing at idle or with engine stopped. The last mark at the far left is for fully advanced timing.

Connect a point checker to the points for the right cylinder (marked with a letter "R"). Rotate the engine in a counterclockwise direction (as viewed from the left side) until the ignition points just open. The timing mark on the rotor should line up, exactly centered, between the two "F" marks.

NOTE: BECAUSE OF THE WAY THE IGNITION POINTS PLATE IS CONSTRUCTED, THE RIGHT-HAND CYLINDER POINTS MUST ALWAYS BE ADJUSTED FIRST.

If an adjustment of the timing is necessary, turn the shaft until the timing marks are aligned between the two "F" marks. Then loosen the two base plate lock screws and turn the *entire* base plate until the right cylinder points just begin to open, as shown on the point checker. Retighten the base plate lock screws and recheck by rotating the engine through several revolutions and back to right-hand cylinder timing mark alignment. Then attach the point checker to the left cylinder ignition points and check them in the same manner. If they do not begin to open with the timing mark aligned between the "F" marks, loosen the locking screws for the *left* ignition points only and adjust them. Then retighten and recheck.

A timing light enables you to check the timing in a dynamic manner, including action of the advance circuit. At idle, the strobe action of the timing light should "freeze" the timing mark at the two "F" marks. Once engine rpm are high enough to allow the advance weights to fully extend, the timing mark should align with the mark at the far left.

To adjust the valves, turn the engine until the timing mark is lined up with the "T" mark on the housing, One of the cylinders' pistons is now at TDC. The cylinder with both valves closed is the one to work on. It will have clearance between valve stems and adjusters.

You'll need a special wrench for adjusting the valves (available at the dealer if it isn't in the tool kit on the bike). To adjust, break the lock nut loose with a wrench and check the gap between the tip of the valve stem and the actuator with a feeler gauge. The correct clearance is **.002 inch (0.05mm)** for the intake valves and **.004 inch (0.10mm)** for the exhaust. After you have the proper clearance set, carefully tighten the lock nut while holding the adjuster with the special wrench. Then rotate the engine through one cycle of operation and recheck.

NOTE: THE LISTED VALVE CLEARANCES ARE THE "COLD" CLEARANCES, TO BE SET WHEN THE ENGINE IS COLD. SETTING TO THESE CLEARANCES WITH THE ENGINE HOT WILL RESULT IN WRONGLY SET VALVES AND POSSIBLY ENGINE DAMAGE.

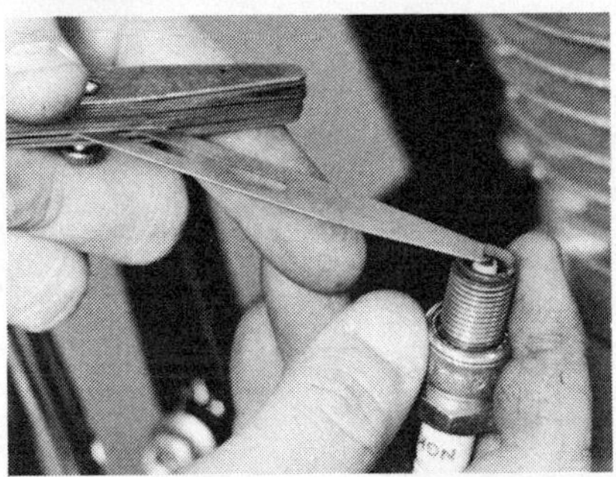

Examine and replace or clean spark plugs as necessary. The correct gap for the plugs is **.020 to .024 inch (0.5-0.6mm).** After gapping, reinstall the plugs with a fresh plug gasket and torque to **230-250 inch/lbs.**

To set the idle on the carburetors, lower engine rpm by turning the throttle stop screw clockwise until the engine is running at its lowest possible speed. Then turn the idle air screw to the left or right until the engine speeds up. Repeat the procedure several times, until little or no gain is seen. Then readjust idle speed to the correct rpm.

Honda XL 350 XL 250

DOING TUNE-UP WORK ON THE 350 SINGLE GIVES YOU THE INSIDE LINE ON HOW TO DO THE SMALLER HONDA XL 250 FOUR-STROKE SINGLE TOO.

The first step in tuning the XL 350 is to get some of the parts out of the way. Lift the seat and take off the gas tank to gain enough room to adjust the valves. Don't forget to shut off the fuel valve on the tank before disconnecting the line to the carburetor.

Next, remove the cover over the ignition. Be sure to position a catch basin of some sort under the bike, as Hondas drain some oil with this cover off. Then remove the small covers on the cylinder head that give access to the valves.

Crank the engine over by putting a wrench on the nut in the center of the generator rotor. Slowly rotate the rotor counterclockwise while watching the intake valve. When the valve goes down all the way and starts to come back up, slow down. You're getting close to piston Top Dead Center (TDC). To get TDC exactly, align the index pointer inside the lip of the generator opening with the "T" mark on the rotor. At this point you can adjust the valves.

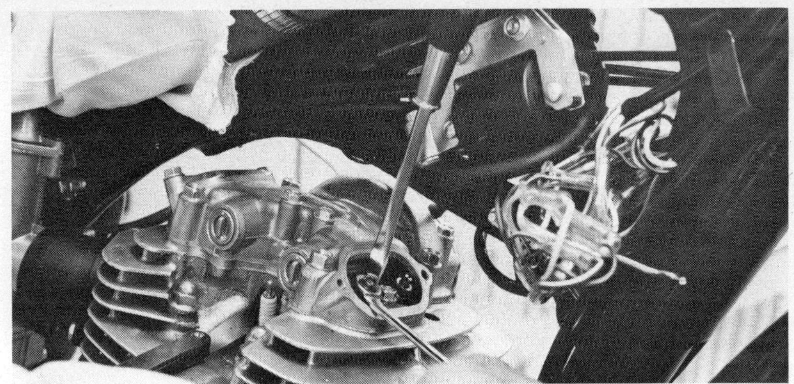

Check the clearance of both sets of valves (there are two intake valves and two exhaust) by inserting a feeler gauge between the valve stem and the tappet adjusting screw. The proper clearances are: **.002 inch (.05mm)** for intakes and **.003 inch (.08mm)** for exhaust. To adjust a valve, loosen the lock nuts and turn the tappet adjusting screws in or out as needed. When tightening the lock nuts, be sure that the adjustment is not disturbed.

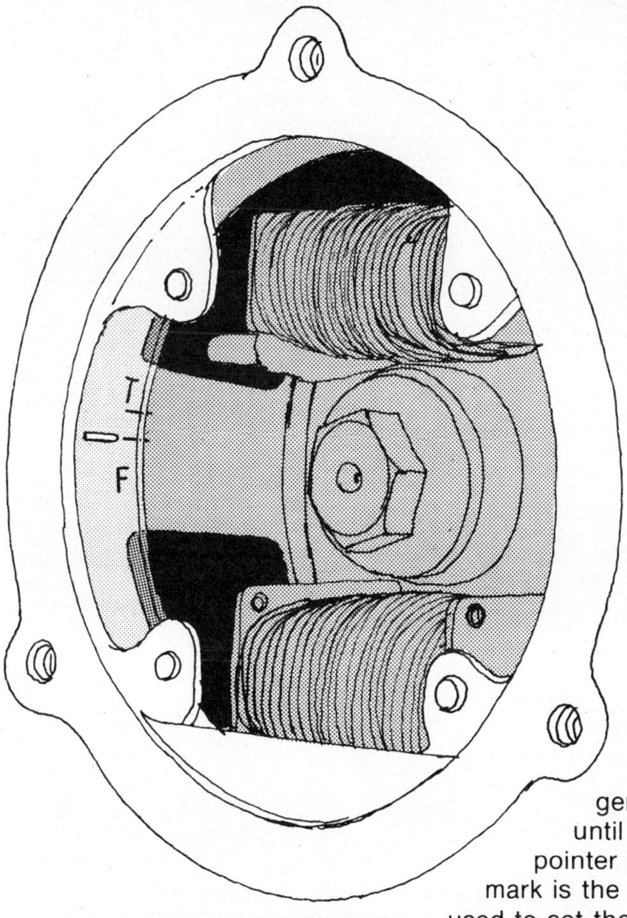

To set ignition point gap, remove the cover over the points. Rotate the engine by turning it with the generator rotor until the points are at their widest opening. After checking them for wear or arcing, set the gap with a feeler gauge to **.012-.016 inch (0.3-0.4mm).** Adjust by loosening the locking screws on the breaker plate and moving the point plate until the correct gap is reached.

Set ignition timing by rotating the generator rotor counterclockwise until the timing mark aligns with the pointer on the case lip. This timing mark is the one just below the mark used to set the engine to TDC.

To check the point opening time, use a point checker (buzz box) connected across the points as you turn the rotor to the proper alignment. At the exact moment the timing mark lines up with the pointer, the checker should indicate point opening. If this happens, the timing is correct. If not, align the marks, then loosen the two base plate screws and move the base plate until you see an indication of point opening. Turning the plate clockwise advances the timing; turning it counterclockwise retards timing. After you have set the timing and retightened the base plate screws, run through the process one more time for confirmation.

Honda CB 360T

TUNING HONDA'S LATEST VERSION OF THE FAITHFUL MEDIUM TWIN IS AS EASY AS FALLING OFF A LOG.

Start by removing the breaker point cover and then turning the engine over until one of the two sets of ignition points opens to its widest setting. Use a feeler gauge and a screwdriver to adjust. The point gap should be **.012-.016 inch (0.3-0.4mm).** To set, loosen the locking screws on the breaker plate, then move the breaker plate to obtain the correct gap. When you have one pair of points set, turn the engine counterclockwise until the other set of points is open to its widest gap, then check and set as necessary.

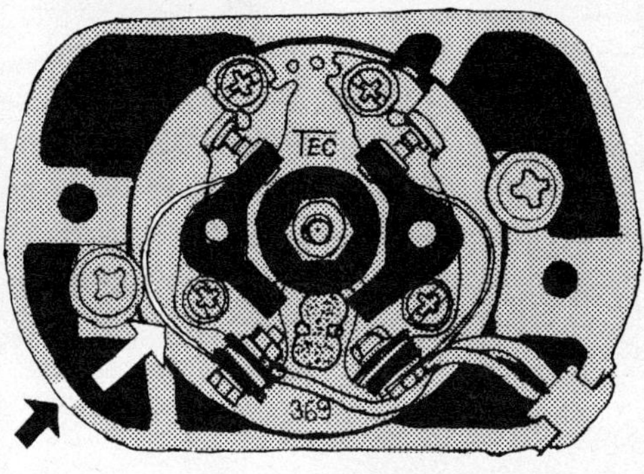

To aid in setting the static timing, connect a buzz box or point checker across the set of points for the cylinder you are checking. The checker will give you an accurate indication of point opening. Some checkers light up to indicate point opening; others make a noise.

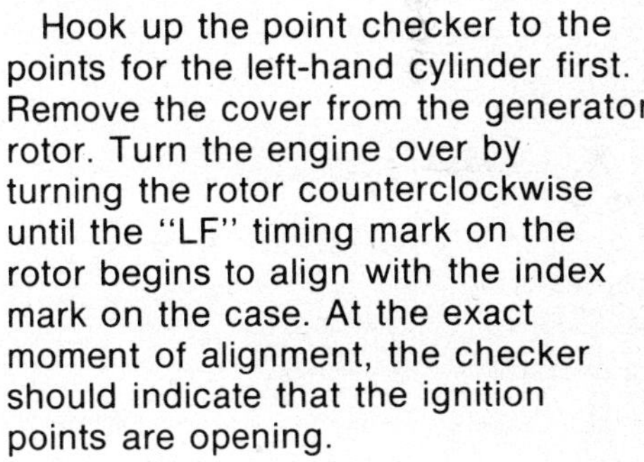

Hook up the point checker to the points for the left-hand cylinder first. Remove the cover from the generator rotor. Turn the engine over by turning the rotor counterclockwise until the "LF" timing mark on the rotor begins to align with the index mark on the case. At the exact moment of alignment, the checker should indicate that the ignition points are opening.

If the ignition timing is not correct, loosen the base plate locking screws and turn the base plate until you get an indication of point opening. Retighten the screws and recheck the timing for that cylinder.

To set the timing for the right-hand cylinder points, reconnect the point checker to the set of ignition points for the right-hand cylinder. Then turn the engine counterclockwise until the "F" mark (for the right cylinder) aligns with the index mark. At the exact moment of alignment, the checker should tell you that the points are opening.

If not, then align the "F" mark with the index mark and loosen the right breaker point locking screws to adjust the right breaker plate until the points open exactly on the mark. Once you have the setting made, retighten the screws and recheck the point gap and the timing for that cylinder. It is important that the ignition point gap remain within its specified limits *after* the timing is set.

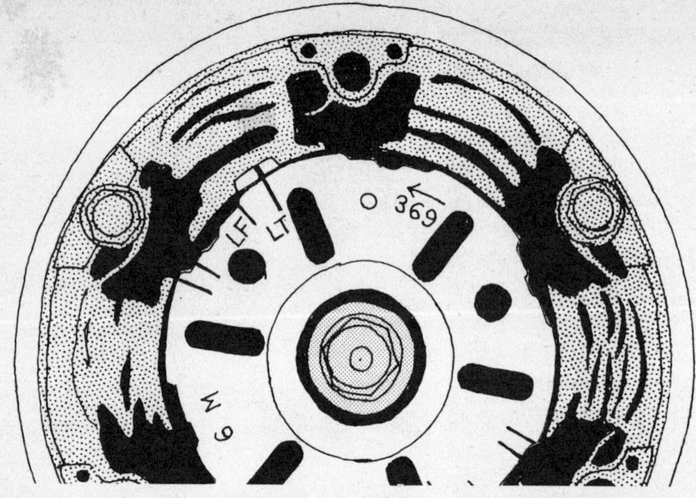

To adjust the valves on the CB 360 T, first take off the valve covers. Then turn the generator rotor in a counterclockwise direction until the left cylinder intake valve tappet starts to go down. When the intake valve tappet starts to lift again, bring the "LT" mark into line with the index mark. The left cylinder piston is now at TDC (Top Dead Center), and both intake and exhaust valves for that cylinder are fully closed.

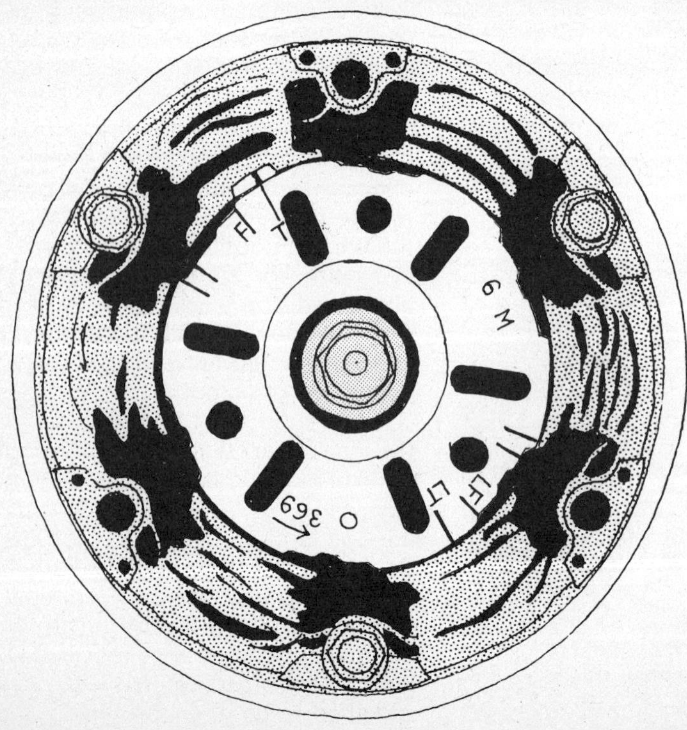

Set the valve clearance by inserting a feeler gauge between the tip of the valve stem and the tappet adjusting screw. The correct clearance (cold) is **.002 inch (.05mm)** for the intake valve and **.003 inch (.08mm)** for the exhaust valve. To adjust clearance, loosen the lock nut and turn the adjusting screw until you can detect a slight drag on the feeler gauge when it is withdrawn from the gap. Retighten the lock nut.

Adjust the valves for the right-hand cylinder in exactly the same manner, with one exception: The index mark on the case must line up with the "T" mark opposite the "LT" mark, so that the valves for the right cylinder will both be closed completely.

About the only worthwhile external carburetor adjustments possible without expensive test equipment are the pilot air adjust and the idle speed.

To adjust the idle speed, turn the large screw just under the pilot air screw (the one being adjusted in the photo) until the tach shows 1200 rpm. Never set idle speed until after the engine has reached operating temperature. Then adjust the pilot air screws on each carburetor until they are at the point of highest rpm. You may have to go back and forth, making this adjustment several times, before the carburetors are equalized and you get everything right.

Critical adjustment of the carburetors on the Honda requires a specialized vacuum gauge of the type shown here. This is a bit expensive for the average home tuner. Take the bike to the dealer for this kind of work.

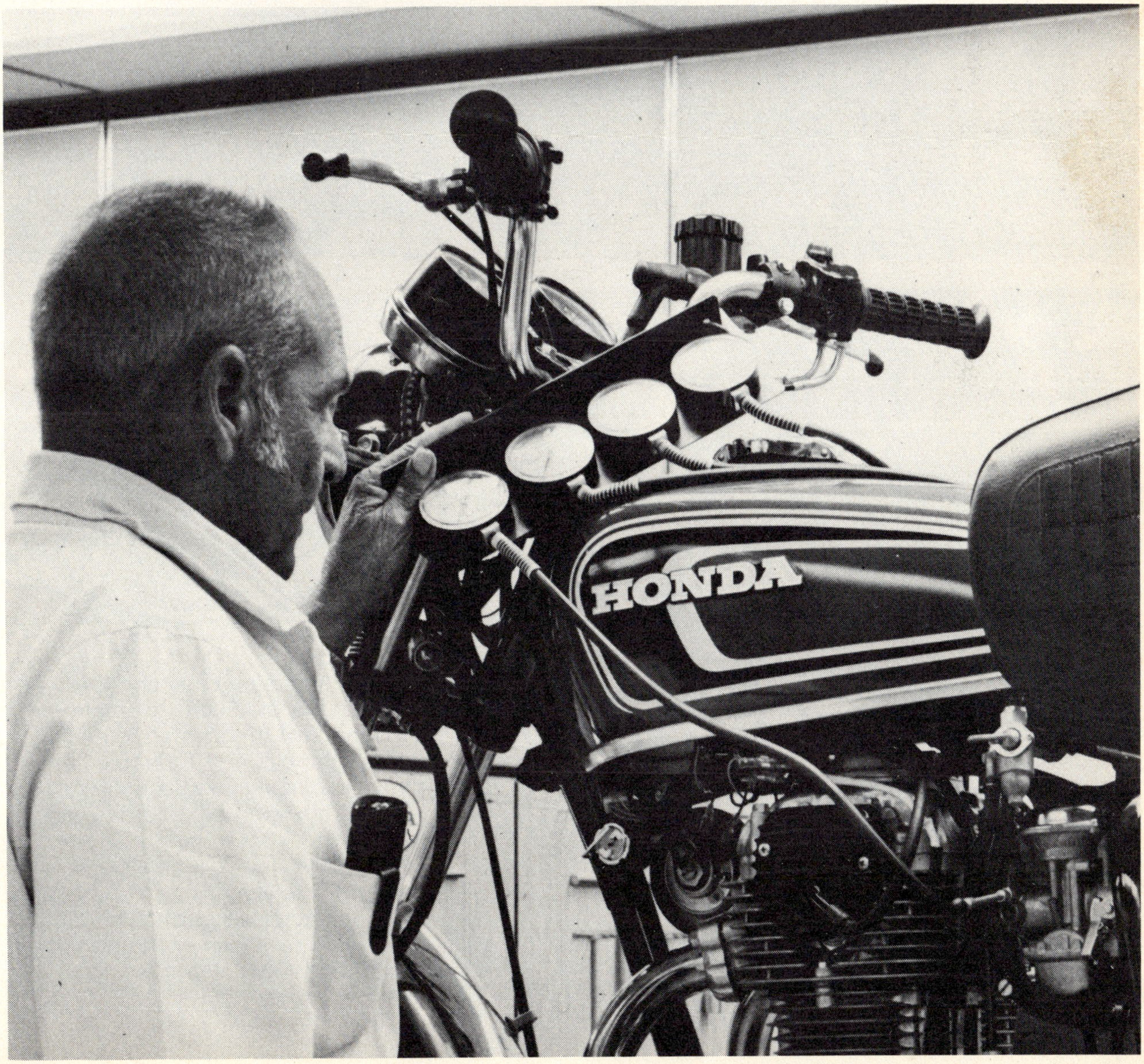

Honda CB 500T

FOLLOWING IN THE FOOTSTEPS OF THE FAMOUS AND RELIABLE HONDA 450, THE CB 500 T IS RUGGED AND EASILY TUNED.

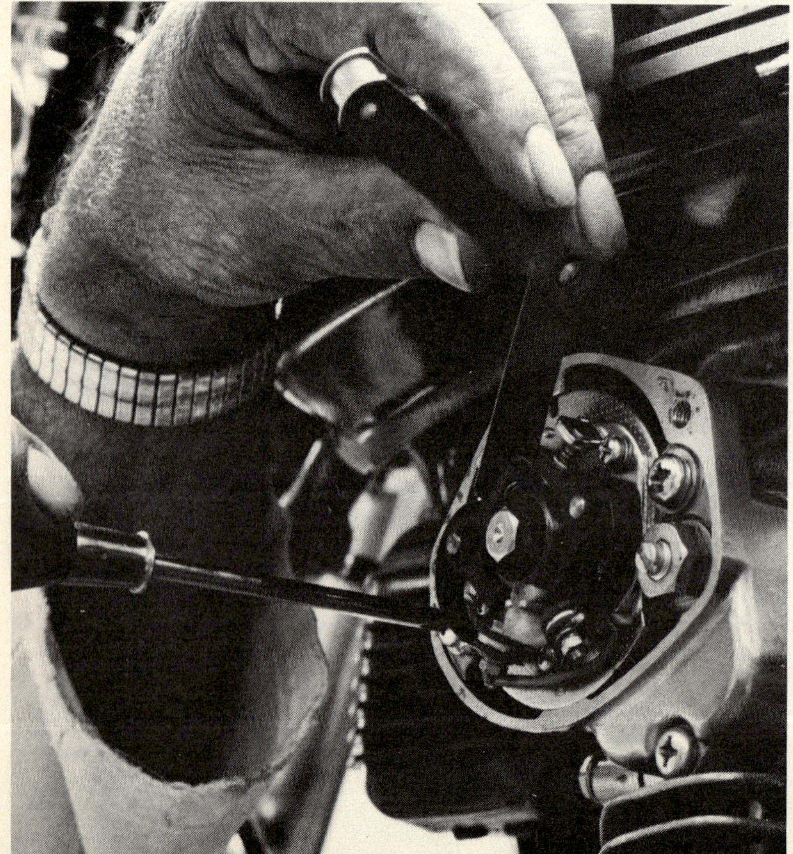

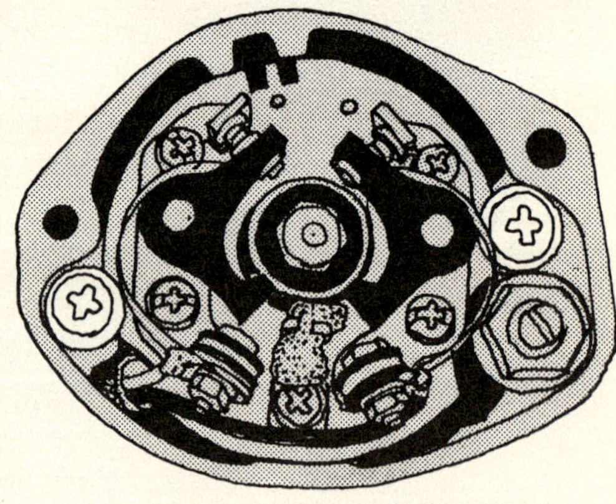

The first step in setting the ignition on the 500 is to rotate the engine until the points are at maximum gap. Turn the generator rotor counterclockwise until the points are open as wide as possible. Then check for a gap of **.012 to .016 inch (0.3-0.4mm).** If change is required, loosen the screws holding the contact breaker plate and move the plate carefully until the point gap is correct. Retighten the screws and then recheck. Adjust both left- and right-hand points in the same manner.

With a point checker or meter connected across the set of ignition points being timed, turn the rotor counterclockwise until the "F" mark aligns with the timing mark. Starting with the left-hand side set of points (for the left cylinder), turn the rotor to the position shown in the picture.

If ignition timing for that cylinder is correct, the point checker will give an indication of ignition point opening at exactly the moment the left "F" mark aligns with the timing mark. If not, align the marks and then adjust the ignition timing by loosening the base plate locking screws and turning the base plate (as you did to set the points) until you get an indication of point opening. Tighten the screws and recheck.

To set timing for the right-hand cylinder, repeat the same procedure as for the left cylinder, with one difference: Rotate the rotor counterclockwise another 180° to bring the right-hand "F" mark into alignment with the timing mark. If the right-hand ignition points open at the exact moment the marks align, no further adjustment is needed. If the timing is off at all, adjust by loosening the screws for the right-hand plate and adjusting within the limits already set for point gap to bring the timing into alignment. Retighten the screws and recheck.

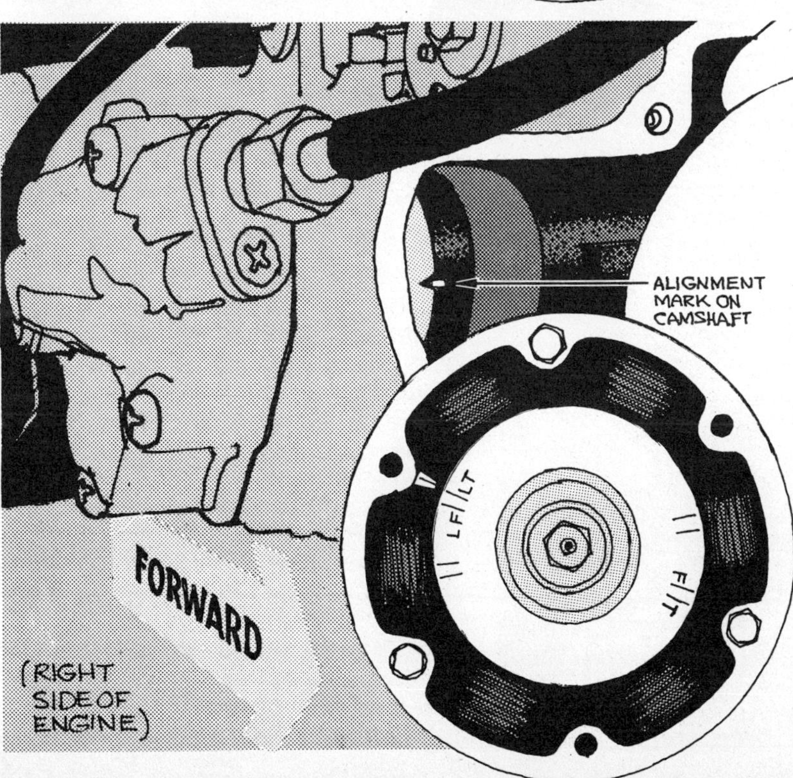

Adjusting the valves on the CB 500 T requires removal of the fuel tank for best access to the valve train mechanism, but for illustration purposes we did not do this. To adjust the intake and exhaust valves for each cylinder, turn the generator rotor until the "T" mark aligns with the timing mark. The rotor must be turned counterclockwise. With the left-hand "T" mark aligned with the timing mark, check the alignment marks on the camshafts to see if they line up with the marks on the cam stands. If they do, the engine is at TDC on the *intake* stroke instead of the *compression* stroke, and the rotor must be moved through one full revolution to put the piston at TDC on the compression stroke.

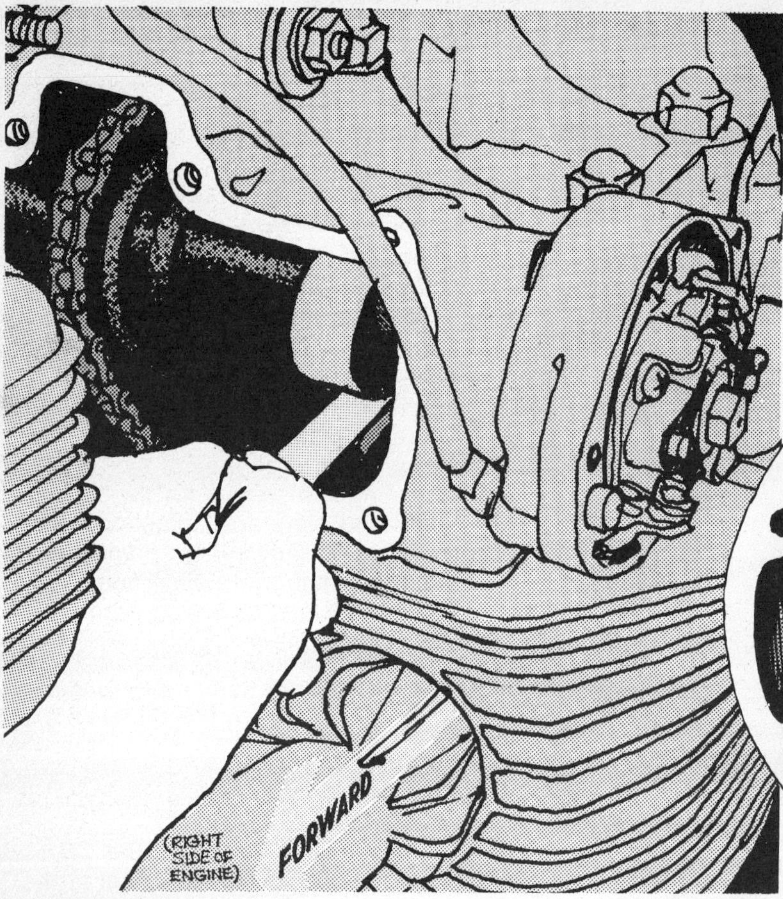

When the piston is at TDC on the compression stroke, adjust valve clearance by loosening the lock nuts and turning the adjusters (arrow) with a screwdriver. Insert a feeler gauge between the cam and the cam follower. The correct clearance on a cold engine is **.0012 inch (.03mm)** for both intake and exhaust valves.

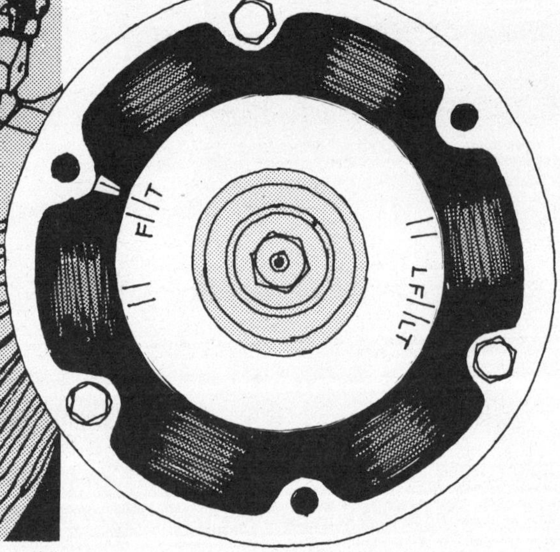

To set the valves on the right-hand cylinder, set the rotor so that the right-hand cylinder "T" mark lines up with the timing mark (the same method as determining compression stroke). Then adjust the valves to the required clearance, as shown in the artwork.

You can set the idle speed and perform a basic idle mixture check as outlined in the owner's manual, but work on the carburetors requires special shop tools such as this vacuum gauge. We recommend that you take your CB 500 T to a dealer for carburetor adjustment.

Honda CB 750

TUNING THE BIG FOUR REQUIRES SOME SKILL AND ALSO SOME SPECIAL TOOLS.

The first step in setting the point gap and timing on Honda's big four is to check the condition of the two sets of points. Gently open them with a screwdriver and look for pitting or wear. If they are good, you can go straight to the gap setting. If bad, then replace the points and the condensers also.

Rotate the crankshaft in a clockwise direction until the points are opened to their maximum width and check with a feeler gauge. Correct gap is **.012-.016 inch (0.3-0.4mm).** If any adjustment is necessary, loosen the single locking screw for the set of points you are adjusting and move the breaker plate until you have the correct gap. Tighten the locking screw and recheck. Repeat with the other set of points until both are within the tolerances specified.

After the point gap is set on both sets of points, position the engine to reflect proper timing for adjustment. Turn the crankshaft clockwise until the "F" timing mark is aligned with the pointer. Hook up a point checker to the Nos. 1 and 4 cylinder points on the left.

If the timing is good, the point checker should indicate point opening just as you reach the "F" mark. If not, align the "F" mark with the pointer and loosen the three base plate locking screws. Turn the base plate very carefully until the point checker just indicates point opening, then lock down the three base plate locking screws and recheck.

This is what it looks like when the "F" mark is correctly aligned with the pointer. After adjusting Nos. 1 and 4 cylinder breaker points, connect the point checker to the Nos. 2 and 3 cylinder points, which are the ones on the right. Then rotate the crankshaft 180° (one half turn) until the Nos. 2 and 3 cylinder points "F" mark lines up with the pointer. As you reach the "F" mark, the point checker should again indicate point opening.

If any adjustment is needed, align the "F" mark with the pointer and loosen the two screws on the right base plate. Adjust the right base plate section until you get an indication of point opening and tighten the screws. Recheck both timing sequences. A final check can be made with a timing light, but with reasonable care, this timing method is sufficient.

NOTE: THE TWO SCREWS ON THE RIGHT BASE PLATE ARE NOT THE SAME AS THE THREE MAIN BASE PLATE LOCKING SCREWS. THESE TWO SCREWS ALLOW ONLY THE RIGHT-HAND PLATE TO BE MOVED.

Setting the clearances on the valves involves aligning the "T" mark (indicating piston Top Dead Center) with the pointer several times, as shown in this picture. You'll need a feeler gauge and a screwdriver and wrench of the correct size to perform the adjustment. First, remove all the

small caps from the valve tappets. You may also want to remove the fuel tank to provide enough clearance to do this job.

Slowly rotate the crankshaft clockwise until the No. 1 cylinder intake valve goes down all the way and then comes back up. As it comes up, watch for the "T" mark that will appear in the window. Align the "T" mark with the pointer. The engine is now at piston TDC on the No. 1 cylinder.

Individual valve adjustment is not hard, but working space is cramped. Use a feeler gauge to determine the valve clearances. Intakes should be **.0019 inch** or **.05mm,** exhausts should be **.0031 inch** or **.08mm.** Loosen the lock nut and adjust the valve tappet screw until the blade of the feeler gauge passes between the adjuster and the stem with just a slight resistance. Do both the intake and exhaust valves for the No. 1 cylinder.

The next step is to reposition the engine, bringing another cylinder's piston to TDC so that its valves can be adjusted. The next cylinder in sequence is No. 4. Rotate the crankshaft one full turn (360°) and again align the "T" mark while watching the intake valve of the No. 4 cylinder, just as you did with the No. 1 cylinder. Repeat the adjustment.

To adjust cylinders Nos. 2 and 3, the procedure is exactly the same, but the "T" mark showing must be the one for cylinders Nos. 2 and 3.

Adjustments to an engine with four carburetors require special tools, such as this vacuum gauge, which is used to synchronize the carburetors' airflow. This tool hooks up to the carburetors by means of hoses, which attach to individual connection plugs on each of the four carburetors. With the engine idling at the proper idle speed (850-950 rpm), the vacuum reading should be **20 to 22 cmHG** (centimeters of mercury). If any carburetors read higher or lower, bring them into balance by adjusting the throttle stop screw.

The vacuum gauge tool set is listed in the shop manual as Honda part #07504-3000100. We recommend that you have the shop manual on hand before doing extensive work on the carburetors.

V/ Your First Two-stroke Tune-up

Two-stroke motorcycles, simple and rugged as they are (having far fewer moving parts than a four-stroke), still need regular preventive maintenance. Though two-stroke engines are simple, they are quite sensitive to small changes in the effectiveness of such parts as spark plugs and carburetors. A regular program of tuning will keep a two-stroke engine in top operating condition and give you much better service.

Gathering together all the necessary parts, tools, and technical manuals is the first step toward a successful tune-up.

PREPARING TO START

The first step is to position the bike in a good work area and gather together the tools and parts you'll need. In good weather a driveway is fine, but if you elect to do the tune-up indoors, make sure that lighting and ventilation are adequate for the job. Poor lighting can lead to mistakes, and bad ventilation can be dangerous. Some of the solvents and cleaners used in a normal tune-up are toxic (poisonous). What's more, during the tune-up you may need to run the engine, and exhaust fumes in a confined space can be quite deadly.

One of the best tools to have on hand for any tune-up is a shop manual or other reference book which gives instructions and specifications for your motorcycle. Tuning by guess does *not* result in a motorcycle that runs well and can cost you plenty of money in repair bills.

At the very least, have handy the owner's manual that came with your bike before you start tearing into complicated equipment.

With this in mind, it's logical that the second step in tuning any motorcycle is to read through a description of the tune-up processes you'll be following before you pick up a single tool. It's best to familiarize yourself with the basic steps before you get started. If you're a beginning tuner, you may find that it helps to move through the procedure step by step as you read, looking at or touching each tool and motorcycle part as it is presented in the book.

Remember too that a manufacturer may call for special tools or techniques to tune a bike. Many beginning tuners have torn a bike half apart before finding that they couldn't complete the job without a trip to the dealer to buy special tools of some kind.

This is one method of cleaning a spark plug. Such commercial cleaners will work on a plug that's not too worn, but discard a really bad plug and install a new one.

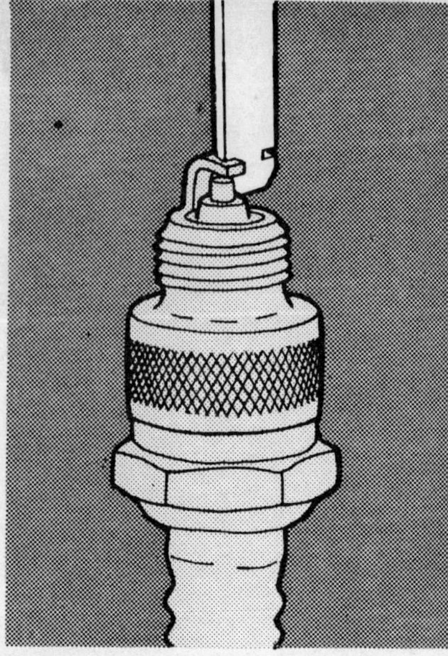

Setting the gap, whether on the old plug after it is cleaned or the new one fresh out of the box, is a very important step in the tune-up. Be sure to use a round wire gauge if you can; it gives the truest reading.

This isn't a bad idea. Spraying a moisture-proofing agent on the ignition wiring can help, especially off-road riders. While you're spraying, take a close look at the condition of insulation. Watch for cracks or burned spots.

SPARK PLUGS

When you actually start to work on the bike, the first step is to remove the spark plug and examine it carefully. A plug tells a lot about what's happening inside the engine, so become familiar with what various spark plug conditions mean. Study the section "Reading Spark Plugs" on page 78. Once you have examined the plug, clean it or simply throw it away and replace it with a new one (not a bad idea; spark plugs are cheap).

In any event, before installing either a new spark plug or a used one in good condition, set the gap between the electrodes with a gauge. This is a critical adjustment which has considerable effect on the way your bike runs. If the gap is set too narrow, the spark path is so short that as the spark jumps between the two electrodes, it won't ignite the air/fuel mixture very well. If the gap is too wide, the spark cannot readily jump across the increased distance, and engine performance goes rapidly downhill as soon as a buildup of carbon and other materials on the plug begins.

In this illustration you can see why a round gauge works best. The underside of the ground electrode can become pitted after use, creating the condition shown. If a blade type of gauge is used on such a plug, the actual gap may not be correct for the plug.

Gap the plug with a good spark plug gauge, preferably the type which uses a round gauge wire to set the gap. After the plug is cleaned and gapped, reinstall it in the cylinder head—unless your ignition timing technique requires putting a dial indicator in the spark plug hole.

Check the wiring at the same time. The wires of the ignition system, particularly the high-tension lead that connects to the spark plug, must be clean and free of cuts, abrasions, or other damage. If a wire is faulty, the plug may not fire well, because the spark can ground to the outside of the engine.

One good preventive measure, and one especially good for off-road bikes, is to treat the wiring with a commercial wiring seal, such as that shown in the photo. This sealant waterproofs the wiring to some degree and helps the ignition system keep its effectiveness.

SETTING IGNITION POINT GAP

Setting the ignition point gap is the next step in tuning the electrical system. Ignition points are inexpensive, and it is often better to replace ignition points that show extreme wear or metal buildup on one contact than it is to attempt to refurbish them with a file or emery board.

Many small two-strokes have a flywheel with only small windows in it to allow access to the ignition points, requiring a tuner to be part contortionist.

Many modern two-stroke engines have a transistorized ignition or a Capacitor Discharge Ignition (CDI) system which has no ignition points to adjust. In these systems, firing the spark plug is controlled by trigger coils rather than the opening of the points, and you have only the timing adjustment to make. See "Ignition," page 50, and "How a Two-Stroke Engine Works" on page 35.

If you have a conventional ignition with points, refer to your owner's manual or shop manual for the correct gap size and setting method before you get started with a screwdriver and feeler gauge. You may find the working space a bit cramped, as many manufacturers hide the points behind the rotor/generator, but with a little effort it can be done.

If you replace the ignition points, always replace the condenser at the same time. The condenser reduces wear and pitting of the points caused by the transfer of electrical energy across the contacts as the points open and close. The condenser is frequently the cause of excessive point contact wear or pitting, so replace it along with the points as a matter of course.

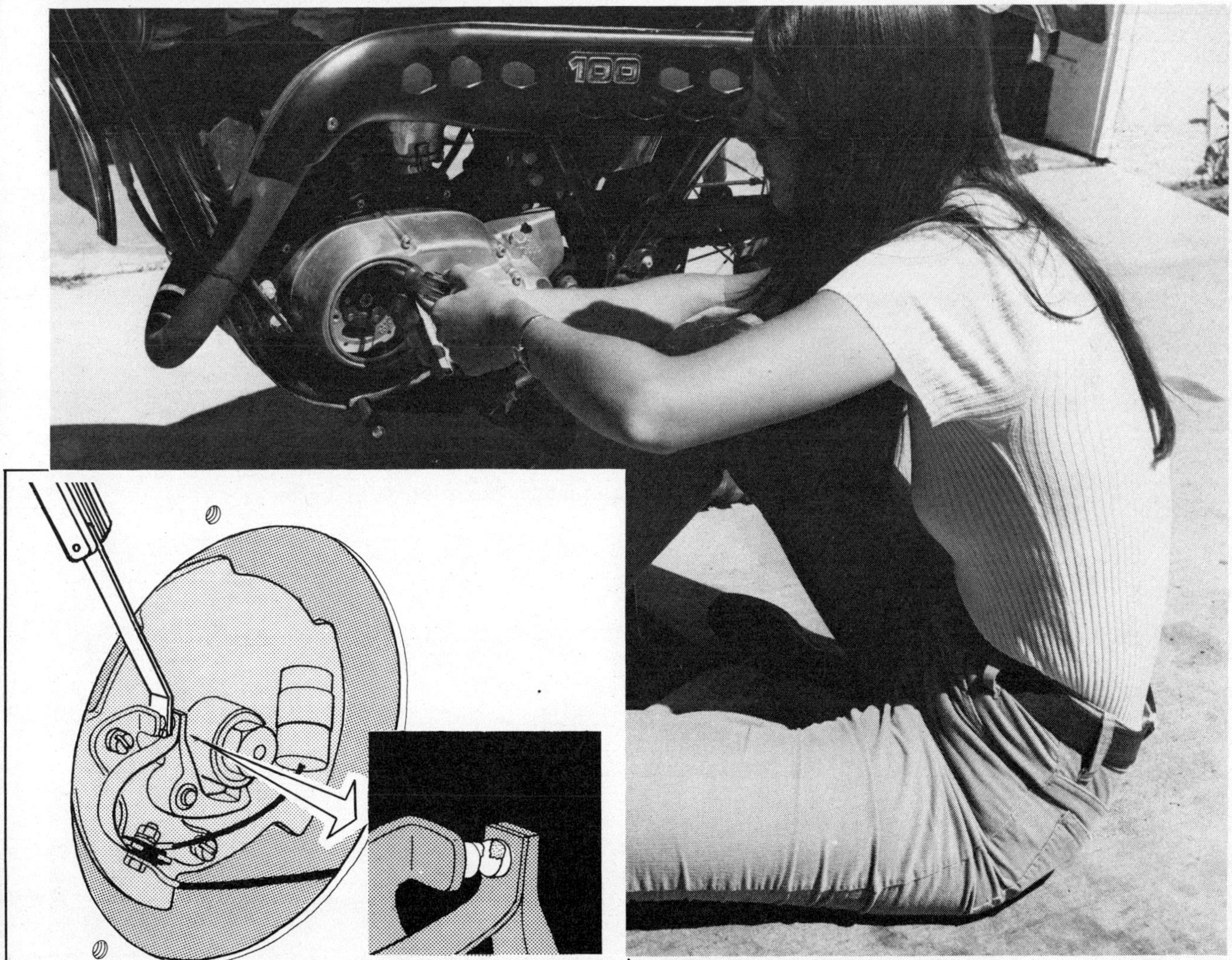

Replace points with worn or burned inner surfaces as part of a routine tune-up. Replace the condenser at the same time as the points to reduce arcing on new point gap surfaces.

Setting point gap requires both a screwdriver and a feeler gauge, both working in a tight space. Be careful to keep the blade angle at a minimum so that twisting doesn't force the gap too large. The feeler gauge blade should fit flat between the contact surfaces.

BATTERY CARE

After completing the ignition part of the tune-up, turn your attention to the battery. It is generally housed under the seat. The seat on most bikes is hinged to give access to the battery and other components. Look over the outside of the battery to see that there is no damage and that connections are tight and free of rust or corrosion.

Corrosion on the battery posts, where the two large cables that handle all of the electrical current from the battery connect, is especially harmful to proper electrical system operation. Usually corrosion appears as a buildup of whitish material on top of the battery in the area of the posts. Remove it. See the chapter "Preventive Maintenance" on page 56.

The fluid level in the battery is important to its operation. If your battery is refillable, it can be topped off with distilled water. Never use ordinary tap water, which contains minerals that harm the battery.

Some batteries have clear sides that let you check the level of the fluid without removing the caps on top of the battery. Others may require you to take off the caps and look inside the holes. In either case, there is a line or lines on the battery to indicate the proper fluid level.

Battery maintenance is part of a tune-up. After checking the outside of the battery for any buildup of corrosion, add water if necessary to bring the electrolyte level up to the mark. Never use tap water; the minerals in it cause problems. Use only distilled water to service the battery.

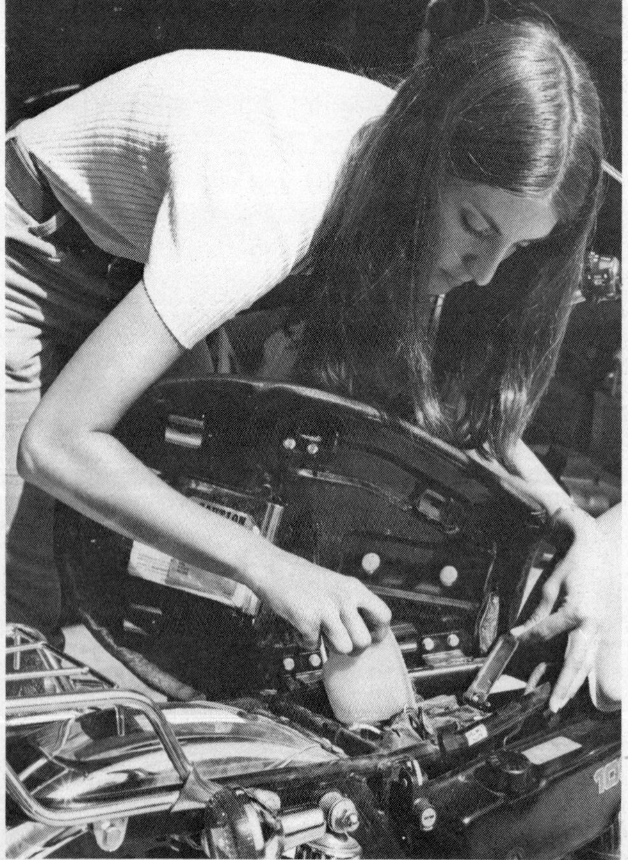

Many motorcycle batteries have a clear plastic case so you can easily see the electrolyte level without removing the filler caps. Fill up to the level mark on the side of the battery or the mark inside filler holes.

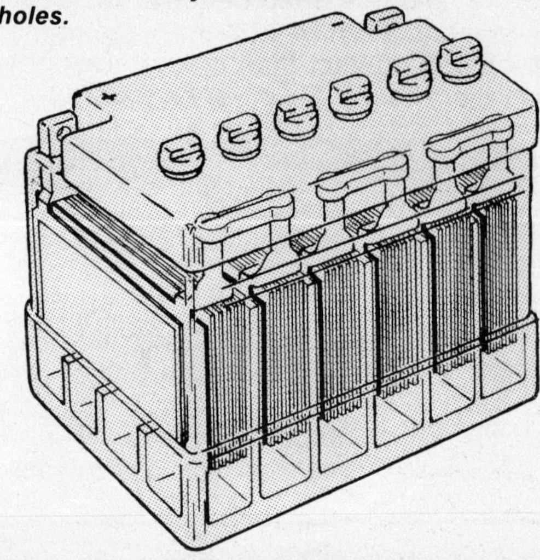

CAUTION: THE FLUID IN THE BATTERY IS AN ACID SOLUTION. AVOID GETTING IT ON YOUR SKIN OR CLOTHES. IF YOU DO GET SOME ON YOU, WASH IT OFF IMMEDIATELY WITH A MIXTURE OF WATER AND BAKING SODA.

One item often overlooked is keeping the battery in a good state of charge. Many motorcycles, especially dirt bikes, spend a lot of time sitting in the garage. The battery can discharge if the bike isn't run often. It helps to get a small home battery charger and charge the battery at regular intervals. These units are not expensive, and they'll go a long way toward making your bike's electrical system more reliable if you ride infrequently.

When using the battery charger, pay attention to the instructions that come with it. Also read any instructions in the owner's manual or shop manual on charging your battery.

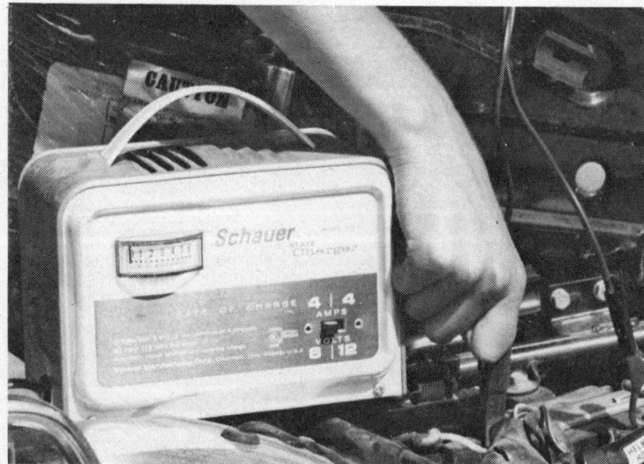

Small home battery chargers known as "trickle chargers" should be used to maintain battery charge if the bike spends a lot of time in the garage. Even better is to combine regular charging with at least weekly riding of the bike to maintain charge.

Adjusting the oil pump on a two-stroke is one step that's missing from a four-stroke tune-up. The oil supply on a two-stroke is not recycled through the engine, so the pump must match the throttle setting to supply the correct amount of oil for proper lubrication at all times.

OIL PUMP

Unless your two-stroke bike is a competition model, it has an oil pump somewhere on the engine to deliver lubricating oil from a separate oil tank to the engine. Two-stroke engines burn the oil during combustion, and the only source of lubrication for the upper end of the engine is this oil, which is mixed with the air and fuel as it passes into the engine. (For a more complete explanation of this, see "How a Two-stroke Engine Works" on page 35.)

The operation of the pump is controlled by the throttle. As you twist the throttle to increase the input of air/fuel mixture, the oil pump also supplies more oil, so that a balance of oil to fuel is maintained across the entire operating range of the engine.

Locate the oil pump on your engine and remove its cover. Then inspect the outside of the pump for leaks or loose parts. The actual adjustment usually consists of positioning the throttle as specified in the manual and then moving the oil pump cable adjuster so that the pump lines up with a mark on the engine case.

NOTE: ON SOME BIKES, YOU MAY HAVE TO ADJUST THE THROTTLE CABLE BEFORE SETTING THE OIL PUMP. SEE THE OWNER'S MANUAL OR SHOP MANUAL FOR YOUR BIKE.

A good first step in fuel system tuning is to check the inside of the fuel tank for a buildup of rust or scale. Then remove the cup at the bottom of the fuel shutoff valve to clean the small screen inside. Don't forget to turn the valve to the OFF position before removing the bowl.

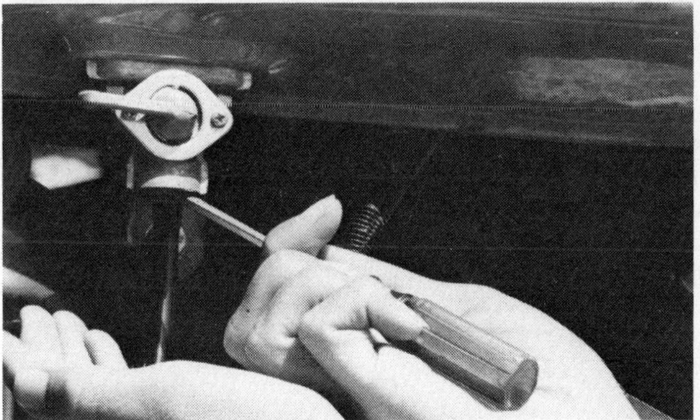

The small brass screen can be pried out with fingernails or a screwdriver, but be careful not to damage it, as it is quite fragile.

Clean the cup and screen in solvent before reinstalling them.

CARBURETOR TUNING

The next area to consider is the fuel system. Before you tear into the carburetor, check the inside of the gas tank with a flashlight to see if there is any buildup of sediment or rust. Then remove and clean the fuel screen or filter. This screen is located in the shutoff valve below the tank. Turn the valve to the OFF position and remove the small cup on the bottom of the valve.

With the cup removed, pry the small screen out of the shutoff valve with a screwdriver. Be careful not to damage it, as it is very fragile. You'll probably find a certain amount of rust or sediment in the bottom of the bowl or on the screen. Get rid of it by cleaning the bowl and screen in some solvent.

WARNING: GASOLINE IS NOT A SAFE SOLVENT FOR CLEANING PARTS. IT HAS A LOW FLASHPOINT (THAT IS, ITS VAPOR CATCHES FIRE EASILY) AS COMPARED TO OTHER SOLVENTS, SO DON'T USE IT. USE OTHER SOLVENTS ONLY IN A WELL-VENTILATED AREA. NEVER SMOKE OR HAVE ANY OPEN FLAME NEARBY WHEN YOU'RE WORKING WITH SOLVENTS.

The next step is the carburetor. Most tune-ups call for only minor external adjustments, but every so often you should take off the carburetor, give it a complete cleaning and install the replacement parts from a carburetor tune-up kit. Unless you intend to change the way your bike runs (either economy or performance tuning), your aim is simply to restore the engine to normal operating levels of performance.

In this case, the main adjustment to the inside of the carburetor is the float level adjustment. Jet changes and other metering adjustments are something to approach carefully, armed with the advice of an experienced mechanic.

In setting the float level, remove the carburetor from the engine (not always strictly necessary; see "Your First Four-stroke Tune-up"). Invert it to gain access to the float chamber. After removing the chamber cover, go ahead and install the new needle and seat provided in the rebuild kit.

Next, set the float level. Usually a small gauge is provided in the kit, but you may have to use a small steel ruler to set the level. On many modern two-stroke engines (and some four-strokes), you gauge the level with a special tool that tells you if the level is set correctly without removing the bowl from the carburetor.

You can see this special measuring gauge at work in several of the individual tune-ups in this book. Basically it's a section of plastic tubing marked with lines to indicate fluid levels. After removing the drain plug or main jet plug on those models which have an outside replaceable main jet, attach the tubing to the float chamber. When held up alongside the carburetor, the gauge fills with gas up to the same level as the inside of the float chamber, telling you the float level.

After any internal adjustments to the carburetor and/or taking it apart for cleaning and installing new parts, certain adjustments are necessary once the carburetor is reinstalled on the engine. These include adjusting the idle speed, the idle air screw and the throttle cable (to remove any slack from the cable which would interfere with the movement of the throttle). Take your time making these adjustments.

Normally, to adjust the idle air you turn the adjusting screw in until it bottoms out and then back it out again a predetermined number of turns. This is an adjustment that must be made cautiously. It's not hard to damage the adjusting screw or the seat it fits into by turning it in too hard. Be careful not to overtighten the idle air screw.

When you've finished working on the carburetor and reinstalled it on the engine, make the idle air and idle speed adjustments before riding the bike. Don't set the idle speed until the engine has been running for a few minutes to warm up to operating temperature.

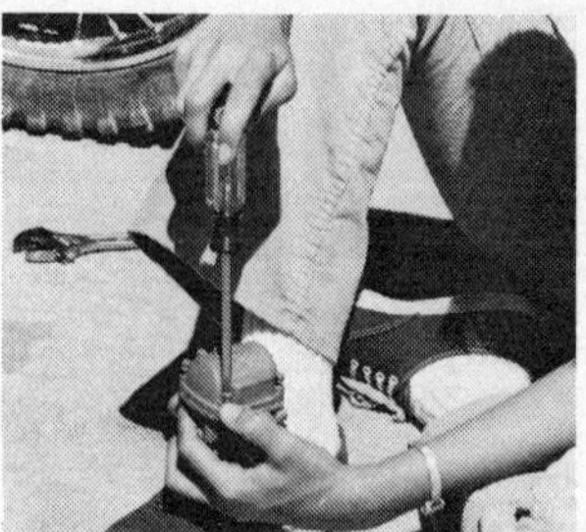

When you've taken the carburetor off the engine (see the shop manual for removal instructions), invert the carb and remove the float bowl. This gives you access to the float and the needle and seat. It's good practice to change the needle and seat valve during a tune-up, and the float level should always be checked and reset.

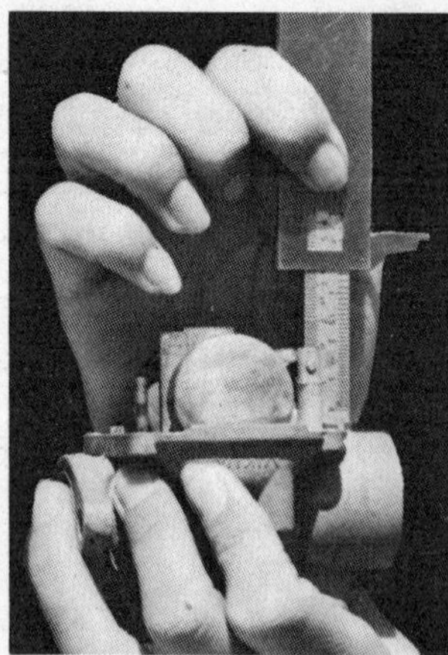

Setting the float level requires precise measurement of the float against some fixed part of the carburetor body. You may have to measure it more than one way to satisfy a single setting.

You'll probably find that the owner's manual tells you to bottom the screw, then back it out about 1½ turns. This is a common setting. You may need to adjust the screw a little to one side or the other of this setting, but 1½ turns out is the best starting place.

As for idle adjustment, the manual normally requires you to start the engine and let it warm up to operating temperature before setting the idle.

The last two items on the carburetor are the air cleaner and the carburetor mounting. Always check the air cleaner and replace or clean it before reinstalling it on the bike. A dirty air cleaner can rob your bike of gas mileage and interfere with your tuning. Most motorcycle air cleaners can be cleaned and reinstalled rather than replaced. You can remove much of the dirt and dust from most of them by rapping them sharply against a solid surface. Other cleaning methods include blowing the dirt off with an air hose or cleaning the filter element in solvent.

CAUTION: NEVER USE TRANSMISSION OIL IN THE ENGINE OR ENGINE OIL IN THE TRANSMISSION CASE. SERIOUS DAMAGE TO BOTH ENGINE AND TRANSMISSION CAN RESULT.

Adjusting the clutch compensates for normal wear and keeps the clutch from being harmed.

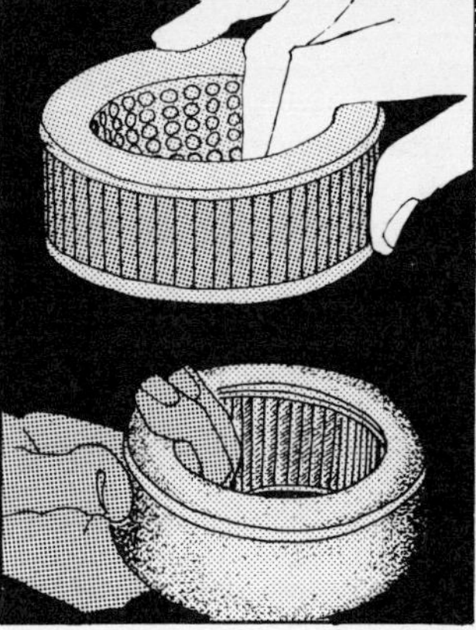

The air cleaner is an important part of the tune-up, especially for bikes ridden off-road. After removing the air cleaner from the bike, clean it in one of several ways or replace it.

Don't immerse paper air filters in solvents—only those filter elements made of foam rubber. Paper elements should be replaced or cleaned with air pressure.

After installing the carburetor kit and cleaning the air cleaner, if you have difficulty tuning the engine or the idle seems rough and the bike has poor power, the first place to look is the attachment point of the carburetor to the engine.

There is a connecting gasket or O-ring between the carburetor and the engine on many bikes. Others have a rubber or plastic hose connecting the carburetor to the engine. A leak here allows air to enter the engine behind the carburetor and upset the balance of fuel and air. This destroys the settings you have made on the carburetor and can make the engine run rough or refuse to idle.

Such things as ignition problems or sediment in the carburetor or fuel lines can also cause this kind of problem, but if you've had the carburetor off the bike, it's a good starting place for troubleshooting.

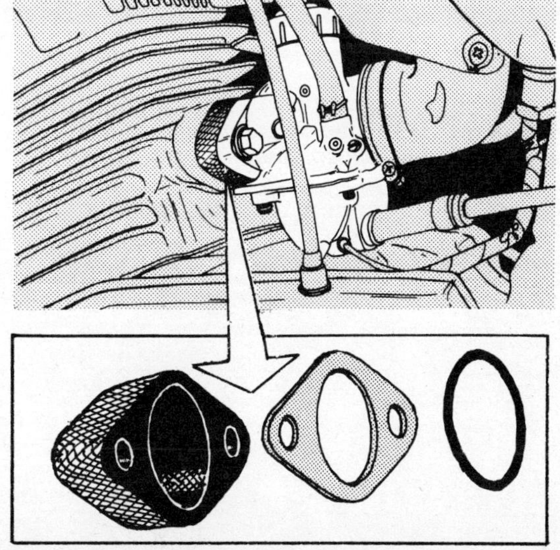

If you experience a rough idle or other tuning problems after having had the carburetor off the engine, be sure to check the seal on the parts behind the carburetor. An air leak here can create a mismatched air/fuel ratio and several tuning problems. O-rings are especially prone to leaking if care is not taken during reinstallation of the carb on the engine.

CLUTCH ADJUSTMENT

Adjusting the clutch is a necessary part of a tune-up. The clutch wears during normal use, and it should be kept in adjustment for maximum service life. The owner's manual will tell you the correct method of adjusting your particular clutch. The general procedure is to take up slack in the cable that would prevent the clutch from releasing all the way when the lever is pulled. You have to leave some slack, however, so that the clutch will completely engage.

After adjusting the clutch a couple of times, it'll become routine. You'll grow sensitive to any slipping or grabbing of the clutch, which is a sign of maladjustment or wear.

Once the lower adjustment is set, take up the slack in the brake cable (if any) at the lever.

The rear brake should be set according to the instructions in the owner's manual.

Front brakes on most bikes intended for off-road use should be set looser than for street use. This prevents the brake from locking up quickly on soft surfaces and dumping the rider.

SETTING THE BRAKES

Getting the brakes set right is important. Not only is it a safety measure, but bikes used for different purposes may require different brake adjustment. For example, your two-stroke bike is probably a dirt bike, or at least a dual-purpose bike capable of being used off-road. This being the case, you may want to set the brakes differently from the way they are normally set for street riding when you go to the dirt.

Street brakes should be set quite tight to give good response, but dirt bike brakes can get you into serious trouble if they react too fast. Many riders prefer to set the brakes on their dirt bikes a little loose. This allows you to squeeze the brake lever a bit harder before the brake comes on. It also reduces the tendency to lock up the brakes. Locking up the brakes on dirt promotes a slide a lot quicker than on the pavement, because it's easier to break the wheel loose in the dirt. Once the tire loses its grip on the dirt, you have virtually no control and you can wind up on your head.

Many riders compromise by setting the front brake a little loose and leaving the back one set much as they would on the street. The front wheel is more likely to break loose anyway, so this is probably the best method for bikes used for both street and dirt riding.

Front and rear brakes are adjustable both on the mechanism at the wheel and at the lever or brake pedal end of the cable. Following the adjustment routine outlined in the owner's manual, set the brakes the way you think they should be (you'll get to test them at the end of the tune-up when you test ride the bike) and then go on to something else.

A bent wheel rim can be straightened (if it's not too badly bent). Inspect the wheels from time to time to be sure they're not damaged or cracked.

TIRES & WHEELS

That something else ought to be tires and tire pressure. As long as you're there, now's a good time to pull out your gauge and check the pressures in both front and rear tires. Again, just as with the brake settings, you may have a good reason to depart from the listed pressures in the owner's manual if you're riding in the dirt.

Lower tire pressures give the tire some flex and increase its ability to bite into the ground for traction. The problem with dual-purpose bikes is the same as with front brakes. Underinflated tires may work well off-pavement, but they're a definite threat to life and limb on the street.

If you've been running low pressures in your tires, check to see that the tire hasn't slipped on the rim. This usually happens on the rear tire, where engine power is applied to the ground. If the tire slips badly enough, the valve stem can tear or be pinched against the rim, resulting in a flat tire.

After you've checked tire pressures, look at the general condition of the tires themselves. Examine them for tire wear, sidewall damage, etc.

Next, take a look at the wheel rim and the spokes. If you've been riding in the dirt, it's surprising how often you'll discover that you have a slightly bent rim. This isn't necessarily a serious problem. If the damage is mild, you can go on riding for quite a while. But if the rim is cracked or badly bent, do something about it before putting any more miles on the bike. There are two types of rims: steel and alloy. A steel rim bends more easily than an alloy one but can be repaired more easily as well. An alloy rim is much tougher, but if bent can only be straightened by an expert (and not often then).

Also check the spokes and tighten them if necessary. Be careful not to overtighten spokes.

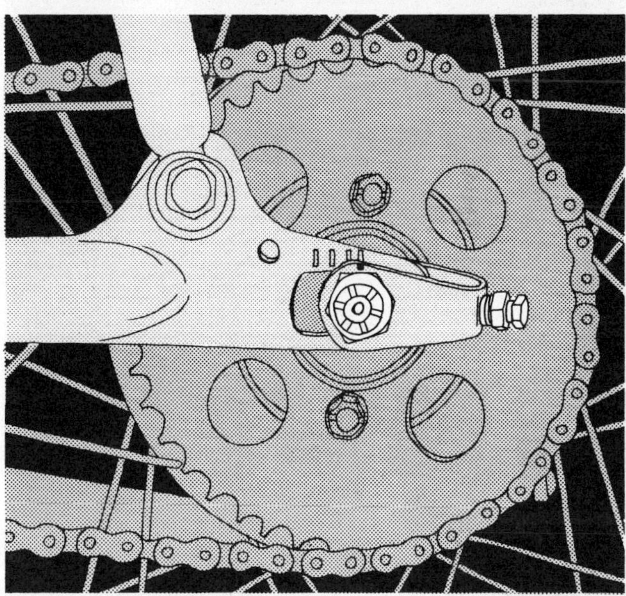

The chain stretches with use. check it and adjust if necessary. Loosen the axle nuts and turn the adjusters at the rear to tighten or loosen the chain as required.

Check the spokes too. They can also become bent and require replacing, but often the problem is that they loosen up from the pounding and vibration of travel. Some motorcycles come with a spoke wrench in the tool kit, and you can buy special ones at the dealer. However, you can do an adequate job with a simple crescent wrench. Read the owner's manual before tightening spokes for any instructions the manufacturer may give, and remember one rule: Don't overtighten. Pulling spokes too tight is almost as bad as letting them stay loose. You run the risk of breaking a spoke or distorting the rim if they are too tight.

Transmission oil should be drained and replaced, following the guidelines in the owner's manual.

CHAIN CARE

To check and set the rear chain, block up the rear wheel with something so that you can turn the wheel easily and bring all the chain around for easy viewing. Be careful about the blocking—a two-wheeled vehicle isn't the most stable thing on earth. Take proper precautions so that the bike won't fall over on you.

With the rear wheel off the ground. put the transmission in neutral and turn the rear wheel to inspect the chain. It may be necessary to remove the chain from the bike from time to time and give it a complete cleaning in solvent. Look for rust or broken links. While you're at it, inspect the teeth on the sprockets for signs of wear. A worn sprocket can damage the chain.

The chain needs a certain amount of slack, measured on the bottom run at about the middle. Usually ¾ to 1 inch of play is about right (check your motorcycle's manual). To adjust slack, loosen the rear wheel in its mounting and slide it forward or back. Then, using a wrench, turn the chain adjusting bolts that stick out at the back of the swingarm.

There are alignment marks on the slots in the end of the swingarm to help make sure the wheel is aligned correctly when you retighten it. Also, you'll have to loosen the axle nuts before you move the wheel with the adjusters; always retighten the nuts after making any adjustment.

A final measure of care for the chain is applying some oil or other lubricant. The drive chain on your motorcycle is really a precision part, and it must run in the worst possible dirt and dust conditions. Many quality commercial lubes come in spray cans. Coat the chain completely, seeing to it that the lubricant penetrates between the side plates and the rollers.

TRANSMISSION OIL & ENGINE OIL

Although it's part of the ordinary preventive maintenance program discussed in that chapter (and in the owner's manual for your bike), changing the oil in your transmission at the recommended intervals is a sound idea.

The best way to get good oil drainage is to drain the oil after the bike has been ridden *and* has cooled off to the point where you won't burn yourself working on it. As long as the oil is still warm, it flows easily. Place a pan under the drain for the transmission and open the plug.

After the transmission has drained completely, replace the plug and add the recommended type of oil. Don't depart from the manufacturer's recommendations on oil. A lot of time was spend designing your transmission, and the engineers who worked on the trans know what kind of oil works best.

Another place to check and refill the oil if necessary is the remote oil tank for the engine.

When adding transmission oil, be sure that it is the proper type and weight, as specified by the manufacturer.

Two-stroke engines burn oil along with the fuel, so oil is not recirculated as in a four-stroke system. Always use oil designated for two-stroke engine operation.

COMBUSTION CHAMBER CARBON REMOVAL

One step that sometimes needs doing is removal of the cylinder head to scrape away the carbon buildup in the combustion chamber. To do this, you must have the shop manual for your motorcycle.

On many bikes, the cylinder head can be removed without disturbing the carburetor or any other part of the engine. A two-stroke engine has no moving parts on the cylinder head as does a four-stroke engine, so the job of removing and reinstalling is made much easier.

When you have the cylinder head off the engine, remove the carbon buildup inside the combustion chamber—with a tool that won't damage the inside of the chamber. Often the carbon is soft and can simply be brushed off with a wire brush or scraped with a pocket knife. If you use a knife, be sure you don't cut or nick the metal. A deep gouge or raised edge left inside the combustion chamber can become a "hot spot," which can ignite the air/fuel mixture at the wrong time.

After completing the tune-up, making sure that all parts are tightened and nothing is left hanging, the last step is to don the proper safety gear and give your bike a test ride. Going around the block will give you an idea of how the engine is running, but a more thorough checkout involves putting a few miles on the bike and watching carefully how it performs.

Engine oil is also important. Add oil at regular intervals, and keep an eye on the level in the tank, because two-stroke engines burn oil with the fuel. It is important to use an oil intended for two-stroke engines. Regular oil will not do the job.

Once in a while, remove the cylinder head and scrape away the carbon buildup inside the combustion chamber. Follow the instructions in the shop manual.

Kawasaki KD 125 KS 125

TUNING THIS TWO-STROKE SINGLE AND ITS STREET-LEGAL BROTHER, THE KS 125, GIVES YOU A GOOD LOOK AT A ROTARY-VALVE TWO-STROKE ENGINE AND HOW IT OPERATES.

If you want to take the trouble to remove the cylinder head, you can use a dial indicator to locate piston TDC for timing, but it isn't strictly necessary.

The points are located behind the magneto flywheel, so you'll have to reach in through a small window to do any adjusting. There is a single contact breaker screw to loosen. Put the screwdriver tip into the notch in the breaker plate and adjust the position of the plate.

Remove the side cover and connect a point checker or buzz box across the points. Because of the location of the points, you'll have to consult the wiring diagram for suitable hookup points for the checker or meter. Turn the flywheel clockwise until the left-hand timing mark on the outer edge of the flywheel lines up with the cast pointer on the case. When this mark comes into alignment with the pointer, the buzz box should indicate that the points are opening. If not, align the two marks and adjust the points until they open exactly on the mark. No exact point gap is specified for the ignition on this motorcycle.

Timing can be checked better by the use of a timing light. With the engine running at idle, the timing marks should line up just as in the static method of timing.

On two-stroke engines, oil pump adjustment is vital to proper operation. There are two sets of marks on the oil pump on Kawasaki's KD 125. The first should line up with the mark on the post when the throttle is fully closed; this is the one used for oil pump adjustment.

Loosen the lock nut on the cable and move the cable adjuster to bring the oil pump mark into alignment with the mark on the cast post. Then tighten the lock nut. To test the pump further, twist the throttle to the fully open position and see if the cast mark on the post now lines up with the second mark on the pump. This tells you whether the throttle is opening fully or not.

On rotary-valve two-stroke engines, the carburetor is located at the side of the engine. Because of this low position, the carburetor is generally protected from dirt and dust by a cover. Removing this cover exposes the carburetor so that adjustments can be made.

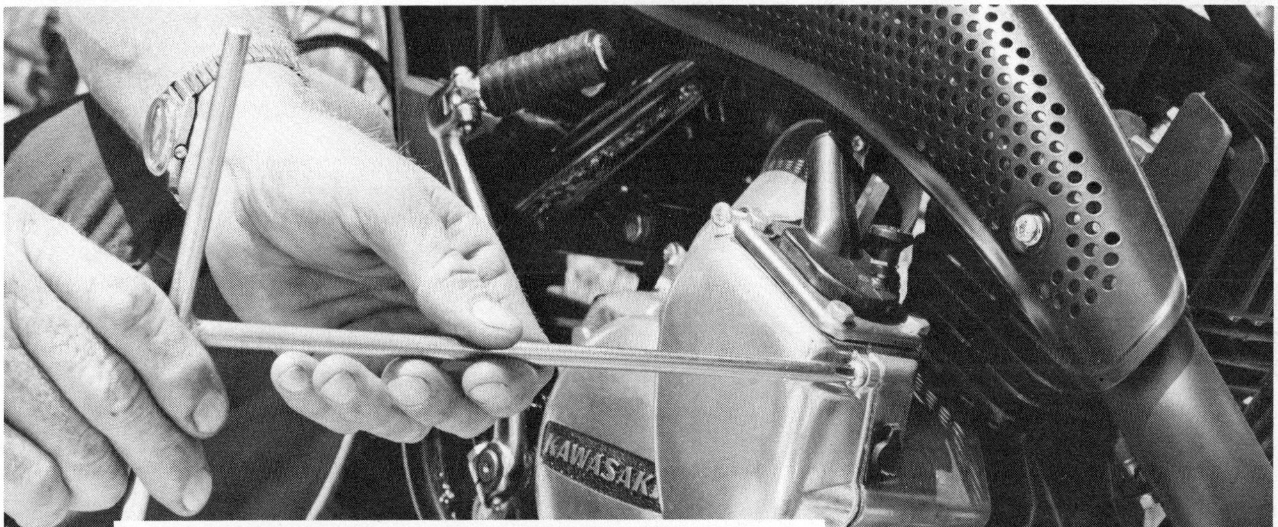

One of the nice things about doing carburetor adjustments and checks on the KD 125 is the outside replacement main jet on the carburetor. You can change jets without disassembling the carburetor. Also, by installing a special tool called a fuel level gauge in the hole where the jet belongs, you can determine if the float level is set correctly without taking the carb apart.

This is the tool for checking fuel level (Kawasaki part #57001-206). It screws into the port for the main jet to check the float adjustment. To use it, shut off the fuel valve at the gas tank and remove the outside cover from the carburetor and the main jet holder. Install the fuel level gauge, then turn the fuel back on. Hold the flexible tube alongside the carburetor as shown while the float bowl refills. The level the fuel reaches will be displayed in the tube. It should reach **.12 to .20 inch (3-5mm)** below the edge of the carburetor body, where the float bowl cover is attached. The tube has millimeters marked on it to make measurement easier. If adjustment of the fuel level (float level) is necessary, remove the carburetor and gently bend the tang to reset the float level.

Idle air screw adjustment is simple. The screw is located on the bell mouth of the carburetor. The basic adjustment is to gently turn the screw in until it bottoms. The key word here is "gently." Too much force will damage the system. With the screw bottomed, back it out 1½ turns. Next, reinstall the carburetor cover and set the idle speed.

With the cover reinstalled, start the engine and let it warm up for about five minutes (until proper operating temperature is reached). Then pull the small plastic plug out of the side of the engine and reach in with a screwdriver to set the idle speed. Proper idle speed is the lowest stable idle speed at which you can get the engine to run—normally around 1300 rpm. After the idle speed is set, replace the cover and test ride the bike.

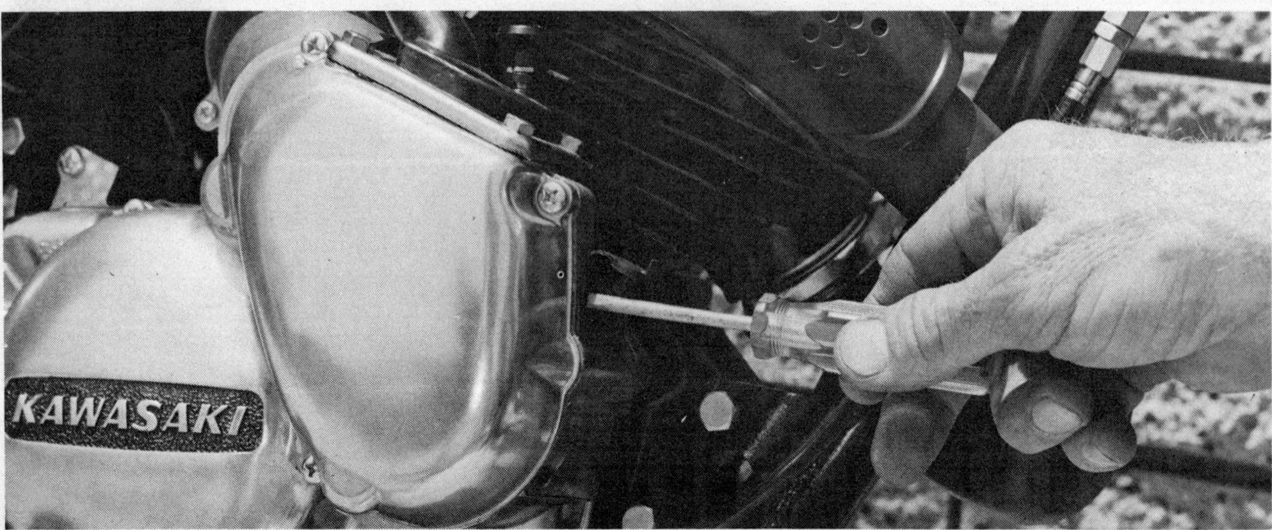

Kawasaki KX 250

THIS MIDDLEWEIGHT MOTOCROSSER IS POTENT BUT EASILY TUNEABLE.

To gain access to the magneto CDI unit on the KX 250, remove the screws from the cover on the left side of the engine. Setting the static timing on the CDI magneto is easy. Just check the alignment of the two marks at the top of the unit. If the marks are not aligned, proceed with the simple adjustment.

Loosen the screws at the top and bottom which hold the magneto base. There are only two of them, and it's an easy job.

To set the ignition static timing, move the magneto base until the two marks near the top screw are lined up. Then retighten the screws. That's all there is to it. A dynamic check can be made by using a timing light, following the shop manual procedure, but it's not usually necessary.

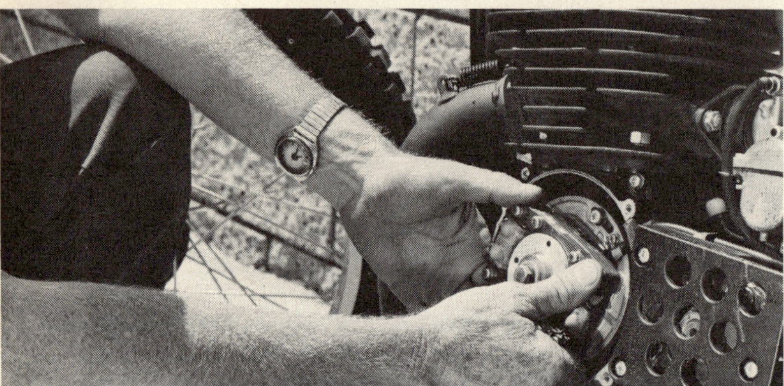

To set idle air, turn the idle air screw in until it bottoms (be careful to do this gently; too much force will damage the screw). Then back it out 1½ turns.

Rather than setting the idle speed for a certain rpm, as you would with a road bike, adjust the idle speed so that the engine dies at zero throttle. You will have to use both a screwdriver and a wrench to adjust the idle speed. Be sure to retighten the lock nut afterward.

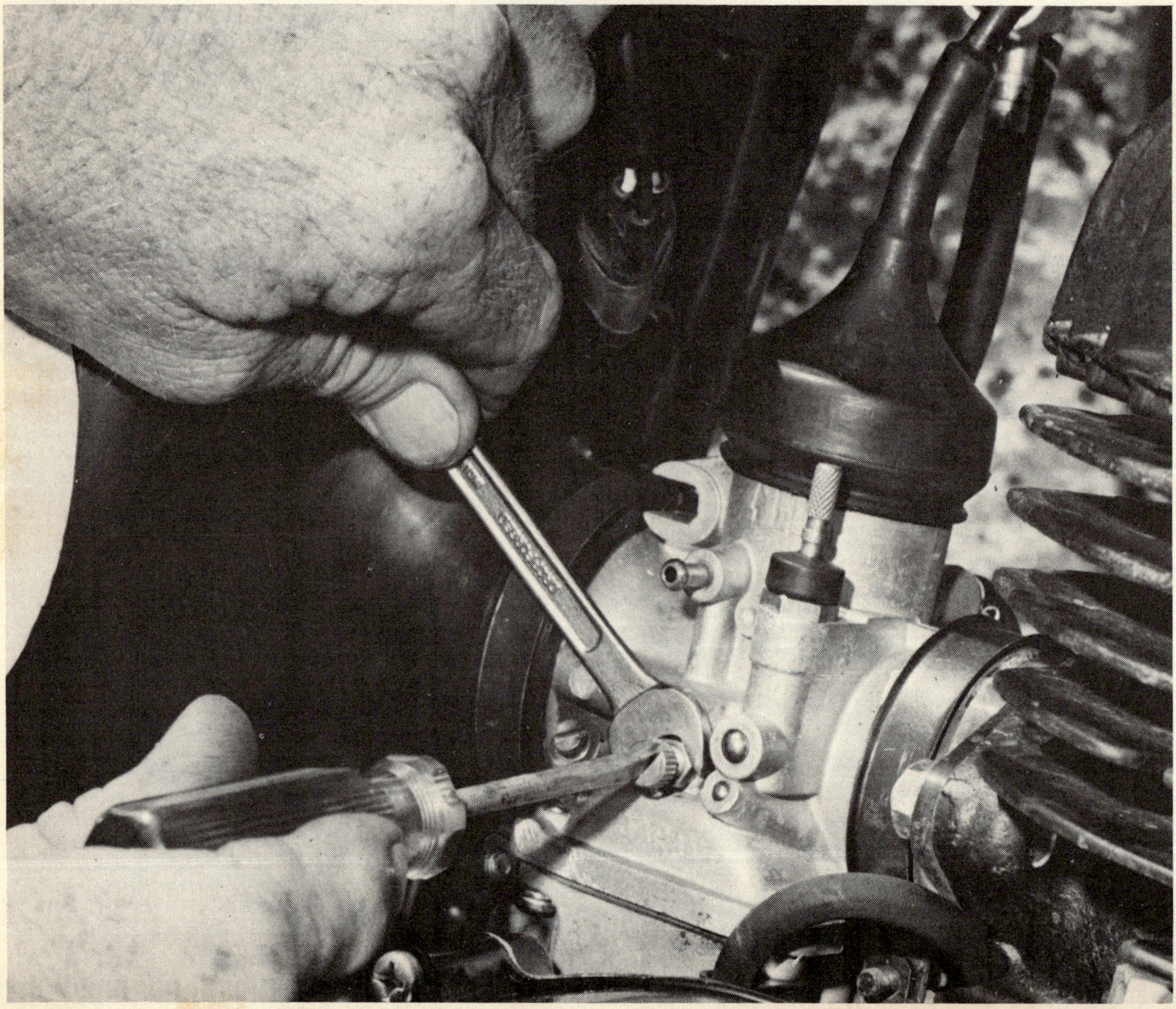

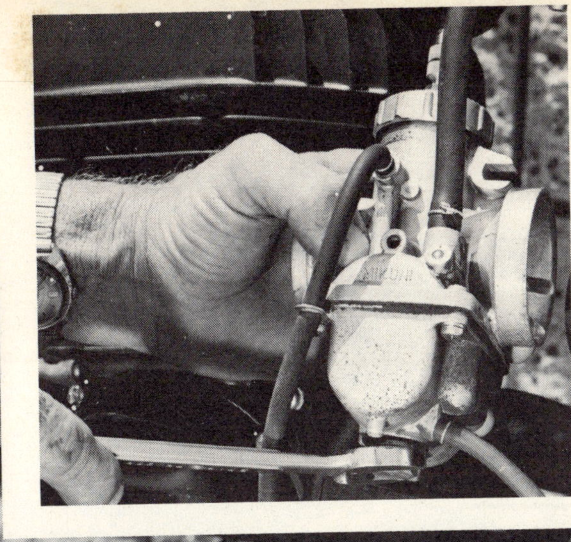

Remove the carburetor from the engine to gain ready access to the drain plug on the bottom of the float bowl. This plug also gives access to the main jet for quick and easy changes between races.

Fuel level in the float bowl is checked by installing a Kawasaki gauge (part #57001-202). With the adapter screwed into the drain plug hole, line up the top ruled line on the gauge with the bottom of the carburetor body at the junction of the body and float bowl. The correct fuel level is **.31 inch (8mm)** below the ruled line.

If the fuel level is off, remove the float bowl and invert the carburetor. Using a screwdriver, bend the tang gently to change the float level. Then reassemble and recheck using the gauge.

NOTE:. SINCE THE KAWASAKI KX 250 IS A PURE RACING MACHINE, THERE IS NO OIL PUMP TO ADJUST. OIL IS PREMIXED WITH GASOLINE IN THE GAS TANK FOR LUBRICATION.

Kawasaki 500 H1 350 400 750

THE TUNING PROCEDURE FOR KAWASAKI'S ORIGINAL SCREAMER IS THE SAME FOR THE 350, 400 AND 750cc MACHINES AS WELL.

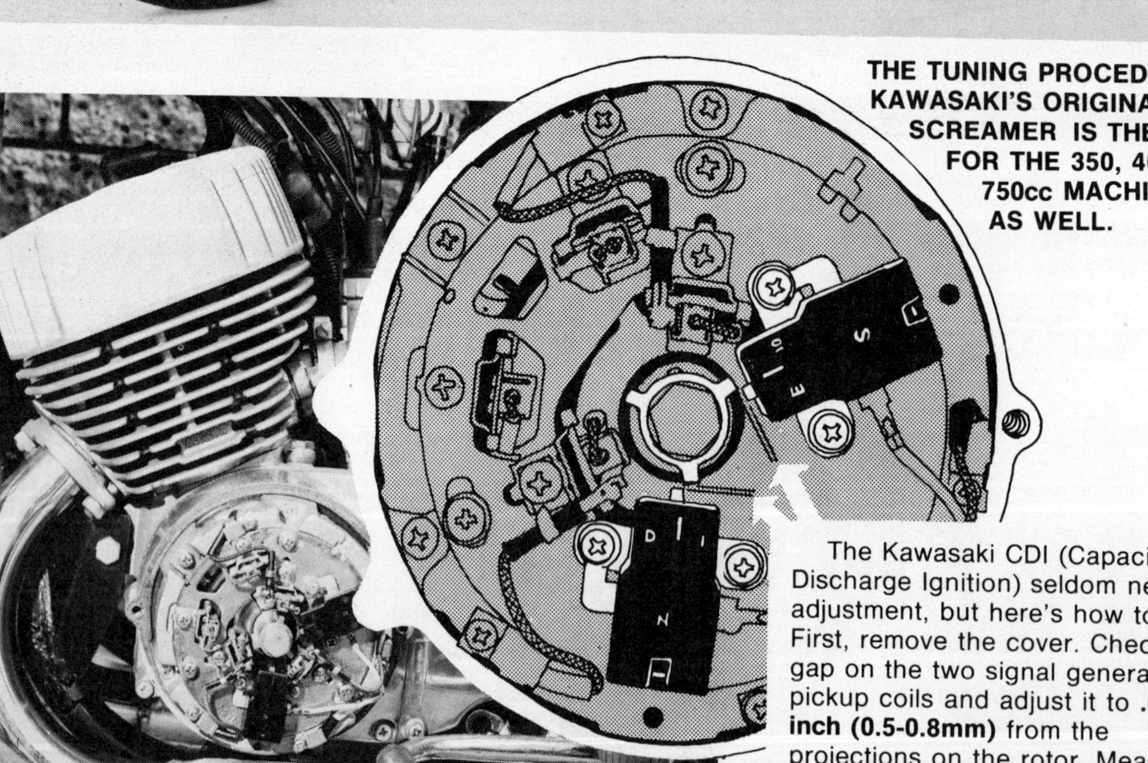

The Kawasaki CDI (Capacitor Discharge Ignition) seldom needs any adjustment, but here's how to do it. First, remove the cover. Check the gap on the two signal generator pickup coils and adjust it to **.020-.030 inch (0.5-0.8mm)** from the projections on the rotor. Measure the gap on each with a feeler gauge, loosen the coil mounting screws, reposition the coils and retighten the screws, if necessary.

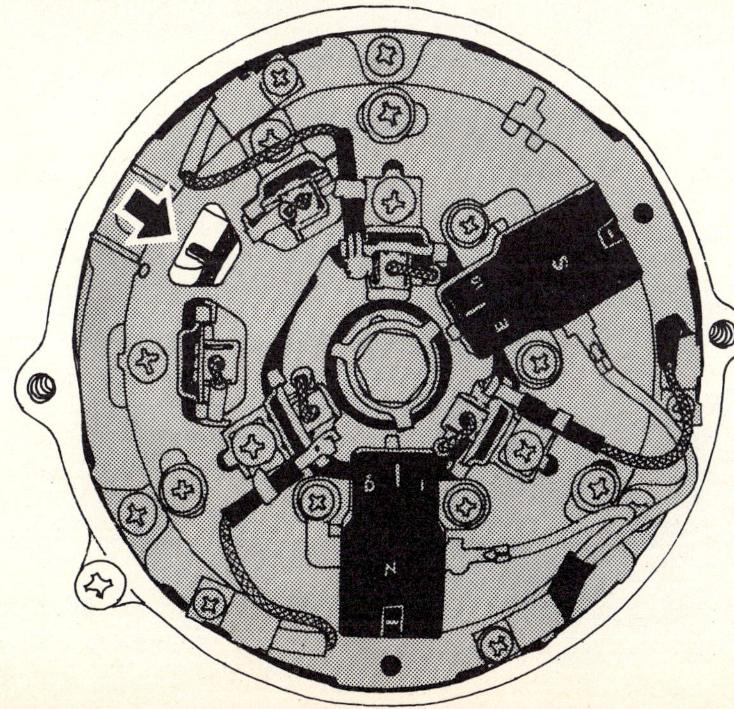

With the dial indicator installed in the spark plug hole on the left cylinder, rotate the engine until the piston is set to **.116 inch (2.94mm)** BTDC (Before Top Dead Center). The pointer on the ignition housing should line up with a mark on the rotor. If the mark doesn't line up, reposition the pointer to bring it into alignment with the mark.

Once you have positioned the pointer, move the crankshaft rotor counterclockwise until a second mark on the rotor is aligned with the pointer. If the timing is correct, the trailing edge of the rotor at the bottom will line up with the leading edge of the projection on the lower pickup coil. If not, loosen the three base mounting screws and reposition the base plate. Recheck the pickup coil gaps.

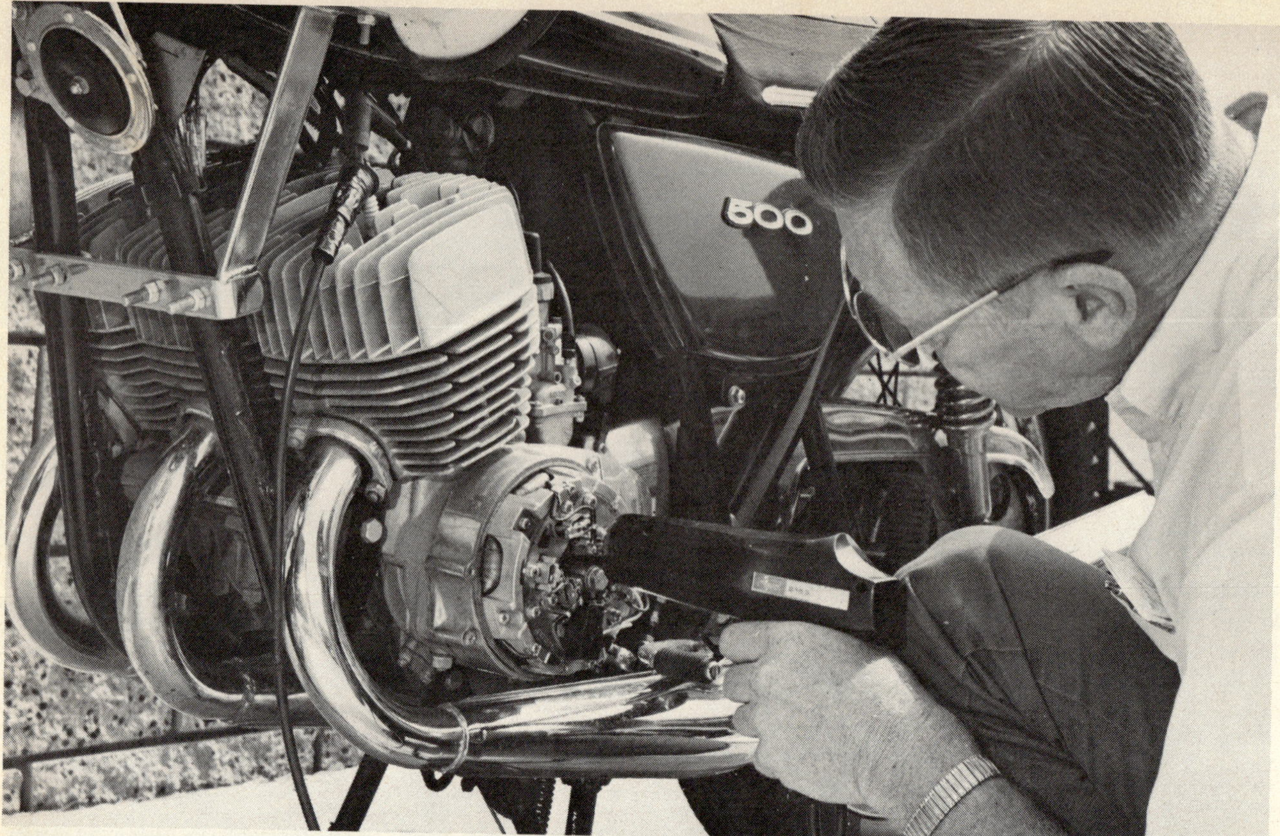

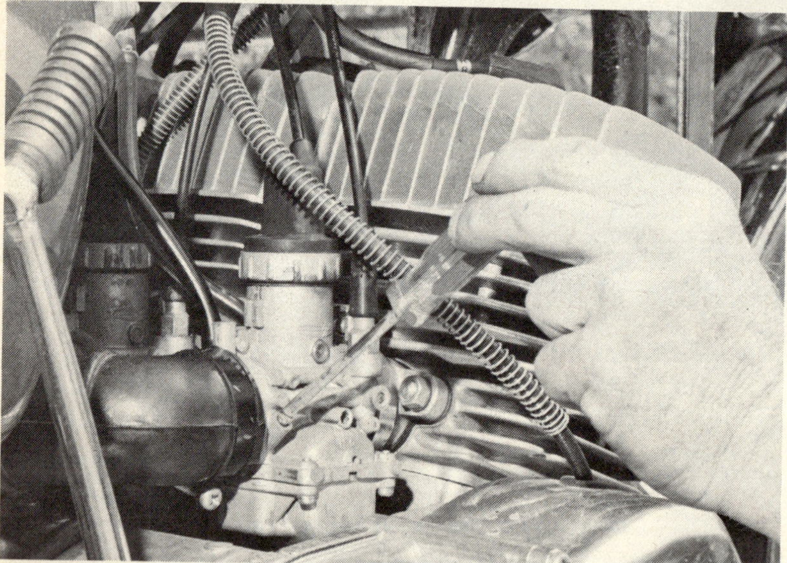

As a final check, use a timing light to determine whether the mark aligns with the pointer when the engine is running at 4000 rpm. This is generally a two-man job, so use a buddy. Remember, a running motorcycle on a stand can be dangerous.

To adjust the idle speed, you must work with both the air screws and the throttle stop screws. First, screw in the air screw fully. Then back it out 1½ turns on each carb. Be careful not to force any adjustment screw; they are easily damaged. When the screws are adjusted, start the engine and allow it to warm up completely before going on to the next step.

After the engine is up to normal operating temperature, adjust the throttle stop screws to give the lowest stable idle speed (usually about 1200-1400 rpm). You can adjust the individual carbs by placing your hand at the exhaust tips and feeling for a difference in exhaust pressure, but using a carburetor synchronizing tool such as Uni-Syn (see the picture) is a better way. With this device, each individual throttle screw can be adjusted to give the same airflow rate through the carburetors. These tools are very helpful to a tuner.

Carb cables stretch, so adjust them every 2000 miles (3000 km). To do this, screw in the throttle screws all the way, then take the play out of the outer sleeve of the carburetor. At the same time, you can use a mirror to make sure the slide height is the same on all carbs. Afterward, readjust the carburetor throttle stop.

Adjust the automatic oiling pump every 2000 miles (3000 km) also. Remove the small cover on the right side of the engine to expose the pump. Check around the pump for any signs of leakage, which would indicate a bad seal, and then adjust the pump. The pump is cable-controlled from the throttle, so the throttle cable adjustment must be checked and/or set before doing the oil pump.

The oil pump must start with the throttles, providing more oil as throttles are opened. To set the pump, loosen the lock nut on the cable, then adjust until the mark on the oil pump lever lines up with the mark on the oil pump lever stop. These marks must be in alignment at zero throttle opening.

CAUTION: OIL PUMP ADJUSTMENT IS CRITICAL TO PROPER ENGINE OPERATION. FAULTY OIL DELIVERY CAN CAUSE ENGINE SEIZING AND DAMAGE.

Yamaha DT 175B

PROBABLY THE WORLD'S MOST SUCCESSFUL DUAL-PURPOSE BIKE DESIGN, THE SINGLE-CYLINDER ENDURO IS SIMPLE TO TUNE.

To start the timing procedure on the DT 175B, take off the engine cover on the left side and remove the spark plug. Install a dial indicator in the spark plug hole. Rotate the engine by turning the magneto flywheel until the dial indicator reverses, informing you that the piston is at TDC. Zero the dial and turn the engine over in a clockwise direction until the dial indicator is at least four complete revolutions from TDC. Then slowly return the engine toward TDC by rotating it in a counterclockwise direction until the dial indicator reads **.071 inch, ±.006 inch (1.8mm, ±0.15mm).**

The advance mechanism must be locked out with a 2.5mm pin or an old carb needle before making the timing adjustment. Use a point checker to establish the exact moment of point opening. If any adjustment is needed, loosen the pan-head screws and gently rotate the contact breaker assembly until the indication of point opening is exactly on the mark.

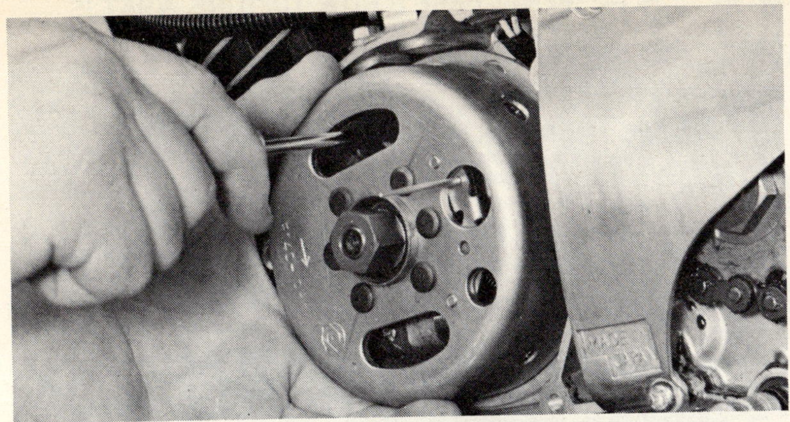

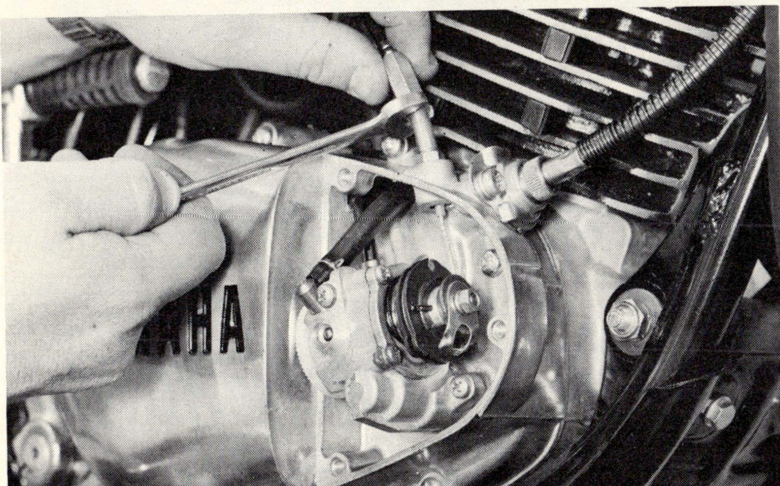

After ignition timing comes ignition point gap. Turn the flywheel until the points reach their maximum opening and check with a feeler gauge. The correct point gap setting is **.012-.016 inch (0.3-0.4mm).**

Oil pump adjustment is simple. First remove the small side cover on the right side of the engine. Then take all the slack out of the throttle cable without moving the carburetor slide. The mark on the pump pulley will line up with the pin sticking out of the side of the pump body if the pump is adjusted correctly. If not, use the oil pump cable adjuster to provide the proper alignment. This job usually requires two people, one to do the adjusting and the other to hold the throttle in the correct position.

Carburetor adjustment is also easy. Idle air is set by gently running the idle air screw in until it bottoms, then backing it out exactly one full turn. Start the engine and let it warm up to operating temperature before setting the idle speed to 1300-1400 rpm. The idle speed screw is located right next to the idle air screw on the same side of the carb.

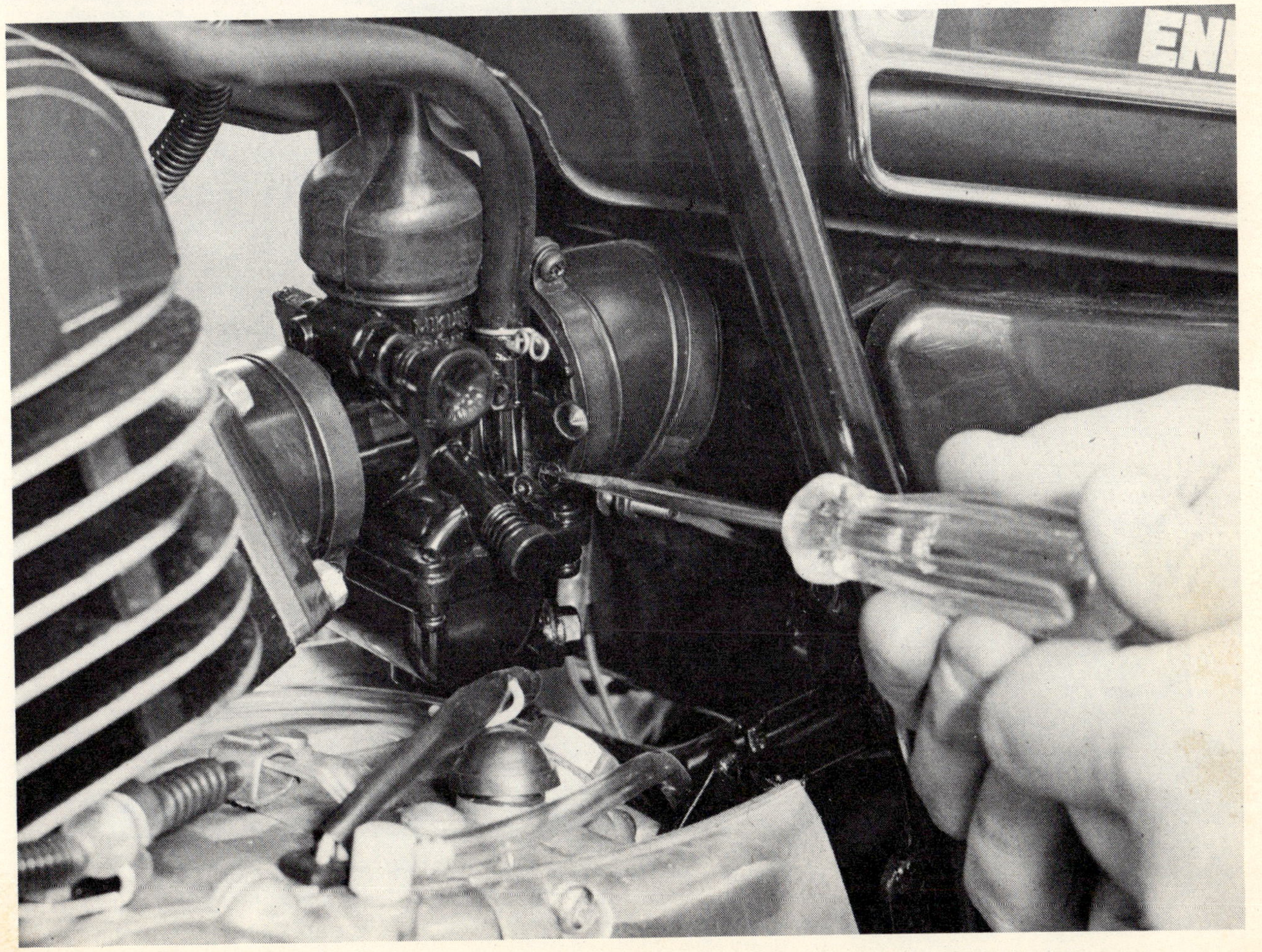

Yamaha RD 350

HERE'S HOW TO TUNE WHAT IS PERHAPS THE BEST LIGHT STREET TWIN ON THE MARKET TODAY.

Access to the ignition on the RD 350 requires removing the engine cover on the left side. Take out the plugs from both cylinders before installing a dial indicator and starting the ignition adjustments. While you have the plugs out is the best time to clean and gap or replace them.

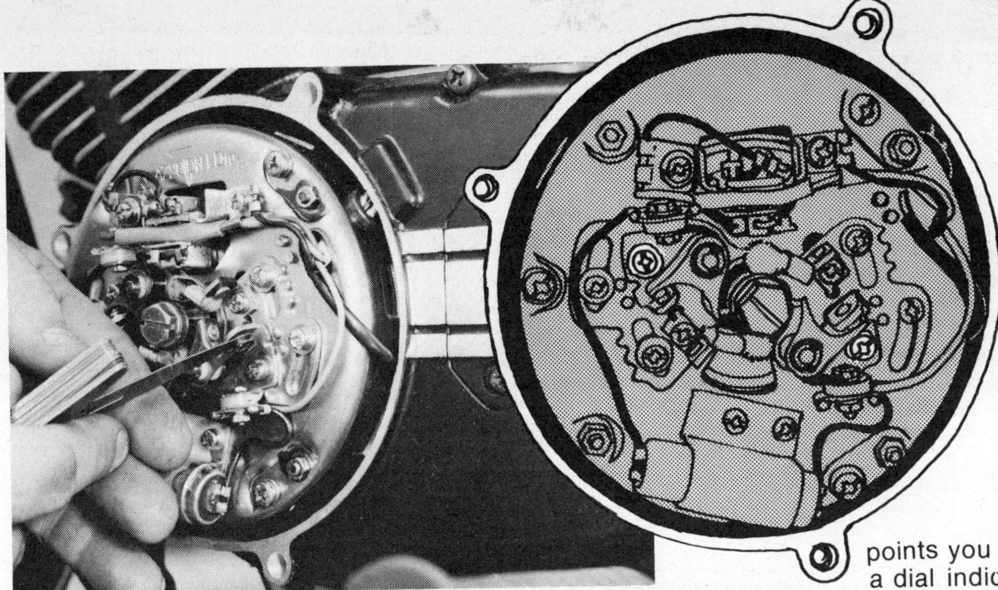

Before setting point timing, set the gap on both sets of points to **.012-.016 inch (0.3-0.4mm).** It's important to get the point gap set right, because it may require some readjustment during the timing process and you'll want to have a good reference point to work from.

First, connect a point checker to the set of ignition points you are setting. Then install a dial indicator in the spark plug hole and zero the dial indicator by cranking the engine over. When you find the exact point at which the dial indicator reverses, indicating piston TDC, zero the meter scale. Then carefully rotate the crankshaft in the direction opposite to that in which it normally rotates until you get a dial reading of **2.0mm** before TDC.

Using the point checker (buzz box), loosen the breaker point setting screw and move the points (very carefully) until the point checker indicates that the points are opening at exactly **2.0mm** BTDC (Before Top Dead Center). Do not fully loosen the screw. The breaker plate tends to creep a bit when you tighten it back down, and it will throw off the setting. Turning the breaker plate in the direction of normal rotation retards the ignition timing, while turning it in the reverse direction advances the timing.

NOTE: WHEN ADJUSTING LEFT-HAND CYLINDER TIMING, ADJUST THE POINTS WITH THE ORANGE TERMINAL. FOR THE RIGHT-HAND CYLINDER, ADJUST THE POINTS WITH THE GRAY TERMINAL.

After the adjustments, turn the engine backwards until you have a reading of 2.5mm BTDC or better. Then reverse direction and bring the engine back toward 2.0mm BTDC. The point checker should indicate point opening exactly at the 2.0mm mark. It may be necessary to repeat this procedure a couple of times to get proper timing on both cylinders and a balanced point opening gap.

To adjust the oil pump, remove the small cover on the forward right side of the engine to expose the pump. Close the throttle completely, then slowly open it until no slack remains in the cable *but* the slides in the carburetors have not yet started to move. At this point, align the pump.

With the throttle cable held at the point described in the previous paragraph, move the oil pump cable adjuster until the small mark on the pump pulley aligns with the pin (see the photo).

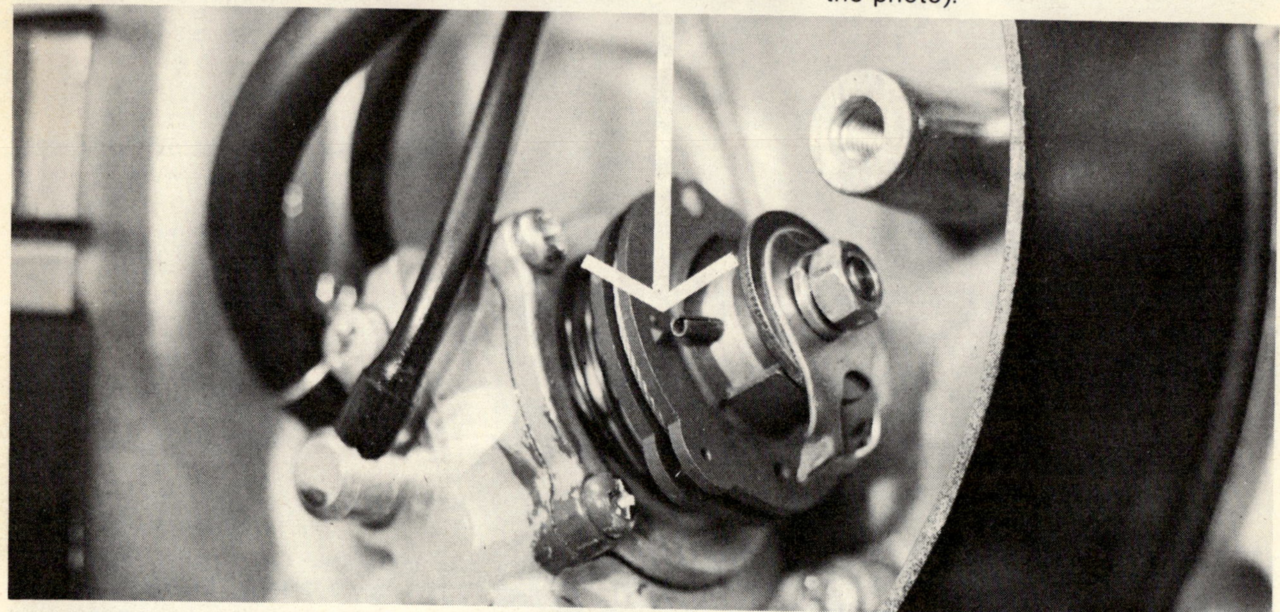

To set idle air, turn the screw lightly until it bottoms, then back it out 1¼ turns. The idle speed screw is hard to see. To adjust it, start the engine and let it warm up, then set engine idle speed to 1100-1200 rpm. Take care to synchronize both carburetors.

YZ 250B
Yamaha YZ 360B

TUNING YAMAHA'S YZ 360B ALSO GIVES YOU THE INFORMATION NEEDED TO TUNE ITS SMALLER BROTHER, THE YZ 250B.

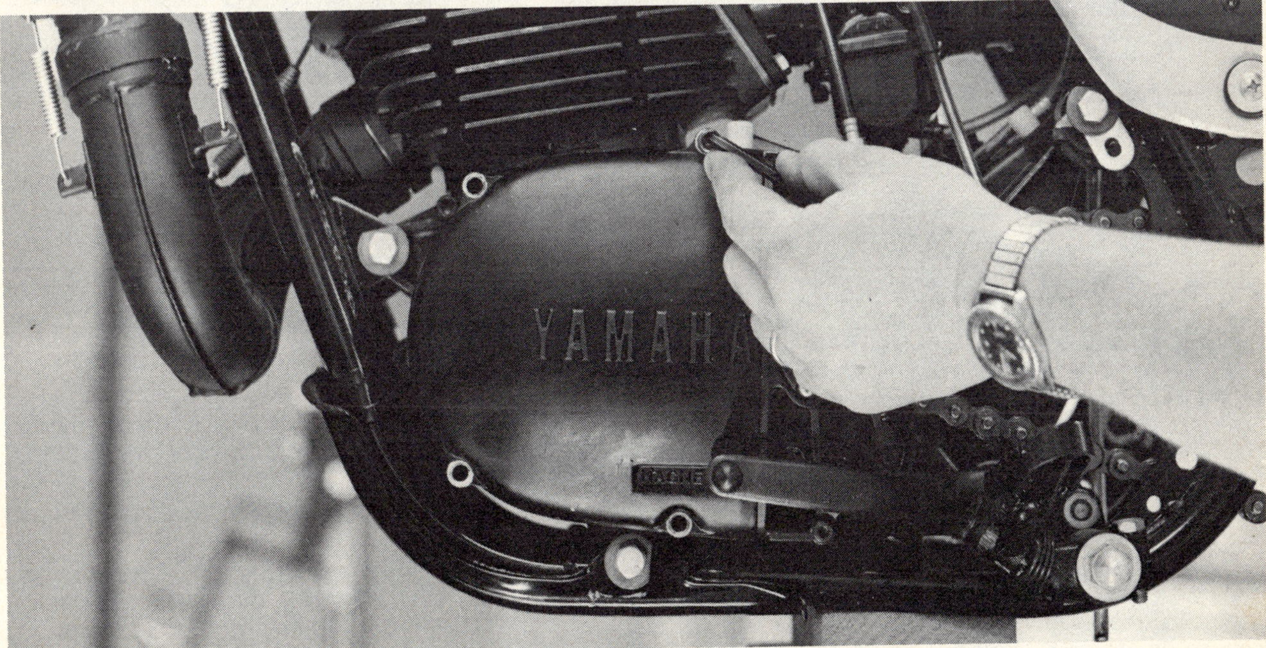

Access to the ignition system on the YZ 360 is gained by removing the cover on the left side of the engine. The screws are Allen-head.

The first step is to make sure that the pulse coil base is centered. The three screws that hold it should be centered in the slots, as shown in the picture.

With the spark plug removed, install a dial indicator in the spark plug hole. Rotate the engine until the piston is at TDC (Top Dead Center). Then set the dial on the indicator so that the dial reads zero at TDC. Rock the engine past the TDC mark several times to make sure of your reading. Starting from TDC, rotate the engine flywheel clockwise until the dial indicator reads **.091 inch (2.3mm)** before TDC.

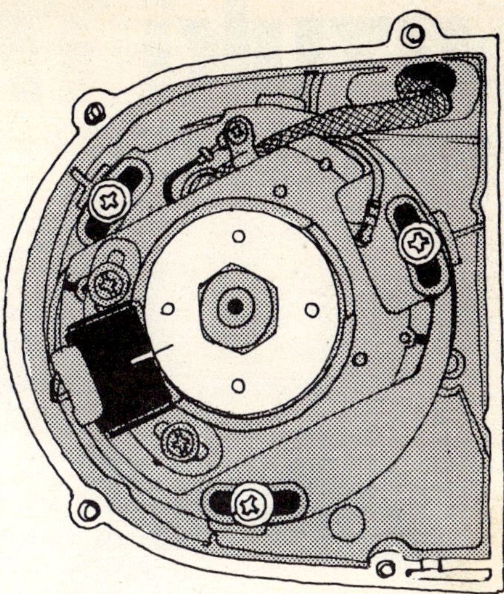

If the marks on the rotor and plate don't line up, loosen the screws and turn the pulse coil plate. Align the timing marks. Retighten the plate screws.

Gap the spark plug to **.016 to .020 inch (0.4 to 0.5mm)** and reinstall, torqueing to between **19.5 and 21.0 ft.-lbs. (2.7-2.9 m-kgs.).**

Adjust idle speed and idle air screws as follows: Idle air—turn gently in until screw bottoms, then back out 1½ turns. Idle speed can be set to rider's preference.

Suzuki TM 125

THE BASIC TUNE-UP ON THIS NO-FRILLS MOTOCROSSER IS A SNAP. THE IGNITION HAS NO POINTS, IS BULLETPROOF AND COMES DIALED-IN FROM THE FACTORY.

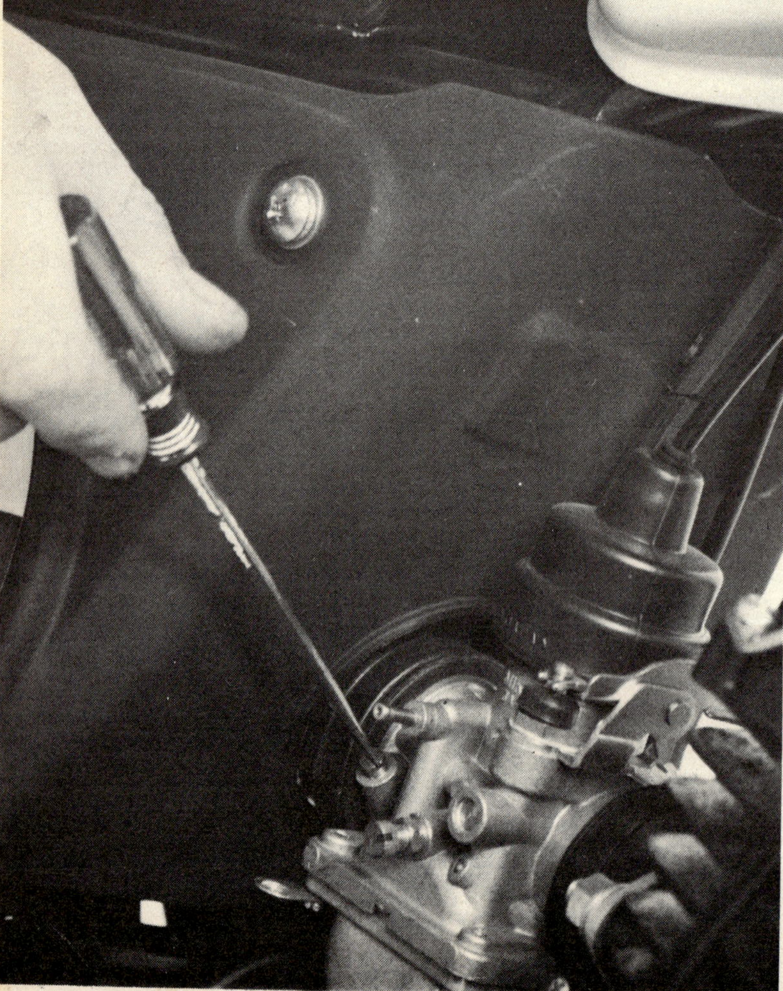

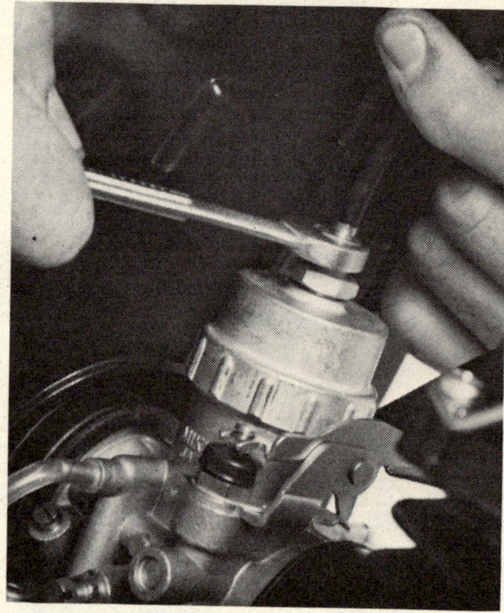

To adjust idle air, turn the pilot air screw in gently until it bottoms out. Then back it out 1½ turns. Set the idle speed by adjusting the throttle valve stop screw just to the right of the pilot air screw. You can adjust idle speed to suit your own desires.

For proper throttle operation, set the throttle cable so that it has **.02 inch (0.5mm)** play at the carburetor. Loosen the lock nut on the carburetor cap adjuster until you have the desired free play, then retighten the lock nut.

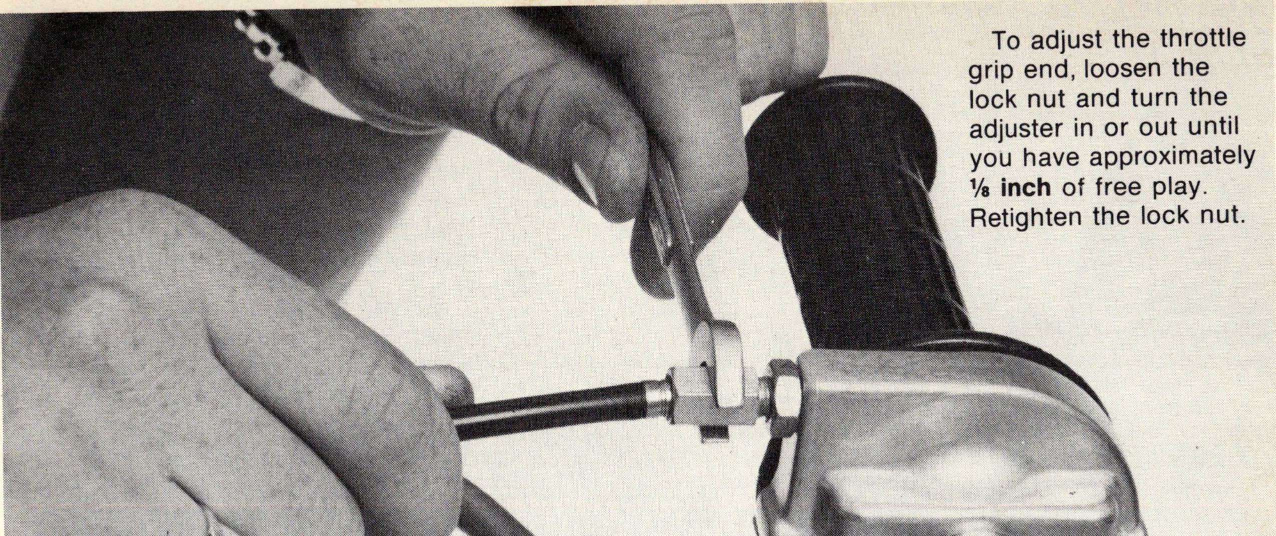

To adjust the throttle grip end, loosen the lock nut and turn the adjuster in or out until you have approximately ⅛ **inch** of free play. Retighten the lock nut.

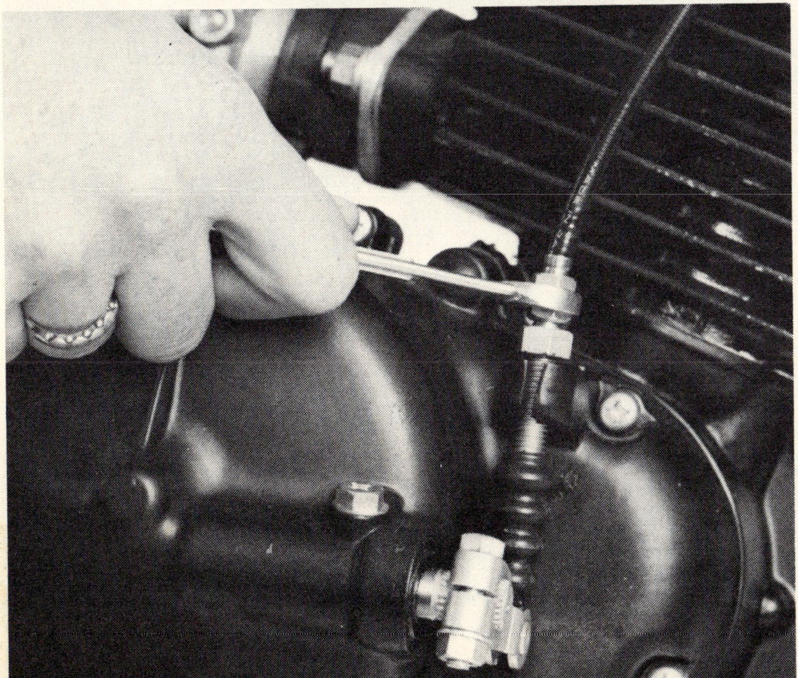

Many all-out racing machines use premixed oil and gas in the tank, but the TM125 has an engine-driven lubrication pump which should be adjusted. To gain access to the oil pump, remove the side cover over the engine sprocket. The oil pump control arm can be seen just behind the sprocket. To adjust, turn the cable adjuster above the pump until the alignment mark on the arm is lined up with the mark on the small post when the throttle is fully opened. That's all there is to it.

Clutch adjustment begins at the cable adjuster on the housing on the right side of the engine. Loosen the adjuster lock nut and turn the adjuster in or out until you have ⅛ **inch** free play at the clutch lever. Retighten the lock nut. Any additional adjustment can be made at the lever end of the cable.

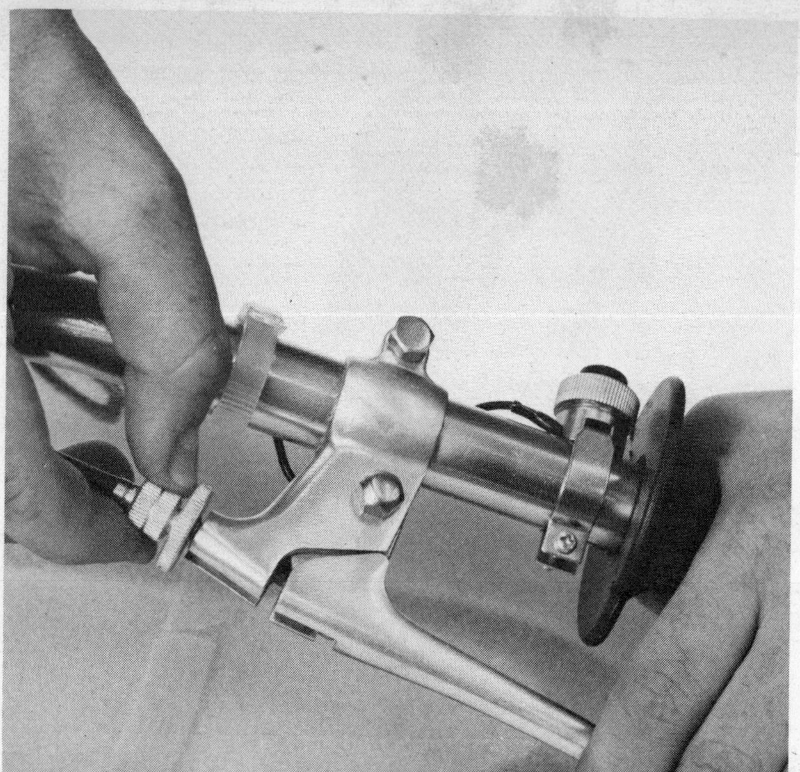

The final adjustment on the clutch is at the lever. If necessary, move the thumb-screw adjuster to get the proper ⅛ inch of free play in the lever. Too little free play can prevent the clutch from locking up all the way, while too much can keep the clutch from releasing completely even when the lever is squeezed.

Setting the ignition is simplicity itself. Suzuki uses an electronic ignition system with no mechanical ignition points, so no real adjustment is possible or necessary. The only external adjustment is timing. This is preset at the factory, but if you wish to check it, attach a timing light and an accessory tachometer (since the bike is not equipped with a tach). With the engine running at 6000 rpm, the center rotor mark should align with the mark on the pulser coil core. If the marks do not align, make sure that the stamped mark on the stator backing plate is aligned with the center of the screw hole.

TC 185
Suzuki TS 185

THE TS 185 IS IDENTICAL TO THE TC 185 EXCEPT FOR IGNITION, AND THESE TUNE-UP INSTRUCTIONS SHOW HOW TO WORK ON BOTH.

To make the pilot air (idle) adjustment, gently turn the pilot air screw in until it bottoms, then back it out 1½ turns.

Before adjusting the idle speed, start the engine and let it reach operating temperature (the book suggests five minutes of warmup). Then adjust the idle speed screw to obtain the lowest rpm at which the engine will idle smoothly.

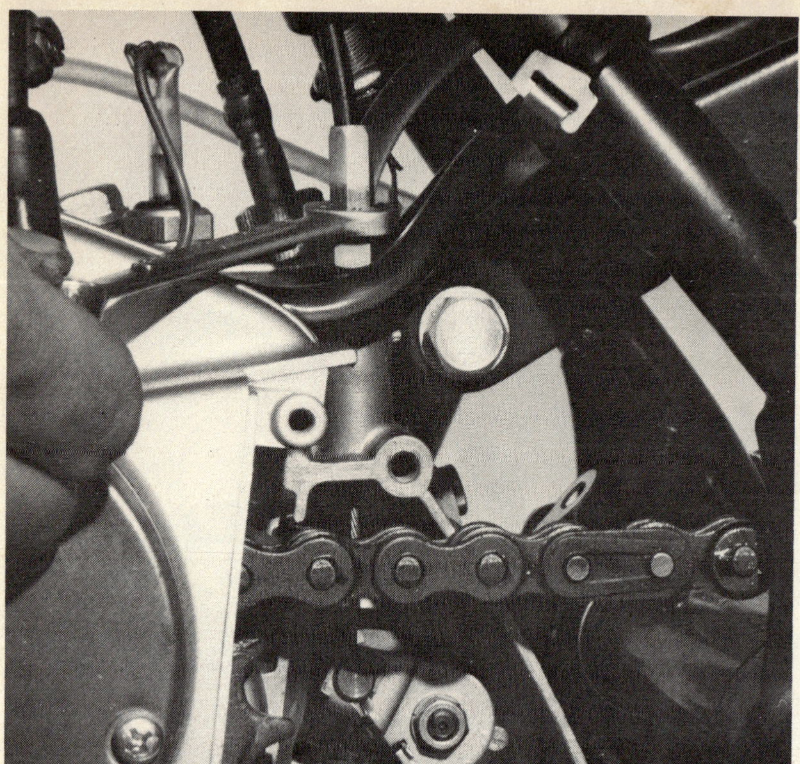

Setting the oil pump requires removal of the small cover over the area of the engine sprocket. To adjust, turn the adjuster until the mark on the pump arm lines up with the mark on the small post at the rear of the pump arm when the throttle is fully open.

Setting the clutch free play takes several steps. First, turn the cable adjusters on the clutch lever and the engine housing all the way in. Then, with the cover removed (on the TS 185; there is an inspection plug on the TC 185), adjust the clutch as shown in the picture.

Loosen the clutch release arm lock nut. Next, turn the adjusting screw in the center with a screwdriver until it lightly bottoms, then back it out ¼ to ½ turn. Tighten the lock nut on the clutch release arm, and then turn the cable adjuster on the housing until there is approximately **⅛ inch (2-3mm)** of free play at the clutch lever.

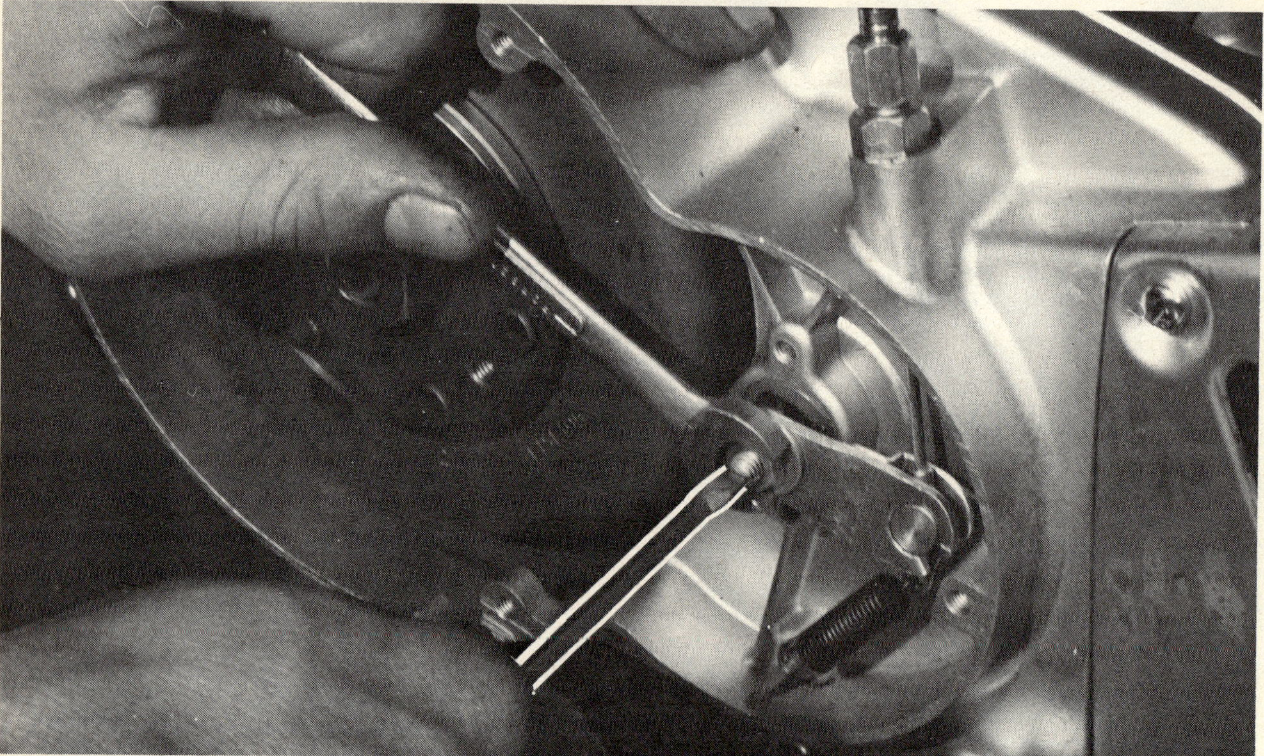

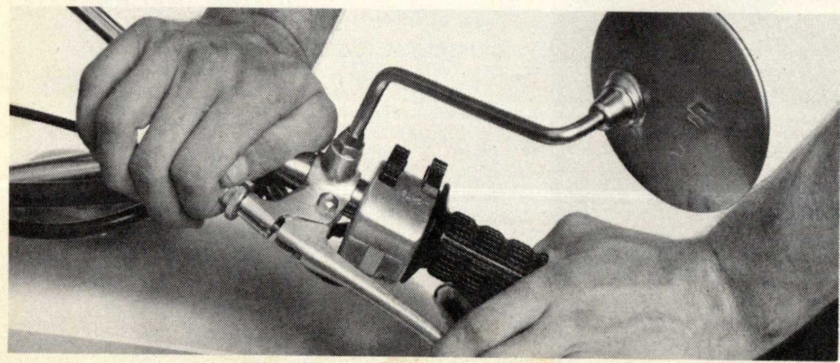

Any additional fine adjustment in the free play of the clutch lever can be made at the adjuster on the clutch lever. Remember, there should be ⅛ inch of free play.

Since the TS 185 is equipped with Suzuki electronic ignition, it requires no point adjustment (the TC 185 does, and it is covered in the next few photos). To check the timing, remove the left engine cover and attach a timing light. There are timing marks on the flywheel and a cast timing mark on the inside of the case. The center timing mark on the flywheel should line up with the casting mark when the engine is running at 4000 rpm.

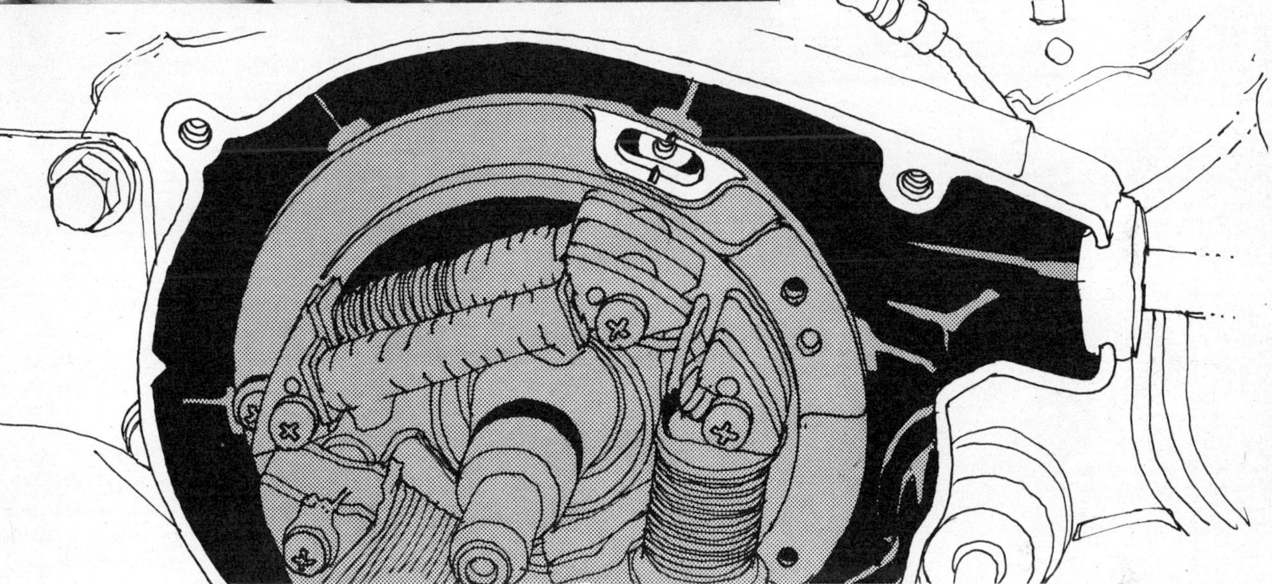

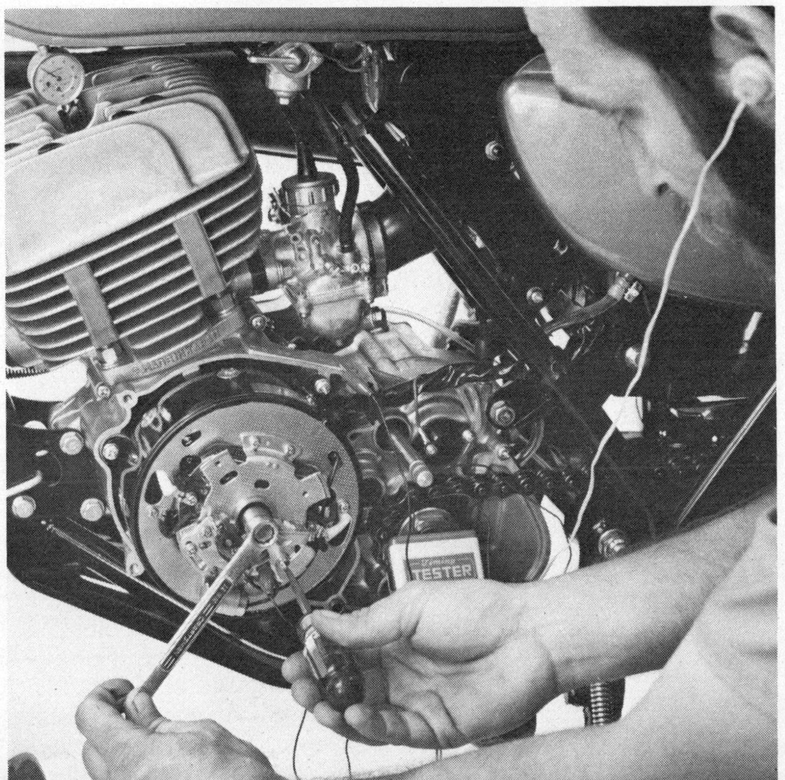

To adjust the timing on the TS 185, first remove the flywheel to gain access to the ignition coils. You'll need a puller to remove the flywheel. The puller is Suzuki part #09930-30713. With the flywheel off, align the stamped mark at the top of the stator plate with the center of the screw hole just above it. Reinstall the screw and check the timing. You may have to repeat this. When reinstalling the flywheel, tighten nut to **45 ft.-lbs.**

To time the TC 185, remove the spark plug and install a dial indicator. Rotate the engine until the dial pointer reverses direction, indicating piston TDC, then zero the meter and turn the engine clockwise until the dial reads slightly past **3.07mm.** At *exactly* this moment, the attached buzz box should sound, indicating point opening. If the adjustment is not correct, loosen the point backing plate and move the point plate until the buzz box indicates point opening. Then retighten the locking screws and recheck.

Suzuki T 500

SUZUKI'S 500 WAS ONE OF THE FIRST BIG TWO-STROKES. NOW IT WOULD BE CLASSED AS A MIDDLEWEIGHT.

Remove the left engine cover. Rotate the engine until one set of points is open to its widest position. For the actual adjustment, loosen the lock screw and then use the screwdriver blade in the adjusting slot on the points. Adjust the gap to **.012-.016 inch (0.3-0.4mm),** using a feeler gauge. Then retighten the lock screw and repeat the steps for the other set of points.

Set the timing by removing a spark plug from one cylinder and inserting a dial indicator. Zero the dial indicator by turning the engine over (use a 12mm wrench on the cam extension for the points) until the dial indicator reverses itself. When the *exact* moment of indicator reversal is reached, the piston of the cylinder you are setting is at TDC. Zero the dial, then connect a buzz box (timing tester) to the set of points for that cylinder. The point set in the forward position (to the left) is for the left cylinder; the points to the rear of the engine (to the right) are for the right cylinder.

Now turn the engine counterclockwise a distance of **3.40mm,** as indicated on the dial indicator. At that exact reading, you should get an indication of point opening from the buzz box. If not, loosen the backing plate screws for the ignition and move the entire plate until it is correct. Tighten the screws and recheck the timing. Repeat for the second set of ignition points.

Although the owner's manual for the T 500 recommends that exacting carburetor adjustments be done by a dealer, the following part of the tuning procedure is simple. To adjust idle air (pilot air), turn the pilot air screw in gently until it bottoms, then back it out 1½ turns. Next, set the throttle cable (see next step). After that, start the engine and allow it to warm up. Then adjust the idle speed screw, which. can be seen just to the right of the screwdriver in this picture. Adjust the idle speed for the slowest idle rpm at which the engine runs smoothly.

Adjust the throttle cable free play to provide between **1/16 inch and ⅛ inch (2-3mm)** of free movement.

To adjust the oil pump output, remove the little cover over the pump so that you can see the oil pump arm. There are alignment marks on the arm and on a small post near the arm. With the throttle opened all the way, the marks should line up. If not, adjust the cable until the marks line up correctly.

To adjust the clutch, first turn the adjuster at the clutch lever and then the adjuster at the case end of the cable all the way in. Next, remove the inspection cap from the left engine case cover and loosen the lock nut. Turn the adjusting screw in the lock nut in until it bottoms out (do it slowly and gently), then back it out ¼ to ½ turn and tighten the lock nut.

The final clutch adjustment is cable free play. Turn the cable adjuster at the case end of the clutch cable to provide about **⅛ inch** of free play at the clutch lever. Any minor adjustment required beyond that can be made at the lever end of the cable.

Suzuki GT 750

SUZUKI'S GIANT WATER-COOLED TRIPLE HAS NO LESS THAN THREE COMPLETE SETS OF IGNITION POINTS, BUT IT'S EASY TO TUNE.

Set the ignition points (there are three sets, one for each cylinder) by first rotating the engine until the set of points you're adjusting is open to its widest setting. Using a screwdriver and a feeler gauge, unlock the lock screw and set the gap to **.012-.016 inch (0.3-0.4mm).** Retighten the lock screw and repeat the procedure for the other two sets of points. Do not attempt to set the ignition timing until you have set the gap on all three sets of points.

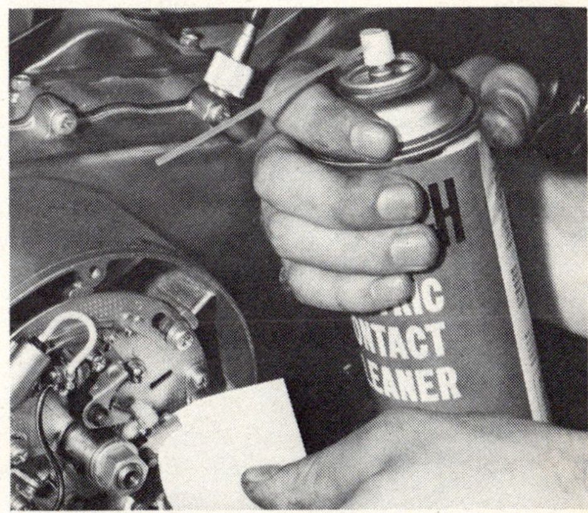

Here's a good tip for cleaning ignition points: Use a good commercial contact cleaner, then draw a thin piece of cardboard between the point surfaces to remove any oily residue.

To start the timing process, remove all three spark plugs from the cylinder head and install a dial indicator in the left cylinder spark plug hole. To turn the engine over to zero the indicator, put the bike on its centerstand. Place the transmission in its highest gear (5th). Turning the rear wheel, rotate the engine until the dial indicator begins to reverse itself. At that point, zero the dial indicator. The left-hand cylinder piston is now at TDC.

Connect a timing tester (buzz box) to the set of points being set, starting with the left cylinder points. The points are marked with letters—"L" for left, "C" for center and "R" for right cylinders. To remove any slack in the timing chain prior to making an adjustment, rotate the rear wheel backwards, *beyond* the desired timing point. Then very carefully bring the engine toward TDC again until you have reached a dial reading of **3.64mm** BTDC (Before Top Dead Center). At the *exact* moment of reaching 3.64mm BTDC, the buzz box should indicate point opening.

For necessary adjustment to the *left cylinder* points, loosen the three Phillips screws and turn the entire point backing plate assembly until the left cylinder ignition points are just beginning to open at the correct setting. Retighten screws and recheck.

Now repeat the procedure for the center and right cylinders. Be aware, though, that the *center cylinder* uses a different dial indicator reading than the outer cylinders. That's because it has a slightly different spark plug hole angle, which changes the indicator shaft angle. Begin by attaching the buzz box to the ignition points marked "C." Then install the dial indicator in the center cylinder. Zero the dial indicator in the same manner as before.

This time bring the final timing measurement to **3.42mm** BTDC. As you reach exactly 3.42mm BTDC, the timing tester should indicate that the points for the center cylinder are just beginning to open. If adjustment is required, loosen and adjust the locking screw for the individual center points set *only*.

The procedure for the *right cylinder* points is the same, except that the dial reading should be **3.64mm** BTDC again, just as with the left cylinder.

Setting the oil injector pump is

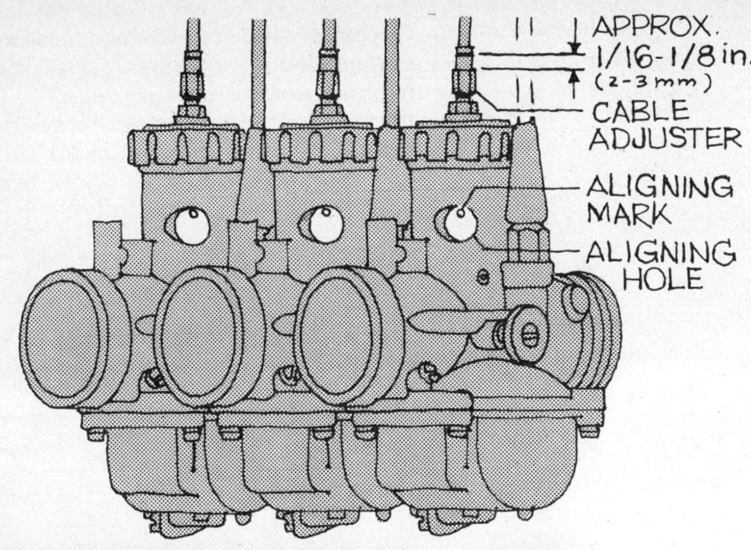

combined with an adjustment of the carburetors. In the upper right part of the photo (arrow), notice the hole in the side of the carburetor body. In the hole is an alignment dot. Before you can set the pump, you must first remove the plug fitted to that hole from each of the three carburetors. Also, adjust the individual carburetor cable play to **1/16 -⅛ inch** on each.

Twist the throttle until the alignment dots appear in the holes. Make sure that all three dots align at the upper edge of their holes, as shown in the photograph. A slight readjustment of one or more of the throttle cables may be necessary to get them lined up.

Finally, adjust the oil pump by seeing that the mark on the oil pump arm lines up with a mark on a cast metal post next to the arm—when the dots are in the position shown. After adjusting, retighten the lock nut on the oil pump cable and reinstall the three plugs in the carburetors.

Adjust the throttle cable assembly at the upper end. With a pair of wrenches, establish approximately **⅛ inch** of free play.

Adjust the pilot air screws on all three carburetors by turning them in easily until they bottom out. Do this gently; too much force can ruin the seat. Then back each screw out 1½ turns.

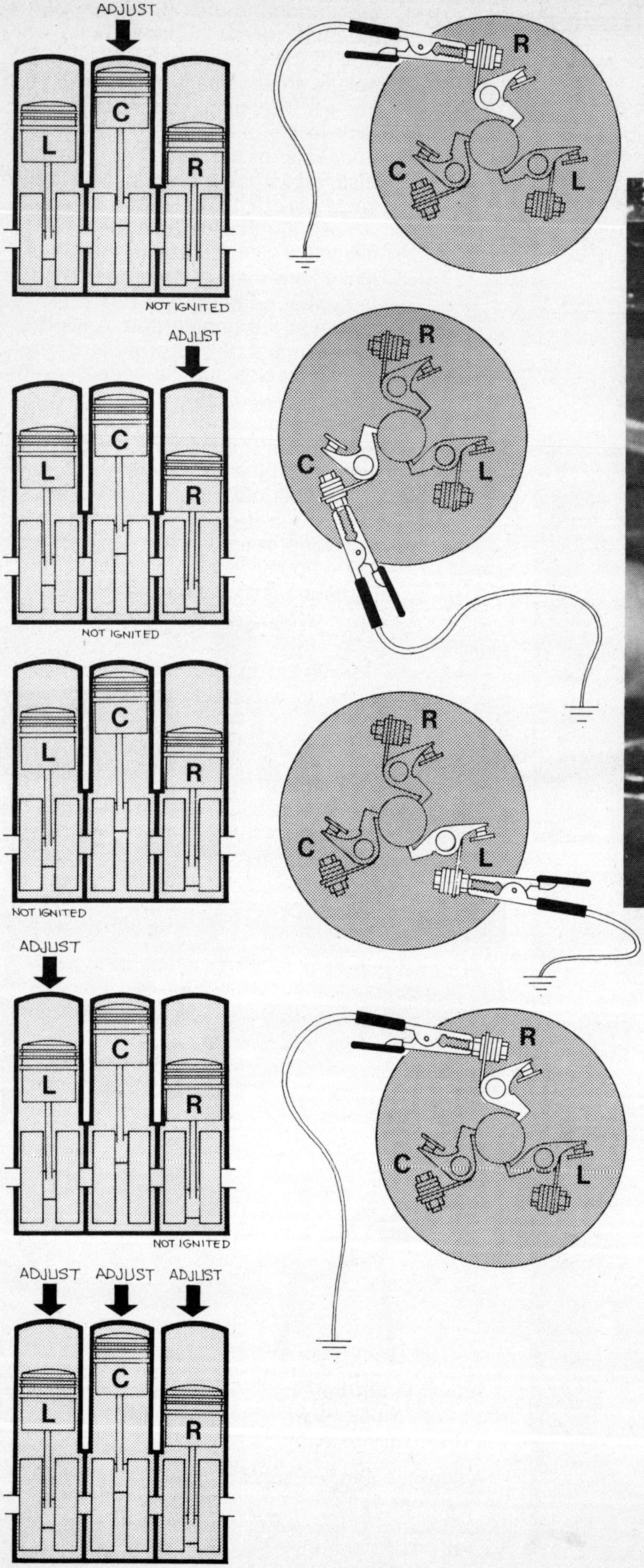

After setting the idle air, start the engine and let it warm up for at least five minutes (or until it reaches normal operating temperature). Then shut the engine off. Adjust all three idle screws by bottoming each lightly and then backing it out 3½ turns.

Next, balance the idle on each carburetor by following the procedure shown in the artwork. You'll need a test lead with an alligator clip on one or both ends. Ground out the ignition points of the right-hand cylinder by hooking the lead from the connection on the points to any place on the engine where you can get a good ground. Then adjust the throttle stop screw on the center carburetor until the tachometer reads 1100 rpm.

Next, repeat the procedure by grounding the center cylinder ignition and adjusting the right cylinder throttle stop screw for a reading of 1100 rpm. Finally, ground the right cylinder ignition and adjust the throttle stop screw on the left cylinder for an idle of 1100 RPM. When you have adjusted each of the three cylinders individually, remove the ground and adjust the throttle stop screws of all three carburetors *equally* to bring the engine to an 1100 rpm idle speed.

To set the clutch correctly, first turn the adjuster at the clutch lever end all the way in. Then turn the adjuster at the engine case end of the cable all the way in. Remove the small cover that fits over the clutch release mechanism. Using a pair of 17mm wrenches, tighten the nuts until there is about **0.2mm** of axial play in the clutch release shaft.

After setting the clutch release shaft, adjust the clutch cover adjusting bolt until you have **⅛ inch (2-3mm)** of free play at the clutch lever. Then tighten the lock nut.

If any additional adjusting is needed to get the required free play, do it with the adjuster on the clutch lever.

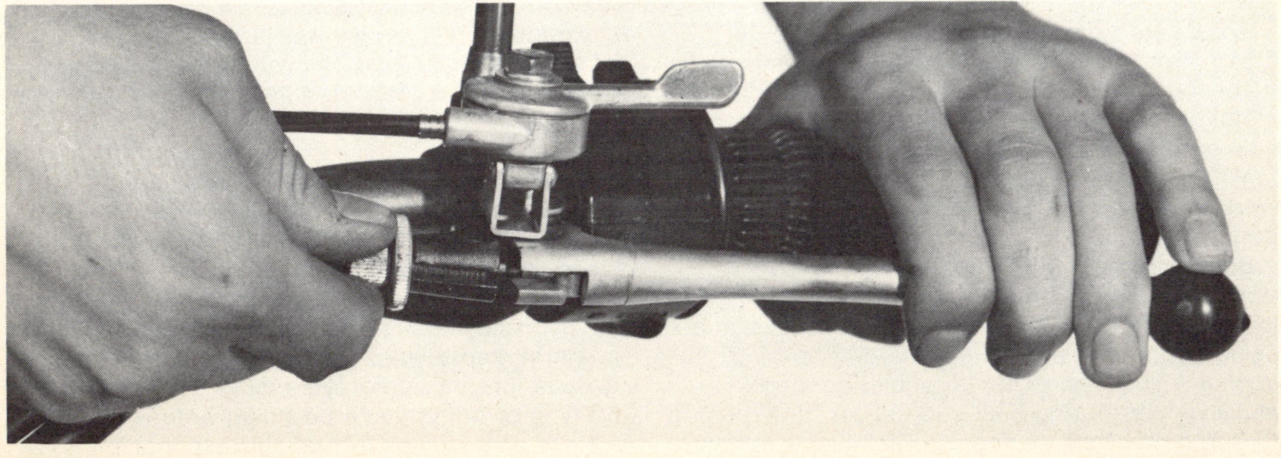

V/Economy Tips

Riding two up is a favorite way to have a good time, but on a small-displacement motorcycle, it can result in a loss of gas mileage. The point is, try to match the motorcycle to the job if you're after high mileage.

A concern common to almost everybody in these days of high fuel prices is getting maximum fuel economy, whether from a car or a motorcycle. While your motorcycle is designed to give better mileage than an automobile, proper tuning methods and materials will give you a head start on getting the best possible mileage (and performance) out of your motorcycle.

Before attempting to improve on the level of economy your motorcycle now provides, take a look at the basic specifications of your bike and decide if it is possible to get the degree of economy you desire. For example, no large, multicylinder touring bike can get (or be expected to get) better mileage than a small-displacement motorcycle of the type used for casual trail riding or short trips to school and the store.

Similarly, if you have a small bike, say under 125cc, and you regularly load it down with a passenger or camping equipment, you might be better off buying a somewhat larger motorcycle as a first step toward getting good economy. It's obvious that the motorcycle must be matched to the type of riding you'll be doing before you can achieve any savings in fuel and expenses.

Your street riding techniques have a lot to do with mileage also. If you like to extract the maximum in performance from your motorcycle or do a little street racing, then don't expect too much from your bike in the way of economy.

This can be the biggest gas thief on your motorcycle. A dirty air filter changes the air/fuel ratio and can really reduce fuel economy. Keeping the filter clean is basic to getting maximum mileage and performance out of your bike.

Riding styles have a great deal to do with economy. No amount of "trick" tuning will save you much gas if your riding style includes shotgun starts from every stoplight in town and riding the bike into its upper rpm limits in each gear.

Another thing that many riders do which lowers fuel economy is riding the bike before it is completely warmed up. This is especially critical with two-stroke engines. They simply do not function well until internal parts of the cylinder and the piston have reached normal operating temperatures. A lot of riders try to get around this by riding the bike with the choke left partly in the ON position, figuring that since the bike is running without stumbling or sputtering, they're doing everything right. This isn't true. Riding a partly warmed-up bike with the choke slightly on may get you down the road, but it destroys economy.

Spend a few minutes reading the owner's manual for your motorcycle. You'll find some interesting information on how to ride in the better ones.

When applying tuning to the problem of fuel economy, it helps to understand one thing quite clearly. Except for one or two minor changes, the tuning you do to improve fuel economy is exactly the same as the tuning procedures discussed in the rest of this book. The most important single step toward gaining the maximum in economy is keeping all critical parts on the bike in good repair. Preventive maintenance is the name of the game.

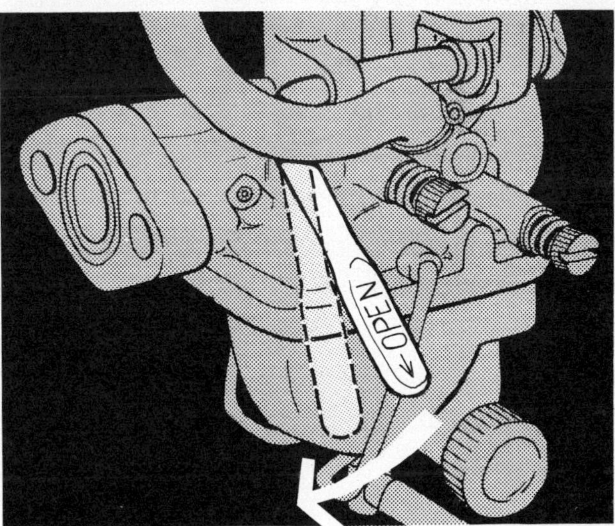

Make sure that the choke is completely off before riding the bike. Riding with the choke partly on does nothing to enhance fuel economy.

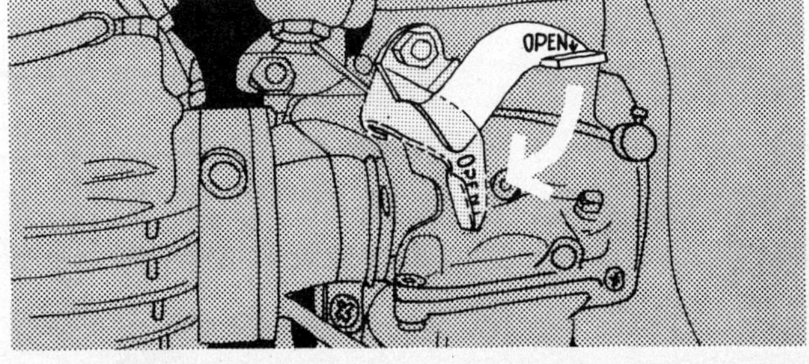

A clogged air filter left over from a weekend spent riding in the desert or a spark plug that hasn't been changed since the bike was purchased last year—these are the kinds of things that steal gas mileage and performance. Bad ignition points or condenser is another electrical problem that can make gas mileage fall off drastically as the bike suffers wear between tune-ups.

Another major potential problem area on your motorcycle is the spark plug. A fouled plug will cost you! Inspect spark plugs often; either clean and regap them or replace them.

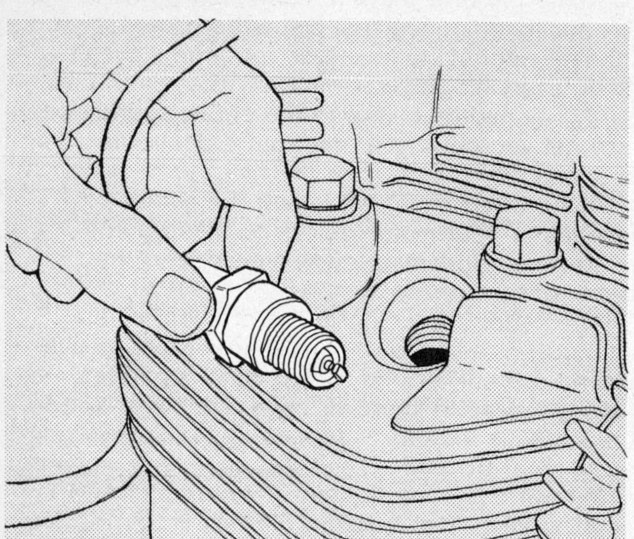

Much the same can be said of ignition points and condenser as of the spark plug. These items wear and can cause severe performance and economy problems. Inspect and tune them at regular intervals, as specified in owner's manual.

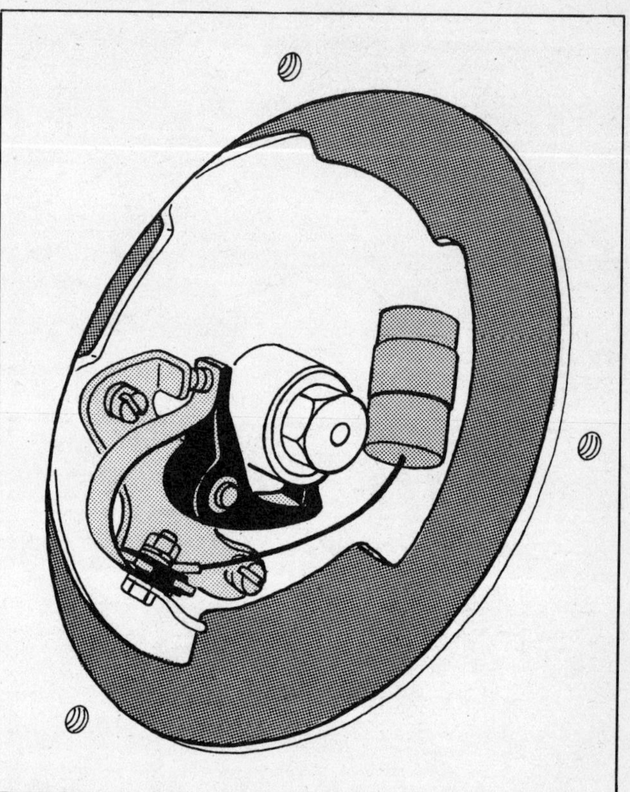

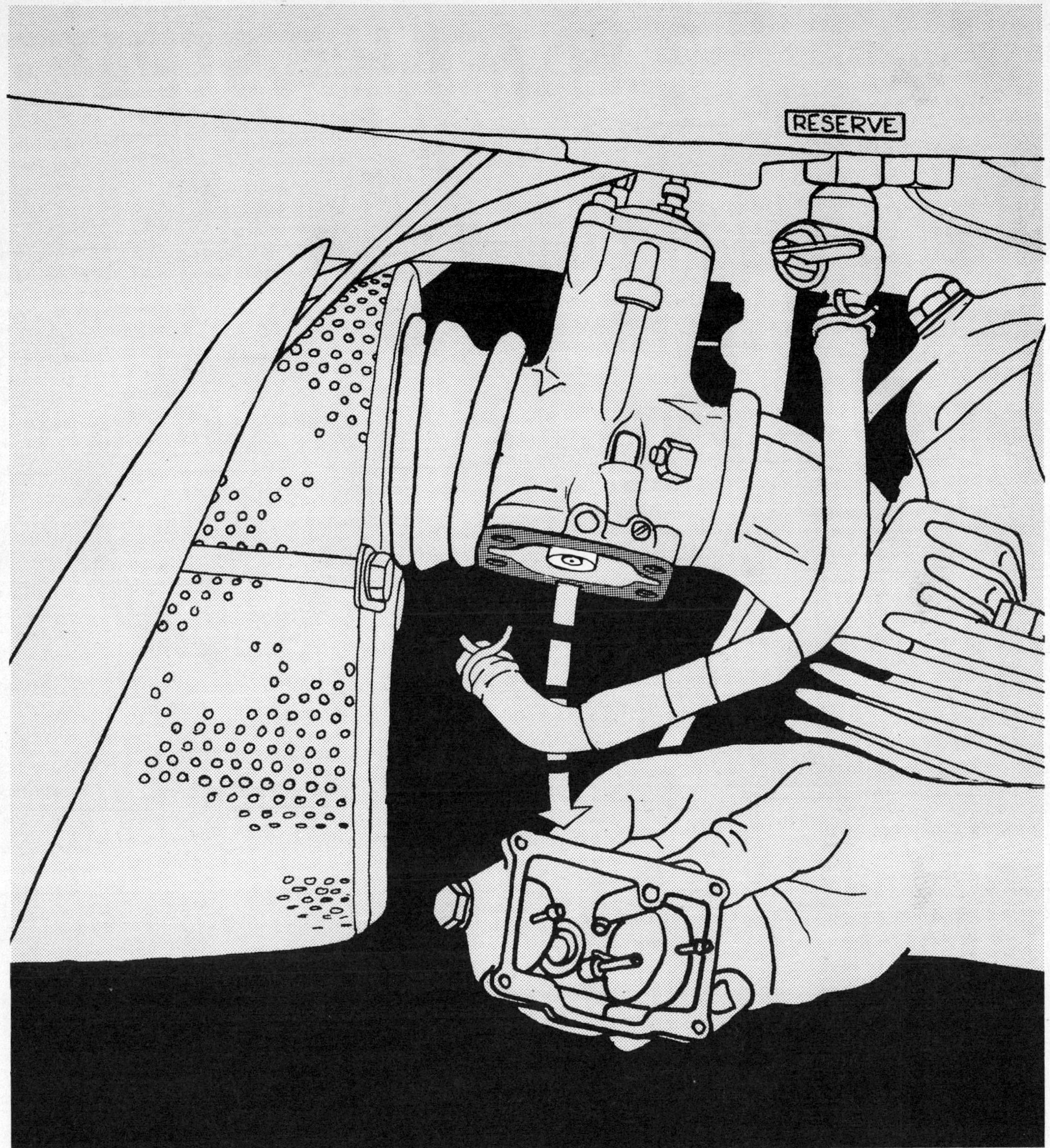

Carburetor jetting changes, though accompanied by a drop in performance, can result in considerable fuel savings. Be careful not to overdo it. Get the advice of an experienced mechanic before changing internal parts of the carburetor.

In extreme cases, you might wish to get better gas economy than the bike is capable of in its present form. This means that you'll have to start making changes in the carburetor jetting. It is the jets (small orifices or openings through which the fuel passes into the airstream in the carburetor) that control the amount of fuel the engine can take in.

Before you undertake such a change, be sure to read the shop manual for your bike and discuss the problem with an experienced mechanic. He may be able to recommend other measures or give you some good information on reducing jet sizes for better economy.

The only way to get the bike to use less fuel than it is designed to use, once you've performed all the routine tune-up steps and have the bike in a good state of tune, is to reduce the intake of fuel by jet changes. You may find that you have to do considerable work and make several test rides to evaluate the results of a jet change.

Keep in mind that any such jet change will alter the power output and road performance of your bike as well. If you're willing to accept a slight reduction in power, you can achieve considerable savings in fuel.

YAMAHA STREET &

YAMAHA RD 200B

MODEL	SPARK PLUG GAP	POINT GAP	IGNITION TIMING	IDLE AIR SCREW (turns out)
XS 650B	.6-.7mm .024-.028 in.	.30-.45mm .012-.018 in.	34-42° (retarded)	¾ ± ½
XS 500B	.6-.7mm .024-.028 in.	.30-.45mm .012-.020 in.	38 ± 3° BTDC	1⅜ ± ¼
RD 350B	.6-.7mm .024-.028 in.	.3-.4mm .012-.016 in.	2.0mm BTDC	1¾
RD 250B	.6-.7mm .024-.028 in.	.3-.4mm .012-.016 in.	2.0 ± .15mm BTDC	1¼
RD 200B	.6-.7mm .024-.028 in.	.3-.4mm .012-.016 in.	1.8mm BTDC	1¼
RD 125B	.6-.7mm .024-.028 in.	.3-.4mm .012-.016 in.	1.8 ± .15mm BTDC	1½
RS 100B	.5-.6mm .019-.023 in.	.3-.4mm .012-.016 in.	1.8 ± .15mm BTDC	1½

ENDURO MODELS (TWO-STROKE)

YAMAHA DT 100B

MODEL	SPARK PLUG GAP	POINT GAP	IGNITION TIMING	IDLE AIR SCREW (turns out)
DT 400B	.5-.6mm .019-.023 in.	none/CDI	2.9 ± .15mm BTDC	1½
DT 250B	.5-.6mm .019-.023 in.	.3-.4mm .012-.016 in.	3.2mm BTDC	1¾
DT 175B	.5-.6mm .019-.023 in.	.3-.4mm .012-.016 in.	1.8mm BTDC (full advance)	1
DT 125B	.6-.7mm .024-.028 in.	.3-.4mm .012-.016 in.	1.8mm BTDC (full advance)	1½
DT 100B	.5-.6mm .019-.023 in.	.3-.4mm .012-.016 in.	1.8mm BTDC	1¼
GT 80B	.5-.6mm .019-.023 in.	.3-.4mm .012-.016 in.	1.8mm BTDC	1½
RD 60B	.5-.6mm .019-.023 in.	.3-.4mm .012..016 in.	1.8mm BTDC	1¾

TRIUMPH

(FOUR-STROKE) NOTE: Do ignition timing at 3000 rpm.

TRIUMPH T160V

TRIUMPH T150V

MODEL	SPARK PLUG GAP	POINT GAP	IGNITION TIMING	VALVES (COLD)	IDLE AIR SCREW
TR5MX	.024 in.	.014-.016 in.	30° BTDC	In .008 in. Ex .010 in.	1½
T100R	.024 in.	.014-.016 in.	38° BTDC	In .002 in. Ex .004 in.	1½
T100C	.024 in	.014-.016 in.	38° BTDC	In .002 in. Ex .004 in.	1¼
TR5T	.024 in.	.014-.016 in.	38° BTDC	In .002 in. Ex .004 in.	1¼
TR6C	.024 in.	.014-.016 in.	38° BTDC	In .002 in. Ex .004 in.	1¼
TR6R	.024 in.	.014-.016 in.	38° BTDC	In .002 in. Ex .004 in.	1¼
T120R & V	.024 in.	.014-.016 in.	38° BTDC	In .002 in. Ex .004 in.	1¼
TR7R & V	.024 in.	.014-.016 in.	38° BTDC	In .008 in. Ex .006 in.	1¼
T140V	.024 in.	.014-.016 in.	38° BTDC	In .008 in. Ex .006 in.	1¼
T150V	.024 in.	.014-.016 in.	38° BTDC	In .006 in. Ex .008 in.	1½
T160V	.024 in.	.014-.016 in.	38° BTDC	In .006 in. Ex .008 in.	1½

NORTON

(FOUR-STROKE)
NOTE: Do ignition timing at 3000 rpm.

MODEL	SPARK PLUG GAP	POINT GAP	IGNITION TIMING	VALVES (COLD)	IDLE AIR SCREW
COMMANDO 750	.023-.028 in.	.014-.016 in.	28° BTDC	In .006 in. Ex .008 in.	1 to 1½
COMMANDO 850	.023-.028 in.	.014-.016 in.	28° BTDC	In .006 in. Ex .008 in.	1 to 1½

NORTON COMMANDO 850

NORTON COMMANDO 750

B.S.A.

(FOUR-STROKE)
NOTE: Do ignition timing at 3000 rpm.

MODEL	SPARK PLUG GAP	POINT GAP	IGNITION TIMING	VALVES (COLD)	IDLE AIR SCREW
B50	.024 in.	.014-.016 in.	30° BTDC	In .008 in. Ex .010 in.	1½
A65	.024 in.	.014-.016 in.	34° BTDC	In .008 in. Ex .010 in.	1½
A70	.024 in.	.014-.016 in.	34° BTDC	In .008 in. Ex .010 in.	1 to 1½
A75	.024 in.	.014-.016 in.	38° BTDC	In .006 in. Ex .008 in.	1 to 1½

KAWASAKI

(FOUR-STROKE)

MODEL	SPARK PLUG GAP	POINT GAP	IGNITION TIMING	VALVES (COLD)	IDLE AIR SCREW
900 Z1B	.7-.8mm	.3-.4mm	20° BTDC @ 1500 rpm 40° BTDC @ 2350 rpm	In .05mm Ex .10mm	1¼
KZ 400D KZ 400S	.7-.8mm	.3-.4mm	15° BTDC @ 1500 rpm 40° BTDC @ 2670 rpm	In .08mm Ex .13mm	1½

KAWASAKI KZ 400S

KAWASAKI F11B

(TWO-STROKE)

MODEL	SPARK PLUG GAP	POINT GAP	IGNITION TIMING	IDLE AIR SCREW (turns out)
MT1C	.4-.5mm	.3-.4mm	1.85mm BTDC	1½
MC1B MC1MA	.4-.5mm	.3-.4mm	1.96mm BTDC	1½
KD 80	.4-.5mm	.3-.4mm	1.96mm BTDC	1½
G3SSE	.6-.7mm	.3-.4mm	1.96mm BTDC	1½
G4TRE	.6-.7mm	.3-.4mm	1.96mm BTDC	1½
G5C	.6-.7mm	.3-.4mm	1.96mm BTDC	1½
KS 125A	.6-.7mm	.3-.4mm	2.52mm BTDC	1½
KD 125	.6-.7mm	.3-.4mm	2.52mm BTDC	1½
KX 125A	.6mm	none/CDI	1.91mm BTDC	1
F7D	.6-.7mm	none/CDI	2.94mm/6 mark	1¼
F11B	.6-.7mm	.3-.4mm	2.56mm BTDC	1¾
KT 250A	.6-.7mm	none/CDI	23° @ 4000 rpm	1½
KX 250A	.6mm	none/CDI	22° @ 6000 rpm 2.90mm BTDC	1
S1C	.6-.7mm	.3-.4mm	2.60mm BTDC	1½
F9C	1.0mm	none/CDI	3.41mm/6 mark	1½
KX 400	.6mm	none/CDI	3.20mm BTDC	1
S3A	.6-.7mm	.3-.4mm	2.60 BTDC	1½
H1F	1.0mm	.5-.8mm	2.94mm BTDC	1¼
H2C	1.0mm	.5-.8mm	3.13mm/L mark	1¾

SUZUKI

(TWO-STROKE)

MODEL	SPARK PLUG GAP	POINT GAP	IGNITION TIMING	IDLE AIR SCREW
TS 50	.6-.7mm .024-.028 in.	.012-.016 in. .3-.4mm	2mm BTDC	1½
TM 75	.6-.7mm .024-.028 in.	.3-.4mm .012-.016 in.	1.56mm BTDC	1½
RV 90	.6-.7mm .024-.028 in.	.3-.4mm .012-.016 in	2.04mm BTDC	1½
RV 125	.6-.7mm .024-.028 in.	.3-.4mm .012-.016 in.	2.41mm BTDC	1½
TC 100	.6-.7mm .024-.028 in.	.3-.4mm .012-.016 in.	2.22mm BTDC	1½
TS 100	.6-.7mm .024-.028 in.	.3-.4mm .012-.016 in.	2.22mm BTDC	1½
TM 100	.6-.7mm .024-.028 in.	none/PEI	29° BTDC @ 3000 rpm	1½
TM 125	.6-.7mm .024-.028 in.	none/PEI	29° BTDC @ 3000 rpm	1½
TC 125	.6-.7mm .024-.028 in.	.3-.4mm .012-.016 in.	2.41mm BTDC	1¼
TS 125	.6-.7mm .024-.028 in.	.3-.4mm .012-.016 in.	2.41mm BTDC	1¼
TS 185	.6-.7mm .024-.028 in.	none/PEI	factory preset	1½
TC 185	.6-.7mm .024-.028 in.	.3-.4mm .012-.016 in.	3.07mm BTDC	1½
GT 185	.6-.7mm .024-.028 in.	.3-.4mm .012-.016 in.	1.83mm BTDC	1
GT 250	.6-.7mm .024-.028 in.	.3-.4mm .012-.016 in.	2.88mm BTDC	1½
RL 250	.6-.7mm .024-.028 in.	none/PEI	factory preset	1½

MODEL	SPARK PLUG GAP	POINT GAP	IGNITION TIMING	IDLE AIR SCREW
TM250	.6-.7mm .024-.028 in	none/PEI	21.5° BTDC @ 6000 rpm	1
TM 400	.6-.7mm .024-.028 in.	none/PEI	22° BTDC @ 3000 rpm	1
TS 250	.6-.7mm .024-.028 in.	none/PEI	factory preset (see shop manual)	1¾
TS 400	.6-.7mm .024-.028 in.	none/PEI	factory preset (see shop manual)	1¼
GT 380	.6-.7mm .024-.028 in.	.3-.4mm .012-.016 in.	3.00mm BTDC	1¼
GT 550	.6-.7mm .024-.028 in.	.3-.4mm .012-.016 in.	3.37mm BTDC	1¼
T 500	.6-.7mm .024-.028 in.	.3-.4mm .012-.016 in.	3.40mm BTDC	1½
GT 750	.6-.7mm .024-.028 in.	.3-.4mm .012-.016 in.	3.64mm BTDC (R & L) 3.42mm BTDC (C)	1½

HODAKA

HODAKA SUPER COMBAT 125cc

(TWO-STROKE)

MODEL	SPARK PLUG GAP	POINT GAP	IGNITION TIMING	IDLE AIR SCREW
ACE 90	.6-.7mm .024-.028 in.	.3-.4mm .012-.016 in.	25° BTDC	1¼
ACE 100	Same as ACE 90.			
SUPER RAT	Same as ACE series except side gap plugs preset at factory.			
ACE 100B	Same as ACE series.			
ROAD TOAD (100cc)	.6-.7mm .024-.028 in.	.3-.4mm	2.4mm BTDC	1½
DIRT SQUIRT (100cc)	.6-.7mm .024-.028 in.	.3-.4mm	2.90mm BTDC	1¼
SUPER RAT 100cc MX	.4-.7mm .016-.024 in.	none/CDI	3.95mm BTDC	1½
WOMBAT 125cc	.6-.7mm .024-.027 in	.3-.4mm	2.4mm BTDC	1½
COMBAT WOMBAT 125cc	.4-.7mm .016-.024 in.	.3-.4mm	2.46mm BTDC	1½
SUPER COMBAT 125cc	.4-.7mm .016-.024 in.	none/CDI	3.95mm BTDC	1¼

HONDA

HONDA CL 360

(TWO-STROKE)

MODEL	SPARK PLUG GAP	POINT GAP	IGNITION TIMING	IDLE AIR SCREW
MT 250	.6-.7mm	.2-.6mm	20° BTDC	1½

(FOUR-STROKE)

MODEL	SPARK PLUG GAP	POINT GAP	IGNITION TIMING	VALVES (COLD)	IDLE AIR SCREW
CB 175	.6-.7mm	.3-.4mm .012-.016 in.	Align "F" mark	.002 in.	1¼
CB 250	.7-.8mm	.3-.4mm .012-.016 in.	Align "F" mark	In .002 in. Ex .003 in.	Balance L & R
CB 360 CL 360	Specifications same as for CB 250 Specifications same as for CB 360				
XL 350	.6-.7mm	.3-.4mm .012-.016 in.	Align "F" mark	In .002 in. Ex .003 in.	⅞ to 1⅝
CB 360T	.7-.8mm	.3-.4mm .012-.016 in.	Align "F" mark	In .002 in. Ex .003 in.	Balance L & R
CB 500T	.7-.8mm	.3-.4mm .012-.016 in.	Align "F" mark	In .0012 in. Ex .0012 in.	Balance L & R
CB 750	.6-.7 mm	.3-.4mm .012-.016 in.	Align "F" mark	In .0019 in. Ex .0031 in.	See shop manual

VI. Glossary

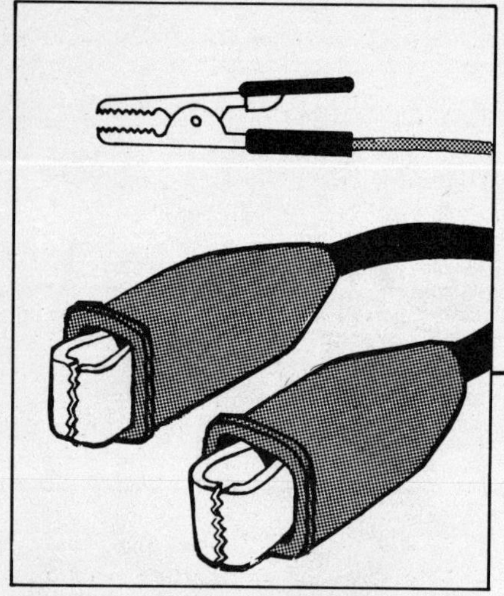

AIR CLEANER—A filter mounted over the carburetor for the purpose of keeping dirt out of the engine, while at the same time offering minimum resistance to vital airflow.

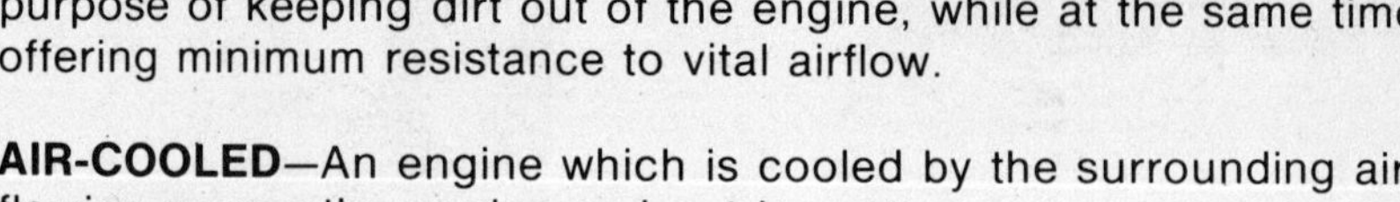

AIR-COOLED—An engine which is cooled by the surrounding air flowing across the engine and not by water.

AIR/FUEL MIXTURE—A mixture of air and gasoline vapor that is burned in the cylinder to provide power.

ALLIGATOR CLIPS—Small, spring-loaded clips that fasten the test leads of the multimeter to the electrical parts to be tested.

ALTERNATOR—Modern electrical current generator used on many motorcycles. Produces alternating current (AC) to power some of the electrical equipment on the motorcycle. Alternating current must be changed to direct current (DC) before it can power the other half of the electrical equipment (see also GENERATOR and RECTIFIER).

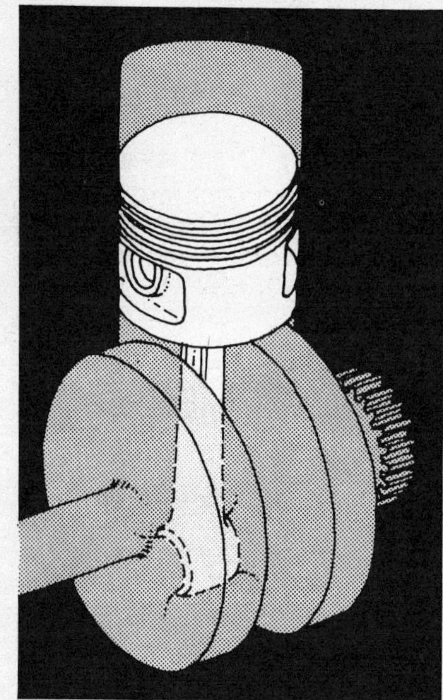

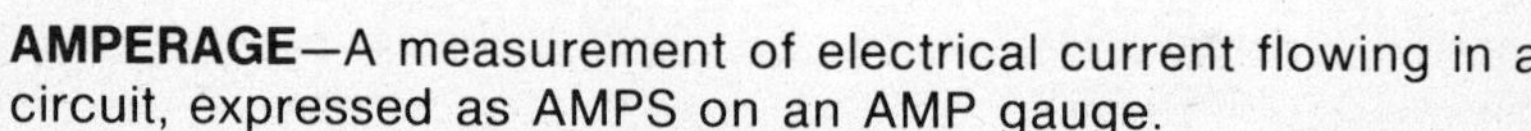

AMPERAGE—A measurement of electrical current flowing in a circuit, expressed as AMPS on an AMP gauge.

AXLE—Steel shaft, supported by bearings, around which the wheels on a motorcycle rotate.

BATTERY—A container filled with lead plates and a mixture of acid and water which stores electrical energy by a chemical reaction between the plates and the acid solution and releases the energy on demand.

BDC—Bottom Dead Center, the farthest downward travel of a piston.

BEARINGS—Special metal balls, needles or rollers housed in a race (channel) and used to reduce friction between the moving parts of the engine and drivetrain.

BIG SINGLE—A motorcycle with a large, single-cylinder engine.

BREATHING—The ability of an engine to draw air/fuel mixture through its intake system and discharge burned gases through its exhaust system.

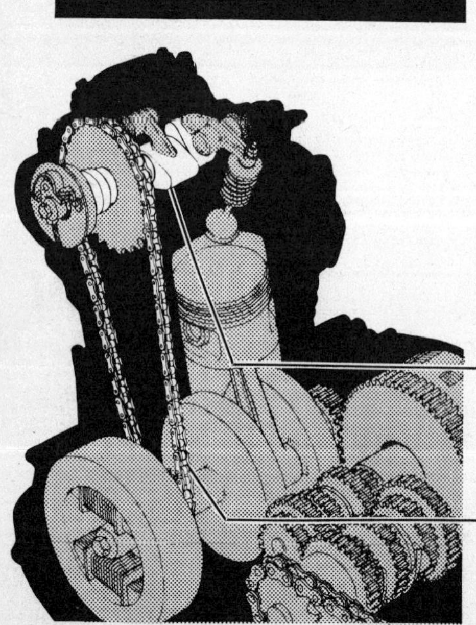

BUZZ BOX—Test unit that tells the exact opening time of ignition points. Used for ignition timing on motorcycle engines.

CALIPER—Brake pad holder which fits over rotor disc. When brake pressure is applied, the piston in the caliper forces the brake pad outward, gripping the rotor disc and slowing the motorcycle down (see also DISC BRAKE)

CAM—Also called **CAMSHAFT.** This is a shaft with egg-shaped lobes on it that open and close the valves of a four-stroke engine. The cam is responsible for the precision timing of valve operation in relation to piston movement in the cylinder.

CAM CHAIN—The camshaft is connected to the crankshaft by a timing chain in most motorcycles (overhead cam). Both camshaft and crankshaft have a gear to mate with the chain. Proper cam chain adjustment is critical to cam timing.

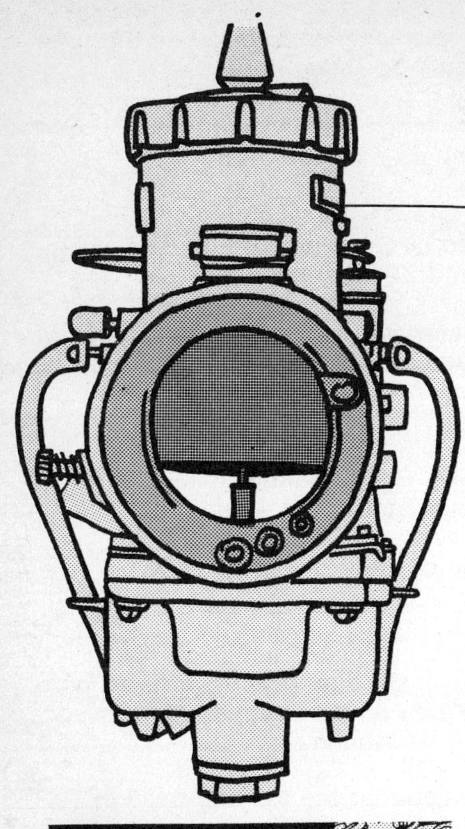

CARBON—A byproduct of burning gasoline that builds up in the exhaust system as a black deposit, especially on two-stroke bikes. If there is too much carbon buildup, the flow of exhaust gases will be restricted, causing poor performance and high gasoline consumption.

CARBURETOR—Mixes gasoline with air for combustion and supplies the air/fuel mixture to the engine, varying the amount of fuel in the mixture to suit changing engine speeds.

CHAIN—Method used to connect engine and rear wheel on most motorcycles. The chain is made up of two types of **LINKS** (see LINKS, PIN and LINKS, ROLLER).

CHAIN BREAKER—Tool used to disconnect links in the chain so that a master link or extra links may be installed or removed.

CHOKE—Device which partly blocks the air intake of the carburetor to provide an extra-rich fuel mixture for easier starting when the engine is cold.

CLUTCH—The clutch is made up of two sets of plates, one steel, the other a fiber material. It connects or disconnects the engine from the rest of the drivetrain for starting and stopping. Clutch action is controlled by the clutch lever, located on the left handlebar on most motorcycles.

COLD PLUGS—Spark plugs used for continuous, high-speed operation, usually racing.

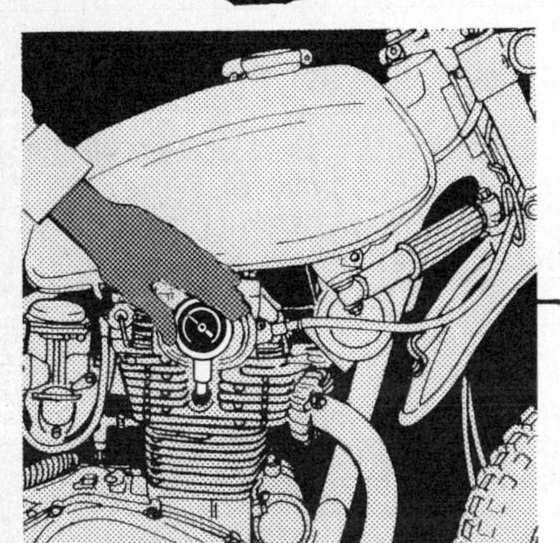

COMPRESSION—The upward movement of the piston in the cylinder compresses the air/fuel mixture to make it burn with great force, providing power. Compression is measured in pounds per square inch, abbreviated "psi." (See COMPRESSION TESTER below.)

COMPRESSION TESTER—Gauge for measuring engine compression. Normally used by removing a spark plug, then inserting tip of tester in the spark plug hole and cranking the engine over.

CONDENSER—An electrical device that reduces the spark between the point contacts in the distributor and prevents burning. If the condenser fails, point wear and burning result.

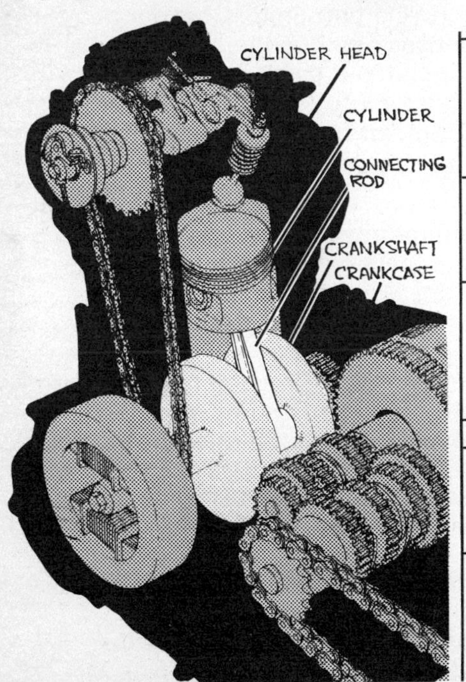

CONNECTING RODS—Attach pistons to crankshaft. They allow forces from the burning air/fuel mixture pressing downward on the pistons to travel down to the crankshaft, changing the pistons' up-and-down motion to crankshaft rotary motion.

CRANKCASE—The housing that encloses and seals off the crankshaft, connecting rods and allied parts. In some motorcycles, it also holds the oil supply.

CRANKSHAFT—Located in the lower half of the engine, the crankshaft rotates, thereby turning the rear wheel. The crankshaft is rotated by piston movement, as transmitted and converted through the connecting rods.

CYLINDER—Portion of upper engine assembly, also called the **BARREL,** which acts as a container for the piston while the piston moves up and down. Exterior of barrel/cylinder is usually finned to draw heat away from the engine as the motorcycle moves.

CYLINDER HEAD—Top of engine. The upper portion of the cylinder and the inside of the cylinder head form the completed combustion chamber, where the compressed air/fuel mixture is burned. In four-stroke engines, the cylinder head also contains the intake and exhaust valves, and on some motorcycles the camshaft.

DIAL INDICATOR—Measuring tool sometimes used to find the position of the piston in the cylinder for timing purposes.

DIMMER SWITCH—Control that switches the headlight beam up or down. Normally located on handlebars near the throttle.

DIODE—Solid-state device which permits the flow of electrical current in *one direction only.* Used in charging systems and voltage regulation (see also RECTIFIER and ZENER DIODE).

DISC BRAKE—Found on some motorcycles. The brake uses a steel rotor disc, which is gripped by pads of brake material held in a caliper, to slow down the motorcycle. More efficient than old-style drum brake (see also CALIPER).

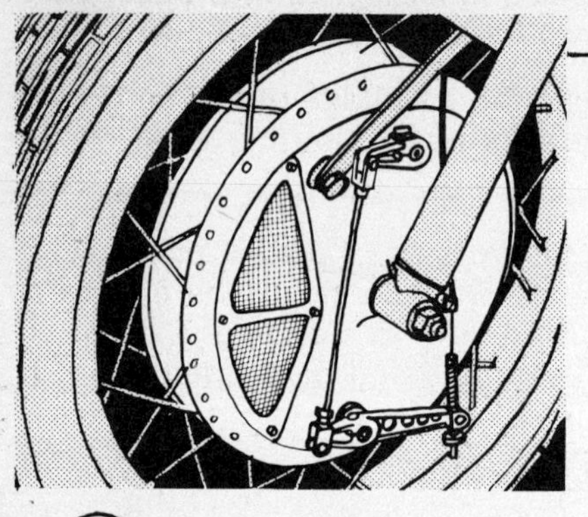

DRUM BRAKE—Older style of brake. Brake material is located inside a steel drum which composes part of the wheel hub. When brakes are applied, the brake material or "shoe" is pressed outward against the inside surface of the drum to slow the motorcycle.

EXHAUST PIPE—Tubing that directs exhaust gases away from the engine to the rear of the motorcycle. On motorcycles, exhaust pipe *length and diameter* are critical. When a well-designed exhaust pipe is installed, exhaust is said to be "tuned."

EXHAUST VALVE—A metal disc, fitted into the cylinder head of four-stroke engines, which opens to let burned exhaust gases that remain after combustion escape from the cylinder, then closes.

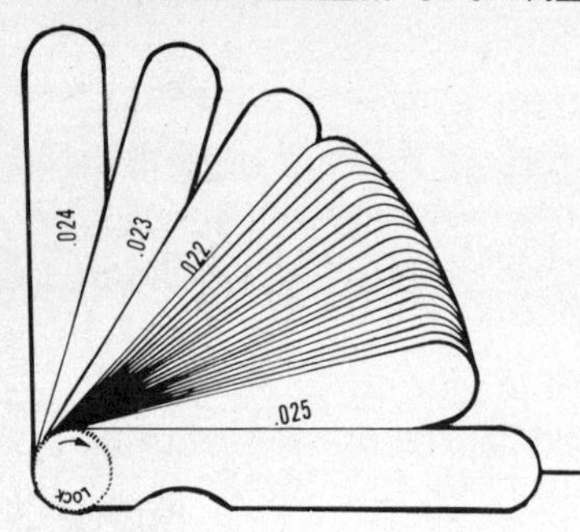

EXPANSION CHAMBER—Type of exhaust pipe used on two-stroke motorcycle engines. Two-stroke engines are sensitive to changes in exhaust backpressure and timing, and the expansion chamber can add considerable horsepower to two-stroke engines if properly designed and maintained.

FEELER GAUGE—Tool for measuring small gaps between parts, such as ignition points and bearing clearances. A feeler gauge set is made up of various diameters of wire or many small blades of steel of various thicknesses. Measurements are usually in thousandths of an inch (e.g. .016 inch).

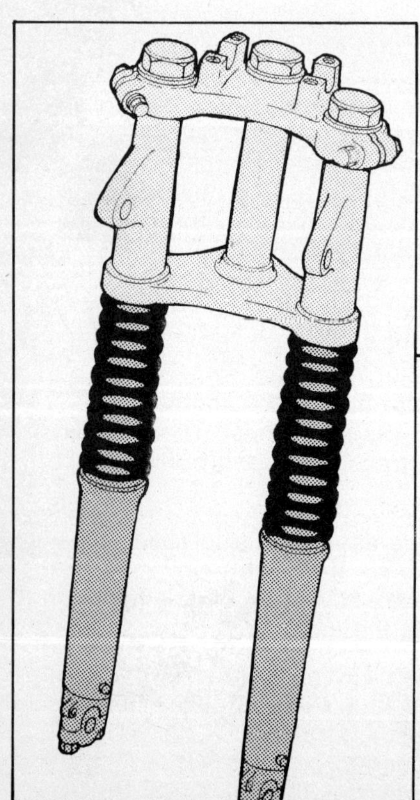

FLOAT, CARBURETOR—Most motorcycle carburetors have a float inside a float chamber. The float senses any change in the level of fuel inside the float chamber and operates a small valve, which controls the flow of fuel from the gas tank to the float chamber. This system provides a constant supply of fuel in the float chamber for use by the carburetor.

FORKS—The front suspension of a motorcycle. The forks are composed of upper legs and lower sliders, which hold the springs and oil for the shock absorber action.

FOUR-STROKE ENGINE—An engine with intake and exhaust valves that requires two revolutions of the crankshaft to complete one full cycle of operation. During these two revolutions, the piston makes two upward and two downward movements—a total of four strokes.

FUEL FILTER—A fine wire mesh, set into the fuel line below the carburetor, which traps particles of sediment or rust and prevents them from passing into the engine.

FUEL TANK—A container that holds the motorcycle's supply of gasoline, made of metal or fiberglass. In two-stroke engines that lack an oil pump, it contains a mixture of gasoline and engine oil.

GENERATOR—Old-style unit for producing electrical power on motorcycles. The generator produces direct current (DC), which does not require rectification like alternator output, but it is not as efficient a device (also see RECTIFIER).

HOT PLUGS—Spark plugs used for short-trip driving with lots of idling. They burn off combustion deposits that might otherwise tend to foul them.

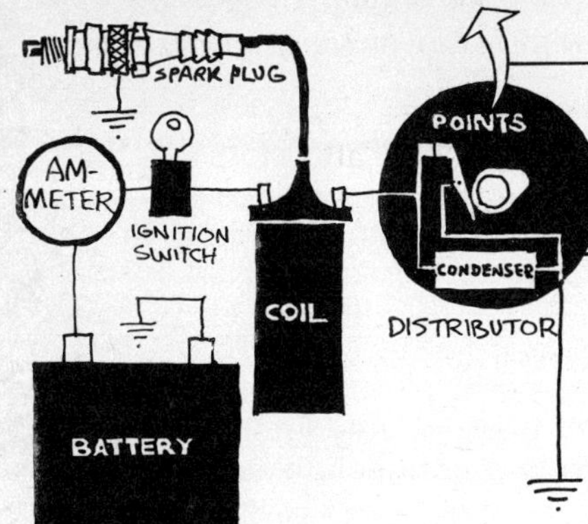

IGNITION POINTS—Small set of contacts which open and close at precisely the right time to fire the spark plug(s) on the motorcycle engine. The points may be operated by either the crankshaft or the camshaft.

IGNITION SYSTEM—Part of the electrical system. It performs two functions: First, it boosts the relatively low voltage of the battery to the very high voltage needed to fire the spark plugs. Second, it controls or "times" the exact moment of firing of each spark plug to coincide with piston movement in each cylinder.

IGNITION TIMING—Setting the operation of the ignition points or other type of firing device so that the spark plugs fire at exactly the right time in relation to piston movement.

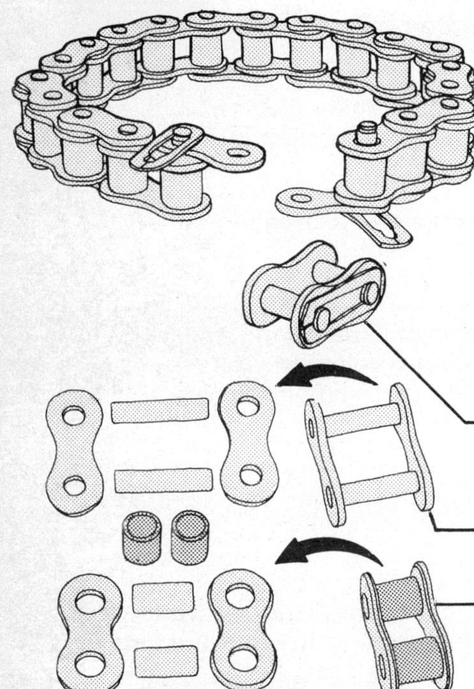

IMPACT TOOL—Hand tool designed to break screws and bolts loose. Used with a hammer to apply sufficient force to loosen tightly bound fasteners.

INTAKE VALVE—A metal disc, fitted into the cylinder head of four-stroke engines, that opens to admit air/fuel mixture into the cylinder and closes for compression and combustion.

JET, CARBURETOR—Special orifice (opening) which controls the amount of fuel that can pass through the carburetor into the cylinder. Most carburetors have more than one jet to control different carburetor functions.

LINK, MASTER—Special link with a removable clip that can be taken apart without using a chain breaker tool so the chain can easily be removed for cleaning.

LINK, PIN—Part of the chain. The pin link holds two roller links together. Alternating roller and pin links make up the entire chain.

LINK, ROLLER—The part of the chain link that touches the teeth of the sprockets. Roller links are held together by pin links.

METRIC SYSTEM—International system of measurement. Metric tools and parts on most motorcycles differ from American sizes.

MUFFLER—A series of baffles and noise-absorbing materials that reduce the noise of combustion and escaping gases coming from the engine and exhaust manifold.

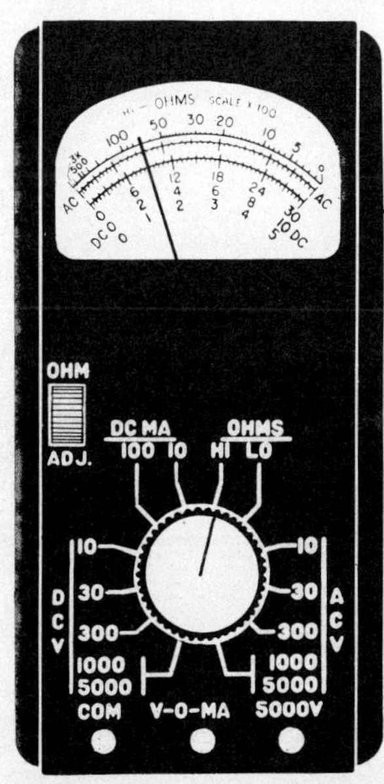

MULTIMETER—Measuring instrument for electrical use. Measures current flow (AMPERAGE), electrical potential (VOLTAGE) and circuit resistance (OHMS). Useful for troubleshooting and can substitute for buzz box in setting timing.

NECK—Also known as the steering head. Portion of the frame where the front forks are fastened.

OHMS—Measurement of the amount of resistance to current flow in an electrical circuit.

OIL COOLER—A small radiator installed on the frame of a motorcycle, through which engine oil is pumped for cooling and then returned to the engine lubrication system to be reused.

OIL PUMP—Pushes oil through passages or galleries to all the moving parts of the engine.

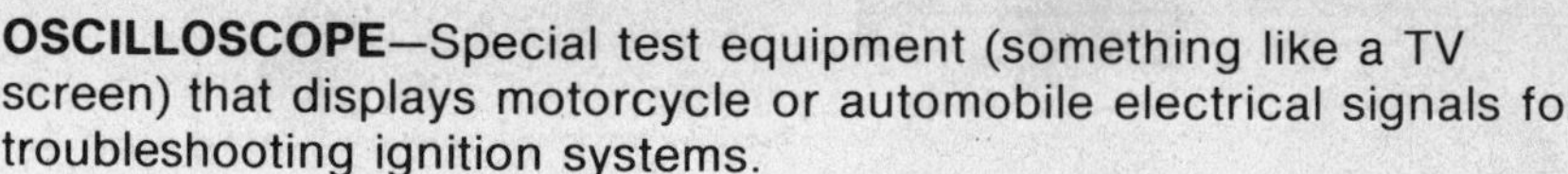

OSCILLOSCOPE—Special test equipment (something like a TV screen) that displays motorcycle or automobile electrical signals for troubleshooting ignition systems.

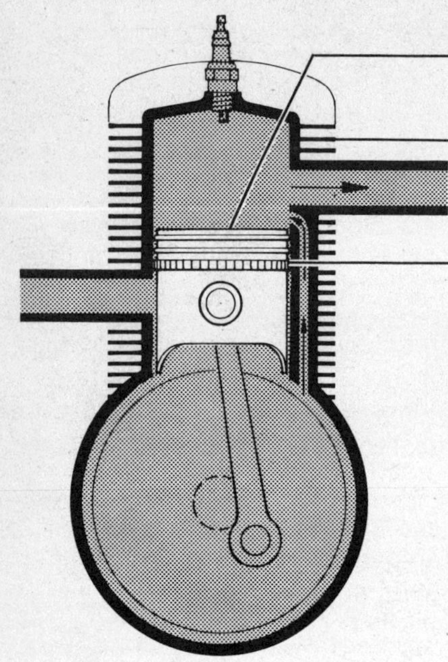

PISTON—A metal plug that fits tightly inside the cylinder and is moved up and down inside it by the force of combustion.

PISTON-PORT ENGINE—Type of two-stroke engine. This is the simplest type of two-stroke engine, with fewer moving parts than other types.

PISTON RINGS—Metallic rings or circles that fit into slots machined (cut) into the sides of the piston. One kind of ring guides the piston along the cylinder walls, while other rings seal and lubricate the cylinder walls.

POINTS—See IGNITION POINTS.

PRESSURE PLATE—Spring-tensioned plate in the clutch which forces clutch plates together to provide a connection between the engine and the rear wheel drive.

PRIMARY CHAIN—Used on some motorcycles to connect the engine to a separate transmission.

PRIMARY COVER—Cover which shields primary chain from dirt and dust. May also be oil-tight if motorcycle lube system pumps oil to the primary chain during engine operation.

RECTIFIER—Solid-state device that converts alternating current (AC) provided by alternator to direct current (DC) for use by headlights, gauges and other electrical systems.

REED VALVE—Valve inserted between carburetor and engine on some two-stroke engines. Improves engine efficiency by reducing backward flow of gases during portion of engine cycle.

RINGS—See PISTON RINGS.

ROCKER ARMS—When activated by the camshaft, they open and close the intake and exhaust valves.

ROTARY-VALVE ENGINE—Type of two-stroke engine which has a disc-shaped valve at the crankshaft that covers and uncovers the intake passageway to allow the air/fuel mixture to enter the engine at the proper time. Rotary-valve engines are easily recognizable, because the carburetor is mounted on the side of the engine and is usually covered.

SAE NUMBER—A measurement of an engine oil's thickness or viscosity. Engine oils are graded according to type by "weight;" thus oil cans are marked "20 weight," "40 weight," etc.

SHAFT DRIVE—Used instead of primary drive chain on some models of large road motorcycles. Similar in operation to an automobile driveshaft.

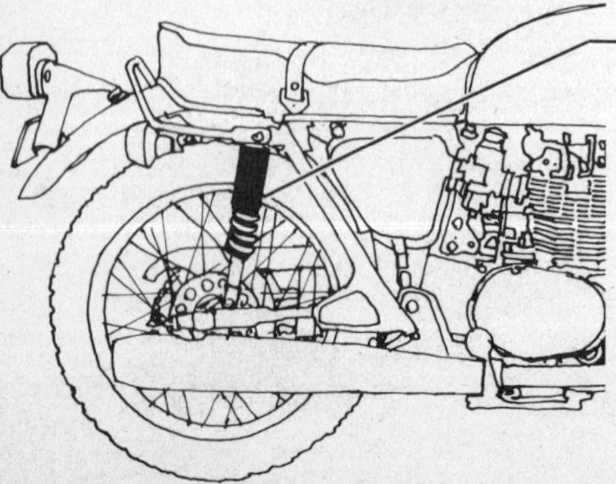

SHOCK ABSORBERS—Oil-filled device on rear of motorcycle for absorbing road shocks. Most motorcycle shock absorbers also have springs mounted on the outside of the shock body. (NOTE: Front forks on motorcycles are also shock absorbers.)

SLIDERS—Lower portion of front forks. Act as shock absorbers by sliding up and down over upper legs in reaction to road shock.

SLIDE VALVE (CARBURETOR)—Main moving part of many motorcycle carburetors. The slide valve, controlled by the throttle cable, moves up and down to vary the intake opening, regulating the flow of air and fuel into the engine.

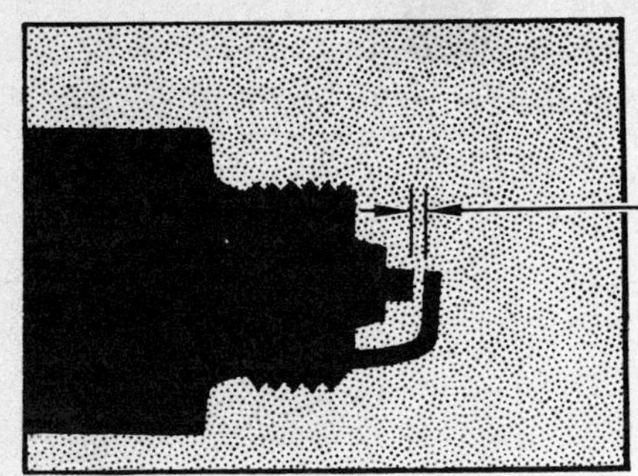

SPARK PLUG—Device which has two terminals or electrodes a short distance apart. An electrical spark jumps between these electrodes to ignite the air/fuel mixture in the cylinder.

SPARK PLUG GAP—The distance between the two electrodes on the spark plug.

SPOKES—Adjustable steel wires which support wheel rims.

SPROCKETS—Toothed wheels which mesh with drive chains and primary chains to drive the motorcycle.

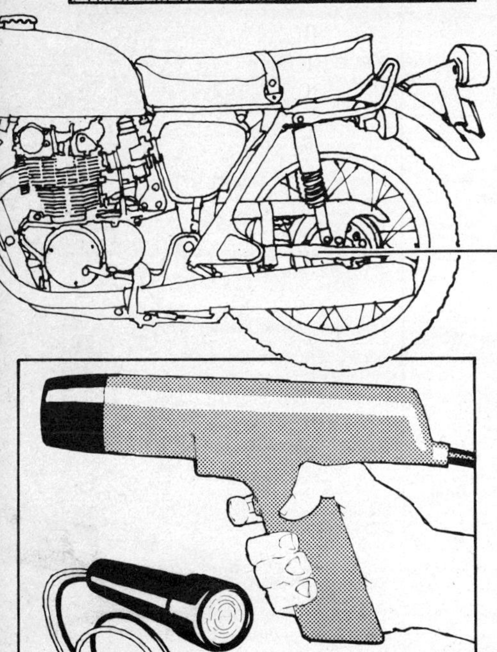

STEERING DAMPER—Fitted to some motorcycles, this is a small shock absorber which connects the front forks to the frame. Dampens violent movement of front forks in rough terrain and softens front end movement on the highway.

STRAINERS—Used for both fuel and oil, strainers are usually small screens for filtering out foreign material.

SWINGARM—Rear suspension of motorcycle. The swingarm fastens to the rear of the frame and pivots on bearings.

TACHOMETER—Gauge that indicates the number of engine revolutions per minute (rpm), a measurement of engine speed. Different from a speedometer, which indicates tire speed in miles per hour (mph).

THROTTLE—Motorcycles use a twist type of throttle, located on the right handlebar, that controls the action of the carburetor by cable, allowing you to change vehicle speed.

TIMING—Precise setting of ignition and camshaft (camshaft on four-stroke engines only) with respect to crankshaft to produce an efficient cycle of operation.

TIMING LIGHT—A test device which operates on the stroboscopic principle, flashing a light in time with spark plug firing. The strobe action makes the timing mark appear to "freeze" so that it may be compared with timing marks on the engine and adjusted.

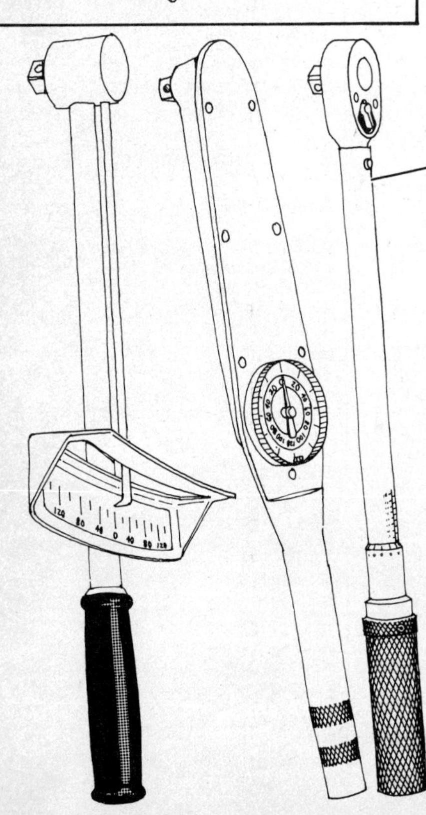

TORQUE—Work force applied in a rotary plane. Used as a measurement of engine power and of the force required to tighten fasteners securely.

TORQUE WRENCH—Special hand tool which accurately measures the torque force applied to fasteners while tightening them.

TRANSMISSION—Cluster of gears contained in the engine (on most models) to vary output shaft speed and torque according to the rider's requirements.

TWO-STROKE ENGINE—An engine which requires only two movements of the piston in the cylinder (intake/compression and power/exhaust) to produce a *complete* cycle of operation.

VENTURI—A restriction in the size of the carburetor opening which increases airflow speed through the carburetor. The increase in air speed produces a drop in pressure (called a vacuum) behind the venturi, which pulls fuel through carburetor jets into the airstream to be mixed with air for combustion in the engine.

VOLTAGE—A measurement of electrical pressure. Batteries are rated by voltage and amperage (see also AMPERAGE).

ZENER DIODE—Special solid-state device found in some motorcycle electrical systems. Acts as a voltage reference point or voltage regulator.

VII/Where To Get It

SERVICE MANUALS

AJS—From Dealer or Write:

WEST: Norton-Villiers Corp.
6765 Paramount Blvd.
Long Beach, Calif. 90723
(213) 531-7138

EAST: Berliner Motor Corp.
Plant Rd. & Railroad St.
Hasbrouck Heights, N.J. 07604
(201) 288-9696

Benelli—From Dealer Only

Cosmopolitan Motors
Jacksonville & Meadowbrook Rds.
Hatboro, Pa. 19040
(215) 672-9100

BMW—From Dealer Only

WEST: Butler & Smith, Inc.
135 East Stanley St.
Compton, Calif. 90220
(213) 638-8508

EAST: Butler & Smith, Inc.
Walnut St. & Hudson Ave.
Norwood, N.J. 07648
(201) 767-1223

BSA—From Dealer Only

WEST: BSA Motorcycle
2745 East Huntington Dr.
Duarte, Calif. 91010
(213) 681-2621

EAST: BSA Motorcycle
P.O. Box 6790
Towson
Baltimore, Md. 21204
(301) 252-1700

Broncco—From Dealer only

Engine Specialties, Inc.
P.O. Box 260
Cornwells Heights, Pa.
(215) 785-3232

Bultaco—From Dealer or Write:

Bultaco Services, Inc.
P.O. Box 433
Silverado, Calif. 92676
(714) 649-2543

Bultaco American Ltd.
2767 Scott Blvd.
P.O. Box 101
Santa Clara, Calif. 95052
(408) 241-4672

Cemoto
P.O. Box 1065
Schenectady, N.Y. 12301

Carabela—From Dealer or Write:

Carabela Moto Imports Co.
172 Freedom Ave.
Anaheim, Calif. 92801
(714) 870-5243

Cooper—From Dealer or Write:

Apache Ltd.
110 East Santa Anita Ave.
Burbank, Calif. 91502
(213) 849-6066

DKW—From Dealer Only

Hercules Distributing
9825 Mason Ave.
Chatsworth, Calif. 91311
(213) 882-8272

Ducati—From Dealer Only

WEST: ZDS Motors
4655 San Fernando Rd
Glendale, Calif. 91204
(213) 245-8695

EAST: Berliner Motor Corp.
Plant Rd. & Railroad St.
Hasbrouck Heights, N.J. 07604
(201) 288-9696

Greeves—Not in Print

WEST: Nicholson Motors
11573 Vanowen St.
North Hollywood, Calif. 91605
(213) 877-7366

EAST: Jeckel Industries
38 Everts Ave.
Glen Falls, N.Y. 12801
(518) 793-5181

Harley-Davidson—From Dealer Only

Harley-Davidson Motor Co.
3700 West Juneau Ave.
Milwaukee, Wis. 53201
(414) 342-4680

Hodaka—From Dealer or Write:

Pabatco
P.O. Box 327
Athena, Ore. 97813
(503) 566-3526

Honda—From Dealer or Write:

American Honda Motor Co.
100 West Alondra
P.O. Box 50
Gardena, Calif. 90247
(213) 321-8680

Husqvarna—From Dealer or Write:

WEST: Husqvarna Motor Corp.
4790 Palm Ave.
La Mesa, Calif. 92041
(714) 460-0884

EAST: Husqvarna Motor Corp.
1906 Broadway Ave.
Lorain, Oh. 44052
(216) 244-1515

Indian—From Dealer or Write:

Indian Motorcycles Inc.
1535 West Rosecrans Blvd.
Gardena, Calif. 90249
(213) 532-7374

Jawa/CZ—From Dealer Only

WEST: American Jawa Ltd.
3745 Overland Ave.
Los Angeles, Calif. 90034
(213) 838-7349

EAST: American Jawa Ltd.
185 Express St.
Plainview, N.Y. 11803
(516) 938-3210

Kawasaki—From Dealer Only

Kawasaki Motor Corp.
1062 McGaw Ave.
Santa Ana, Calif. 92705
(714) 540-9980

Laverda—From Dealer Only

MED International
4225 30th St.
San Diego, Calif. 92104
(714) 460-4289

MZ—From Dealer or Write:

International Accessories
102 Park St.
Hampshire, Ill. 60140
(312) 683-3865

Maico—From Dealer or Write:

WEST: Cooper Motors
110 East Santa Anita Ave.
Burbank, Calif. 91502
(213) 849-6066

EAST: Cooper Maico
Royal & Duke Sts.
Reedsville, Pa. 17084
(717) 667-3970

Monark—From Dealer or Write:

Inter-Trends, Inc.
825 South Victory Blvd
Burbank, Calif. 91502
(213) 845-7601

Montesa—From Dealer or Write:

Montesa Motors Inc.
3657 Beverly Blvd.
Los Angeles, Calif. 90004
(213) 663-8258

Moto Guzzi—From Dealer Only

WEST: ZDS Motors
4655 San Fernando Rd.
Glendale, Calif. 91204
(213) 245-8695

EAST: Premier Motor Corp.
Plant Rd. & Railroad St.
Hasbrouck Heights, N.J. 07604
(201) 288-9685

Norton—From Dealer or Write:

WEST: Norton-Villiers Corp.
6765 Paramount Blvd.
Long Beach, Calif. 90723
(213) 531-7138

EAST: Berliner Motor Corp.
Plant Rd. & Railroad St.
Hasbrouck Heights, N.J. 07604
(201) 288-9696

Ossa—From Dealer or Write:

WEST: Yankee Motor Co.
24030 Frampton Ave.
Harbor City, Calif. 90710
(213) 530-0565

EAST: Yankee Motor Corp.
P.O. Box 36
Schenectady, N.Y. 12301
(518) 372-4727

Penton—From Dealer Only

WEST: Penton West
9604 Oates Dr.
Sacramento, Calif. 95827
(916) 362-4124

EAST: Penton Imports
1354 Colorado Ave.
Lorain, Oh. 44052
(216) 288-1216

Puch—From Dealer Only

Hercules Distributing
9825 Mason Ave.
Chatsworth, Calif. 91311
(213) 882-8272

Raider—From Dealer Only

Marco Dist. Co.
P.O. Box 2826
Idaho Falls, Id. 83401
(208) 523-7373

Rickman—From Dealer Only

WEST: Rickman Division of B.S.A.
2745 East Huntington Dr.
Duarte, Calif.
(213) 681-2621

EAST: Rickman Division of B.S.A.
P.O. Box 6790
Towson
Baltimore, Md. 21204
(301) 252-3400

Suzuki—From Dealer Only

U.S. Suzuki Motor Corp.
13767 Freeway Dr.
Santa Fe Springs, Calif. 90670
(213) 921-4461

Triumph—From Dealer Only

WEST: Triumph Corp.
2765 East Huntington Dr.
Duarte, Calif. 91010
(213) 681-0255

EAST: Triumph Corp.
P.O. Box 6790
Towson
Baltimore, Md. 21204
(301) 252-3400

Yamaha—From Dealer Only

Yamaha International Corp.
6600 Orangethorpe Blvd.
Buena Park, Calif. 90620
(714) 522-9011

Yankee—From Dealer or Write:

EAST: Yankee Motor Corp.
P.O. Box 36
Schenectady, N.Y. 12301
(518) 372-4727

WEST: Yankee Motor Co.
24030 Frampton Ave.
Harbor City, Calif. 90710
(213) 530-0565

SPECS AND CHARTS

Available From:

WEBCO INC.
218 Main Street
P.O. Box 429
Venice, Calif. 90291
(213) 399-7724

FLANDERS CO.
340 South Fair Oaks
Pasadena, Calif. 91101
(213) 681-2581

METRICS FOR MOTORCYCLES

Tool Catalogs and Information Available From:

SNAP-ON TOOL CORP.
8026 28th St.
Kenosha, Wis. 53140

PROTO TOOLS
P.O. Box 3519
Los Angeles, Calif. 90054

CRAFTSMAN TOOLS at all SEARS STORES
and available through their catalog.